Spain and Central America

Recent Titles in
Contributions in Political Science

SPAIN AND CENTRAL AMERICA
Democracy and Foreign Policy

ROBIN L. ROSENBERG

CONTRIBUTIONS IN POLITICAL SCIENCE, NUMBER 288
Bernard K. Johnpoll, *Series Editor*

GREENWOOD PRESS

New York • Westport, Connecticut • London

Library of Congress Cataloging-in-Publication Data

Rosenberg, Robin L.
    Spain and Central America : democracy and foreign policy / Robin
L. Rosenberg.
        p. cm.—(Contributions in political science, ISSN 0147–1066
; no. 288)
    Includes bibliographical references and index.
    ISBN 0–313–27885–7 (alk. paper)
    1. Central America—Foreign relations—Spain. 2. Spain—Foreign
relations—Central America. 3. Representative government and
representation—Spain—History—20th century. 4. Representative
government and representation—Central America—History—20th
century. 5. Socialism—Central America—History—20th century.
I. Title. II. Series.
F1436.8.S7R67   1992
327.460728—dc20   91–824

British Library Cataloguing in Publication Data is available.

Library of Congress Catalog Card Number: 91–824
ISBN: 0–313–27885–7
ISSN: 0147–1066

First published in 1992

Greenwood Press, 88 Post Road West, Westport, CT 06881
An imprint of Greenwood Publishing Group, Inc.

Printed in the United States of America

The paper used in this book complies with the
Permanent Paper Standard issued by the National
Information Standards Organization (Z39.48–1984).

10 9 8 7 6 5 4 3 2 1

To Pepí, Joshua and Daniel

Somewhere a strange and shrewd tomorrow goes to bed,
Planning a test for men from Europe; no one guesses
Who will be most ashamed, who richer and who dead.

W. H. Auden

I cannot believe that God has for several centuries
been pushing two or three hundred million men toward
equality just to make them wind up under a Tiberian or
a Claudian despotism. Verily, that wouldn't be worth
the trouble.

Alexis de Tocqueville

Europa debe ser la locomotora de la multipolaridad en
las relaciones internacionales. De este hecho político
depende la independencia europea. Y también su salud
moral y su participación intelectual en el discurso
heterogénico, policultural, del porvenir. La alternativa
es la muerte; muerte rica, si se quiere, pero muerte al
atesorar fin, pues no hará sino atesorar dinero muerto,
trabajo muerto, cansancio y carcajadas mortales.

Carlos Fuentes

Contents

Preface

Any one of the 50 million people who each year pass through Spain can testify to the intoxicating effects of its culture, the enchantment of its peoples, and the beauty of its natural and man-made landscapes. Political scientists, moreover, often confess to the compelling nature of Spanish politics, whose mix of vulgarity and elegance is perhaps unrivaled in the affairs of other nations.

My intoxication with Spain began in 1979, during a study-abroad experience that led to marriage and a life-long personal and professional fascination with things Spanish. My acquaintance with the Latin American "experience" began slightly earlier in New York; but I quickly found that the two pursuits were compatible, if not mutually reinforcing.

A long-term living and working experience anywhere could quickly disillusion an otherwise romantic perception of a nation's reality. My four years of living and working in Spain coincided with severe economic and social crises that went largely unnoticed by the international media and by most tourists except for those who suffered at the hands of Spain's now infamous petty thieves and muggers. The present study is a result of my sobering experience in Spain from 1985 through 1989; its critical tone is an effort to put Spain's otherwise miraculous economic and political performance into the proper perspective. Much of the critique is justified by the fact that Spanish leaders provoke scrutiny by their unabashed use of the Spanish democratic experience as a vehicle for their own external validation, as well as a means to maximize national power in areas of the world like Central America, where the people are much less fortunate than the new, Europeanized Spaniards. Such an enterprise is, I believe, true to my love for

Spain because it serves as a reminder to leaders everywhere that democracy, like knowledge itself, is an unending search for perfection.

An undertaking of this kind usually involves the collaboration of a great many people, only some of whom are aware of their participation. My appreciation must go out to the many friends and colleagues, both in the United States and Europe, who saw me through difficult times.

To my friends, mentors, and colleagues at the Graduate School of International Studies, University of Miami, who reviewed the manuscript in various phases, I owe a great personal and professional debt. There I received the support and encouragement to become an educator. In particular, I would like to thank Drs. Jack Harrison, Alexander McIntire, and Enrique Baloyra, for recognizing that I could make a contribution; Dr. Joaquín Roy, for sharing Spain, his files, and his friendship; Dr. Carl G. Jacobsen, whose friendship, advice and direction were responsible for my pursuing doctoral studies; Dr. Julian Weinkle, for his consistently warm support and for the wisdom he imparted to me; Ambassador Ambler H. Moss Jr., Director of the North-South Center, for sharing his brilliance, good humor, and his experiences with me—and for coming to Miami to help build a great institution; and, of course, to my friend and colleague, Dr. Jaime Suchlicki, Executive Director of the North-South Center, whose boundless energy, loyalty to his students, and sense of humor are matched only by his generosity.

Special thanks must go to a number of people, including the Luque family of Córdoba, booksellers, whose friendship and bibliographical aid were invaluable; to Dr. Robert H. Kelley of Troy State University, for his unwavering support throughout my stay in Europe; to Captain Juan Carlos Campbell Cruz (U.S. Air Force, ret.) for advice on Spanish geopolitical and defense matters; to Diana Egeler of Troy State University's European headquarters, and to all the Troy field representatives throughout Europe for their kindness and logistical support; to Greenwood Press for their patience and for recognizing my contribution to the study of democratic development; to Beth Zurzolo, North-South Fellow, for the index and other aid with the manuscript; to an anonymous reader for the extremely constructive criticism of the manuscript; and to Jane Marchi of the *Journal of Interamerican Studies and World Affairs*, whose contribution to my personal and professional development can never be adequately described. None of the aforementioned friends and colleagues shares the blame for whatever blunders may follow.

Introduction

This book is a modest attempt to integrate a number of recent scholarly trends that have dominated the field of international relations during the 1980s. Clearly, the "big" issue in the literature is the democratic transition from authoritarianism, which in the 1990s has been expanded into an exploration of democratic transitions from totalitarian regimes. Probably less has been written on the normative aspects of foreign policy and the relationship of democracy to the foreign policy behavior of nation-states. But recent events in Eastern Europe and the Middle East, not to mention Panama, have emboldened the never quite defunct rear-guard of the scholarly community that made a vocation of criticizing the dogmatic aspects of modern political realism. The apparent strategic alignment of the superpowers around democratic outcomes across the globe added some strange new voices to the chorus against dogmatic realism. Moral spillovers from the Gulf War and the perception of success in U.S. interventions in Panama, Nicaragua, and elsewhere fueled a nationalist urge to use international norms like democracy as a vehicle for national power. Many saw the U.S. president's call for a "New World Order" as a repudiation of the rules of *realpolitik* and as a harnessing of U.S. strategic power as an agent for the imposition of international norms. *Realpolitik* had become too conservative for the new conservatives.

The trend would be gratifying for those normative analysts who have labored for years to convince scholars and policy-makers that realism was self-prophetic and inimical to the establishment of global institutions—if it were not for the fact that there may be a Trojan horse somewhere in the onslaught. Are global institutions like the United Nations the vehicle through which U.S. power is maximized and global hegemony is effected? Only the realists would be gratified if that were indeed the case.

Spain, a middle-power whose democratic "model" and integration into Europe helped carve out for her a new international role, cannot aspire to global hegemony. But her pursuit of international norms in places like Central America may be no less an effort to maximize national power in the international sphere. Without decisive military and economic policy resources, Spain has been able to take advantage of moral, cultural, and historical linkages by employing the Spanish model of democratic transition as a foreign policy vehicle.

The appeal to the international norm of democracy has won Spain some influence in a region traditionally dominated by the great powers. Although the establishment of democracy is rarely, if ever, the work of external actors, Spain's identification with democratic outcomes ensured Spanish business, commerce, and politicians a place in Central American affairs. While the success of such diplomatic initiatives has been tempered by a lack of tangible policy resources in the form of trade and aid, Spain nevertheless facilitated Europe's return to a region dominated by superpower politics.

The case of Spain goes to the heart of the paradox between *real-* and *idealpolitik*. That there is no contradiction between Spain's support for democracy in Central America and its pursuit of international political and economic power may be due only to the flexibility that being a middle-power affords. But the lessons may be important for superpower actors as well.

The focus on the Spanish case is important in other respects. When a national experience such as democratic transition is used as an international metaphor, the image of that experience is divorced from its own context. In this work I felt it necessary to link the image and substance of Spain's democracy with the country's foreign policy. A study of Spanish reality suggests that the establishment of "congruence" between Spain's internal democratic project and external foreign initiatives has been jeopardized by social and economic problems at home as well as by the sometimes undemocratic practices of the government and political elites. Spain's foray into Central American democratic development provides her leaders with a source of external validation that aids attempts at home to exercise political hegemony.

Moreover, Spain's initiatives in Central America have come precisely at a time when foreign policy resources are being exhausted by the geopolitical pull of the European Economic Community and by close strategic and defense cooperation with the U.S.-led Western alliance. The European orientation of Spain and its "autonomous regions" has resulted in the declining importance of Latin America as a trading partner and as an area where Spanish aspirations would be realized. It is my intention to show how the asymmetry between rhetoric and tangible development cooperation, together with the incongruity between the image and the reality of Spanish democratic behavior at home and abroad, damages Spain's prestige and disappoints and deceives less fortunate, often desperate, Central Americans. More importantly, these asymmetries and incongruities weaken the moral power of Spain's democratic projection in the world and detract from its otherwise significant diplomatic accomplishments in the Central American context.

In attempting to integrate the major trends in the literature on democratic transition, foreign policy, and normative frameworks for international politics (while focusing on "democratic" Spain's new international role), a rather sweeping methodology must be employed. In Part I, a case is made for the validity of democratic models in the international context. Thus in Chapter 1, the notion of the exportability of a democratic model is explored in the Latin American context. This commerce of democratic models has been a constant feature of Latin and Central American politics, whose intellectual framework was established by the *pensadores* and *libertadores* at the onset of Latin American independence in the Nineteenth Century. Spain then enters the market with a successful democratic experience that Spanish policy attempts to exploit.

Then the Spanish model itself must be established as a legitimate international good. Chapter 2 analyzes the Spanish transition as an international phenomenon, a metaphor whose major elements can be promoted—perhaps—as a coherent package. And in Chapter 3 the contents of that package—the actual performance of Spanish democracy—are examined empirically to test the "symmetry" or "congruence" between the international and national projects.

Part II of the book presents the international context in which the Spanish model and Spanish foreign policy are oriented. In Chapter 4, the crisis in Central America, the "target area," is explored in its strategic dimensions, thus establishing a "strategic space" for the initiatives of the lesser-powers. Chapter 4 also surveys democratic prospects in Central America, the "moving target" of democratic policy initiatives. The discussion of the target area leads to a point of departure at which Spanish policy-makers determine that the national experience can serve as a framework for foreign policy. Chapter 5 addresses Spain's "push outwards" from the confines of its own democratic experience.

In Part III, the geopolitical and operational aspects of Spanish foreign policy in Central America are explored. Chapter 6 treats the years of Spain's relationship with Europe. This relationship is central to Spain's international behavior inasmuch as European ties condition efforts elsewhere—especially in Central America.

Chapter 7 investigates the parameters of policy under the Socialist government after 1982; and Chapter 8 analyzes the operational aspects of Socialist foreign policy in Central America and the use of the democratic model as a foreign policy "vehicle." This section also evaluates the effectiveness of Spanish policy, its ability as an external actor to influence the transition to democracy in Central America, as well as assesses the relative importance of Central America in Spanish foreign relations.

The conclusions in Chapter 9 offer some insights on the connection between the image and substance of Spain's democracy and Spanish foreign policy, the lust for external validation of Spain's political leadership, the democratic aspirations of Central Americans and Spaniards, and the democratic prospects in Central America and Spain.

A NOTE ON SOURCES

The documentation herein reflects my preference for primary sources of information. Much of the analysis is based on field research and four years of living and working experience in Spain.

Apart from my own eye-witness accounts, interviews, and analyses, the work is drawn from mostly Spanish primary and secondary sources. Official information is still difficult to obtain in Spain, and it is often unreliable. Government officials are characteristically reluctant to divulge information, either for political reasons or because they simply do not possess it. Like myself, officialdom uses the Spanish and international media as primary sources for its information and analyses.

Much of the documentation on the Spanish aspects of this study is taken from *El Pais*, the internationally recognized newspaper of record for Spain. Other reliable sources, including *La Vanguardia* (Barcelona), *Diario 16*, *Tiempo*, and *Cambio 16*, are also employed in cases where coverage is unique or exclusive. Implicit in the use of such sources is the proper degree of content and frequency analysis. Wherever possible and appropriate, U.S. and European newspapers of record are also used.

Every effort was made to keep the work as up to date as possible, given my publisher's deadlines, the scope of the study, and the fluidity of events in Central America, Spain, and strategic affairs. In the search for an appropriate juncture, I opted for the July 1991 Ibero-American summit in Guadalajara, Mexico, which was held after mid-term elections and new peace initiatives in El Salvador, a major cabinet reshuffle and local elections in Spain, and the winding down of the Gulf War.

While the important scholarly contributions to the theoretical aspects of this work are accounted for and incorporated, my preference for an empirical focus is manifest. If there is a lack of emphasis on secondary sources in the discussion, it reflects not only the theoretical weaknesses of the field but also my own desire for originality.

Part I

The Democratic Market

Spain and Latin America: Democratic Models and the Search

Efforts to establish a democratic agenda for the behavior of nation-states are by no means new to political science. Much progress has been made in identifying the components of foreign policy that are related to promoting a country's conception of democracy. It has been observed that in practically all modern nation-states there exists a model of democracy, which becomes a major part of the foreign policy content. The "Democratic Revolution" of 1989 in Eastern and Central Europe, the evolution and reform of authoritarian regimes in Asia, as well as the recent implantation of formal democratic regimes in Latin America, have helped raise expectations that the ideals of democracy would definitively penetrate great-power foreign policy concerns. Whereas in the past the very fact that the model tended to differ from state to state accounted for much of the inherent conflict in the international system, by the early 1990s there was reason to hope that at least the great powers agreed on the *telos* of foreign policy and intervention.

The behavioral approach in political science has nevertheless sought to account for actual deviations from established patterns of behavior that result from a foreign policy agenda being held hostage by a nation-state's notion of democracy. The majority of foreign policy analyses in the post–World War II period has tended to discredit the idea that a nation-state's behavior is a function of its view of democracy. Behavioralists have observed—and documented—the disparity between a country's vision of democracy and the actual behavior of that country in the international sphere. In an effort to discredit the "moral approach" to politics, which has as its major goal the establishment of democratic systems, some have gone so far as to warn of the normative tendencies of an approach to foreign policy whose point of departure is a model of politics to which there may be only one subscriber.[1]

Realists, moreover, have dismissed the notion of the democratic agenda as hopelessly naive and inherently dangerous. Inasmuch as there is no concurrence of democratic thought in the hostile international environment, an approach to national power that is based on the nation's view of democracy will, at best, satisfy only a psychological desire on the part of its adherents. In the worst case, a foreign policy agenda based on democratic wishful thinking will ignore the more important aspects of maximizing national power, thus leaving untended vital national interests and objectives.[2] Efforts to explain the inherent contradictions in U.S. foreign policy have focused on the counterpoint between the *idealpolitik* of those who see America's power as a function of its democratic credentials and the *realpolitik* of those who fail to find a democratic echo in a competitive and hostile international system.[3]

Realistic observers and practitioners alike have rejected the constraints that normative thought would place on both analysis and decision-making in foreign policy. If nation-states seek to maximize their power, as Morganthau asserted, then their major concerns would have less to do with upholding certain norms in the international sphere than with securing the material advantages necessary to that power. These advantages may be intangible—psychological oneupmanship, "crazy man" gaming—but, for the most part, they are measured by alliances, territories, deployments, and economic wealth. The promotion of a democratic model in the international sphere will often be somewhere in the policy mix, perhaps even underlying all other initiatives; yet a practitioner of power politics would be reluctant to regard the realization of the model as the end in itself.[4]

The explosive dawn of the post-Cold War era only serves to reinforce the realist assumptions. At first glance there seemed to be a *convergence* of political goals and values across the old Cold War axis. Superpower intervention was tolerated—if not exhorted—if the perceived goals were the establishment of democratic regimes. Suggestions of approval of Soviet intervention in the 1989 Romanian revolution (made by none other than U.S. Secretary of State James Baker), were more than a *quid pro quo* for Soviet restraint in its critique of American intervention in Panamá. Such suggestions, which were seconded by other great powers (notably France), seemed to herald a new strategic harmony where democratic goals would be pursued from both axes of the Cold War divide.[5]

For the realists, the popular wisdom that "politics makes strange bedfellows" has some validity here. If the promotion of a democratic model is the dominant component of foreign policy—and hence, national strategy—then how is one to account for the seemingly bizarre relationships that have cropped up over the years? The Soviet Union's self-proclaimed model of socialist democracy hardly found an echo in the anti-communist, authoritarian and militaristic political system in Iraq. The liberal establishment in the United States still recoils at the thought of close relations between the U.S. and authoritarian Pakistan, while the right wing is no longer alone in its dis-comfiture with U.S. strategic cooperation with communist China after the so-called Tiananmen Square massacres. And perhaps more problematic was the presence of despotic Syria in the U.S.-led anti-Iraq coalition, which was built on the rhetorical assumption that it would usher in a "New World Order." In all of these cases, the motivating factor is not the confirmation of democratic ideals or the commerce of democratic models, but the quest for political, strategic, or geopolitical advantage *vis à vis* an international competitor.

There may be, however, cases where the realistic goals of power maximization would call for precisely the kind of policy agenda that would have as its first priority promoting a democratic model. Such an unlikely overlap would not often be found within the ranks of the great powers, much less among the superpowers. It is more likely to be observed among the foreign policies of the lesser powers, whose political, strategic, and economic concerns are usually administered to by alliances or clientships led by a great power or superpower. The security afforded by such protection allows a nation to develop a foreign policy agenda whose priorities reflect a concern for democratic promotion.

Even without this protection from the direct pressures of the international system, a nation-state might not possess any other means of exerting its influence on other states. The Scandanavian model, whose greatest international purveyor is the Kingdom of Sweden, has by no means provided an exception to Morganthau's iron law of political realism. Like all nation-states, Sweden seeks to maximize its power; the fact that it uses its political and economic model of democracy as the frontpiece of its foreign policy does not alter the fact that Swedish society and the Swedish government secure international advantages. The political realists may assert that these advantages are mostly intangible: prestige, notoriety, good-will. Yet it would be hard to imagine what Sweden would achieve if it were to use only economic, political, and military might to maximize power. Despite its relative economic and social health and its sophisticated armed forces, Sweden's *real* power is dwarfed by the international nuclear giants.

Thus there is a case to be made for those lesser powers, whose task of power maximization in the nuclear era demands that they put forth something other than goods, services, capital, soldiers, and missiles. The subject of this study, Spanish foreign policy, is at present the most attractive case example of a nation-state whose international behavior appears to be guided primarily by the desire to promote a democratic model.

SPAIN'S CATAPULT OF POWER

Spain's democratic transition after the 1975 death of authoritarian ruler General Francisco Franco has become the subject of much international scrutiny and scholarly effort. While most studies concentrate on the transition model itself, some attention has been given to the international role of Spain's new democracy. Much of the energy for this scholarly and political activity comes from two sources: the trauma and debate surrounding the Spanish Civil War of 1936–39; and the almost desperate search for new solutions to the worsening crisis in Spain's former colonial domains in Latin America.

For much of the international intellectual community, the Spanish Civil War left an open wound in international political consciousness. While the Allied victory over German and Italian fascism in Europe and Japanese imperialism in Asia served to vindicate democratic aspirations the world over, in Spain Francoism was regarded as an unresolved political and moral problem. For the practitioners of post-war international politics, Franco's Spain was, at best, an inconvenience and embarrassment. As liberal democracy in Europe flourished in the United States-led post-war period and was called upon to confront Soviet power, Spain remained isolated from the political and economic life of the West. The enlistment in 1953 of Spain as an anti-communist bulwark through the Eisenhower/Franco base pact only served to heighten the contradictions. Europe refused to allow Spain to participate in its most sacred political, military, and economic institutions. Spain would have to acquire democratic credentials before being admitted to the NATO alliance or the European Economic Community.

The peaceful democratic transition after Franco's death immediately became a model for comparative politics. Much of the energy was emotional; after forty years of Francoism there was bound to be celebration, no matter what the ultimate view of the model. Observers and participants tended to see the confirmation of their own democratic ideals; many would later be blind to the model's own internal problems. There remains a real need to address the model on its own terms by noting its internal successes and failures while at the same time evaluating its role as the major component for Spain's foreign policy in Central America. There will be, of course, a major dichotomy. As an operational guide for foreign policy, the model needs to be successful internally. If there is considerable doubt as to the success of the model itself, then an analysis of the model's international role must take into account these weaknesses. The important thing, nevertheless, is that the practitioners and decision-makers of Spanish foreign policy behave in such a way that suggests that *they believe the model is working.*

The other force contributing to the political and academic importance of the Spanish model is the desperation that has accompanied recent efforts at peace-making and democratic development in Central America. Even with "northern winds" blowing after the Soviet strategic retreat from the hemisphere, the stunning Sandinista defeat at the February 1990 Nicaraguan polls, and the militarily decisive U.S. intervention in Panamá, new and greater expectations are yet to be fulfilled. While an analysis of the crisis' roots, *sui generis*, lies beyond the scope of this study, one must nevertheless observe that the most important and decisive actors in Central American politics—Cuba, the Soviet Union, the United States, and the Central American countries led by Costa Rica—all have proffered their political models as a panacea for the region's problems. Even the Soviet model made, and the Cuban model continues to make, the claim that their alternatives represent true democracy. Costa Rica's Nobel laureate and former president Oscar Arias may have succeeded, through his Esquipulas II peace initiative, in establishing a framework in which conflict remains within national borders; but it remains to be seen if the traditional actors in the region, with the erratic support of the United States, a superpower overwhelmed by events in the Near East, can muster the kind of inspirational and transcendent appeal in their approaches that would sow the seeds for a more lasting peace and—perhaps more important—an enduring prosperity.

One of the fundamental suggestions of the present study is that such a commerce in democratic models in Central America is both contributor to—if not the cause of—conflict, and a source of hope. For the superpowers, the costs of direct confrontation in the nuclear era make such conflicts a normal part of the output of the international system. The shift to the Third World of multi-level competition has been exhaustively argued and documented. The portrayal of Central America as a region caught in a "strategic squeeze" has elicited reactions from around the globe. If there was such a "stalemate" in superpower competition, then there must have been room for less powerful actors. It is as if the market for democratic models were expanding for not only the monopoly players but also for the small purveyors.

It is precisely within this strategic and ethical space that Spanish foreign policy has operated. With its democratic model as its battle flag, Spain's Socialist government of Felipe Gonzalez boldly entered the policy picture in Central America. Spain's experience with democracy would thus become the vehicle through which aspirations—national, international, and personal—could be fulfilled by the Socialist prime minister.

But it is not the purpose of this study to make a case for the *decisiveness* of Spanish policy in the Central American context, despite what official Spanish propaganda would have us believe. Spain lacks the resources and "realistic" policy instruments to profoundly alter the economic, political, and strategic situation on the isthmus. What is significant is the phenomenon in and of itself: that a nation-state would establish its foreign policy on the basis of a democratic experience; that policy-makers would operationalize such an experience as an international experiment; and that a country such as Spain, with its own democratic development only partially accounted for, would have as big an impact on events in such a distant region.

This study, therefore, is not simply of the Spanish transition or of development in the Third World. The effort herein is as much an analysis of the psychological and abstract content of foreign policy as it is an attempt to find alternative solutions to chronic international crisis. Inasmuch as the transition in Spain is by no means complete, as this study will endeavor to show, the relationship between the international role of the Spanish democratic model and its domestic role will remain central to the study. From an analysis of this relationship comes one of the primary theses of this work: that the adoption of *pro forma* democratic structures and reforms is no guarantee of a democratic society; and that there is often a grave risk in evolutionary transitions from authoritarianism to democracy. Spain looks toward rich and powerful partners in the European Economic Community to bury her weaknesses and shore up her democratic achievements. Central America, as we shall see, has no such geopolitical advantages.

The warning about dangers of evolution from authoritarianism should by no means be construed to mean that a revolutionary approach is being advocated or that authoritarianism is being presented as a desirable system. The thesis points to larger questions of political change, the first of which is the role of economic development and the international economic system in the search for democracy. The author is well aware of the temptations of reductionism, or the short-cuts of economic determinism. In deciding "which came first, the chicken or the egg," the evidence in Spain, the model, seems to suggest that economic development must precede the institution of democratic structures or else those very structures will be put at risk by anti-social, revolutionary, and external forces. Central America already enjoys the presence and influence of a home-grown democratic model in Costa Rica; yet the failure of this democratic model to spread to neighboring countries, despite the undeniable influence of its leaders, suggests that Costa Rican democracy lacks something outside of the political sphere. Costa Rica remains a political success story, but its international weight is held hostage by a less than miraculous economic performance and an acute vulnerability to the dicta of outside policy actors, especially the United States.

One may just as convincingly argue that democratic political institutions are necessary for economic development. But in the final analysis we must, at the very least, observe the *reciprocal relationship* between economic and political structures. No democratic model with international prestige could erect its democratic structures on the foundations of poverty. Socialist and other Soviet-type models are no exception; it is prosperity that is the basis for new social relationships, or in socialist terms, 'the abolition of scarcity.''

The differing paths to abundance and prosperity that characterize the struggle between capitalism and socialism suggest another of the larger questions that the present study's thesis would pose. It is no accident that the revolutionary transformations advocated in the Cuban, Soviet, and other socialist models are accompanied by a healthy dose of authoritarianism. Revolutionaries of the Third World are faced with the formidable obstacles of backward social behavior inherited from generations of historical and socioeconomic experience and passed on through powerful family and clan cultures. The countervaling socialization process imposed from above by the revolutionary regime is usually characterized by coercive methods and authoritarian techniques. Even the peculiar revolutionary strain found in Sandinista Nicaragua shared the authoritarian character of an embattled political elite, which attempted through coercion to socialize its people into an alien political and economic framework.[6]

Profound social and political change in a capitalist framework has as its goal the elimination of authoritarian political structures. The Spanish model, the transition from "dictatorship to democracy," reserves no place for the authoritarian politician; authoritarianism was recognized as the major obstacle to democratic aspirations. Yet the new democrats are still faced with the same backwardness and intransigence in the general population—as well as within their own ranks—as the revolutionaries. What means are available to the capitalist democrat if authoritarian measures are precluded? What will save society from "eating itself" if deteriorating economic conditions and radical social transformations present democracy from above with a new set of enemies?

In such a situation, the society must arm itself with a measure of authoritarian control or find a way to eliminate the economic problems that give birth to anti-social behavior and radical political challenges. The use of authoritarian means is usually out of the question, though it will be shown that such measures still abound in "democratic Spain." One would hope that the confluence of international, domestic, and transnational economic factors is such that at least gradual solutions can be found for the economic problems. Within Europe, Spain may enjoy such a confluence of factors that would help it to muddle through and stave off anarchy. The question remains as to whether the countries of Central America enjoy the same advantages.

DEMOCRACY AS METAPHOR

At this point the reader may ask for an explanation of the term "democracy." And as with most political science discussions, only an operational definition can be offered. When democracy is referred to in a study that involves decision-making and implementation in foreign policy, the best operational definition is the one the actors themselves use. In the case of the Spanish democratic model there is no single version of the democratic project; but there is a shared point of departure. At the very minimum the model seems to call for some sort of "popular selection" of leaders from a pluralistic political party system in free elections, and for a state of law—*el estado de derecho*—which emanates from constitutionalism.[7] These criteria may seem meager for European and North American countries with long democratic traditions, but for much of the Third World, the institutionalization of such a system would constitute a political miracle.

The type of economic system that is advocated in the Spanish model is not entirely clear. There is clear reference in the Spanish Constitution to a market system (Article 38) but no specific guidelines for the amount of state regulation and intervention. It is assumed that the selection of a political party will reveal a preference for the degree of state control over the means of production. That preference will make its way in the context of opposing ideologies and economic programs that make up the political system, from Eurocommunism and European democratic socialism to neo-liberalism. While each party would like to see its vision reflected in the democratic model being purveyed internationally, there is no presupposed type of economic system tied to the model.

The existence of a predetermined economic system is important both for the politics of transition within Spain and for the target countries of the model. A perusal of the democratic landscape in Spain will show that the unfinished business of the Spanish transition leaves open the possibility that the democratic model itself will change.

The Spanish model, nevertheless, would be of little interest if it were being utilized as a foreign policy vehicle in a context that is incapable of echoing, on any level, the democratic appeal. Contexts, so problematic for comparative politics, must be addressed at the outset; a case for the validity of democratic models in the Latin American context must be made. There must be a market for democracy, just as there must be the national democratic energy necessary to exploit a democratic model as a foreign policy tool.

LATIN AMERICA, DEMOCRATIC MODELS, AND THE SEARCH

There may be a scholarly imperative here; for too long, the business of democratic models has remained firmly in the hands of intellectual historians. Political science, in its behavioral trajectory, has tended to ignore the aspirations of human beings if those aspirations were not manifested in concrete material or institutional concerns. The struggle for democracy is a dramatic process. It hardly needs to be portrayed as a battle of ideas fought by intellectual generals commanding troops that are, more often than not, ignorant of the nature of the struggle. It is not without justification that most scholars and observers focus on the massive political and socio-economic transformations that accompany the democratization process. Nationalism, economic aspirations, and the lust for power make dramatic enough stories on their own merit; they are often presented with only a passing reference to the intellectual dimensions of the struggle and an almost obligatory concession to the desirability of democracy as a possible outcome. The importance and power of the intellectual dimension is left unaccounted for, while an operational definition of democracy is not even casually proffered.

The history of Latin American politics exemplifies the importance of the intellectual struggle for democracy. Nowhere has the commerce of democratic models been more central to the political debate. That this debate has been at the level of the political and social elite only serves to strengthen the argument for the power of democratic models. The body of modern research on political change in Latin America admits to the decisiveness of the "elite" in practically all phases of the democratic struggle.[8] Whereas the participation of the masses is seen to be something of a desperate groping for economic improvement or an emotional and intuitive rejection of current social relationships and power arrangements, the movers and shakers of Latin American society have almost always spoken the language of democratic models. The fact that this elite is primarily responsible for political change, from socialist revolution to fascist "organic democracy," makes the intellectual and conceptual dimension of conflict in Latin America a central area of concern.

Democratic yearnings in Latin and Central America were ignited by the American Revolution in 1776 and fanned by the French Revolution ten years later. The inspiration that these two international events afforded cannot be underestimated in any analysis of the history of the Americans. The fact that they occurred so far from the centers of political change in Latin America accounts for the idealization of the models. Time and space served to abstract these events and detach them from the binds of culture, race, and history. For early Latin American democrats, the models were operational; Spanish colonialism was doomed. Theory would be put into action. The *libertadores*, like George Washington, would be the agents of inevitable, yet controllable change.[9]

Simón Bolívar, the great South American *libertador*, knew the difficulty of transplanting democratic models to areas that have unique historical experiences. He marveled at the success of the federal system in the United States but stopped short of recommending it for South America. Pointing to the different geographical, cultural, and social inheritance of South America, he was perhaps the first to suggest that political models could not easily be translated from one people to another:

[And] it is a marvel to me that its model in the United States has operated so successfully . . . In spite of the fact that freedom was their cradle, that liberty was the air that they breathed, and the food they ate . . . that in many respects this people is unique in the history of the human race, still I do repeat: it seems a marvel to me that a government so weak and complicated as the federal system should have endured . . .[10]

The difficulties of establishing one great Latin American nation, Simón Bolívar's lifelong dream, obsessed him. He confessed that such a project "is not possible because extremes of climate, geographic differences, opposed interests, distinct characteristics divide our America. Unless Latin Americans could acquire the talents and political virtues which distinguish our brothers of the North, entirely popular systems, far from favoring us, will become our ruin."[11]

While his visionary fervor is most celebrated, Bolívar's political realism was perhaps his most endearing quality. He knew that a democratic project could not be consolidated without a concurrence in the international political system. Predicting the Monroe Doctrine as far back as 1815, Bolivar suggested that democratization was a local project that could not be transplanted from other lands and peoples, but it could be fostered under favorable international conditions:

> As soon as we are strong, under the auspices of a liberal nation which lends us its protection, the world will see us cultivate with a single accord the virtues and talents which lead to glorious accomplishment. Then we shall move majestically forward towards the great prosperity and development for which our South America is destined.[12]

What Bolívar suggested throughout his life has come to form a preliminary body of theoretical thought regarding the role of democratic models in the international system. His writings and exploits point to two main areas of concern in the transfer of democratic institutions over national borders: (1) the differing characteristics of human beings and the peculiar local conditions; and (2) the need for favorable conditions in the international sphere that would help foster the process of democratization.

Within the scope of the first set of factors are the anthropological, historical, and sociological experiences that distinguish one nation or region from another. Although the social sciences have tended to aggregate groups and peoples in order to make universal generalizations, more recent scholarship in international affairs and political science has turned its focus on the *sui generis* aspects of political and historical events, thus admitting to the difficulties of transferring standards, values, and ideas across national boundaries. The case of Central America is perhaps the most illustrative of this trend in scholarship. Policy positions must be aware of such a variety of confounding factors to principles confirmed elsewhere that specialized skills must be developed for policy formulation in that area of the world.

The second set of concerns refers to the political and strategic realities that characterize the international system at any given time. Bolívar, of course, saw the array of forces in function of Spanish imperial power; he looked toward Great Britain and the United States to change the balance of power in the Western Hemisphere. Under this strategic umbrella would be constructed the great South American democratic project. His sensitivity to these strategic factors was reinforced by military reality; the business at hand was the liberation of South America from the Spanish Crown. Yet his hopes for a favorable international arrangement went beyond the concerns of the long, drawn out war against Spain. Bolívar's writings suggest that he considered victory over the Spanish as a tactical battle in a larger struggle for the construction of a new American society.

Although Bolívar remains as Latin America's first and foremost *pensador*, the legendary character of his exploits is what most impresses the student of Latin American affairs. If indeed Bolívar was the "George Washington of South America," as the cliché would have it, then we should be most impressed by his hard-headed realism. Unlike many revolutionary leaders, Bolívar was concerned with what lay ahead for Latin American society. His vision was comparative and dynamic. In contrast to later revolutionary leaders, Bolivar was interested in the process of revolution with all its national, regional, and international dimensions. Victory was not in the simple expulsion of the Spanish or in the defeat of the *federales* as Zapata saw it, or in the overthrow of Somoza as Edén Pastora's revolutionary zeal led him to believe. The authentic triumph is the establishment of a democratic project that would be able to withstand the myriad social, cultural, and political-strategic forces that seem poised to demolish it.

The concern for democratic models on the part of the early Latin American *pensadores*, then, does not represent a utopian current in the literature of an emerging civilization. On the contrary, a healthy dose of realism usually accompanies these impassioned visions of future Latin American society. One of Central America's own *pensadores*, José Cecilio del Valle, the principal author of Central America's declaration of independence in 1821, harbored no illusions about the ability of Central Americans to survive without establishing international structures that would ensure economic and political development. The Honduran's emphasis on economics was his most distinguishing characteristic. Well-entrenched in Central American reality, del Valle's vision extended to the rising independence movement throughout Latin America. He envisioned an Inter-American system that would foster economic progress in places where the Spanish empire had wrought havoc on the land and the people.[13]

The intellectual contributions of the Latin American *pensadores* were anything but romantic visions of an unattainable future. The most important *pensadores* were great lovers of liberty, yet their analysis of the situation in the Americas was tempered by an overriding realism. Andrés Bello, the Venezuelan-born leader of the "Generation of 1842," could not be convinced of the debt that the Latin American *libertadores* owed to the republican models purveyed by France and the United States. Arguing that the heroism of the *caudillo* revolutions against the Spanish Crown had its roots in the same heroism and spirit that earlier "reconquered" the vast territories of Iberia and America, Bello suggested that independence for the Americas arose out of a natural desire for self-government, whatever form that might take. The warning implicit in Bello's analysis is that one should not confuse "inde-

pendence"—or in a modern sense, "sovereignty"—with political freedom
and democracy. It can be argued that the examples of the Cuban and Nicaraguan Revolutions amply demonstrate the merits of this view.[14]

From his privileged view as Latin America's foremost educator, Bello
identified the major challenge to Latino democrats as one of education. The
Spanish Empire had denied democratic opportunities by systematically limiting education to a tiny elite. A wide gulf existed between the democratic
pretensions of Latin America leaders and the ability of the general populace
to carry out social and political activities in ways that would safeguard the
pro forma gains embodied in constitutions and the like. Unlike their North
American neighbors, Latin Americans were not exposed to the value system
inherent in democratic politics. North Americans were introduced to democratic values through primary education. Latin Americans had such values
thrust upon them from above. Bolívar's and other liberators' struggles with
local *caudillos* and chieftains, who sometimes sided with the Spanish Roy-
alists, were logical outcomes of generations of educational discrimination and
neglect.

What Bello and others—including the Argentine president and *pensador*
Domingo Faustino Sarmiento—suggested was a problem of "reciprocation"
of democratic values. Constitutions and statutory reforms could democratize
only the sectors of the population that were able to respond, through self-
interest or appeals to ingrained values, to the challenge of democratic society.
In most polities, and especially in those that have suffered harsh colonial
experiences, this reciprocation can be found only in educated sectors of the
middle-classes. In places where the educational gulf is widest, as in Central
America, democratic projects are quickly abandoned in an effort to restore
political authority over a populace that has failed to reciprocate in its democratic responsibilities. Authoritarianism becomes the preferred choice of
political leaders who develop an arrogance and cynicism with respect to their
own people's ability to perform democratic tasks. The authoritarianism has
appeared in the form of military interventionism, personal dictatorships,
oligarchical rule of economic elites, as well as leftist statism. Even Bolívar
doubted the capacity of the people to achieve democratic goals in a federal
republican framework; it was "overperfect and demands political virtues and
talents far superior to our own."[15]

The limits to the romantic democratic visions are nowhere more evident
than in the Mexican Revolution. To deny the Mexican Revolution's impact
on Latin Americans—and Central Americans especially—would be to deprive
the present-day democratic movement in the Americas of much of its spirit.
Even the ethnocentric Soviets, whose Bolshevik Revolution had become the
ultimate democratic model on the world market, admitted to the Mexican
Revolution's being the first genuine "people's revolution." The alliance
between the middle classes, the urban workers, and the rural peasants was

unprecedented; but history has shown that there was no body of thought, no specific program that would make the Mexican Revolution a complete and saleable package. Indeed, the *mystique* of the revolution is what prevails, along with the utopian vision of rapid and profound social transformations that later served and is serving the spiritual needs of Central American revolutionaries. Beyond land reform, the nationalization of natural resources, a labor code, and restrictions on Church power, there was no specific ideological content to the Mexican Revolutionary experience. Certain figures like the revolutionary populist Lazaro Cárdenas stand out, yet his nationalistic populism was by no means an ideological package.

Efforts by the diplomatic community in Latin America to "disarm" revolutionary movements, such as *Sandinismo*, by pushing them towards the Mexican "model" only reinforce the point.[16] But what is important here is that the Mexican model is still very much in currency in Central America. Mexican policy continues to work through this vehicle, despite its theoretical and practical limitations. Moreover, the theoretical and practical implications are precisely what we should be concerned with when attempting to establish parameters for the role of democratic models.

Together, the impassioned realism of the *pensadores* and the spiritual inheritance of the Mexican Revolution can be seen as forming a kind of analytical framework for studying the role of democratic models in Central America. The *pensadores* were preoccupied primarily with six things: (1) the unique and local characteristics that make Latin American institutions, societies, cultures, and rulers different from those in other parts of the developed and underdeveloped world; (2) the international political system and the strategic realities in the Western Hemisphere; (3) the establishment of uncontested political authority by regimes as a condition of national sovereignty; (4) the need for a spiritual and moral driving force for Latin American democracy; (5) the educational chasm between elites and the general populace, which inhibited democratic reciprocation; and (6) the primacy of economic development in the quest for democracy. While the Mexican Revolution would suggest the fourth concern, it also contributes to the framework a definition of the struggle that would later be formalized by Marxist interpreters: the notion of a class struggle that sets the people (*el pueblo*) apart from the ruling elites. This notion is perhaps the most problematic insofar as it suggests that some kind of revolutionary transformation is a *requirement* of democracy in the Latin American context. In perspective, however, the idea of revolutionary change need not conjure images of unacceptable totalitarian alternatives; indeed the revolutionary aspects of political change in a place like Central America may well take the form of a bourgeois revolution. We must nevertheless account for those Central Americans, like the Sandinista leaders, who saw in any democratic framework a requirement that any change must be a revolutionary push up the path of socialism,[17] even if there are those in the thick of the Nicaraguan conflict who believed that Nicaragua's problems could adequately be addressed within the traditional capitalist economic framework.

As guidelines that would help us evaluate the potential role of a democratic model, the aforementioned concerns are observable political and social variables that can be broken down to identifiable and measurable units of analysis. The bulk of recent scholarship in Latin American affairs has addressed these concerns either on an individual country basis or as regional problems. That knowledge will be used here, in conjunction with scientific guidelines, to evaluate the potential role of the Spanish democratic model in the Central American context. By looking at the historical concerns of democratic advocates as a framework of analysis, it is possible to arrive at a set of necessary conditions for the success of a democratic model. And if the foreign policy of a nation state is predicated on the prestige of its democratic model, then it would be possible to evaluate that nation state's foreign policy role in the Central American context.

Yet the framework is still incomplete. Certainly the wisdom of the *liber-tadores* and the democratic visionaries of yesteryear touched on the most fundamental variables. But there are a number of other, perhaps more recent, concerns that must be included in any analytical framework. Some of these variables will emerge from the discussion of the Spanish model itself; others will reveal themselves in the ensuing discussion of democratic models in the contemporary Latin American context.

At this point it is necessary to address the more contemporary magnets of democratic thought. It can be seen that democratic models have an established role in the political and social life of the Americas, and that they account in good part for the revolutionary spirit in places like Central America. As "political goods," they are almost necessary imports. Their power to influence change in weak societies has caused them to be the loci of much national and international conflict. By the same token, they are also regarded as the potential salvation from chronic and often desperate political and social conditions.

DEMOCRATIC MAGNETS

Ideological conflict in Central America can no longer be simplified or reduced to the struggle between dictatorship and democracy. In many cases dictatorships have given way to democratically elected regimes, yet profound problems persist in destabilizing the entire isthmus. It is no longer instructive to depict the struggle of the Central American people as that of popular uprising against quasi-fascist rule, as if we were once again living in the days of Georgi Dimitrov's Popular Front.[18] Today the struggle is multidimensional. The hearts and minds of the Central American people are being pandered to by a number of political forces, behind which there are distinct political and economic alternatives. Three of them—U.S. style liberal democracy, Cuban Marxism-Leninism, and Costa Rican social democracy backed by European social democrats—account for practically all the ideological conflict on the isthmus.

While a comprehensive evaluation of these contemporary models lies beyond the scope of this study, the more salient features of their appeal in the Central American context will become apparent during ensuing discussions on democratic politics and strategic affairs. What is perhaps most interesting about the models, however, is the fact that their *content* may not be of any decisive importance. Rarely, if at all, is there an intercontextual analysis of the actual performance of the model itself. What is of importance is the *image* of the model—the hope and promise that it holds out for oppressed or poverty-stricken people who have become increasingly aware of their predicament.

The Weight of History: The U.S. Model

While the United States has certainly lost its revolutionary appeal over the course of almost two hundred years of intimate involvement in the affairs of Latin America, it still remains a democratic magnet for perhaps the most decisive sectors of the Latin American population. The infatuation with U.S. institutions, so evident in the writings of 19th Century Latin democrats, has given way to a more realistic appraisal of the United States and its undeniable role in fostering democracy in the Americas.[19] If the behavior of the United States in the Western Hemisphere has complicated the U.S. role as a democratic model, then one must find some other way to account for the considerable attention given to the U.S. democratic experience in the political debate in the Americas.[20] While there remains some fascination with the institutional aspects of U.S. democracy and the peaceful nature of social, economic, and political change therein, most of the attractiveness seems to come from the image of wealth and power that the United States projects. It is safe to say that, while most Latin Americans are familiar with the many faces of U.S. power, it is the economic aspect of the U.S. role that is the center of the democratic debate, especially in the 1980s. It was never lost upon the Latin Americans that prosperity is needed for the construction of the welfare state, and that no major economic system, including socialism, could be built on the foundations of poverty. There are marginal revolutionary groups in Latin America that preach the kind of dignified poverty that came out of the Maoist experience, especially those groups that have roots in Indian highland communities.[21] But even the unique revolutionary experience of *Sandinismo* in Nicaragua has yielded to the demands of economic improvement.

The United States still holds out the hope of efficiently using natural and human resources to develop a nation-state. The notion of prosperity has become synonymous with democracy. As long as the United States is seen as the mecca of economic choice and opportunity, many of the democratic demands are satisfied. Many admirers of the United States and its democratic model would choose to focus on the vast expanse of economic and social opportunity and political freedoms while ignoring the equally vast array of crushing social problems, from drugs, crime, and inadequate health care, to corruption, divorce, and suicide.

Socialism and the Cuban Challenge

The separation of content from image of a model is by no means unique in the democratic marketplace.[22] In the Cuban case, the successes and failures of Fidel Castro's social experiment do not necessarily establish the content of the Cuban model. The attraction of the Cuban model can be found in its foreign policy posture in the Americas and across the globe.[23] The perception on the political left that Cuba stands for the ideals of Latin American democracy, national liberation, economic development, and non-alignment accounts for the Cuban model's continuing presence in the marketplace of democratic models. Castro's ability to speak to the issues, to exploit, however cynically, the legitimate aspirations of the Latin American masses creates an image of an island of freedom amidst an ocean of despair. There is no need or opportunity for further investigation of Cuban reality on the part of the naive intellectual or impoverished *campesino*. Just as there is often only a vague idea of what parliamentary democracy involves and demands, there is an ignorance of the workings and implications of socialism. Although disenchantment with Cuba's performance, especially in the economic sphere, seeped down to popular levels during the 1980s, in the desperate situation in which many Latin Americans live, there hardly seems time for such details.[24]

There are Latin American political leaders who have embraced the Cuban model in all its Marxist-Leninist dimensions. These loyal few in the revolutionary left were weaned on the Cuban revolutionary experience during a generation in which democratic alternatives were not easily grasped. The Cuban Revolution, the hemorrhage of Latin American nationalism, the mystique which propelled the myth of the guerrilla war, all served to fashion a generation of revolutionaries whose idealism would never be tempered by harsh reality. Some of these revolutionaries even trained in Cuba, or spent long periods of exile there. In Nicaragua, Sandinista officials at the highest levels shared this generational inheritance; a few remain outspoken admirers of Cuban socialist reality and maintain personal relationships with Castro himself.

But even among the Sandinistas who dreamt and still dream of a *Nicaragua Socialista*, or of a Marxist-Leninist Central America, there is a growing realism. As the Sandinistas, like any other Central American leadership, came to terms with the dimensions of their country's economic problems, they became less enamored by a model whose economic failures are evident even to the most optimistic observer.[25]

On the democratic left in Latin America there are those political leaders who have found that certain compromises with Castro's positions on Latin American affairs can assure them significant, and often widespread, support. Populists like Alan García of Peru found Castro's policy on debt repayment to be a convenient shield for his less extreme, but nonetheless radical positions. The Mexican presidency has always sought this shelter, as it provides the revolutionary character that is missing in practically all the regime's other policies. And as the middle-ground in Latin American politics became more and more narrow, the nature of the compromise with Castroite policies and approaches became more profound. Such is the case with the entire social democratic movement in El Salvador. The polarization of Salvadoran society was such that social democrats like the late Guillermo Ungo or left-wing Christian Democrats (Social Christians) like Rubén Zamora were forced to throw in their lot first with insurrectionary labor, civil and religious groups and finally with the Marxist-Leninist guerrilla groups and their Cuban sponsors. (The association with the guerrilla groups complicated the attempt by Ungo and Zamora to represent the democratic left in the February 1989 and March 1991 mid-term elections). Political phenomena of this sort account for much of the ambiguity in Central American politics.

If Castro has been able to rally to his cause an impressive array of Latin American leaders, it is at the expense of an equally profound alienation of many other elites. Where Cuban policy intervenes directly, as in Guatemala, Colombia, El Salvador, and within counterrevolutionary sectors of Nicaragua, the Cuban model is rejected outright. This is particularly the case in the Latin American business community, the military, and among oligarchical economic elites. If Castro appeals at all to these sectors, it is only through the most primitive messages of Latin American nationalism, anti-Americanism, and anti-imperialism. An occasional echo is received by an embattled military dictator, such as Panama's Manuel Noriega; but most conservative forces prefer isolation to any form of association with Cuba's international role.

It should have become evident by now that the Cuban model's presence in the Latin American marketplace is made possible by an underlying current of nationalism and a latent hostility toward interventionism, which often takes the form of anti-Americanism. If there often seems to be a scandalous silence in Latin American chancelleries after Castro's pronouncements, it is because there exists a natural sensitivity to the issues that the Cuban leader addresses. The theory that Latin America is "twenty countries but one people," as former Dominican leader Juan Bosch once said, has some operational significance here. It accounts for the fact that the Cuban model, a bankrupt and empty shell, continues to exert a subtle but nonetheless pro-

found influence on the politics of Latin American democracy and development. Its influence rises in direct proportion to Latin America's problems;
and its presence will evaporate as soon as Latin Americans, together with
their northern neighbors, begin to find solutions to these problems.

The Weight of Costa Rica: Towards Social Democracy

Costa Rican social democracy, which, along with Venezuela's political
system, serves as a vehicle for the involvement of European democratic
socialists and social democrats, emerged from the turbulent, revolutionary
1960s as the only stable, viable democracy in Central America. This model's
longevity is its most prominent selling point. Costa Rica has suffered the
same developmental problems and economic downturns as other Central
American countries, yet its democratic institutions have withstood the stress.
When being evaluated as a model in the Central American context, few
observers look to Costa Rica's specific economic and social accomplishments,
which in certain respects can be as dubious as those of its less fortunate
neighbors.

In fact, Costa Rica's achievements belong to that abstract world of international democratic politics where the criteria for success are somewhat intangible. The safeguarding of human rights, it might be argued, is hardly
intangible proof of democratic credentials; yet if one would expand the
operational definition of democracy proffered for the purposes of this study,
Costa Rica would come up short on most aspects of economic democracy.
The well-entrenched climate of political pluralism in Costa Rica is amply
documented. The rigorous defense of constitutionality by the judicial system
may well be the heart of the matter in the context of Latin America's de-
plorable record of making paper constitutions a political reality.[26] But Costa
Rica remains a Central American country: her social fabric is woven by the
same developmental issues as her neighbors'. She borrowed herself into
financial oblivion; she has made herself vulnerable to great power diktat.
Her tenuous economic base has not been immune to the revolutionary politics
that characterize the rest of the isthmus.[27]

Indeed, the popular suggestion that Costa Rica was the "Switzerland of
Central America," often heard during the 1960s and 1970s, reflects only a
superficial analysis of Costa Rican reality. Even the notion that Costa Rica
remains a truly neutral country is somewhat suspect. In a sea of turmoil and
upheaval, Costa Rican society has been a lighthouse of stability and a magnet
for exiles the world over. But the realization that Costa Rica cannot hide
behind the problems of others slowly dawned on the elites and political class
of San José.[28]

As a political model, Costa Rica may offer promise and hope, but it has
yet to yield permanent results outside its own frontiers. One may honestly
ask why it is that the sufficiently lauded accomplishments of Costa Rican

democracy have not taken root in any of the sister republics on the Central American isthmus. And the answer, while complex, will have something to do with the more sober perception of not only Costa Rica's performance as an economic and political entity, but also of its relative weight in the international system.

What, then, is this sober reflection? It has to do with the very factors that burden any democratic model in the current context. Democratic models are in the eye of the beholder. It is the *image* of the state that is, in most cases, competing in the democratic marketplace. The foreign policy apparatus of the state must then respond by creating and cultivating such an image.

And that image may have little to do with the reality of national politics and economics. As we shall see in the case of Spain, Costa Rica uses its democratic system as a vehicle for its foreign policy. The moral power of such a foreign policy is indisputable.[29] Oscar Arias, the former Costa Rican president and Nobel laureate, brought Costa Rica's democratic experience to Esquipulas, Guatemala in August 1987 and achieved a peace accord that had been beyond the reach of Latin American, European, and North American leaders for over five years. The leadership of the Costa Rican president in Central American affairs is rarely brought into dispute. Yet is significant that the peace accords, whose successful implementation was still in doubt over three years later, only establish the *pro forma* framework for democratization of Central America. The absence of civil and regional wars, and the cultivation of political pluralists, all embodied in the Esquipulas II accords, may make the region more *safe for democracy*, but they will hardly defend the fragile Central American region from the cruel realities of underdevelopment, debt, and declining terms of trade.

Central Americans may well ask if Costa Rica is prepared to provide the capital, trade, and technology needed to lift the region out of economic desperation.

DEMOCRATIC CONTEXTS

The foregoing survey of the market for democratic models in Latin America establishes a context, however ambiguous, for the functioning of current democratic models in the region. The possibilities, as well as the limits, of democratic alternatives in Central America are suggested by the historical experience the hemisphere has had with democracy. From this experience emerges a number of factors to which policy makers, who are using their democratic model as a foreign policy vehicle, must be sensitive.

These factors are contemporary manifestations of the rather general concerns that one sees within the Latin American intellectual tradition. For the present purposes, however, one must specify the actual manifestations of these historical concerns, thereby establishing a context in which foreign policy operates. Such a task involves an analysis of the rules of the democratic game in Central American and international politics. Thus, after an analysis of the Spanish Democratic Model as an international political "metaphor," and an empirical evaluation of the model's "contents," the focus will return to the context in which this model, insofar as it is a foreign policy vehicle, operates.

Groping for Theory:
The Spanish Democratic Model
as an International Metaphor

The optimism and energy radiating from international media and intellectual circles concerning the Spanish democratic experience belie a more sober concern for the state of theoretical knowledge about the process of democratization. The search for a coherent theory of democratic transition is perhaps the most noble and urgent pursuit in political science. If the field has retained any of its normative concerns throughout the behavioral deluge, these concerns were primarily teleological. But behind even the most rigorous behavioral methodology was an underlying concern for democratization. Amid the most bare-bones analyses of conflict and confrontation there always seemed to be a suggestion that democracy held out the possibility for conflict resolution. Even among the most reluctant scholars, the standard by which the politics of their subject nation-states were to be judged was the notion, however utopian, of democracy.

There is no need here to review the ambiguity of the term democracy. Whether it means different things to different observers is not material.[1] What is important is that Western scholarship has revealed a profound, almost metaphorical, concern for democracy. The myth of democracy, like that of El Dorado, has motivated and sustained even the most stark appraisals of international political reality. It should be pointed out that, ironically enough, the only environment in which the rigid scientific requirements of behavioral methodology could be fulfilled is within the context of democracy. Any other environment would be hostile to such an "objective" pursuit.[2]

Despite the overriding concern, social scientists have been hard-pressed to find coherent theories that would accommodate empirical reality. The march towards democracy, moreover, has not been rapid. The post-World War II experience in Europe and Japan, while encouraging, did not provide the means to explain democratic transition elsewhere—especially in the emerging nations of the Third World. Positive developments in Austria, Japan, Germany, and Italy, for example, did nothing to explain the resilience and longevity of the Franco dictatorship in Spain, which remained an open wound in the European democratic psyche. The death of models during the 1960s and 1970s, precisely when social science scholarship was coming into its own, injected a current of pessimism and cynicism into an area that otherwise demonstrated a good deal of empirical momentum.

Meanwhile, theoretical work stagnated under the burden of functionalist approaches. Scientific rationality demanded *cause and effect* explanations for political phenomena. The seminal essays in the field, which include work by S. Lipset and Jaros and Grant,[3] were concerned with identifying the functional preconditions or requirements for democratization. Independent variables such as income levels and technological development were identified in an effort to find a causal relationship between certain functional aspects of society and the flowering of democratic institutions. The strength of these approaches rested on the *measurability* of these variables; most indices of technological and economic modernity are reasonably reliable. Certainly there would be little argument over a *correlation* between these variables and democracy.[4]

By the 1970s, the variables were widened to include such political-cultural notions as democratic heritage and certain political institutions. These variables, though not as easy to observe and measure, were later incorporated in the more dynamic theoretical models that came to the fore in the early 1970s as an alternative to the purely functional approaches. The critique of the functionalist onslaught not only focused on the mirage of certain variables, such as economic and technological modernity, but also on more subtle but equally fallacious arguments that pointed to things like the size of the middle class, political culture, and other aspects of socio-economic development as explanatory factors.[5] As Robert Dahl has pointed out, "the evidence simply does not sustain the hypothesis that a high level of socioeconomic development is either a necessary or sufficient condition" for democratic development.[6]

The partially satisfactory dynamic models, first put forth by Dankwart Rustow, attempted to build a flexible system within which the democratic transition process could occur. Certain stages of this process have survived subsequent critique and now form part of the language of analysis in later studies.[7] Yet by the mid–1970s, it was apparent that whatever the methodological requirements, the analysis itself would be bound by the unique aspects of the national experience in question. The *sui generis* approach was consistent with the development in the international relations discipline of a greater concentration on area studies and distinct national experiences. There was less of a concern for comprehensive theories that could embody all national experiences with democratization and the transition from authoritarianism to democracy. With so much empirical territory to explore, there hardly seemed time to establish historical laws that would explain political developments.

As scholars focused on the unique experience of their subject nation-states, they retained a strong impulse to view political transitions as inevitable teleological processes. Democracy becomes the final cause, the ultimate destiny. Society moves towards this goal despite massive setbacks. The march of history is a crusade toward Democracy; the obstacles that democrats encounter on the way will eventually be eliminated by the implacable assault of democratic actors and institutions whose belief in the myth of democracy is so staunch that torturers or generations of dictatorship cannot stamp it out.

It is not unfair to point out that those scholars and observers who—however implicitly—subscribe to the inevitability of the democratic process often resemble the Communists who were still patiently waiting for the inevitable victory of socialism over capitalism. They, too, attempted to explain away the setbacks—in Chile and Guatemala—as minor detours with historical significance for the socialist project. However subtly the inevitability thesis is incorporated into an otherwise empirical analysis, the result is ideology: democratic ideology, but ideology nonetheless.

Recent efforts to develop a comprehensive body of theoretical knowledge on democratic transitions have been characterized by methodological eclectisism. While Herz's studies[8] reflect a renewed concern for the functional *breakdown* between the authoritarian or totalitarian regime and the requirements of society (the independent variables or conditions of democracy), there is also a tendency toward empirical analysis of distinct, and unique, historical experiences.[9]

The most expansive effort to date is that of O'Donnell and Schmitter, whose seven-year study of regime transition includes the work of twenty-two contributors. The studies present the view of democratic transition as an elite enterprise without addressing democratic motivations from below. The transitions are national projects of elite self-protection that are self-contained. According to Daniel H. Levine, a critic of this approach, "the editors and many of the contributors seem to consider the major motivation behind transitions to democracy to be fear and a healthy respect for opponents . . . there is much conflict in these pages and lots of tactical maneuvering, but little passion or commitment."[10]

THE SPANISH CASE

The new empiricism did not deter the great surge of intellectual energy that the death of dictator Francisco Franco released in 1975. After all, Spain was hardly a marginal Third World country. The economic boom of the 1960s had placed Spain firmly in the ranks of the industrial powers. Its strategic links to the United States, which had become increasingly important to the NATO alliance as well, made Spain an integral part of the West. Europe was precisely the subject area where scholarly activity on democratic transition had borne the most fruit; Spain's opportunity was not to be ignored.

Unfortunately for the cause of objectivity, the Spanish case was wrapped in a tremendous cloud of emotion. The historical memories of both the actors and the observers of the democratic transitions were set in play. The unresolved issues of the Spanish Civil War were like live wires shooting sparks into already dry tinder. Spain had been the meeting ground for all the competing ideological, political, syndicalist, religious, and secular forces of the Twentieth Century. During the Civil War it had become the battlefield for all of them.

The forces released after the death of Franco in 1975 attested to the fact that the battlefield had not been a graveyard of ideas. Franco had muffled, stifled, and stiltified but had not wiped out the ideological diversity of the Spanish nation. He boasted of keeping things well tied down (*bien atadas*), but he was able only to repress not eradicate. Moreover, the Spanish Civil War had been an international event, and there was a great number of firsthand witnesses outside the country—along with tens of thousands of political and economic exiles.

It is therefore not surprising that the best studies and accounts of the transition were to come not from Spanish authors, but from British and American scholars.[11] As was the case with the histories of the Spanish Civil War, Spanish authors were able to find neither the distance nor the resources to properly analyze the momentous transformations that their society was undergoing. Despite the apparent detachment of foreign observers, they, too, were vulnerable in one way or another to the emotionalism of the historic phenomenon.

POLITICAL MYTHOLOGY

The first effect that the intellectual energy field had on interpretations of the Spanish model was to create the kind of environment from which myths and metaphors spring forth. Any time so much emotional and political energy surrounds a phenomenon, there is a tendency toward abstraction. Not many observers have time to fulfill the rigorous requirements of political and sociological analysis. It is not surprising, then, that the Spanish model of democratic transition has been abstracted from its own reality. As with any abstraction, detail is no longer important. Scrutiny of the model is not necessary to give it weight as an international metaphor for the Third World. It should be remembered that such metaphors are greeted in a context of profound democratic longing bordering on desperation. The message must be simple and uncluttered by theory. It must be generic without being formulaic. It must have immediate and direct appeal.[12]

It is within this process of abstraction that actual scrutiny of the model is all but abandoned. Not only is analysis of the transition dynamics lost, but a continuing evaluation is no longer necessary. There is a popular consensus that the transition in Spain is still transpiring in the 1990s and that any evaluation would be hasty. The symbolics involved in imputing a consolidation of democracy to the overwhelming victory of the left in 1982 (as Socialist Prime Minister Felipe González has often suggested) are, again, indications that there are and will always be interpretations of the transition that are based on the historical experience of individuals and parties.[13] The left's return to power after 44 years of repression, exile, and clandestinity certainly does complete an emotional and—more objectively—historical cycle. But it is not the only test. The Socialist government in Madrid, beset by intractable problems of corruption, tax evasion, crime, drugs, unemployment, terrorism, and environmental emergency certainly wished that its return to power were the only criterion. Nevertheless, the Spanish people, who remain quite optimistic, have always demanded a more detailed accounting.

This detailed accounting is certainly necessary for the continued legitimacy of the ruling party within Spain, but it is not quite as urgent for Spain's new international role. While this study must be concerned with both versions of the model—the domestic interpretation and the foreign policy vehicle—Spanish foreign policy-makers are quite content with the myth. They do not wish to see their model put to the kind of test that, say, U.S. democracy must endure on a continuous basis. The power of the metaphor, like the good-looks of the transition's greatest leaders, prime minister Felipe González and former prime minister Adolfo Suárez, is much more convincing.

Recent scholarship, moreover, has not been able to arrive at a consensus on the most effective interpretation of the democratic transition in Spain. The existing interpretations offer a wide variety of alternatives, from the reductionist economic inevitability thesis to the proposition that the transition was effected by an elite leadership meeting behind closed doors in smoke-filled rooms. There is room here for practically all hypotheses and sub-hypotheses, from royal *deux ex machina* to the integral role of Adolfo Suárez's dentist. This study is not intended to resolve the debate; nor is it disposed to resort to the typical social science solution of declaring that the Spanish democratic transition is a complex phenomenon that can be explained only by a combination of the available interpretations.

What is of importance here are the prevailing interpretations that are *perceived* by countries that look toward the Spanish model as a source of hope. It is necessary to touch on these views before examining the conduct of Spanish foreign policy in Latin and Central America.

Of the major works available, the studies by Raymond Carr and J. P. Fusi, José Maravall, and Victor Alba, have set the tone and the standards for subsequent analysis.[14] In *Spain: Dictatorship to Democracy*, Carr and Fusi present a fast-moving political adventure fueled by democratic momentum.

The entire cast of characters is presented to the reader in an effort to communicate a complex historical process. The stage is set after a thorough
analysis of the pre-transition society of Francoist Spain. An ineluctable process emerges from the economic explosion of the 1960s, wherein the notion
of democracy is unavoidable. The economic *apertura* is followed by a democratic opening, which begins to bloom while the dictator languishes on his
deathbed.

To the careful reader, the clever sidestepping and colorful detail cannot
disguise an emergent central thesis: Spanish democracy was born in the
economic explosion of the 1960s when the floodgates of liberalism were
opened and the authoritarian regime collapsed under the weight of worker
involvement in the increasingly competitive workplace, the tourist deluge,
and the insatiable demands of consumer society. Carr would later recant this
thesis, rejecting the fallacy of economic determinism.[15] Nevertheless, his
book contains an underlying economic logic that seems to overshadow the
operational aspects of the events. One is sure from the beginning that democracy will triumph, if only because prosperity and consumerism were
eating away at the foundation of Franco's authority.

In what seems an effort to set the record straight, Carr later offered a more
dynamic thesis: the economic forces had their political manifestations within
the old regime, and these politicians shaped the transition process in a
unique—and perhaps unrepeatable—way. The skills and blunders of the
political elite, acting in response to vague, yet incessant, economic impulses
from the society at large, were what characterizes and explains the Spanish
democratic transition. Thus, amid the democratic "inevitability" there is
room for anecdote, dialogue, and idiosyncrasy.[16]

Maravall's work, on the other hand, is much less colorful but much more
challenging in its thesis. There is no underlying process here; everything is
out in the open. The author subscribes to Rustow's first two stages of the
democratic transition process, claiming that, in the Spanish case, these two
stages of the process are sufficient theoretically to explain the Spanish experience with democratic transition. For Maravall, the transition in Spain
can be explained by the interplay of "strategies of reform from above" and
the strategies of "pressure and demands from below." This methodology,
which is followed with sufficient empirical detail, reflects the author's credentials as a sociologist while providing him with a vehicle to display his
intimate knowledge of opposition politics, which his position as a Socialist
insider and cabinet member easily afforded.

Not surprisingly, Maravall's sociological methodology works, at least
within the context of his study. In such a methodology, details may be
inserted into a tightly bound process whose dénouement, the triumph of the
Spanish Socialist Workers Party (PSOE) in 1982, he almost overtly predicts.
Under the rubric of "pressures and demands from below" he is able to include
economic and ideological pressures, as well as interest groups and public

opinion. In the "strategies of reform from above" category, one finds the elite machinations of the old regime, as well as the often amateur maneuvering of reincarnated or newborn political parties that arose as a logical response to the democratic demands from below. Thus, Maravall's approach is compatible with the more recent "corporatist" approach of Foweraker and others.

Maravall observes that the Spanish process, though apparently systematic, has its idiosyncrasies. He is careful to detach it from the Latin American experience, thus limiting the applicability of his thesis as a contribution to political science. It is fair to point out, however, that Maravall was concentrating solely on the Spanish case and made no overt attempt to generalize his analysis. The Spanish case is clearly distinguished from the Latin American experience of reform and liberalization:

Contrary to some experiences in Latin America, the political change (in Spain) did not consist simply in liberalization, which for example has so far been the limit of *distencao* in Brazil. That is to say, the political changes in Spain did not merely open up the arena of political participation, but also created a competitive pluralist situation which could lead to alternatives of power.[17]

Writing before the triumph of the Spanish Socialist Workers Party in the 1982 elections, Maravall saw the momentum of pressure from below coalescing in the form of a leftist party.[18] The environment of pluralism created in the context of the above/below counterpoint assured the possibility of "alternatives of power." The inference here is that while some degree of political participation is possible in Latin America, the kind of pluralism necessary to permit "alternatives of power" remains elusive. As to what exactly is the ingredient necessary for the pluralistic environment, Maravall provides few clues. It is here that the analysis of the Spanish experience with democratic transition becomes *sui generis*.

While less empirically rigorous than Maravall's work, and certainly more historical, Victor Alba's analysis of the transition follows a similar methodology. The major difference is that in Alba's approach the idea of a sociological process is much less explicit. Reflecting his leftist background, Alba focuses more on the incessant demands and pressures from below, ascribing to them an inevitable momentum. The strategies of reform from above are unavoidable concessions by a political elite faced with unrelenting democratic force from below. Thus the players remain somewhat faceless in the context of an inevitable process. Only King Juan Carlos I seems to possess the qualities necessary for drama, though his legitimacy, according to Alba, is conditioned on his relationship to the masses: he and Spanish democracy will eventually have to pass the test. The King, who was instrumental in the "bourgeois-democratic revolution," will have to ride with the tide of a non-violent and undramatic "socialist revolution."[19]

Recent scholarship has emphasized the complexity of the transition process, without providing the kind of conclusive analysis necessary for further
generalization to other democratic experiences. Both Richard Gunther[20] and
Andrea Bonime-Blanc[21] see the central problem in democratic transition as
one of establishing new rules to govern the game of politics. Gunther, whose
work primarily deals with the institution-building inherent in party politics,
makes it clear that he regards the transition process as something "related
to but distinct from the process of founding a competitive party system."
While the creation of new parties and the transformation of small, weak,
and clandestine ones was an "all-important task," something essential
needed to precede it.[22]

Bonime-Blanc identifies this essential ingredient as the politics of constitution-building. Breaking down the "process" of democratic transition
into an evolutionary schema, she recognizes the importance of the political mobilization from below, which is termed "pluralization." Socioeconomic policy then becomes liberalized by these social pressures from
below.[23] The process culminates in the "constitutionalization" of political
activity, which in turn serves to liberalize and democratize an otherwise
resistent bureaucracy. The central role of constitutionalization of politics
receives the most attention in an analysis that includes scrutiny of the actions of the major elite actors, who moved from above through well-defined stages of the constitution building process. The final result, the
Spanish Constitution of 1978, reflects a number of functional formulae for
democratic coexistence.[24]

What emerges from Bonime-Blanc's analysis of the Spanish transition is
a clearly defined system or model of political change. It is evident that
the Spanish transition was chosen only as a subject for analysis and that
the effort is intended to advance a theory of democratic transition. This
admirable, if risky, venture counts among its major assets the success and
endurance of the Spanish constitutional regime. But it is important to
note that when the model is submitted to the unavoidable comparative
analysis, the only comparisons drawn are from Europe itself. The formidable challenges that the Third World would present to this model are
side-stepped in a way that draws attention to the model's major weaknesses.[25]

The most glaring of these weaknesses in the face of Latin America's
abysmal experience with democracy is that there has been no shortage of
excellent constitutions. What there has been a shortage of, however, is the
kind of mobilization and "pluralization" that characterized the Spanish experience. What conditions are necessary for such a process? Whatever they
are, they were present in Spain in 1975. Are they or will they be present in
Central America?

Despite its pretentions, Bonime-Blanc's analysis is by no means prescriptive. The "policy-oriented framework" for constitution building is instructive to aspiring democrats, but the context in which Spain's experience is supposed to serve as a model is, in most cases, generations away from the kind of political mobilization and pluralization of the model's first stage. Here we may want to make the distinction between Central America and the more promising prospects in the Southern Cone. The gratitude of many Chileans towards the Spanish model suggests a more developed political culture than what one would find in Central America.

In *The Triumph of Democracy in Spain*, Paul Preston[26] reenacts the drama and fury of the transition process, fleshing out the major actors in a journalistic yet analytical fashion. Written for a wide audience, especially for Europe, Preston's book avoids any particular methodology and allows the drama to unfold in a natural, almost literary way.[27] Empirical data is slipped in along the way, illuminating the path, and at times startling the reader with some particularly revealing facts, including the role played by ex-president Adolfo-Suárez's dentist.[28] Although Preston is a foreigner, it is clear from the beginning that the tale is being told by an insider who is emotionally involved in the outcome.

There are, nevertheless, a number of underlying theses that propel Preston's study. One is that personality, or leadership from above, played a key role in the transition. Another is that "popular commitment" to democracy was always characterized by leftist politics, leaving the right wing of the political spectrum with little more than an honorary role. Preston, like three-term prime minister Felipe González, believes that democracy was consolidated in the 1982 elections with the victory of the PSOE.[29] The 1975–82 period was the "transition" period, wherein centrists and rightists merely did their duty to heed the call from a decidedly leftist popular majority. This insinuation, which begins to take on momentum during a discussion of the crucial Adolfo Suárez phase of the transition, becomes part and parcel of an emerging central thesis: that the democratic impulse in Spain was a constant drumbeat whose inevitable triumph could only take the form of democratic socialism.[30]

Although Preston's central thesis does have some merit, its exposition in a rather literary or dramatic methodology leads to an *a priori* feel to the study. The aura of victory permeates the book, making it suspect from a purely academic standpoint. Preston is guilty of the typically Latin crime of *triunfalismo*, which, for our purposes, means an essentially *a priori* approach tainted with the subjective energy of celebration. More important, however, is the fact that any kind of *triunfalismo* implies a certain inevitability. Thus the work is guilty of presenting the march of democracy as an essentially inevitable process when much of the world's experience does not seem to prove this conclusively.

In all fairness, the scope of Preston's work is limited to Spain. There is nothing prescriptive in his analysis; and, more importantly, there is no pretention of creating a "model" for democratic transitions. Like most works in the field of history, the analysis is limited to its subject.

THE SPANISH DEMOCRATIC PACKAGE

The body of scholarly literature on the transition to democracy in Spain betrays a striking lack of consensus or a convincing political or sociological explanation for one of the most significant events in modern politics. Observers do not seem to agree on the actual dimensions of the transition or even upon its duration. Some, like Maravall and Preston, assert that the transition ended in 1982, when the Spanish Socialist Workers Party (PSOE) convincingly won the national elections. Others suggest that the transition is still in progress; the profound changes that have been experienced on the political level have not been undergone by a society still characterized by ideological polarization and economic dislocation. Many suggest that the democratic process was inevitable without committing themselves to an explanation of what specific forces fueled the democratic furnace. Most seem resigned to the fact that to explain such a complex phenomenon with one simple thesis would be to take the risk of being accused of reductionism, the worst of which being economic determinism.

The impressive body of empirical data that has been compiled through the years is still in search of a coherent theoretical framework that would be of use to students of comparative politics. Bonime-Blanc comes closest to this goal, providing a "model" based on the Spanish experience. Yet her stages for the democratic process do not go far enough back in the causal chain to address the requirements for setting her model in motion. She takes for granted that the subject nation would have the degree of political and social mobilization that Spain has had during the transition period. Hence, she does not answer the most important question in comparative politics: What accounts for the type of political and social mobilization that would lead to a democratic outcome? What is the essential ingredient(s) that distinguished Spain from the rest of the undemocratic world in 1975?

This central question is not answered by any one student of the Spanish democratic transition. There is, nevertheless, a suggestion of possible answers in those analyses that seem to be driven by the "democratic inevitability" thesis. There is no shortage of suggestions that social and economic changes in Spain during the 1960s and the political/economic/strategic context of Europe in the 1970s provided the bases for meaningful democratic change after the death of the dictator. The thesis thus becomes merely an invisible assumption, as the authors then go about the task of analyzing what amounts to a *sui generis* phenomenon.

Of course, one should never discount the possibility that the peaceful transition to democracy in Spain is a unique political phenomenon that could not be used as a kind of capital good in the production of similar democratic experiences elsewhere. The case for a *sui generis* analysis is just as strong as any of the contending theories of democratic transition, perhaps even stronger. Prime Minister Felipe González seems to have taken this stand in an effort to lower foreign expectations; in his three terms as prime minister the only specific requirement of democratic transition to which he has referred is that of a market economy. As the embodiment of the new Spain, Felipe González must contend with the internal and external pressures that Spain's successful image engenders. Early euphoria has given way to a more *sui generis* approach. Spain will provide inspiration, not democratic technology. For the reborn nations of Central and Eastern Europe who are looking toward Spain for guidance, González preaches caution. After all, Spain's transition began with a market economy; the post-Communist regimes in the East have a much larger task ahead of them.

Ascertaining the truth about democratic transition may be the goal of most social science inquiry, but to resolve this debate here would be to deviate from the course of the present study. A theoretical framework for democratic transitions may emerge from this inquiry, but it will not be taken simply from an analysis of the Spanish experience. As Bolívar suggested in the 19th Century, our scope must be global. Only from a truly comparative analysis can we assemble the foundations of a model.

That "model," moreover, need not be as defined as most social scientists would prefer. What is of fundamental concern for a democratic model is its image, not necessarily its reality. The only content that it must necessarily have is the image of its success; and this image may be held exclusively by foreigners, particularly the investment community. The model becomes a metaphor, a mythical inspiration to aspiring democrats. If there is prescriptive content, it would not be easily within the grasp of embattled political and social elites. Sometimes the metaphor suffices. Wiarda has pointed out the power of the Francoist metaphor in Latin America even when it communicates a distinctly undemocratic alternative under the guise of fascist "organic democracy."[31]

For a nation-state, especially a newly reborn country, the metaphor becomes a major foreign policy vehicle. In the coming chapters it will be shown how Spain has been able to exploit the idea of democratic transition in the context of Third World politics. It will become evident that there has been very little concern for communicating the actual content of the model, and even less concern for describing the current reality of "democratic" Spain.[32] As for the model's efficacy, theoretical work has discounted the influence of international factors. According to Abraham F. Lowenthal, most of the studies done on democratic transitions point to the primacy of national forces and actors.[33] But the interest here is not the efficacy *per se*, but the establishment of a foreign policy vehicle for an emerging power. Thus, both the reality and the image of the democratic model must be discussed.

Packaging the Model

The effort to maximize nation-state power through the instruments of foreign policy does not by itself protect a modern democracy from the possible internal disequilibrium that is a result of deviations from the democratic course. These deviations can be internal or external; a foreign policy decision that is perceived as undemocratic or a failure to consolidate democratic legitimacy at home can each produce a diminution of international status. If both the international and national images are threatened simultaneously, either a democratic breakdown will be imminent or a change in regime will be imperative. The safety-net afforded by integration in the EEC protects Spanish democratization from such a breakdown, but chronic crisis in the Socialist government of Prime Minister Felipe González suggests that public pressure for greater congruence or symmetry between the internal and external democratic projects cannot be ignored.

Spain has taken the risk of using the vague and ambiguous idea of democracy as a vehicle for its foreign policy. The use of such a vehicle in the policy sphere exposes Spanish nation-state interests and its own democratic institutions to the threat of incongruity and disequilibrium when realistic national interests intrude on *pro forma* policy declarations. At the outset of the first Socialist government in 1982, former foreign minister Fernando Morán heralded the "congruence" or overlap of the internal and external political projects for Spain. Yet Spain's behavior has been inconsistent on the international front. There are also signs on the domestic front that democracy is by no means consolidated. The price the ruling PSOE party must pay for this disequilibrium may only be that of giving up majority rule. But insofar as democratization requires the optimism and participation of Spanish subjects in political processes, the image of hypocrisy and incongruity may be a threat to the democratic system itself.

The Spanish democratic experience has shown its capacity to tolerate deviations, abuses of power, as well as direct threats to the democratic system of government. Much inconsistency can be excused when held against the criteria of almost forty years of brutal dictatorship, but the effect is cumulative. A governing party that has used democratic legitimacy as its trump card throughout its rule is extremely sensitive to any criticisms of its abuse of authority or to its inconsistencies in domestic or foreign policy.

The domestic issues are the more pressing insofar as foreign experiments for a lesser power do not provoke major responses from the international system. Those countries that do possess the ability to punish or destabilize Spain for its foreign policy "errors" see no interest in doing so. The European Community, which has taken some of the credit for Spanish democracy, has little interest in destabilizing the Spanish government despite any irritation some members might feel over Spain's almost utopian obsession with European unity or its efforts to inject a North-South dimension to the European dialogue. The Socialists in Spain have flattered the Europeans with this obsession; Spanish foreign policy and democratic project are dependent on European approbation and cooperation. "It is impossible to separate the internal priorities from the external ones," according to Felipe González.[1]

The United States has had little or no interest in destabilizing the Socialist regime despite the apparent lack of ideological compatibility. U.S. policy has achieved some major victories from the Socialists on security policy. Spain's commitment to NATO remains intact with Spanish collaboration on every level except for the integrated military command. Spain's strategic cooperation with the United States in the Gulf War, which, apart from important intelligence, entailed the use of Spanish bases by U.S. naval and air forces (including B–52s), was undertaken at serious risk to the Spanish government's domestic political position.[2]

The bilateral treaty with Spain, signed in 1988, extended the agreement to eight years from the usual term of five years, eliminated the leverage that came from U.S. payment of rent and aid for bases, and provided language to rule out Spain's denial of port visits and temporary transport of U.S. nuclear assets. The fact that the agreement was made with a Socialist government insures continuity with future Spanish ruling parties, whose position has been historically more pro-American. The removal of the U.S. Air Force 401st tactical air wing from crowded Madrid was a small price to pay in this larger context.

THREATS TO DEMOCRATIC LEGITIMACY

External Deviations

The Socialist government and Spanish democracy are much more vulnerable to the internal destabilization that results from a general *desencanto* (disenchantment) with the way Spain is being ruled. The inconsistencies and outright hypocrisies of Socialist foreign policy are a major part of this disenchantment, as Spaniards question the legitimacy of the ruling party to represent Spanish democracy abroad. For the most part, Spanish public opinion cannot see beyond the rhetoric of foreign policy, especially with regard to the hyperbolized relations with Latin America. But on certain key points, the Socialists' credibility has been seriously damaged.

In May 1987, press reports accused the Socialist government of being a major supplier of armaments to countries in a state of war and to some known to be notorious human rights abusers. Spain was already under pressure since 1985 from Amnesty International and other human rights groups to stop shipments of arms to governments that systematically abuse human rights. Spain was supplying South Africa with small arms; Chile with anti-riot equipment, 21 CASA 101 jet aircraft, and ground and naval transports; and a number of Arab states with modern equipment.[3] There were artillery shipments to Stroessner's Paraguay as well as 2,000 tons of arms for Libya.[4] In 1985, the Socialists were able to explain away these arms transfers as commitments acquired from previous governments, but the 1984 contract with Chile for modern aircraft was a glaring hypocrisy in light of the government's stated position regarding the democratization of Chilean society. The Socialists had imposed a boycott of arms sales to countries in armed conflict, but there were no provisions to prevent the resale of other arms transfers to countries such as Iraq and Iran. In May 1987, *El País* broke the story of massive Spanish arms sales to Iran and Iraq through third parties. Over 5,883 tons of bombs and munitions had made their way to the Iran-Iraq war from Spanish ports after brief stopovers at third party destinations.[5] Earlier reports had linked Spanish chemical exports to Iraq's poison gas production capacity, and subsequent investigations found evidence of a Spanish company's involvement in supplying chemical-capable munitions that were used against Iranians who were later treated at a Madrid hospital. Technology for the much-feared fuel air explosion bomb was also released by Spanish companies through third parties, and Spanish "merchants of death" began to figure prominently in the round of investigations of similar export violations in the United States.[6] To these accusations, the Socialists could only declare their inability to prohibit third party transfers of important industrial goods to war zones. Critics pointed to the involvement of Spanish state-owned companies as the government moved to tighten controls.

The suspicion that *realpolitik* had intruded on democratic socialist values was further reinforced by the Socialist government's duplicity in its policy towards post-Tiananmen China. EEC sanctions were approved under the Spanish presidency at the 1989 Madrid Summit. Nevertheless, the Spanish government proceeded to violate the spirit if not the letter of the sanctions by maintaining hundreds of millions of dollars in credits as well as high level contacts. It was no surprise that in November 1990, the Spanish foreign minister Francisco Fernández Ordoñez would be the first EEC foreign minister to visit Beijing since the Communist crackdown.[7]

The Socialists could survive such scrutiny of the government's actual behavior with respect to arms transfers to far off military and civil conflicts as well as morally bankrupt business relationships with oppressive foreign governments, but affairs closer to home would threaten the government with an unforgiving public perception. This time it was its relationship with the United States that tarnished the Socialist image as the embodiment of Spanish democracy. The 1986 referendum on NATO membership approved Spanish "permanence" in the Atlantic Alliance with three major conditions. One of those conditions was the prohibition of the introduction, transport, or deployment of nuclear weapons on Spanish soil. This constraint was directed toward the U.S. military presence, which included regular port visits of U.S. aircraft carriers at Rota and elsewhere, as well as the occasional stopover or overflight of B–52 bombers. Spain insisted on language that would reiterate the referendum's conditions in the Spanish-American 1988 bilateral treaty. But the Socialist government also conceded the inclusion of a clause that literally pledged the Spanish commitment to not ask U.S. military authorities if ships or planes were carrying nuclear weapons. U.S. and NATO policy in such cases is to neither confirm nor deny the presence of nuclear weapons.

There was no doubt that this move was a flagrant violation of the principles of a democratic referendum. Felipe González could be applauded in Western capitals for his commitment to nuclear deterrence, but the hypocrisy of the decision in its domestic context was not lost on the Spanish public.[8] Criticism of the move put González on the defensive.[9] Later, in the context of heated passions over Spain's participation in the Gulf War, the decision to allow landing, refueling, and reloading of nuclear capable B–52 bombers at the U.S. facilities in Morón, Seville would reopen the wound.[10] In the past, as practically all sectors of Spanish society assailed the government's hypocrisy, the Socialists hoped that other matters would divert attention from their untenable foreign policy position. But with fears of upheaval in the Maghreb and the resultant threat to Spanish interests there, the Socialists' moral legitimacy in foreign relations was seriously tested.

Institutionalization of Democratic Politics

To be sure, throughout the 1980s and into the 1990s, there was no shortage of internal matters to occupy the attention of Spanish citizens. These threats to democratic consolidation were not of any one specific nature. Problems were to be found in the social, economic, and political spheres, thus providing a continuous backdrop of crisis to democratic life. Despite over five years of strong economic growth since 1985 and the resurgence of Spain on the

international political and cultural scene, Spanish society was still in a fragile
stage of transition as it entered the final decade of the century.

Not all of these weaknesses were apparent to observers from overseas.
International attention was caught up in the charisma of King Juan Carlos
and Felipe González, as well as with the novelty of Spanish democratic
culture as it was marketed in travel brochures and promotional campaigns
for Spanish products and industries. The Western press lauded the Socialists
for their pragmatism and for their conservative economic program. Only those
living in Spain were aware of the abuses of power, the lingering signs of
authoritarianism, and even worse, the maintenance of old habits in a new
democratic garb. Spain was telling the world that it was democratic, but the
Spanish themselves remained skeptical. They were the victims of the arbitrary administration of justice, abuse of basic human rights, backward
institutions, and cronyism. Most of all they were the victims of the protracted
economic crisis that had begun in 1976–77. From London and New York,
Spain appeared a country with a bright and secure future, a place to invest
and grow. Only major disturbances, such as a military coup attempt, could
cast doubt over Spain's sunny skies.[11]

Constitutionalism

The Spanish experience seems to support the assertions of Bonime-Blanc
and others who see the triumph of democracy in Spain as a matter of successful constitution-making. With little fanfare, Spain commemorated the
tenth anniversary of the constitution in November 1988. The most remarkable thing about the 1978 constitution is not the fact that a broad spectrum
of politicians, from Francoists to Communists, sat down and agreed to a
lasting document, but that ten years later only a few lonely voices of Republicanism declared that the document needed reform.[12]

The general feeling of contentment with the constitution should not,
however, be misinterpreted. There are still those, including the government
itself, who flagrantly violate its articles of faith. The climate of conservatism
with regard to the constitution reflects, perhaps, a fear that any change in
something so delicate could unleash the "natural forces" of Spanish society,
as Pérez Gáldos, the perennial literary voice of the Spanish national character,
would warn. The major political forces in Spain seem to find in the constitution just enough political space to put forth their respective political projects. The Socialists, for example, were happy to put their aspirations of
Republicanism and Federalism on the back burner as soon as they were sure
that the constitution would facilitate their consolidation of power. As long
as this remains the case for the major political parties, there will be no
movement for constitutional reform.

It should be noted that the Spanish constitution defined the structure of
Spanish democracy as that of a constitutional monarchy. Aspiring democrats

in Latin America, already embittered by the worthlessness of the many great Latin constitutions, are quick to draw the conclusion that Latin American countries were brought up in the grand tradition of 18th Century republicanism. There are no men who would be king in Latin America. Democratic institutions would have to fend for themselves.

Praetorianism

At first glance, the "Spanish miracle" seems to have achieved the impossible: the complete subjugation of military power to civilian authority. After 1985, even the wary Socialists, reared in the shadow of repression and exile, were quick to declare that the dangers of a military coup had disappeared.[13] Much of the credit is owed to Narcis Serra, the Socialist minister of defense from 1982–91 and former mayor of Barcelona, whose smooth and apolitical style has glossed over many of the troubling differences that the Socialists were bound to have with the bloated and arrogant armed forces.[14]

But a closer look would show that the Socialist experience with the praetorian armed forces (which before 1985 still included the national police and the Civil Guard) is a dangerous model for other democratic aspirants. In many ways the Socialists surrendered to the power of these factious forces.[15] Though the police and the Civil Guard were put under civilian control in 1985 with the organic law of State Security Forces, the Socialists felt that the best way to control them was to unleash them on common enemies. These enemies included strikers, demonstrators, and more importantly, terrorists. In May 1984, ten Civil Guards refused to appear in court to face charges of torturing political prisoners. The government supported the refusal, backing the guards' claim that they could not neglect their daily duties.

Reports of torture by Spanish police continued to make the Spanish press and the human rights reports of the 1980s. The government's anti-terrorist law gives police wide powers that suspend practically all constitutional rights for terrorist suspects. Under the law, the police have committed acts of torture and execution. Although international pressure was brought to bear on the González government to stop the abuses as far back as 1984, the government decorated four heroic Civil Guards in September of that year while accusations of torture against them were still being investigated.[16]

Nevertheless, the case that finally put the government on the defensive did not surface until 1988. Three members of the national police were tried and found guilty of involvement in the "disappearance" of Santiago Corella, alias *El Nani*, a common criminal to whom was applied the anti-terrorist law. Corella's body was never found, but the trial revealed that the application of anti-terrorist law to cases of common criminals was a common practice. One of the defendants admitted that the police had solicited the application of the anti-terrorist law (which, among other things, allows ten days of detention without the right of *habeus corpus*) to common criminals accused of

robbery and other crimes on "hundreds of occasions" and that the then
Minister of Interior, José Barrionuevo, "never turned down" the requests.[17]

For their part, the armed forces were challenged to professionalize. But
the challenge was not in itself political. The Socialists used bureaucratic
mechanisms to thin out the officer corps and redirect praetorian energies.
Forced retirements sent young officers home with fat pensions and time to
embark on new enterprises. The strengthened ties with NATO gave the
remaining officers a new sense of mission, which Narcis Serra eloquently
purveyed to the Spanish people. A special military section of the Supreme
Court was set up to try and convict the authors and perpetrators of the 1981
coup attempt, taking away from the military justice system a key privilege.
Even so, the government did not risk the prosecution of any more than the
key figures in the conspiracy, and the sentences and conditions of detention
were lenient given the gravity of the offenses. By 1988, one of the *golpistas*,
the general Luis Torres Rojas, was given parole well before his twelve-year
sentence was completed. And there was talk in the Ministry of Defense of
seeking amnesty for the remaining prisoners (except for Civil Guard Lt. Col.
Antonio Tejero) before the end of the decade—a distinct possibility given
the parole of Rojas. The democratic intent of a sweeping amnesty law for
older and infirm prisoners confirmed the suspicion: General Jaime Milans
de Bosch, a co-conspirator was released from a military prison in July 1990,
to the dismay of many defenders of Spanish democracy. A growing fear that
Spain would once again become a magnet for dictators and fascists escaping
justice rippled through the public opinion. Spain was seen as setting examples that Carlos Menem in Argentina would later follow. In January 1991,
released Argentine military junta member Jorge Videla's plans to retire in
Spain caused an outpouring of public revulsion at a time when the Spanish
government was attempting to recover from major internal shake-ups while
confronting storms of protest over Spain's role in the Gulf War.[18]

Agrarian Reform and Land Tenure

Spain ranks in the top ten among the Western industrial powers in production, yet its politics are to a great extent rural. The issues of agrarian
reform have always polarized the country, as Spain's landed estates, especially in the southern areas of Andalusia and Extremadura, were notorious
for their size and political presence. The *latifundia* system that today plagues
much of Latin America has its roots in Spain. To this day great estates, some
productive, others underused, comprise the better part of the agricultural
area of Andalusia. Rural unemployment levels outstrip those of most major
industrial centers, especially after planting and harvests. If desperation can
be seen in "typical Spain," it is in the rural areas of Huelva or Seville where
entire villages are either teeming with idle farm workers or literally empty
of all citizens except for the very old.

The irony, however, is that this desperation for work and land remains a local issue that is not able to affect national politics. The reasons for this remoteness are primarily economic. Spain produces a surplus of most agricultural goods, except for certain cereals and meat products. New EEC quotas are squeezing smaller farmers out of the picture as Spanish agriculture modernizes and realizes economies of scale. By 1990, agricultural production in Spain was still in a state of increasing returns, and investment—both foreign and domestic—has gone toward large exploitations. There is less and less room for the small farmers or cooperatives that would result from a systematic agrarian reform.

The autonomous governments of Andalusia and Extremadura, nevertheless, embarked on moderate—but controversial—land reform programs. The main thrust of the programs is to redistribute large plots that are underproductive or in disuse. Many of the estates in Andalusia, for example, have been used traditionally for bull raising for bullfights, or for private hunting parties. Peasants in the rural areas who are organized in anarchist, socialist, or communist labor federations clamored for the redistribution of such estates and other fallow land; expectations were high when the Socialists took power in 1982.

The Socialists first clashed with the desperate agricultural workers, whose "impossible dreams" and utopian notions had led them to believe that democracy in Spain would mean an escape from unemployment and misery. In the rural areas of Extremadura and Andalusia this "old story" of Spanish politics began to be played out once again.[19] Large underused or unused estates were occupied by militant field workers who saw their actions legitimized by the agrarian reform legislation promulgated by the regional authorities. But instead of supporting the legitimate aspirations of the workers, the Socialist authorities unleashed the reactionary local security forces and broke up demonstrations, highway blockades, and spontaneous squatting. By 1986 about 350 field workers were facing criminal charges of public disorder. Some of the leaders served short prison sentences. In most cases, fines and embargoes further impoverished these workers. Pedro González, a hero of the struggle in the province of Seville, elected to serve his six-month sentence instead of appealing to the supreme court. His case has galvanized the agricultural workers throughout Andalusia, making the rural areas difficult electoral territory for the Socialists.[20]

The agrarian reform movement, meanwhile, continued apace. Large landowners scurried around to either sell their tracts to willing producers, or develop them by themselves. The force of the right wing on the movement was considerable as legal procedures slowed the pace of the expropriations and the creation of worker cooperatives. By the end of 1988, only a fraction of the hundreds of thousands of hectares included in the reform legislation was actually being administered by the regional authorities.

Opposition to the agrarian reform measures was widespread and broad based. The difficulties were not only legal, political, and constitutional but also economic. Without exaggerating the parallels with pre-Civil War Spain, when the agrarian reform issue led to the first sparks of irreconcilable civil conflict (the 1932 anarchist uprising in Casas Viejas—now Benalup—in Cádiz is often referred to as the first battle of the Civil War), the landless agricultural class is perhaps the only truly explosive revolutionary class in Spain. The Socialists have drawn outrage from all sides of the political spectrum, including their own union front the General Union of Workers (UGT). Many activists on the left would agree with the right-wing and pro-landowner mouthpiece *ABC* that "in the face of the Europe of the 1992 Single Unitary Act it is incongruous that Andalusia sail against the wind and tide with an agrarian policy ready-made for the 19th Century, when the reforms that our society needs are to be found on quite different paths."[21]

The desperation of the Spanish *peones* would inevitably facilitate political corruption and inefficiency. Socialist plans to provide unemployment benefits for those who could prove 60 days of field work were complicated by local fraud and rebellion. Even fellow Socialist municipalities punched fraudulent time cards to get the unemployed masses minimum coverage. In many places, especially in Andalusia and Extremadura, there was little or no possibility of finding the minimum 60 days work necessary to qualify.[22]

The European Economic Community, moreover, has given indications that Spanish law will not hold up in European courts. The EEC land-retirement plan, so dear to the agricultural and environmental planners of the European Commission, will probably stop the Spanish agrarian reform plan dead in its tracks. The economic logic of overproduction and high-cost subsidies will in the long run overwhelm whatever political momentum the agrarian reform has retained after years of bitter struggle. The PSOE's own "Euromania" and lust for liberalization of the marketplace will, ironically enough, sabotage its efforts at addressing historical injustices in the Spanish heartland.[23]

It is obvious, therefore, that the Spanish experience with agrarian reform cannot furnish the Latin Americans with a model to eliminate the destabilizing nature of land redistribution. If the Socialists have survived the damage wrought by the agrarian reform program, it is simply because rural politics, while explosive, are relatively less important in Spain. In Latin America, democratic legitimacy is still linked to bold agrarian reform initiatives, as the political aspects of Latin American agricultural society are much more important than the economic issues of efficiency and economies of scale. In both societies, agrarian reform is a political metaphor for correcting historical injustices and inequities. But in Spain, the economic tidal wave of liberalization, generated by the weight of the EEC, will drag Spain away from the politics of underdevelopment.

THREATS TO THE MODEL

Subversion

The democratic euphoria in Spain, fanned by the feigned optimism of the ruling Socialists, often creates an environment in which mortal threats to the democratic system are minimized. Only tragic events, which involve considerable carnage and loss of human life, serve to remind the Spanish people of the fragility of their new democratic system.

Like many Latin American countries, Spain is engaged in a war against armed insurgents whose mission includes the destruction of the democratic system. These insurgents share some of the ideological proclivities of their Marxist-Leninist counterparts in Latin America, but their desire to kill is fueled more by nationalist sentiments than by any particular vision of a socioeconomic future. Basque, Catalan, and Galician terrorism in Spain is intimately linked to issues of regionalism and separatism in Spanish politics.

If Franco achieved any legitimacy during his long and harsh rule, it was due in part to his unambiguous position regarding autonomy for the many distinct nationalities contained in Spain's geographic endowment. To the Francoist, Spain was indivisible; thus there was nothing artificial about Madrid's dominance of political affairs. To concede autonomy to regional subdivisions would be tantamount to the destruction of the "one, great and eternal Spain." The granting of limited Catalonian and then Basque autonomy under the Second Republic was undoubtedly a major cause of the Spanish Civil War.

After eliminating the threat of roaming bands of anarchist and Communist guerrillas after the war, the Franco regime was confronted with the first signs of political and military vulnerability. The Basque separatist guerrilla group, Euskadi ta Askatasuna (Basque Homeland and Freedom), known as ETA, began its attacks on military and security figures in the 1960s. The 1973 assassination of Franco's right-hand man and chosen government successor, then Prime Minister Admiral Luis Carrero Blanco, brought home the vulnerability of Francoism in the face of democratic momentum.[24]

As a definitive air of crisis swallowed up the Franco regime, the Spanish people toasted ETA in the seclusion of their homes. The aspirations of ETA were identified with the legitimate democratic aspirations of Spanish society. ETA's self-professed Marxist-Leninist ideology and nationalistic fanaticism were ignored by those who, blinded by decades of pent-up democratic hopes, could not distinguish attacks against the state from attacks against the dictatorship.

It took a good part of the transition years and hundreds of bombings and assassinations by ETA to finally convince the Spanish people that the ETA project had little to do with democracy. As late as 1990, the Socialist government was still talking of "reinsertion" of ETA political prisoners into democratic society, as if the problem were one of democratic *convivencia*, or living together. By 1987, however, even the Socialists, who had entertained notions of answering ETA's political challenges, were characterizing the group as a band of common criminals. The basic strategy of ETA had been to destabilize Spanish society by provoking the armed forces and police into a military coup. The repression of the military and police would produce a revolutionary situation in which the Basque region would achieve its own sovereignty. A workers vanguard, presumably led by ETA and its legal political party front Herri Batasuna, would rule the newly formed state under the principles of socialism. According to the twisted logic of ETA, the 1979 statute of autonomy, and the regional autonomy guaranteed under the Spanish constitution of 1978, were only ploys by the Castilian authorities to prolong the unjust rule of Madrid over the free peoples of the Basque Country.[25]

With such utopian goals, ETA has employed a strategy of bombings, kidnappings, extortions, and assassinations. But Spanish democracy, as fragile as it is, has convinced most Spaniards that political aspirations can be achieved by peaceful means. ETA's brand of terror, which is designed to unite Spaniards against the repression of the dominant Madrid authorities, has provoked only disgust and rejection in Spanish public opinion. The cold-blooded communiques that follow each bombing have isolated Herri Batasuna and ETA not only in the rest of Spain, but also within the Basque community. As ETA's strategy becomes more and more removed from practical political goals, its credentials as a legitimate political-military group dissolve. Out of touch with political currents and forces, as well as with the popular will in the Basque Country, ETA has degenerated into a band of criminal terrorists whose murders and destruction are ends in themselves.

This kind of terrorism, nevertheless, has presented the government and state with an ongoing crisis that tests the authorities' capabilities of defending the democratic state without resorting to undemocratic methods. Even the small Catalonian guerrilla group Terre Lluire and the smaller Galician Exército Guerilleiro do Pobo Galego Ceibe (which drew blood for the first time with a February 1989 assassination of a Civil Guard) have proven relatively invulnerable to police and security measures. *Etarras* work in extremely small cells that are virtually immune to police infiltration. The international ties to PLO dissidents, the Libyan regime, and the various and sundry of the revolutionary terror network afford them shelter, arms, cash, and a secure career.[26] In pursuing a political course, that included the offer of direct negotiations as well as reinsertion and amnesty, the Socialists embittered the Spanish military and police, especially the Civil Guard, who are the objects of most of the terrorist attacks. The shift to a policy of police action after 1986 was aimed as much at the loyalty of the Spanish armed forces and police as at the inpenetrable terrorist bands. The Socialists began to turn a deaf ear to reports of human rights abuses under the anti-terrorist law as a concession to the factious official forces that were perhaps more of a threat to Spanish democracy than ETA.

The government's helplessness was made even more manifest during the prolonged kidnapping of the Madrid-based industrialist Emiliano Revilla. Revilla had sold his food processing empire to foreign interests and then amassed a greater fortune in the booming Madrid real-estate market. His 1988 kidnapping created an outburst of public outrage at the authorities' inability to discover even the most insignificant detail of his whereabouts. The government warned the Revilla family that to pay ransom to the *Etarras* was a crime under the anti-terrorist law; much of the ransom paid was thus intercepted by the Spanish or French authorities. As the months went by and ETA demands for money continued, special police forces followed up unreliable tips by storming apartments where only innocents were housed. Revilla was eventually released, but the government, under tremendous strains (*el desgaste*) from this and other democratic weaknesses, relieved the embattled interior minister of his duties in a governmental reshuffle in July 1988.

Negotiations with the terrorist band had only proven that political solutions with criminal forces were difficult propositions. When hopes were dashed by ETA intransigence in talks in Algiers in 1989, the Spanish authorities ruled out political negotiations. But Felipe González was under constant pressure to reiterate the government position, as reports circulated that secret government contacts with ETA were continuing in Santo Domingo.[27] Yet there remained differences of opinion within the prime minister's own cabinet, as Justice Minister Enrique Mújica watered down the government's stricter criminal justice penalties with a defense of the concept of "reinsertion" for those terrorists and drug traffickers who want it.[28]

The impotence of the authorities, however, was not the only aspect of the government's anti-terrorism policy that forced the reshuffling of Felipe González's cabinet. Bubbling under the surface of the crisis was a much greater threat to Spanish democracy: official connections with paramilitary assassination squads. Latin American countries are no strangers to the threat that paramilitary "death squads" pose to democracy. Their existence in a political system usually signals one or more of the following weaknesses: (1) that a praetorian military holds effective power; (2) that certain oligarchical groups with connections to the military hold enough power to perpetrate such actions with impunity; (3) that the political threat to the system from terrorism or subversion is significant enough for certain interest groups to act without government sanction; or (4) that democratic institutions are either too weak or too inefficient to engage the threats effectively. A democratic government that tolerates such activity is admitting its weakness in the face of threats to the system; a democratic government that relies on such activities as part of its war against subversion is itself subverting the democratic process.

In Spain, the famous *caso Amedo* has produced a climate of doubt about the Socialists' actual commitment to democracy. A Spanish interior ministry official, José Amedo Fourcey, together with another Spanish policeman was linked to the 1987 murder of Juan Carlos García Goena, a Basque political exile whose connections with ETA are yet to be definitively proven. The two policemen were allegedly on a mission for the anti-terrorist paramilitary group Grupo Anti-terrorista de Liberación (Anti-Terrorist Liberation Group, GAL), a right-wing Basque extremist organization active in assassinations of known ETA militants in Spain and France.[29] The incident would have been little more than another transgression by the overly assertive national police if it were not for the subsequent revelations that Amedo was operating with money from the executive's own secret discretionary accounts. A furor was raised over the existence of these *fondos reservados*, and then Felipe González himself, after justifying their existence in a democratic system, refused to offer details of the secret accounts. The new government in July 1988 made its position perfectly clear: there would be no investigation of GAL and no discussion of the secret funds "under the law of state secrets."[30]

While the Amedo affair dragged on through the courts, the GAL remained undeterred. In November 1989 the paramilitary forces of GAL shocked the nation with a bold assassination attempt at a Madrid hotel. This time the targets were Spanish parliamentarians from the ETA political front group Herri Batasuna. One was killed, another seriously wounded, and a third escaped death when the perpetrators ran out of ammunition. The subsequent investigation revealed what the Spanish public had feared: one of the assassins was a national policeman linked to the Coordinadora Nacional Antiterrorista de Fuerzas Armadas y de Seguridad (Conafays), an ultra-rightist terror group within the Spanish security forces. For Baltasar Garzón, the Spanish judge who presided over both the Amedo and the Conafays cases, the investigations and trials would be perhaps the greatest challenge to the Spanish democratic *estado de derecho*."[31]

It is no doubt true that democracy lacks the tools to combat certain threats. Democratic requirements restrict authoritative decision-makers in their actions, making their efforts transparent, slow, and carefully measured. Against a group like ETA, which does not play by the same rules, the democratic state may seem helpless. In its desperation for victory over anti-democratic forces, the democrats themselves will employ undemocratic methods. Realism would justify the application of special funds to paramilitary operations by asserting the Clausewitzian logic of war as a continuation of policy by other means. The restriction on methods is a normative imposition, demanded by the values of a democratic system. The logic of democracy, however, is self-protecting; for many democratic advocates it is an article of faith. If the society and its institutions are strong, the adversary's strategy is bankrupt. He can kill and maim but he cannot destabilize the system. At first it appeared that the Socialists would test the Spanish faith in democracy by "ignoring ETA to death"; but somewhere on the way it seems they panicked. The *caso Amedo*, and the murders of the Herri Batasuna deputies by a member of the security forces, attest to the fact that even the ruling party, for all its blustering, does not believe that democracy has been consolidated in Spain.

By 1991 the only source of optimism was evidence that the Spanish security forces were sharpening their skills against the terrorists. Though embarrassed by the return in 1990 of tiny Galician EGPGC, after the authorities claimed that it was completely disarticulated, and renewed terror by the ultra-left Grupos de Resistencia Antifascita Primero de Octubre (GRAPO), whose infrastructure was reestablished after the release in 1989 of 18 members, the security forces could at least claim a decline in the number of victims of terrorist attacks.[32] As spectacular as they were, the EGPGC bomb attacks in 1990 were directed at narcotraffic interests that had turned Galicia into a major point of entry for heroin and cocaine. Like the release of the GRAPO commandos, this embarrassed the government, but the security forces could, by the end of 1990, claim that they had cut the deaths from ETA attacks down by over half since 1985, from 70 to a reported 23. The police had stopped dozens of bomb and assassination attempts, avoiding what Interior Minister José Luis Corcuera said could have been "the most tragic year ever."[33]

Also to be considered are the causes of violence. The nationalism that produces ETA or the tiny Galician and Catalonian groups is the simple result of democratic paralysis. The State of Autonomies is a handy modality for temporarily channeling nationalist energies in peaceful ways. Nevertheless, the extreme nationalist outbursts that erupt from practically every region are a product of centuries of neglect and repression whose historical wounds will not heal completely under the present system. Spanish political leadership, which has been decisive throughout the transition, does not wish to tamper with the present system of regional autonomy. But political leaders unconsciously desire a more stable arrangement that would drown out the impulse of separatism. The PSOE has put its project of federalism on the back burner, as it did with its original desires for a republic. But the Socialists' almost naked plunge into Europe suggests that the party sees the great cultural and regional bath of Europe as the way to drown Spanish regionalism without destroying Spain's own delicate system. The Europe of Regions will replace the Spain of Regions.

Life at the Top: The Decline of Party Politics

The view of the Spanish transition as a process of party formation and competition advances a concept of democracy that suggests that all ideologies and aspirations be represented on the political spectrum, and in a parliament, by organized political parties with access to power.[34] The ruling party must be confronted by an opposition capable of preventing the monopoly of power.

The electorate must be presented with credible alternatives if the pluralism that underlies democracy is to survive.

When in 1982 the Socialist Party was swept into power by a surge of popular demands for change—*un cambio*, democracy appeared to have achieved the ultimate victory. A party that suffered from an historic failure during the most decisive era of the century, branded as an enemy of "eternal" Spain, had emerged from the shadows of clandestinity with a distinctly different political program, and took power with an absolute majority. The ballot offered a complete menu of ideologies and personalities. As far as party politics were concerned, democracy in Spain had passed the test.

After a few years of this democratic experience, however, there was concern that the criteria of pluralism were no longer being met. The structure of the party and parliamentary system, while formally intact, did not address the deficiencies of the parties themselves with respect to democratic behavior. The focus was on the behavior of the ruling party, which wielded uncontested power by virtue of its absolute majority.

By 1985 one could speak without reservation about a hegemonic political party that had penetrated all sectors of public administration with party militants. Observers on the right warned that the conservative economic program of the Socialist government was merely a smokescreen for a Gramsci-like strategy of social and political hegemony.[35] The Eurocommunist strategy was encharged to deputy prime minister Alfonso Guerra, whose control over the new "socialist class" and state apparatus was in many cases absolute. Guerra would become the "lightning rod" of the Socialist administration, undaunted by his ever declining popularity. His crude rhetoric and direct provocations of the opposition embarrassed his close friend and senior colleague Felipe González, but he deflected criticism from the prime minister and appealed to party militants in the leftist authoritarian sector, who came to be known as *Guerristas*. Unscathed by the opposition, the Socialists acquired the arrogance of power that can only be associated with authoritarianism.

The authoritarian agenda began with an attack on the only remaining dissidence within the party. The historical inheritors of the party's truly socialist left wing, led by the *criticos*, whose spokesman Pablo Castellanos managed to stay in the party through 1987, had been decimated. Known as the Izquierda Socialista or Socialist Left, these dissidents claimed that they were the true guardians of the spirit of the PSOE's 19th Century founder, the revolutionary socialist Pablo Iglesias.[36] The divisions in the party dated back to 1979, when the *Felipista* wing of the party rejected Marxism with González's Willy Brandt-style resignation and subsequent restoration on a non-Marxist platform. The old PROMARX wing of the party, led by Castellanos, Francisco Bustelo, and Luis Gomez Llorente, had struggled to keep Marxism within the party program, rejecting the *Felipista* social democratic compromise that reserved for Marxist ideology only one place among the many "theoretical instruments of analysis."[37] The *criticos* maintained their position among the Socialist Youth movement and in regional party groupings, but the *Felipistas* alone decided national economic, social, and foreign policy. The momentum of Felipe González's leadership led one *critico* to remark that trying to stop the *Felipistas* was like "shooting a BB gun at an elephant."[38]

Apart from supporting the "no" position on the NATO referendum—its last stand as it turns out—the Izquierda Socialista was outraged by the government's economic program, which it felt was not oriented toward wealth redistribution. Nevertheless, the original architect of the economic program of readjustment and reconversion, then economics minister Miguel Boyer, never relented. And the *Felipistas*, along with the *Guerristas*, justified their internal repression with references to "reasons of state." In power, the PSOE would have to transcend party ideology and become the government of all Spain. In a 1985 interview, Felipe González asserted that he "had lost his freedom so that others could have it," a reference not only to the limits on his personal life that the presidency had imposed but also to the ideological sacrifice that power had meant to his party.[39]

But González's invocation of reasons of state did not satisfy the parliamentary opposition, which was being trampled by an artificially imposed discipline of vote in the Cortes. Parliamentary debates became exercises in futility, as González and his cabinet ministers ridiculed and derided the opposition with an arrogance that embarrassed most of the few remaining viewers who followed the legislative sessions on national television. The discipline of vote imposed by the party leadership guaranteed the passage of any legislation the government saw fit. The practice within the party, where electoral lists were manipulated by the party executive[40] and where dissent was either ignored or assailed directly,[41] was being transported to the Cortes. The move dismayed the legendary leaders of the Spanish transition, who fruitlessly attacked the government's performance before near empty aisles.

Many prominent Socialist commentators saw this process as inevitable and systemic, one resulting from the weaknesses of the parliamentary system of representation and from the age-old political science notion that power itself corrupts. Bureaucracies become "conveyor belts of power" in the Stalinist sense. But many Socialist insiders were genuinely concerned with the deteriorating image of Spanish "socialism." Ignacio Sotelo, a socialist insider and former member of the party executive, warned Spaniards in 1986 that nothing was being done to prevent the "institutional power and social hegemony" of the ruling party.[42] Sotelo has since lost his access to power, but his scathing critiques of Socialist hypocrisy remain as primary sources of Spanish political reality. According to Sotelo, whose leftist position finds strange bedfellows on the right, the relationship between the governed and the government has not improved: "No one has figured out how to reconcile authority with being alongside the people in the street. The reverencial and authoritarian sense of State power has been maximized to the extreme."[43]

The right-wing opposition has gone so far as to accuse the Socialists of being the only "sociological inheritors of Francoism."[44] Surely Socialist behavior reflects the trauma of the Franco years, when the PSOE was forced to operate outside the country or in tight-knit clandestine groups within Spain. Trust in political adversaries is non-existent, as the persecution complex has entered democratic politics. Socialist isolation in Spanish society is for the most part self imposed. By rejecting alternatives with a derisive arrogance and distrust, the PSOE has provided a *continuismo* with the authoritarian past. Their self-concept as a democratic party does not allow the kind of reflection that would modify political behavior.

Some of this behavior is no doubt deliberate. The Socialist policies are a mixture of moderate social democracy combined with supply-side economics and monetarism. This ideological flexibility results in an unprecedented pragmatism in Spanish politics. But it also results in ideological confusion. With its broad range of policies, the PSOE has occupied every space between the extremes on the political spectrum. The Socialists have taken customers away from both the left and the right, while decimating the center. Those voters who contemplate a change in their vote find only weak, divided parties in the opposition or frightening ghosts of the Francoist past.

The decline of the Communists preceded the Socialist victory in 1982, yet the PSOE never relented.[45] The bitterness of the Civil War years, during which the growing Communist Party took control of the Second Republic away from the Socialists and paved the way for Soviet penetration, has not dissipated. The Socialists are loathe to recognize the historical contribution that the Communists and their unions played in the Spanish transition, a role that was in many ways more primary than that of the exile politicians of the PSOE. Socialist policy, which still pays lip service to the left, has facilitated the divisions in the Spanish Communists, virtually neutralizing them as an electoral force.

The collapse of Adolfo Suárez's center-right coalition, the Union of the Democratic Center (Union del Centro Democrático, UCD) in 1981–82 made the right wing party Alianza Popular (AP) the strongest opposition force in the country. Led by the charismatic and personalistic Manuel Fraga, the former Franco minister and the major conservative force in the Spanish transition even before Franco's death, the AP joined with the Liberals and the Christian Democrats in a center-right opposition coalition. But Fraga's Francoist past and his unabashed authoritarianism could never capture more than about 5 million votes, half that of the PSOE. By 1987, the coalition collapsed, and the three parties each went into a tailspin. The Liberals and the Christian Democrats (whose historical failure as one of the governments of the Second Republic still haunts them) disappeared as credible political alternatives. For his part, Fraga "retired" from the party leadership, went to Strasbourg as a Spanish delegate to the European Parliament, returned to his native Galicia to prepare his candidacy for the regional presidency, only to reclaim his leadership position in the AP in a typically authoritarian maneuver to oust the younger leadership in 1988. The generational and ideological struggle between the *Fraguistas*, the old-guard of authoritarianism and obsolete conservatism, and the younger followers of Antonio Hernández Mancha, the moderate party president from Andalusia was hardly a contest. Fraga swept his way back into the party leadership, restructuring the alliance of center-right politicians into the more integral Partido Popular (PP). When again it was time to choose a younger successor for the 1989 elections, Fraga cleared the way for his protege, José María Aznar, the dynamic and forward looking president of the Castilla and León regional government. The PP hoped to go beyond the 5 million votes (25 percent) that under the parliamentary representation system would keep them far away from power.

For the PSOE had taken practically all of AP's potential voters away with pro-business policies and high growth rates that benefited the upper and upper-middle classes. In a nation of lower middle-class workers and professionals, the expectations of "trickle-down" kept the votes with the government, as Spanish voters invested their confidence that neo-liberalism would create the wealth that was necessary before any kind of redistribution could take place. Reaping the benefits, the managers, bankers, and landowners that lead the Right retreated to their provinces and enterprises confident that national economic policy was favoring their economic and social class. A "regionalized Right" replaced the national aspirations of those who only 15 years before wielded absolute centralized power. The Right, which had never held stable power in a democratic regime, was condemned to a future that, however prosperous economically, did not include national political power.[46]

One need only think of Mexico's almost desperate social and political reality to be instructed about the dangers of the institutionalization of one-party rule in a democratic system. According to José Antonio González Casanova, the Catalan scholar and collaborator on the 1978 Spanish constitution, "the absence of an alternative to the PSOE would be deadly for democracy and democratic socialism."[47] The ballot box gave the PSOE a mandate to run the country. But their momentum and style, coupled with the inexperience of the political elite in democratic politics, have produced an unprecedented social and political hegemony that is stifling the political, economic, and social life of a resurgent nation-state.

Fighting Back: Social Conflict and Popular Protest

With the political future well established in Madrid, the steam created by the Socialists' tough economic policies was let out in localized but nonetheless violent incidents in industrial and rural areas. The reconversion of Spanish industry forced thousands of breadwinners into the unemployment lines as González's 1982 promise to create 800,000 jobs became a source of nationwide ridicule. The most sensitive places were the state-owned companies in the National Institute of Industry (INI), where Socialist election propaganda had promised not only to save jobs but also to create more. In 1983, a government decree put over 18,000 workers across Spain on notice that their jobs would disappear. For its part, the private sector was hemorrhaging jobs as factories and businesses devastated by the economic crisis shut down. Shipbuilding, mining, and steelmaking were hardest hit, as the international economic situation for these industries was particularly difficult.

By the winter of 1987, the lay-offs, forced retirements, and canceled apprentice programs in the national shipyards had produced an explosive situation. The *guerra de Puerto Real*, the protracted social upheaval in the Bay of Cádiz area, began in January 1987 with a series of strikes and highway blockades that were broken up forcefully by riot police. Every Tuesday in the shipyards of the state-run Astilleros Españoles (AES), and every Thursday in the town of Puerto Real, workers would block highways and demonstrate. Hundreds of fully equipped national riot police would attempt to unblock highways and clear streets. On Tuesdays at the shipyards, the AES workers, joined by workers from the nearby shipyards of San Fernando and Cádiz, would turn the workplace into a battleground, slinging heavy bolts in homemade slingshots in addition to the usual barrage of rocks and bottles. The police responded with tear gas and rubber bullets. On Thursdays in town, the police would get their revenge on the workers as the grid-like streets of the village trapped the fleeing protestors. Innocent bypassers were grabbed off the streets and beaten by the police, and the normal functioning of the bay area was seriously altered by the desperate workers. Dozens of workers, their wives, and policemen lost eyes, or suffered traumatisms, gas intoxications, and burns.[48] Drug addicts, criminals, and anti-social elements joined Anarchist, Socialist, and Communist labor groups in constructing homemade bazookas and molotov cocktails.[49]

A lock-out by the AES administration in late April provoked a 24-hour battle that began in the shipyards and ended in the barrios of Puerto Real. Hundreds of riot police, backed by rubber bullets shot from helicopters overhead, formed battlelines across the national railroad tracks. The town was ablaze with burning cars and barricades while the shouts of the workers were punctuated by the gunshots of police sent in from as far away as Extremadura.[50]

Meanwhile, in the steel and mining centers of Cantabria, violence also replaced the slow, painful reconversion program. In Reinosa, the death in early May of a protesting worker who had been the victim of a police tear gas attack brought national attention to the social conflict that was springing up throughout industrial Spain. The situation in Reinosa, however, received practically all of the media attention (until the situation in Puerto Real

became so completely out of control).[51] The government-run television network ignored the almost revolutionary situation in Cádiz, focusing instead
on northern matters in Cantabria.[52] The violence during the management
lock-out at AES finally made the late news and the back pages, about four
months after the "war" had begun. In May, a well-known leftist journalist
filed the first investigative piece for the Madrid daily *El País*.[53] Labor leaders
and politicians across the country used the deliberate lack of coverage to
fuel an already well-oiled campaign against the government's control over
national television and radio. Former prime minister Adolfo Suárez later
called for a "Moncloa Pact" (a reference to the landmark 1977 economic and
social accord reached under his government) on the administration of public
TV and radio. He also supported concessions for the private station licenses
projected to come on line in the early 1990s.[54] Like most political metaphors,
the Moncloa Pact seemed unrepeatable in the rarified social climate of the
1980s.

The climate of social conflict, or *conflictividad social*, continued well into
1988.[55] The shipbuilding sector in Galicia and Viscaya, as well as the mines
and related industries of Asturias witnessed violent strikes and police repression in a crescendo that peaked around May Day 1988. The economics
minister, Carlos Solchaga, cited high growth rates and lower inflation as his
justification for continuing austerity measures and the streamlining process
in Spanish industry.

By the government's own conservative estimates, a little over three million
Spaniards had taken to the street in protests over the course of 1987 alone.[56]
Socialist and opposition politicians appealed for a "little bit of calm" from
both the society and the government in order to reflect objectively on the
government's performance—which was not without success on many fronts.[57]
But few seemed to be listening in workplaces and homes across the country.
The violent character of the demonstrations, moreover, suggested that the
Socialist message was not reaching the sectors that once made up the party's
constituency. Young people were a special problem; pent up energies and
frustrations from dim employment prospects made youth-oriented issues
particularly volatile. The international media acquainted the world with the
1987 student riots in Madrid, where dubious anti-social characters like the
legendary handicapped "punk" known as "El Cojo" joined university and
high-school students in violent protests against the government's imposition
of higher standards for university admission and against the generally "Third
World" nature of the educational system.[58]

In 1988, it was the underpaid and overburdened teachers' turn to protest.
The 1987–88 school year on all levels was almost completely lost as students
used the teachers' strike to launch their own boycotts and demands. The
government's only substantial concession after months of bitter bargaining
was the replacement of the embattled education minister, the scholar José
María Maravall, in the July 1988 cabinet shuffle. In September 1988 teachers

returned to their jobs with slightly higher pay and some added benefits but with essentially the same poor social status that generated the conflict.

OBJECTIVE AND SUBJECTIVE CONDITIONS: CREEPING AMBIGUITY

The *desencanto*, or disenchantment, with democracy that so many observers of the transition warned about in the late 1970s was even more a reality in the late 1980s. The ruling PSOE benefited politically from the apathy, but their democratic legitimacy was being slowly eroded by social conflict and a profound atmosphere of cynicism on the street. Crime, completely out of control in the major cities, took its toll on democratic consciousness. The increasingly violent nature of this criminal activity made the comparison between U.S. inner cities and certain parts of Madrid, Barcelona, and Seville a valid one. Spaniards on the right of the political spectrum lacked the democratic sophistication to weigh the price of political freedom against that of individual security in the street. Instead, a resurgent nostalgia for the security of the old authoritarian regime, where everything was *atado y bien atado* (tied down and well tied down), replaced democratic aspirations.[59] A good part of the police force boycotted the situation in a vain effort to debilitate the Socialist government. Petty thieves were at first detained and then released. Later, pickpockets and purse snatchers were often set free without arrest.[60] Only when tour operators in London and New York, along with travel guidebook publishers, began to issue advisories for certain Spanish cities did the local authorities commence a crack-down. In Seville, where tourism and the 1992 Universal Exposition and V Centenary of the Discovery of America projects were gravely threatened, a crackdown in 1988 improved the quality of life drastically, if only temporarily. In cities such as Madrid, however, citizens were forced to form local community patrols to make their barrios livable.[61]

By the mid–1980s, there was no family in urban Spain that was untouched by crime. In the big cities, only a fraction of the robberies and muggings go reported. In October 1987, a public opinion poll put crime behind only unemployment and terrorism as one of Spain's three main problems.[62] From 1985 to 1988, the number of homicides had practically quadrupled from a "European" 370 per year to a more "American" 1,281.[63]

It was no surprise to those who sensed the threat to democratic freedom that in late 1990 the Ministry of Interior would come up with draft legislation on Protection of Citizen Security, which would empower police to suspend basic civil rights for anyone suspected of committing a crime. Protected by an unwitting shield of public opinion that was clamoring for expediency in dealing with crime, the authorities faced only legal and constitutional obstacles to getting the law passed. Again, the young and already overburdened

Spanish judicial system was pressured to make crucial judgments that would have profound implications for the future of Spanish democracy.[64]

As in the United States, the crime problem goes hand in hand with the drug problem. And the drug problem in Spain has frightened the Spanish with its multi-leveled assault that begins with the once inviolable family and ends at the very center of political power. Any analysis of the drug problem in Spain, moreover, must take into account that the devastating effects drugs have on even the most developed industrial societies will here be magnified many fold. Much of Spanish society, though transitional, is immersed in traditional lifestyle and culture. The liberal ideas that fuel modern capitalism did not begin creeping into Spain until the 1960s. The political transition after Franco's death in 1975 was accompanied by breathtakingly rapid social change, but Spain's older generations were never able to keep pace. The distance that separates the generations has never been greater. Youth alienation, which has its objective causes in the economic and political environment of *desencanto*, cannot be treated in the home. The young person often goes straight toward the most addictive drugs in an effort to confirm the profound alienation that he or she is experiencing.

Fear of heretofore unknown social ills has paralyzed any societal capacity to deal with the problems of drug addiction. Heroin addiction in Spain is still a taboo subject that receives little objective scrutiny. For the police and the authorities, its dimensions are purely criminal, as drug addicts are not known to vote or engage in political protest. They and the millions of youths who smoke hashish habitually or drink liters of beer on the streets have for the most part dropped out of the political process, wherein they would probably either censure the government with their vote or join in the nearest street protest as they did during the 1987 Madrid student riots. The popular wisdom is that it is convenient for the PSOE to keep a significant portion of the most vulnerable and volatile sector of the society outside the political process.

Official Spanish statistics on the drug problem reflected only the tip of the iceberg. In 1986, the Ministry of Health and Consumption reported about 125,000 heroin addicts, about 500,000 amphetamine addicts, 350,000 persons addicted to hypnotics and 1.8 million daily users of cannibis derivatives.[65] Most Spaniards would suggest a significant amount of underreporting. Some more reliable private agencies give figures for heroin addiction that are well above 250,000.[66] In certain towns and cities the heroin problem is so obvious that local warnings are issued to residents and tourists to avoid walking barefoot in parks or on beaches where junkies often leave their dirty needles. In railway stations and in the backstreets of the big cities, discarded syringes tell the tale of perhaps the most profound type of human misery.[67]

International trends have made Spain even more vulnerable to this modern scourge. Interdiction efforts in the United States and elsewhere have caused a shift in distribution activities to southern Europe. European prices, which are at least 100% higher on the wholesale level than in the United States, have attracted drug profiteers to the relatively untapped European markets. Spain's proximity to North Africa and its cultural and language ties to the producing countries in Latin American have made the country one of the major drug conduits of the world. The problem in the Costa del Sol reached such proportions that tourism began to plunge and the area became known to Europeans as the Costa del Crime.[68] Drug pushers supply the European markets from the relatively safe haven of Spain, where law enforcement is weak and vulnerable to corruption. Entire customs units have succumbed to bribes and kick-backs, from Algeciras in the south to Galicia in the north. And the vast amounts of illegal narcotics bound for Europe have afforded local Spanish drug users a constant supply for domestic consumption. Only the fear of AIDS, whose major victim in Spain is the intravenous drug user, has helped curb the abuse of dangerous substances.[69]

The profound social disintegration that Spain has been experiencing has not tainted the sunny image that the country enjoys overseas. The impact of some of the problems is amplified in the domestic context by the fact that modern Spanish society had never experienced such phenomena before the democratic transition. The incipient democratic consciousness also creates a new awareness of the situation and attempts to hold the new political class responsible. Spanish society is by no means near a complete breakdown—paradoxically, there is a high degree of optimism—, but there is a fear that in the long run these intractable problems will be associated more and more with the concept of democracy. Already, the ultra-right has used law and order, drugs, and family issues to keep the once moribund anti-democratic forces alive.

Most Spaniards, however, are willing to pay the social price that democracy exacts. Their hopes are directed toward the modernization of the police and security forces to provide protection from democratic spillovers. To the nostalgia of authoritarian culture, which continues to claim that *vivíamos mejor con Franco* ("we lived better under Franco"), the new Spaniards respond with the conviction that democracy is worth the price.

The Macroeconomic Onslaught

Given the evidence of social distintegration, which was so obvious to the local observer by the end of the 1980s, one may legitimately question the sunny image that Spain has cultivated for itself in the international press and travel bureaus. Much of the good press that Spain and the Socialists have received reflects satisfaction with the progress of certain macroeconomic indicators and the positive climate for foreign investors pursuing high margins, low wages, or high interest rates on government debt.

Spain has been experiencing the longest period of economic growth since the booming 1960s, with high growth rates since 1985, when the economy emerged from the crisis that had begun in 1975.[70] Integration in the EEC during 1986 spurred economic growth of 5.2 percent in 1987, the highest rate in the Community; and since 1988, growth has averaged over 3 percent.[71] Inflation, which was in double-digits at the beginning of the decade was cut to a manageable 5 percent in 1988, though many Spanish consumers would argue with the government's methodology in producing vital statistics, and the "overheating" economy began to push prices up sharply by the end of the year.[72] Foreign capital has flooded the Madrid stock exchange and made its way into speculative real estate holdings, joint ventures, and takeovers of state and private companies in massive sell-offs of public and private Spanish assets. Multinationals have expanded their presence with the purchase of plant and equipment, thus modernizing and internationalizing Spain's industrial base.

In 1987 Spain overtook the United States as the largest earner in the tourist trade. Over 50 million tourists each year were passing through Spain, with yearly increases averaging over 20 percent until 1990 when the high peseta and the crime problem provoked a 12 percent plunge in revenues.[73] This tourism, along with the capital inflows, kept the peseta strong: the Spanish currency actually rose against the Deutsche mark during the 1987–88 period, and its gains against the dollar have been consistent with that of other major currencies. Spain's reserve position, which reached $53 billion at the end of 1990, trailed only that of Italy and Germany in the EEC.[74]

Foreign and domestic companies were being attracted by the boom in Spanish domestic demand, which in 1988 expanded at an 8 percent annual rate.[75] Integration into the EEC opened up markets for Spanish agriculture and multinational companies that were based in Spain. Even some domestic industrial firms that were modernized during the government restructuring program were penetrating European markets. But the multinationals and foreign investors were clearly the biggest winners: in 1987 alone $9 billion in long-term capital entered Spain; by 1991, as Spanish interest rates remained well above those of European and Western competitors, over $5 billion in long-term capital entered Spain in the first two months of the year.[76] Aid from the EEC has gone into modernizing Spanish agriculture while Spanish farmers began to benefit from higher Community prices. Spanish agriculture, moreover, remained in a state of increasing returns in the 1990s. The Madrid stock exchange ended 1988 with a 20 percent average gain in stock prices, despite the bearish sentiment that prevailed after the October 1987 market crash.[77]

In fact, there were fears at beginning of 1988 that the economy was overheating.[78] The non-inflationary growth that Spain had experienced since 1985 was put at risk by the soaring internal demand and the extraordinarily high investment rate, which was around 10 percent in 1988.[79] After having shed jobs in the early 1980s, Spain's economic recovery after 1985 created over one million new jobs.

To the disenchanted, the course of these positive economic data should have seemed implacable. Spain's "conservative, jet-set managers" had made Spanish public and private industry leaner and meaner through a long-term reconversion plan; sold off moribund public companies to foreign and private investors willing to modernize; tamed inflation with tight-money policies that would have made the Bundesbank seem loose; attracted massive amounts of foreign direct and portfolio investment that bolstered the peseta and generated confidence in Spain's financial position; and created over one million jobs in over five years of high economic growth. Banks and businesses posted record profits throughout the last half of the 1980s, and EEC accession, for which the Socialists took much of the credit, afforded Spain a positive balance in Community contributions. Even Iberia Airlines, the perennial symbol of money-losing state-owned enterprise, posted profits beginning in 1986, the carrier's first profits for ten years.[80]

THE RECKONING

In the boardrooms of multinational companies and Spanish banks as well as in the executive offices of the Moncloa Palace, the Spanish economy looked sunny. With disarming arrogance, Socialist economic planners led by the controversial economics minister Carlos Solchaga pressed forward with their economic program, winning praise in European and North American circles and harvesting *kudos* in international newspaper and magazine editorials. By late 1988, "economic euphoria" enveloped the halls of power in Madrid.

On the streets of Spanish cities and villages, however, the positive macroeconomic performance was receiving little applause. The average Spaniard had seen his household economic situation actually deteriorate under Socialist rule.[81] The more sober economists pointed to important economic data that seemed to offset the gains that had been made since 1985. Opposition politicians from all sides of the political spectrum suggested that if the advances of the mid–1980s were indeed undeniable, then those gains were far from evenly distributed throughout the Spanish society.

Spanish headlines in May 1987 announced the painful economic reality that the average citizen had been experiencing for over ten years: Unemployment in Spain had reached the "psychological barrier" of three million workers.[82] The barrier had actually been reached in late 1986, but a revision of the accounting methods left hundreds of thousands of unemployed young people, women, and elderly off the rolls.[83] In 1986, Spanish unemployment peaked at about 22% of the work force; at the end of 1988, official statistics put the number out of work at almost 19% of the workforce, the highest rate in the industrial world.[84] By some estimates, even if 1.5 million jobs were created in the next five years, unemployment would still not dip below 15 percent.[85] The rate will remain high throughout the 1990s as the baby-boomers of the 1950s and 1960s swell the labor force, along with women who are seeking jobs to head households or improve declining living standards. Unemployment insurance covers well under half of the workers, and in most cases, the benefits are for less than two-year terms.

The social repercussions of chronic unemployment are difficult to exaggerate. Aside from the crime, drug abuse, and anti-social behavior that is so obvious in Spain, the frustration and hopelessness that this situation has produced in the ranks of the young will affect Spain's future ability to compete in a single European market. For Spain's future generations, *desencanto* in the 1980s and 1990s will result in a cynical, less educated, poorly motivated, and maladjusted class of workers and leaders.

Inflation may have been controlled for the bankers and foreign investors, but Spanish workers have not been able to keep up with the cost of living. Spanish consumers, moreover, have paid the price for whatever improvements there have been in the inflation rates: Spain suffered, and would continue to suffer, under elevated interest rates, which at 12–17% for businesses and up to 21% for consumers were some of the highest in the West.[86] Despite gains on inflation, Spanish labor leaders and opposition economists claim that the working class lost two points of purchasing power in 1988 alone. This decline set the stage for spiraling wage increases in the first few years of the 1990s. The view from the shop floor was that Spanish competitiveness had been achieved by the progressive lowering of the Spanish worker's standard of living.

The new-found competitiveness of Spanish firms, moreover, is by no means a foregone conclusion. Spanish wages are at least a third lower than in other EEC countries, yet Spain's trade balance has been hemorrhaging since the January 1, 1986 accession to the EEC. The receipts from tourism help keep the current account balance from deteriorating commensurately, yet Spain's current account deficit in 1988 was the country's first since 1983. Export growth was strong (seven percent in 1987 and about twice that in 1988), but Spain's unfavorable terms of trade seem to have condemned the Spanish economy to a future of massive trade deficits.[87] The government points out that new capital equipment for modernizing the Spanish productive base accounts for much of the surge in imports. Yet there is no guarantee that Spanish industry will be able to take on its stronger European competitors in a single, unified market.[88] Many fear that Spain will be paying for its BMWs with Valencian oranges and Almerian zucchini and cucumbers for many years to come. While Spanish agriculture remains in a state of increasing returns, extraordinarily high increases in agricultural exports will help pay for some of the expensive manufactured imports. But as returns diminish and EEC quotas and agricultural reforms take their toll, only competitive industry and growing tourism will be able to avert a major crisis in the external sector.

By late 1988, Spain was pleading with the EEC to allow a transition period to help protect the over 800,000 manufacturing jobs that would be threatened through the elimination of trade barriers by 1992.[89] The then secretary of state for commerce Pedro Pérez's unfortunate choice of figures was not lost on the Spanish opposition: Felipe González had promised to create 800,000 jobs in the 1982 campaign; from 1982–85 more than that many were lost. And the million or so jobs created after 1985 could not accommodate the women and young people that were joining the job market.

Even the "objective" statistics suggest that the booming economy in Spain had not benefited all Spaniards. Economic growth in 1986 was uneven on a regional basis, with growth of over the national average in wealthy regions like Madrid, Catalonia, Aragon, and Valencia; the poorer areas of Andalusia, Extremadura, the two Castillas, Galicia, and even the once prosperous Basque country grew by less than half the national rate. Asturias, the mining and industrial heartland of the north, experienced negative growth. The economic recovery had done little to bring rich and poor Spain closer to one another.[90]

It is evident, therefore, that the economic reality of Spain is not without its ambiguities. One can see more luxury automobiles and cooperative apartments as well as more sea-side chalets. But at the same time one sees hordes of bored youths in the streets with liters of beer and *porros* of hashish, alongside rows of cars with windshields smashed by last night's foragers. Luxury department stores and expensive boutiques play host to an unprecedented frivolity while once prosperous mining and industrial villages become ghosttowns. A letter to *The International Herald Tribune*, responding to the report of a major contract between the state-owned telephone company Telefónica and Moscow to revamp Moscow's phone system, summed up the ambiguity: "Come here to rural Spain, Muscovites, before you shell out rubles to Spain's national telephone company. You will find that on its home ground, helpless clients are incommunicado prisoners of a monopoly's malfunctioning dictatorship. It's a system reminiscent of Stalin."[91]

On December 14, 1988, Spanish society collectively put an end to this state of ambiguity. A general strike, led by the two major union confederations, paralyzed Spanish society, shutting down everything but a small sector of the official public administration. City streets were deserted, and all commerce came to a halt. Only luxury department stores remained open, despite the pickets of protesting workers. The government, which had spent most of November and December trying to unravel support for the strike, recognized the action as a "major blow" to its economic and social programs.[92]

What disturbed the government the most was the rupture with its labor front, Union General de Trabajadores (General Workers Union, UGT), the historical force behind Spanish socialism.[93] The UGT had joined the communist Workers Commissions (Comisiones Obreras, CC.OO.) in calling the general strike against Socialist economic and social policy, invoking the wrath of González, whose use of a Hawkings-inspired physics metaphor ("the policy of UGT is sliding toward the Red") rarified the atmosphere.[94] The three years of family feuding with UGT and his once close friend, union general secretary Nicolás Redondo, had turned into bitter and open political warfare. The ostensible issue was the Socialist youth employment program, which contemplated the creation of hundreds of thousands of jobs in Spanish industry at about half the normal wage and with social security benefits paid by the state. For the unions, this latest foray into "Thatcherism" and Reaganomics was unacceptable; with hundreds of thousands of adult breadwinners laid off, the program seemed to be yet another gift to employers.[95] The government vowed not to give in to demands that early elections be held, even though there still was no political alternative to its rule. Redondo compared the anti-strike efforts of the PSOE secretary of organization, José María (Txixi) Benegas to those of the Nazi mastermind Goebbels.[96] With characteristic arrogance, both Benegas and González predicted the failure of the strike, which in their view followed a bankrupt Communist, if not anarchist, strategy.[97]

The government was visibly wounded and shocked by the success of the general strike. Humbly, the Socialists vowed to negotiate in good faith with the unions on all aspects of economic and social policy. Among other things, the unions demanded wage adjustments to meet higher than expected inflation, an increase in the coverage of unemployment benefits to half the idled population (in 1987, coverage was given to only 27% of the unemployed workforce),[98] and a withdrawal of the youth employment plan. Tough bargaining lay ahead for the embattled executive.

IN THE SHADOW OF 14-D (DECEMBER 14)

In the Socialist ranks, however, there were those who chose to ignore the message from Spanish working people. Those who showed the most sensitivity to negative public opinion and the plight of the working class were isolated or ousted from the party ranks by *Guerristas*, the followers of then deputy prime minister Alfonso Guerra, whose own rhetorical leftism was compromised by his cultivation of the monolithic party apparat. Along with top party officials, Guerra believed that the figure of Felipe González would be enough to win national power. A healthy block of votes would come from the new "socialist class," the literally hundreds of thousands of people that owed their livelihood to Socialist patronage. The rest, and enough to put Guerra and González back in the Moncloa Palace, would come from the grand stature of the Prime Minister himself, who had developed the hardest teflon finish of all Western leaders with the exception of outgoing U.S. President Ronald Reagan.

Safe in the assumption that despite the declining popularity of Socialist style and policies there would be no challenge to the Prime Minister, the Socialist leadership exercised a voluntarism that served only to keep the government in constant crisis. Economics minister Carlos Solchaga kept to his package of austerity on monetary and wage policy, refusing to give in to worker demands to keep up with inflation—even though less than $2 billion separated the government from the union position.[99] Socialist leaders were increasingly strident or defensive, disqualifying their opponents with provocative accusations that belonged to another, more remote political era.

The definitive split with the PSOE's socialist union front, UGT, signalled an ideological shift away from the precepts of European social democracy. The authoritative Madrid daily, *El País*, which was always perceived to be ideologically close to the government, spoke of the "death of Social Democracy" and the beginning of chronic confusion.[100]

Meanwhile, Spain's leaders continued to bask in the warm praises they received from international financial and business circles. To the *Financial Times*, Felipe González was "the Left's saving grace," a closet Thatcherite in socialist garb.[101] The peseta soared in foreign exchange markets, bolstered by Solchaga's monetarism and the interest of multinational companies and "hot" drug money bidding up Spanish assets. By the end of 1990, the peseta was at the top end of the European Monetary System range—well above the Deutsche mark—despite a massive and growing trade deficit. More disturbing was a growing current account deficit, a rarity in the past decade or so of Socialist rule. By 1990 the deficit was 3.5 percent of gross domestic product (GDP), reflecting the 12 percent drop in income from tourism. In February 1991 alone, the current account deficit practically doubled. Only foreign capital inflow could offset the deficit; but the foreign investors bid up the peseta beyond its 6 percent range against the Deutsche mark in the European Monetary System (EMS). The high peseta hit exports and tourism hard, keeping the unemployment rate in early 1991 above the 15 percent mark. In the money market, however, foreign investors were getting close to double the rate of return of other European, Asian, and North American markets.[102]

Profits for foreigners, however, did nothing to guarantee the Socialists' fortunes at home. The efforts to freeze the overheating economy that began in 1989 with stratospheric interest rates and, later, direct credit controls, brought economic growth down from 5.1% in 1989 to 3.5% in 1990. The pace of job creation had slowed to a trickle, despite the fact that more people were entering the job market.[103] An unjust tax system, in which massive fraud was perpetrated with virtual impunity by business and financiers, added to the perception that the economic benefits of democracy were only for the few.[104]

DEFLATING THE MODEL: CORRUPTION AND ELECTION FRAUD

First and foremost among the privileged few were the "jet set" Socialists themselves, whose ascent from rags to riches produced strong undercurrents of bitterness and envy. The Socialist elite could defend itself from the standard criticism of the new rich by the reactionary old rich, but the attacks were broad-based and revealed an underlying bitterness. Although the PSOE never received even half of the votes in any of its three election victories, its absolute majorities in the Cortes translated into uncontested domination of national institutions. Without opportunities for scrutiny, Spain stood by helplessly as the system of patronage became a web of corruption and influence peddling, or *trafico de influencias*. The prime minister's popularity made it impossible for the opposition to hold the executive responsible for the extensive local transgressions, but eventually the revelations of corruption would fracture the party and bring the government to the brink of collapse.

As early as 1989 the Socialists sensed that the coming economic slowdown combined with *desencanto* would hurt the party at the polls. Early elections were called in October 1989, as the ruling party hurried to head off possible electoral disaster. As expected, the PSOE returned to the Cortes, or legislature, with an absolute majority, but they had given ground to both the United Left coalition, and to the rejuvenated center-right Partido Popular. Only one vote separated the PSOE from the need to form a parliamentary coalition or a minority government.[105]

But the October 29, 1989 election results were not what they seemed. Opposition parties immediately presented legal challenges to thousands of election "irregularities" across Spain. At least 22 deputies in the 350-seat Cortes were in dispute. For the next six months the Socialists would have to defend themselves against charges of ballot stuffing and other fraud as the election authorities were put to the test in a systematic, nationwide investigation and recounting of votes.

The Socialists managed to survive the challenges in most election tables, albeit by a much more narrow margin. But the opposition challenges in Melilla, the Spanish North African outpost and smallest constituency, bore fruit: repeat elections were held in March 1990, and the Popular Party managed to end the Socialists' absolute majority in the Cortes. The combined opposition was left with 175 seats, enough, in theory, to head off the PSOE's absolute majority.[106]

Ironically enough, anti-democratic forces would again complicate the opposition's effort to reign in the Socialist abuse of power. Herri Batasuna, the political front for the Basque terrorist group ETA, continued to refuse to take its four seats, effectively leaving Felipe González with a majority. The PSOE, the party that claimed to be the fulfillment of Spanish democracy, was now ruling the country with the tacit approval of the nationalist forces that sought to destroy that same democracy.

The Socialists' moral descent into election fraud has had profound implications for the development of Spanish democracy. The revelations of electoral fraud and the lengthy recount and investigations came at a time that Spain was sending observers to Central America to monitor important elections there. Surprisingly, few in Spain were shocked by the revelations; to many this was only the tip of the iceberg of official corruption. The demoralization of the democratic system was cumulative. The executive could, again, blame overly zealous local party militants for the illegal activities but inevitably the iceberg would melt down to the leadership itself.

In January 1990, after a flurry of holiday press reports, the biggest scandal in the eight years of Socialist rule exploded in the Cortes. On February 1 the Popular Party called deputy prime minister Alfonso Guerra to the Cortes to explain what just about everyone already knew: that the corruption went all the way to the Moncloa. The allegations were based on evidence that after the first Socialist election victory, Alfonso Guerra's brother, Juan, had been given an official office in the Seville delegation of the national government, in order to serve, in this own words, as "personal assistant to the vice president during his trips to the [Andalusian] regional Community." Juan Guerra, who had spent the preceding few years in the unemployment lines, had used his surname and the official office to conduct personal business that involved, among other things, the procurement of official building permits and licenses, the laundering of illicit funds, prevarication, and the embezzlement of government property. In short, Juan Guerra had used his brother's influence and an official office to become one of the most powerful entrepreneurs and brokers in Andalusia.[107]

Alfonso Guerra's denials of involvement fell on deaf ears. There was overwhelming evidence that he had been informed of his brother's activities by the police and his party as early as 1987. In March, Felipe González revealed that his vice president and deputy prime minister had presented his resignation in January, but that it had been rejected. For the next year or so, Felipe González and members of the government executive stood fast as piles of evidence in the *Caso Juan Guerra* mounted against whatever domestic prestige was left. Amid the crisis, González hinted at the long awaited separation and autonomy of the government and state policy from the party apparatus; but he continued to protect his old friend and colleague Alfonso Guerra despite widening rifts in his party between the now desperate and wounded *Guerristas* and the more state oriented members of this government, who like economics minister Carlos Solchaga, were not members of the party executive directorate.[108]

The *Guerristas*, meanwhile, went on the counterattack. Alfonso Guerra returned from a long hiatus in December 1990 to lash out at his critics in the opposition and at the press, saying, in his characteristically caustic style, that "democracy has to tolerate freedom of expression, and even the freedom of [press] manipulation," and that "there are those who understand democracy in a certain way, perhaps because they feel nostalgia for the past, but it's not of consequence, except for the fact that the voters will later keep it in mind."[109] What is of importance is what the urns say, not what this one or that one says."[110]

And it was precisely fear of what the voters would say in the spring 1991 local elections that would lead to important changes in the Socialist government. On the eve of the Gulf War, Felipe González accepted the resignation of Alfonso Guerra, leaving the former deputy prime minister and vice president with his party functions, as well as his seat in the Cortes, which would, he hoped, provide him with immunity from criminal prosecution in the *Caso Juan Guerra*.

The long-awaited cabinet reshuffle took place in March 1991. The *Guerristas* were the big losers, as González fulfilled his promise of a greater separation of party and state. The Andalusian clique of González-Guerra-Yañez, *et. al.* was finally broken up, and the government made way for an influx of Catalonian technocrats and functionaries with weaker party associations.

It had been obvious that as far back as the general strike of December 14, the Socialist honeymoon as the sole international and domestic representatives of the new Spanish democracy was over. The 1990 corruption crisis, moreover, had debilitated Spanish foreign policy by keeping Spain's primary policy resource, Felipe González, bogged down in domestic and party strife. The word was out that Third World politics still plagued democratic Spain. For Felipe González, the painful decision to oust Alfonso Guerra, an historic figure in the party and close friend, was an effort to save not only his own credibility but that of Spanish democracy as well.

The move by González headed off a massive defeat in the May 1991 local and regional elections. As expected, the PSOE again received a relative majority of the overall vote, but support throughout the country was uneven, and voters in the strategic provincial capitals rejected the Socialist mayoral candidates. Spaniards in many cities were forced to wait until July to find out the outcome, as election irregularities again plagued the process and the lack of clear majorities in the major cities opened a tense round of negotiations for ruling coalitions. A disaster for the PSOE was averted when the conservative regional Catalonian Party, Convergencia i Unió (Convergence and Union, CIU) failed once again to form a coalition with the conservative national party, Partido Popular (PP). But Barcelona remained the only strategic stronghold for the Socialists: Madrid was taken by the PP, after the collapse of the centrist CDS candidacy; Valencia fell to the PP, and Seville, the platform for the Socialists' Ibero-American aspirations in 1992, was wrested away from the PSOE by a center-right coalition headed by the regional Partido Andalucista (PA) and its mayoral candidate Alejandro Rojas Marcos.

The blow in Seville was particularly cruel for the Socialists. The PSOE believed that a national figure, Luis Yañez Barnuevo, who after giving up his post as Secretary of State for International Cooperation in the March 1991 government reshuffle, also surrendered his job as president of the state commission for 1992 celebrations of the V Centenary of the Discovery of America, would insure that a Socialist mayor would inaugurate the 1992

World Exposition and Celebrations in Seville. Yañez was forced to open a legal battle to recover his largely ceremonial post as president of the state commission of the V Centenary, while leading a humiliated Socialist opposition in the Andalusian capital.

When Felipe González left in July 1991 for the first Ibero-American summit in Guadalajara, Mexico, his party's domestic position was seriously eroded. To the injury suffered at the polls in late May was added the insult of an investigation a few days later of major corruption in party finances. As a backdrop, ETA violence continued unabated, the "social pact" with business and labor to restore national "competitiveness" was ever more remote, and the *caso Amedo* trials began in June with devastating revelations of government involvement in GAL anti-terrorist activities.[111] Before his trip to Guadalajara, González moved to restore internal party unity with an uncharacteristically authoritarian crackdown on party dissent. Even King Juan Carlos felt compelled to issue unprecedented warnings on the corruption in public affairs and its potential to destroy Spanish democracy.[112]

Felipe González went to Guadalajara as the representative of a model of peaceful democratic transition from authoritarianism; but that burden had become increasingly more difficult to shoulder in light of his party's glaring democratic weaknesses. The King's presence at the Guadalajara summit, however controversial domestically and internationally, held out the promise that the image of Spain as a democratic *state* would prevail over the aura of corruption and crisis in the elected government.

Part II

Reconnoitering the Target

> The consolidation of Latin American democracy is of strategic importance to Europe...
>
> —*Felipe González*[1]

The limited progress made in the theoretical inquiry into democratic transitions becomes even more limited when we consider the immense variety of nations and cultures that form the major laboratory for testing this rather tenuous knowledge. Latin America's diversity and richness of historical experience is one of the most well-documented aspects of Third World studies. The breadth of its range, from quasi-European society in Argentina to Afro-American culture in the Caribbean, presents problems for any theorist with only a slight suspicion of the *sui generis* aspects of political phenomena.

Even Central America presents a wide range of historical experience and cultural diversity. From the "meso-American" character of the Guatemalan highlands to the Creole culture of Costa Rica, there is diversity at every geographical juncture.[2] Afro-America asserts its complicating presence in Panamá and the Nicaraguan Atlantic coast and again makes its appearance in Belize. Central American nation-states grapple with the entropy implicit in the powerful combination of racial/cultural distinctions and geographical isolation. Development in the isthmus is often held hostage to social integration at the most basic level.

Nationalism, that most powerful of political forces, is still a pending issue in some Central American republics. The curative powers of nationalism have been displayed by the history of the last two centuries, and most remarkably in Eastern Europe's escape from Soviet domination. Great challenges have been met by harnessing these forces in a developmental effort.

Third World nationalism, however, has limitations deriving not only from the ideological disposition of its leaders but also from the centuries-old separation of different races of people by geographical barriers, which only development would overcome. It is not surprising, therefore, that the most fervent nationalists on the isthmus, the Nicaraguan Sandinistas, would alienate the Indian peoples on their isolated Atlantic coast. The Third World radicalism of the Sandinistas in Nicaragua and the Marxist-Leninist guerrilla groups in El Salvador, Guatemala and Honduras may be the ostensible reason for the regional conflict, but it would be hard to deny that such conflict is built into the backwardness of Central America's social, political, and economic institutions.[3]

Despite the challenges of the Central American context, the democratic agenda remains open. Like Bolívar in the 19th Century, one must attempt to impose a democratic blueprint on the complex and often tumultuous map of Central America. One must take account of the dimensions of Central America's problems and prospects in order to evaluate the recent democratic models that offer hope for a democratic future. In Part II, the Central American target will be reconnoitered, using the Latin American *penasadores'* rough guide for surveying democratic prospects.

Democracy's Moving Target: Central American Prospects and the Strategic Dimension

> One should not disillusion these men, who are fully aware that they have restored democracy at the cost of lowering their standard of living. Such a letdown can have consequences as grave as a return to totalitarianism.
>
> —*Claude Cheysson*[1]

> These are the days of lasers in the jungle, lasers in the jungle somewhere.
> —*Paul Simon*[2]

The foreign policy of nation-states answers certain needs that can be both domestic and international in origin. Domestic sources are usually the result of the ruling regime's effort to retain or advance its political power in the face of opposition. International sources arise from the characteristics of the international system and the nation-state's particular position within that system. The complex international and domestic dynamics complicate the policy process to such an extent that the foreign policy of a nation-state often does not respond logically to international stimuli, even when vital economic or security issues are involved. And when economic or security issues do not impinge directly upon the nation-state, the policy process must be fueled by deep-rooted nationalist impulses, or it risks being given low priority in national affairs.

The realist assumption is that the deepest of national impulses, the one that motivates all nation-states, is maximizing national power in the international sphere. This "holy law" of foreign policy can be proven empirically even in cases where vital economic or security issues cannot be found. An ever-present impulse toward influence, if not predominance and hegemony, can be found among even the smallest of states. Such impulses are what realists and geopoliticians point to when analyzing the foreign policy of nation-states, however much the capacity for influence is limited. This impulse may never have to be manifested in actual deeds; often the leadership will create an image of influence in a particular area of the world, a psychological victory to legitimize current rulers.

Spain's preoccupation with the politics of Central America answers the fundamental need on the part of a democratic nation-state to exercise influence on an international scale. Historical bonds of language, culture and religion help form a platform for influence, but these are, relatively speaking, ancient vehicles.[3] In its democratic transition, Spain has found a modern vehicle for its foreign policy. The use of this vehicle answers not only the natural urge of the nation-state to embark upon an international role but also the domestic compulsion to validate a new-found identity with democratic politics. However psychological the need may be, Spain's foreign policy attempts to express it through the policy instruments available to the state and society.

As fundamental as these impulses are, the nation-state still must grapple with character of the international system in the region of interest and must seriously evaluate the realities there. It must come to terms with the inevitable asymmetries that arise from international relationships and hence become aware of the means available to achieve foreign policy goals. Inasmuch as democratic outcomes are ostensibly the goal of Spanish foreign policy in Latin America, Spain must seriously evaluate the prospects for democracy in an area in which repression, revolution, and armed conflict have characterized politics for many generations.

In making such an assessment, Spain would be following the advice of those Latin American *pensadores* who suggested that there would have to be certain basic preconditions for a democratic experience to transpire. If it can be shown in the ensuing chapter that strategic opportunities exist for the West—if only for strategic self-preservation—then what can be said about the conditions on the ground? Bolívar suggested that strategic opportunities would only pave the way for bold democratic initiatives. Much of the burden would then fall on the Latin American people, who already carry the weight of centuries of backwardness and repression.

In evaluating democratic prospects in the Central American context it is easy to succumb to a pessimism that is far from subjective. Whatever the methodology, the outcome seems to be the same: Central America must endure prolonged inter-state conflict, economic crisis, chronic instability, and outside intervention.

Yet events on the ground never cease to surprise observers for their fluidity and their propensity to rebound from failure and to break loose from deadlock. Few would have thought that in August 1987 Costa Rican President Oscar Arias would revive a moribund peace initiative and produce the first document that commits the Central American nations, by treaty, to peace and democratization. The peace initiative went beyond the Contadora vision of regional security through state-to-state guarantees and the elimination of foreign support to insurgencies; effectively, the Contadora initiative would have left all governments, including the Sandinista regime in Nicaragua, intact. The Arias plan addressed the issue of irregular forces and foreign aid while at the same time insisting on concrete measures to insure democratization through negotiated settlements between insurgents and governments, as well as through free elections. Indeed, as hopes diminished for the speedy implementation of the Esquipulas II peace plan, the first anniversary of the accord passed unnoticed in the Central American capitals.[4] Nevertheless, a growing realism among the actors in the Central American crisis brought the feuding parties back to the negotiating table. That realism is a result of the conclusion that armed conflict is not succeeding as a means of securing political goals, especially in the context of global relaxation of ideological confrontation. In the world of *perestroika* and an emerging *yankeetroika*, there seems to be no alternative to peace and democratization.

THE THEORETICAL QUAGMIRE

For the policy-maker as well as the image-maker, the task of evaluation must begin with a theoretical inquiry into the nature of democracy and the preconditions and conditions for its establishment and consolidation. This is a problem with which political philosophers since Aristotle have been grappling. Modern political science has regionalized the analysis considerably and has arrived at some valid, if tentative, conclusions for Latin America.

Two major schools of thought dominate the debate. One is a rather sophisticated brand of economic determinism that sees democracy conditioned on the nature and characteristics of economic production. The other school, which includes most students of democratic transition, focuses on autonomous decision-making by individuals and the *pro forma* aspects of democracy as the decisive factors involved in the establishment of democratic regimes.

The students of democratic transition begin by recognizing that political democracy exists in many countries in which economic inequality and even extreme disparity can be found. In emphasizing the formal aspects of democracy, including constitution-building and the establishment of democratic rules of the game, these political scientists draw attention to the voluntary acts of political elites to establish democracy. Such voluntary, autonomous action takes place regardless of otherwise unfavorable economic and social conditions. The logic of this line of inquiry is that, if democratic experiences are studied and compared in enough detail, a pattern or technology of transition to democracy will emerge. John Peeler, for example, finds proof of the primacy of the voluntaristic aspects of democratic transition in Columbia, Costa Rica, and Venezuela. He shows that formal political democracy can function even while economic crisis and even extreme social disintegration (as in the case of Colombia) transpire.[5]

The economistic school, of which M. Needler is the most prominent voice for Latin American studies,[6] sees democratic prospects arising from the nature of economic production and the distribution of wealth. This analysis differs from that of Marxist or New Left scholarship only insofar as it does not postulate the ultimate emergence of socialism or the inevitability of class conflict. It simply employs a comparative methodology that evaluates "ecological-structural subregions" of Latin America, noting certain variables such as climate, population, land tenure, the organization of economic production, and the degree of coercion involved in maintaining the economic *status quo*. The degree of social inequality arising from the structure of economic production will determine the degree of political democracy in a given country. In places where coercion is manifest (as in El Salvador, Honduras, Guatemala, *et al.*) or where slavery existed (the U.S. South), the possibilities of liberal political democracy—representative institutions, free elections and popular selection, a climate of civil liberty—will be minimal. Where the degree of coercion resulting from such structures as land tenure is low (as in Costa Rica) or absent, political democracy will take root.[7]

In order to minimize the deterministic aspects of this analysis, some non-economic conditions are deemed necessary. These include a favorable international climate (not unlike Bolívar's strategic requirement), and the legitimization of the regime. The process of legitimization involves not only the validation of the ideas and principles of the regime but also a popular judgement on the regime's economic performance.[8]

Certain preconditions do exist for democratic outcomes that are assumed to be present in regions where democracy flourishes: the limitation of economic power on the political system; the subordination of military power to civilian authority;[9] and the limitation of foreign influence on the state. In the Latin American context, Needler includes the psychological liberation of the peasantry as a necessary precondition. To be sure, all democracies fail in some respects to satisfy one or more of these preconditions, but what is more important is the popular illusion that these conditions can obtain. With that illusion, emergency measures that restrict democratic freedoms and destroy democratic conditionality can be tolerated for long periods of time without regime breakdown.[10]

Ultimately, the major difference between the two schools of thought discussed above lies in the conditionality of the economistic perspective. For Peeler and other students of democratic transition, democracy can be established regardless of economic and social conditions as long as there are bold initiatives from influential and dynamic political elites. Needler joins the Marxists and the New Left analysts in conceding that formal democracy cannot exist without "an appropriate social environment," which, in this case, refers primarily to economic conditions.[11] There is, however, a place for economic issues in the transitionist school; "socioeconomic pacts" are the building blocks of formal democracy, and they represent a decisive "moment" (in the Gramscian sense) in the transition process.[12]

For the present purposes, the debate between the transitionist and the economistic school need not be resolved. Nevertheless, some choices must be made if we are to account for a foreign policy that pursues democratic outcomes in the region. As compelling as the economistic perspective is, it does not lead to optimistic appraisals of democratic prospects in Central America. A brief survey of socioeconomic conditions on the isthmus would result in bleak forecasts. Moreover, it may not withstand the empirical test in the Costa Rican case: the socioeconomic conditions and climate in this country did not differ so radically from the other Central American countries as to provide for such a distinct outcome. At best, the egalitarian nature of Costa Rican economic production is subject to debate.[13]

The transitionist argument, on the other hand, seems empirically weak insofar as it ignores the potential for democratic regime breakdown when economic conditions deteriorate or when the legitimization process involves a judgement of the regime's economic performance. A major alarm has sounded in the Americas as nations that have experienced recent democratic transitions (Argentina, Guatemala, Brazil, Nicaragua, *et. al.*) fight for their economic lives under the weight of debt and underdevelopment. Will formal democratic institutions suffice? Will political democracy be sacrificed as the regime, through attrition, breaks down and increasingly attractive authoritarian or totalitarian alternatives emerge?

Despite the momentum that the transitionists have mustered in explaining the process by which authoritarian regimes undergo peaceful democratic change, many observers and political leaders fear that formal democracy is not enough. Recent scholarship in this school has repeatedly shown that "no recent process of political transition to democracy has been predicated on comprehensive socioeconomic reforms," yet these same analyses warn that the issue cannot be ignored.[14] The socioeconomic bases that the economistic school discusses will either have to have existed before the transition to democracy or they will have to be created during the transition. Otherwise, the regime's days will be numbered, and thus the study of democratic transitions risks becoming strictly academic.

Given the restrictions of both perspectives on democratic development, it would seem as if an integration of the two approaches is needed. This would, indeed, satisfy at least some of the requirements of theory; yet a combination of such demanding requirements would probably make the democratic project seem completely out of reach of the Central Americans. It is precisely at this juncture that the Costa Rican model proves its enormous scholarly value. By whatever combination of socioeconomic conditions and the voluntarism of democratically-oriented political elites, Costa Rica has achieved political stability within one of the most volatile regions in the world. The economic crisis during much of the 1980s threatened this democratic stability, yet Costa Ricans have refused to succumb. Any strategy or foreign policy concerned with democratic prospects in Central America cannot avoid being inspired by this performance.

Hence, the process of political transition continued throughout Central America despite an almost crippling pessimism. There is progress and there are setbacks, but no one can deny that transition is occurring. Authoritarianism, which exists in both the military and oligarchical form in Guatemala and El Salvador, in the military form in Panamá, in the traditional military-oligarchical form in Honduras, and in a leftist revolutionary modality and rightist military form in Nicaragua, is everywhere under attack. In El Salvador and Guatemala, armed revolutionaries subvert the system while the United States and Latin American democrats search for viable substitutes for traditional authoritarian rule. In Panamá, a military dictator who had exploited his ties to U.S. security agencies hung on to an ever more slender thread of legitimacy in the face of fierce and united civic opposition and pressure from U.S. foreign policy—until, finally, U.S. troops were sent in to oust him. In Nicaragua, the pressure on the Sandinista regime to democratize was relentless; the entire Western political and strategic establishment demanded no less as a condition for non-intervention. That same pressure has been felt by the *Contra* rebel organizations, whose politics were under similar scrutiny. While both the Sandinistas and the rebel movement seem to have taken steps toward such democratization, their divergent ideologies, perceptions, and interests have made the democratic coalition government of Violeta Chamorro weak and vulnerable to internal and external events.

SCANNING THE TARGET

Any foreign policy that uses democratic transition as its vehicle must look closely at events on the ground and respond to their fluidity. Spanish foreign policy, as will be seen in the following chapters, has been involved to varying degrees in the process of transition in Central America, all the while regarding events as fluid and promising. What Spain sees in Central America may be conditioned by domestic issues, ideology, and a certain ignorance of Central American affairs. Yet Spain continues to focus on the target.

The particular vision that Spain's foreign policy establishment holds is of considerable interest. For the purpose of the present analysis, however, it is more important to develop an objective perspective on the prospects for democratic transition in Central America. A look at democratic developments in Guatemala and Nicaragua, as well as the strategic implications of the 1989 Panamá invasion and Soviet reform on the civil war in El Salvador, will suffice to show the progress and the setbacks in the process of democratization on the isthmus. The analysis will address the concerns of the *pensadores* and both the transitionist and economistic schools of scholarship on Latin American democracy by showing how political movements and socioeconomic issues are intimately linked. In the particular choice of subjects there is no implicit judgement that the process is not transpiring in other Central American countries. Even in war-torn El Salvador, where setbacks outnumber successes, it has been shown that a slow process of transition to democracy is underway.[15]

ON THE GROUND IN GUATEMALA

By virtue of Guatemala's role as the geopolitical linchpin of Central America, her politics will reverberate across the isthmus and exert their influence wherever Guatemalan commerce, communications, and demographic presence can be found. Before Nicaragua and El Salvador upstaged it in the 1980s, the Guatemalan scenario was the political and strategic focus in Central American affairs. The historical role of Guatemala in Inter-American affairs is well documented and need not be discussed here.[16] That role may seem somewhat diminished today, but that is only because the crisis had become so acute in places like Nicaragua and El Salvador. Whether or not the world's attention is on Guatemala, it continues to be the largest, most populous, richest, and most geopolitically sensitive Central American country.

Guatemala's experience with authoritarianism during this century is rivaled by few other nations. In the early 1980s, the Lucas García dictatorship became known to the world as one of the worst human rights violators in history.[17] United States policy, which has always been intimate with Guatemalan affairs, gradually saw its options being limited to the search for democratic solutions. Authoritarianism would no longer suffice to serve U.S. strategic interests as it had done since the 1954 U.S. intervention against the Arbenz regime.

The Reagan Administration's semi-confidential strategy in Central America, known as "Project Democracy," employed a combination of covert and conventional policy instruments that eventually bore fruit in Guatemala.[18] U.S. policy and the courageous work of Guatemalan democrats paved the way for the 1985 elections that brought an end to decades of *de facto* military rule. In peaceful and free elections, Vinicio Cerezo led the embattled Christian Democratic party to power. This victory was an important boost to European Christian Democratic activists in Central America as well as to Napoleon Duarte's Christian Democratic (PDC) regime in El Salvador. Christian Democracy had been under seige across the isthmus; West German activists had been fighting a losing battle against authoritarianism of the right in El Salvador and Guatemala and that of the left in Sandinista Nicaragua. Labor activists from West Germany were especially rewarded by the triumph of Christian Democracy in Guatemala and El Salvador.[19] The Guatemalan party, which had been decimated by repression,[20] won a resounding victory at the polls, thus inspiring other regional activists. Democratic links were again forming in Central America.

As president of a country that was experiencing the effects of civil war, economic stagnation, debt, the anti-democratic machinations of the recalcitrant right, and the questionable loyalty of the right's military allies who were unused to life in the barracks, Cerezo faced seemingly insurmountable odds. But he and his administration were not content to be judged solely on their ability to survive. The major task in the transition to civilian rule was to replace the arbitrary rule of violence with the rule of law without diminishing the military's ability to maintain the upper hand against a still formidable guerrilla insurgency. There was only one way to achieve even limited success in this area: to sacrifice democratic principles by not prosecuting military and civilian perpetrators of human rights violations during the military dictatorships of the late 1970s and early 1980s. If the practitioners of democratic transition have learned anything from experience it is this fundamental rule of thumb. In unstable conditions, armed forces with a praetorian history, or praetorian pretentions, must not be directly provoked. Their power base and legitimacy will often decline in proportion to the degree of democratization taking place within the country.[21]

Democratic legitimacy was strengthened by a foreign policy that displayed a reticence toward involvement in regional conflicts. Guatemala would be outspoken on the need for peaceful and democratic resolution of the Central American crisis but would maintain a policy of equidistance between the major ideological poles. The position included an almost automatic distancing from U.S. policy in the region. Cerezo's fragile political base did not permit continuity in Guatemala's regional role. The new government in Guatemala City could not afford to bolster the perception that Guatemala has historically played the role of a U.S. client state in the region and that Cerezo could not resist being enlisted in Washington's hemispheric strategy. Guatemala had long been the center of leftism in Central America; the democratic consensus in the country included those members of the democratic left who had survived the repression of the military dictatorships. The appearance of a tacit alliance with U.S. policy would not only have jeopardized this consensus but it would also have served the propaganda interests of the four-group guerrilla alliance National Guatemalan Revolutionary Unity (Unidad Revolucionaria Nacional Guatemalteca, URNG), which counts among its ranks prominent social democrats with international connections.[22]

On the socioeconomic front, the new government moved cautiously. Political space was opened for labor organizing before the 1985 elections, when the American Institute for Free Labor Development (AIFLD) labor initiative formed the quasi-legal Guatemalan Confederation of Labor Unity and was able to put labor leaders on electoral lists. For their part, the Christian Democrats succeeded in placing one labor leader in the National Assembly, from where labor's voice was heard for the first time since the 1944–54

Guatemalan Revolution. The virtual elimination of systematic labor repression, which was so rampant under the military dictatorships, served to isolate not only the armed leftist rebel groups who recruited from radicalized labor unions, but also rightist paramilitary groups who have preyed on democratic labor leaders since the appearance in the 1960s of organized death squad activity.

The inevitable confrontation with the powerful Guatemalan oligarchy and business groups was delayed long enough to allow the incorporation of parts of these sectors into the democratic process. Some still remain disloyal and continue to maintain direct contacts with dissident elements of the military as well as with the right-wing paramilitary groups. This constant feature of Guatemalan politics can only be addressed by a slow incorporation of these sectors into democratic life. Cerezo harbored no illusions about these groups, yet he proceeded cautiously lest his policies should provoke a military coup.

A long-sought tax on the wealthy business sectors was successfully imposed in 1987. This tax was a true test of democratic strength, as the imposition of fiscal pressure on these hitherto unburdened sectors was more than a manifestation of rational fiscal policy. Such taxation had become the symbol of democratic defiance of those who had controlled Guatemala since its independence. The Interamerican Development Bank warned, nonetheless, that the tax reform was watered down by strong private sector pressure, and that it "failed to mitigate the regressive nature of the system or to reduce the dependence on foreign trade taxes."[23]

The financial resources, moreover, are badly needed. Like all the Central American countries, Guatemala has been slow to recover from the economic crisis of the early 1980s. Its economy, despite boasting the only significant industrial base on the isthmus, is no less dependent on agricultural and primary exports, for which international prices have not improved significantly from the abysmal levels of the early 1980s. Unemployment and underemployment remained high, especially in the capital where refugees and peasant migrants have flocked during the 1980s. In the rural areas and highlands, the effects of the military's relocation program for refugees complicated economic production and added extra costs to an already overburdened and underfinanced state.[24]

Guatemala's foreign indebtedness at the end of the 1980s was not as dramatic as that of other Latin American or Central American countries, but the burden of debt service has demanded austerity measures that are bound to be unpopular over the long term. Debt and democracy are intimately linked in Latin America, as recent scholarship has suggested.[25] Guatemala is already well past the point at which the government must heed the rising expectations that the democratic revolution has engendered. This may lead to one of the great paradoxes of modern democratic transitions in the Third World: the leader, in order to avoid the Scylla of unfulfilled expectations that would threaten democratic order, may choose the route toward Charybdis—confrontation with international monetary authorities whose capacity for destabilization is well documented.[26]

There are, moreover, a number of issues which remain taboo in Guatemalan politics. The main one, and the one which historically has provided the excuse for cycles of revolution and repression, is that of land reform. As a Christian Democrat raised in the context of Central American underdevelopment and poverty, Cerezo was aware of at least the superficial linkages between land tenure and democracy.[27] Even if he was not convinced of a causal relationship between the two, he knew the perception on the part of the masses that democracy promises the possibility of land redistribution. In the short term, while the war against the insurgency continued, the government could sidestep the issue for security reasons. The eventual showdown with the landholding oligarchy cannot, however, be delayed forever.

The new government's strategy of allowing democratic momentum, as slow as it is, to carry out difficult policies rewarded it with years of relative stability. Yet there was little doubt that the military would eventually respond to what constituted an assault on the traditional power structures of the country. During the first few years of democratic rule, the government was careful to cede almost entirely the political and military prerogatives related to the war against the still active guerrilla groups. Thrust into this professional role, and relieved of domestic political duties, the Guatemalan military began to carve its own niche into the democratic life of the republic. Its success against the guerrillas and the renewal of low-level U.S. military aid raised the morale of the troops and officer corps, thereby facilitating a new military professionalism.

Yet there were limits to the amount of change the Guatemalan militarists were willing and able to absorb. In April 1988, dissident officers led an army division down the mountains toward Guatemala City in what looked like the realization of the seemingly inevitable military coup. The country braced itself for another round of military repression. But the coup attempt lost steam before it reached the capital. Democratic officers first isolated, then dismantled the coup without violence or opposition. The Cerezo government and the military justice system quietly handled the case together. Democracy, it seemed, had been sown in the armed forces; the Guatemalan military had come to the defense of the republic, refusing the temptations of political power and privilege. But the perception proved illusory, as another failed coup attempt led to the dismissal of the army chief of staff in exchange for the promise to break off direct talks with the guerrilla groups. The refusal to negotiate directly with the guerrilla alliance was no doubt a violation of the spirit, if not the letter, of the Esquipulas II peace plan that Cerezo had helped sponsor in meetings on Guatemalan territory. Such a decision only confirmed suspicions that the coup attempts had forced Cerezo to hand over effective control of the police and security forces to the military.

With the military effectively back in power, it was not surprising to see

right wing paramilitary activity continuing to terrorize the *pro forma* democratic political environment. The attacks may not have been coordinated
from an office in the Presidential Palace, as they had been during the military
dictatorship of Lucas García, yet the government seemed powerless in the
face of well-organized and well-connected right-wing terrorist groups. The
year 1988 saw an exponential increase in death-squad activity, with confirmed
reports of over 1,700 disappearances.[28] During his trip to Mexico in May
1990, Pope John Paul II denounced the conditions in which about 30,000
Guatemalan refugees live in Chiapas on the Guatemalan border.[29] Displaced
by the Guatemalan civil war and distrusted by the Mexican authorities, the
primarily Indian refugees represented only a fraction of tens of thousands
of Indian families who were taken from their villages and relocated.

Talks between the government and the guerrillas, moreover, were falter-
ing. After the last direct meetings in Madrid in 1987, under the Esquipulas
II framework, an independent but government-backed National Reconciliation Commission met with the rebels in Costa Rica in early 1989. Talks
between the guerrilla alliance and the commission resumed in Oslo in March
1990, where both sides called for direct intervention by the United Nations
secretary general. But no agreement on a truce was reached. Amid inten-
sifying violence by the guerrillas in the Guatemalan highlands, remote jun-
gles, and the strategically important coastal plains, the commission met with
the URNG again, this time in June 1990 in El Escorial, the famous monastery
outside Madrid. The talks yielded no cease fire, but the "El Escorial"
agreement promised no guerrilla interference in the upcoming elections
scheduled for January 1991 and eventual URNG participation in a new
constitutional assembly.[30]

Meanwhile, the human rights situation continued to deteriorate. The legitimacy of civilian rule was called into question as Guatemalans saw a
correlation between democratic politics and left-wing and right-wing violence.[31] The guerrillas, apparently aided by drug traffickers in rebel strongholds who supplied them with sophisticated weapons, were dispelling any
myths about their strategic defeat.[32] On the right, Cerezo seemed powerless
to prosecute high-level officials of the security forces for human rights abuses.
According to Americas Watch, "human rights abuses have essentially been
viewed as a public relations problem under President Cerezo."[33]

Cerezo's public relations problem, nevertheless, went so far as to alienate
his natural allies in the White House. After renewing military and economic
aid after the 1986 elections, U.S. policy was confronted with the increasingly
troublesome implications of the Cerezo government's weakness. On the one
hand, the military had been given a free hand in the guerrilla war, thereby
raising confidence in the prospect of a "Guatemalan solution," or all-out,
total war for problems of insurgency. On the other hand, the human rights
abuses were affecting children and U.S. citizens. Covenent House, the U.S.
charity organization, denounced the systematic violation of children's rights

during a brutal police anti-crime sweep of Guatemala City in June and July 1990. The official crackdown on street crime gave the green light to death squads, who began to clean the streets of homeless children.[34] The U.S. ambassador was recalled on one occasion in 1990 in protest of human rights abuses (and perhaps as retribution for Cerezo's regional peacemaking role),[35] and in September 1990 the United States threatened to cut off military aid if official links to the June murder of a U.S. national were not investigated.[36]

In a climate of declining confidence in democracy's ability to solve pressing political and socioeconomic problems, Guatemalans went to the polls in January 1991 in a final election run-off between two conservative presidential candidates. A reinvigorated justice system had kept the popular former military dictator Efrain Rios Montt from the election lists, but the El Escorial pact did not survive the polling, as the guerrillas conducted ambush and sabotage operations in the highlands. The final election results gave a clear victory to Jorge Elías Serrano, a center-right protestant evangelist whose popularity soared as a result of his participation in the National Reconciliation Commission and his populist promises to end the violence and repression. Ironically enough, his minority party, the Solidarity Action Movement (MAS), received crucial votes from the frustrated supporters of Efrain Rios Montt, who is also a born-again Christian.[37]

Lack of confidence in Guatemala's civilian leadership was reflected in the extremely low turnout for the election run-off. With about half of the electorate abstaining from the vote, Serrano faced the same daunting problems that his Christian Democratic predecessor was unable to address. The populist leader's promise was to prosecute anyone who violated human rights, "even if he is dressed in uniform." The promise was backed up with reassurances that he would govern the shattered country with divine inspiration.[38]

What is certain is that in the absence divine intervention, the problem will not go away by itself. Incorporation of the right-wing extremist groups into a democratic project may prove more difficult than the incorporation of armed leftist groups. This is the case not only in Guatemala, but in Nicaragua and El Salvador as well. There remains the alternative of physical elimination, but that depends on the relative strength of these groups, whose financial resources sometimes rival those of the state. Here is where, perhaps, outside influence can help the democratic state in isolating and weakening these formidable threats to democracy.

ON THE GROUND IN NICARAGUA

If any country today symbolizes the peculiar mixture of romance and desperation that characterizes the struggle for democracy in the Third World, it must be Nicaragua. Its struggle against authoritarianism is lendendary; yet its particular historical fortune seems to condemn Nicaraguan society to a process akin to exorcism as the beast of repression and authoritarianism takes on new forms that span the political spectrum from right to left. The 1979 Sandinista Revolution triumphed over the 45-year Somoza dictatorship, a particularly brutal strain of Central American right-wing authoritarianism. The leftist regime that emerged from the civil war then manifested the same tendencies: an unwillingness to accept the inevitable pluralism of democratic institutions made it the target of both local and foreign democratic forces that endeavored to keep the democratic dream alive in Nicaragua.

The injection of Marxist-Leninist ideology into Central America through the agency of an official government was bound to provoke a strategic crisis in the region. As unique and peculiar as the Sandinista program was, it was still perceived largely as a foreign body in the Central American geostrategic context. In fact, the first armed opposition to the Sandinista regime was organized by Latin and Central Americans (former Somoza national guardsmen, Honduran militarists, and Argentines); later, when Argentine support diminished as a result of the breakdown of U.S./Argentine strategic cooperation during the Falklands/Malvinas War, the U.S. Central Intelligence Agency inherited what came to be known as the *Contra War*.[39]

At first, the initiative was only thinly disguised as a democratic venture. According to the CIA director, William Casey, who presented an agency finding on the *Contra* initiative to President Reagan in 1981, the purpose of the rebel force was that of "interdiction" of Sandinista aid for Salvadoran rebels. It took the intense international scrutiny of *Contra* activities over the years to convince rebel leaders of the need to identify their strategic goals with those of democracy. The *Contra* leadership would later complain bitterly about Reagan's characterization of them as "freedom fighters" and "the moral equivalent of our founding fathers," which opened them up to ridicule when abuses of human rights were detected. There is no doubt that among the opposition to the Sandinista regime there were those who followed a more personal and selfish agenda; nevertheless, the main goal of the local and international pressure was to force the Sandinista regime to make good on their pre-revolution promises of democracy and pluralism.

It is a fact of life in parliamentary politics that every government that enjoys an absolute majority tends toward abuse of the that power, and often the regime begins to take on authoritarian character. But this was not necessarily the concern in Nicaragua; in the controversial 1984 elections, when the U.S.-backed opposition candidate Arturo Cruz pulled out of the race, the Sandinistas won an overwhelming two thirds of the popular vote. The fear in Central America was that this control, combined with radical Marxist-Leninist ideology and significant Soviet-Cuban penetration, could result in another totalitarian nightmare in the Caribbean. As Sandinista hardliners slowly recovered ideological and strategic control over the revolution, that outcome seemed ever more plausible.

Any analysis of the movement toward democracy in Nicaragua must address events in the regional context, inasmuch as the political space in Nicaragua was limited for organized opposition. The Sandinista regime, moreover, had a tendency to react only to international and regional stimuli because its hegemony in Nicaraguan economic, social, and political affairs was virtually uncontested. Efforts to democratize Nicaragua were more credible when they came from outside the country, although the existence of an internal opposition was crucial to the legitimization of outside actors.

Nicaragua's position as a poor, underdeveloped, dependent Third World nation-state was only reinforced by the Sandinista experiment. The international system affects Nicaragua in very unsubtle ways; other nations' capacity to injure the Managua regime or cause economic deprivation is tremendous. The Sandinistas were extremely sensitive to the effects of regional and international politics on their power inside Nicaragua. Their vision was regional and international, yet their problems, which they either ignored or denied, were internal.

The democratic opposition from labor, business groups, and the Church was by no means negligible. Such opposition played an important role within Nicaragua, along with a growing level of popular discontent with the economic situation.[40] Nevertheless, after ten years of Sandinista rule one could only begin to talk of an institutional drama of democratic transition transpiring within the country. Democratic transition in Nicaragua had become a regional and international phenomenon with strategic dimensions. The *dramatis personae* were as far away as Moscow and Washington, and as near as San José.

The economic state of affairs within Nicaragua deserves attention insofar as deterioration of living standards was a major variable in the regional negotiating process. The Sandinistas were not insensitive to the suffering of the Nicaraguan people. Their move to the bargaining table in Esquipulas during 1987 was generally interpreted as the only means by which they could begin to address the critical economic conditions in the country. The revitalization of regional trade and the alleviation of the defense burden of the *Contra* war were tangible goals to help address serious economic problems. Along with the concessions toward democratization in exchange for an end to *Contra* hostilities was the revision of some of the economic policies that had helped cause the economic collapse of the country.[41]

Faced with the threat of losing popular hegemony as a result of the widespread economic and social discontent, the Sandinistas showed signs of democratizing their economic decision-making. Even such Leninist hardliners as Interior Minister Tomás Borge began to admit serious errors in the administration of economic affairs. The list is, unfortunately, long; so long that Borge himself states that "an encyclopedia would need to be written" if one were to count them all.[42] Apart from an irrational agrarian reform program, which led to the "insanity" of nationalizing too much land, the mismanagement of international economic aid ("we ate it up instead of investing it," according to Borge),[43] the irrational agricultural procurement program that further impoverished the already suffering Nicaraguan peasant, and discriminatory credit policies that afforded Sandinista sympathizers ridiculously low interest rates and all others unpayable three-digit figures, the Sandinistas sacrificed trade opportunities by pursuing what appeared to be strategic links with the Soviet bloc. The general disarray of Nicaraguan finances, moreover, did not attract trade opportunities, as partners feared that payment for goods would not be forthcoming.

By 1989 the Sandinistas had already begun to experience serious defections as a result of their economic policies. Although the revolution had been able to withstand some crucial departures in the past, including the defection of junta members and Sandinista officials, there was concern in Managua over this new political attrition.[44] This time, however, the deterioration of living standards, which by 1988 approached the levels of the 1950s, threatened the very spirit of the revolutionary movement. The Sandinista goals of *poder popular*, or popular power, were impossible to meet when the daily concerns of the populace were primarily economic, not political. The crude logic of survival replaced the revolutionary élan of earlier, more utopian, days.

The shift in popular momentum from political participation to survivalism represented a turning point in the Nicaraguan Revolution. Despite their obvious elitism and sectarian approach to politics, the Sandinistas remained in contact with the Nicaraguan masses. Their particular brand of Central American authoritarianism had been forged through constant exposure to the Nicaraguan peasantry, making the regime the most politically sensitive on the isthmus. The intimacy of this relationship was always threatened by the ideological challenges of the opposition and the armed assault of the "counterrevolution"; but such adversity only proved the loyalty of Sandinista cadres and of Nicaragua's underprivileged classes. Popular support would narrow, and some cases would completely dissipate or defect to the *Contra* ranks, but Sandinista leadership would be even further legitimized in the eyes of the true believers. Such adversity would be functional; ideological premises would be confirmed by the behavior of the opposition and its foreign supporters. The process of revolutionary identification of the party with the masses would be reinforced.

Nevertheless, as the already serious economic crisis reached a critical point, energy for political participation dissipated. Within the party ranks, cognitive dissonance began to break down revolutionary discipline. High-level defectors, beginning with Major Roger Miranda Bengoechea (the defense minister's chief aide), left their positions and either joined the internal opposition or conspired with the Sandinistas' foreign enemies. Moisés Hassan, a legendary Sandinista militant, former government minister, and junta member, broke with the party in April 1988. Hassan noted the irony that, under the Sandinistas, "for the first time in the history of this country, people are feeling hunger."[45] The disenchantment of the masses thus led to a corresponding breakdown of a regime that relied on the uncritical, almost blind support of the people. In allowing the economy to deteriorate to such an extent, the Sandinistas violated the intimacy they enjoyed with the Nicaraguan masses.

Under normal, peacetime conditions, such regime breakdown would result in the emergence of political alternatives. In Nicaragua, however, the regime's emergency powers, which were always suspected of being merely a cover for totalitarian designs, did not permit the organization of viable alternatives to Sandinista rule. An opposition rally in the small town of Nandaime on July 10, 1988, was violently broken up by Sandinista security forces and civilian supporters. The Sandinistas arrested thirty-nine protesters and expelled the U.S. Ambassador, Richard H. Melton, and seven other U.S. diplomats. The opposition newspaper, *La Prensa*, and the radio station of the Catholic Church, *Radio Catolica*, were shut down; the nation's largest private enterprise, the San Antonio sugar mill, was also expropriated.[46]

The freezing of internal democratic activity inside Nicaragua responded to the mortal threat posed by the economic crisis. Sandinista hardliners, led by the radical ideologue and Commander of the Revolution Bayardo Arce, feared that the strategic opportunity to defeat the underfunded *Contra* rebels would be missed if the regime permitted "the right-wing to take over the streets." In Arce's view, the Revolution could not afford to "confront the war with scorpions inside its shirt."[47] In the face of uncertainty over U.S. policy after the presidential elections in November 1988, the Sandinistas preferred to return to extreme positions from whence concessions would be easier to make.

THE LONG ROAD TO ESQUIPULAS

The Sandinsta crackdown violated the spirit and letter of the Esquipulas II accords, whose provisions for internal democratization of Central American countries were being slowly carried out. The Sandinistas were already working under their "own interpretation" of the provisions, according to opposition critics.[48] Yet some Western leaders, including Spanish vice president Alfonso Guerra, had praised Managua for its progress toward democratization.[49] The radical measures came at a time when Latin American leaders were predicting an "internalization" of the Central American crisis. In April 1988, the Mexican vice-chancellor, Víctor Flores Olea, expressed his government's view that "the problem of Nicaragua had entered into a process of nationalization in which the conflict can be resolved by the Nicaraguans themselves."[50]

Such optimism about democratic prospects notwithstanding, by the spring of 1988 there were already signs that the peace and democratization initiative was fatally stalled. Internal dissent within the Sandinista ranks over President Daniel Ortega's concessions to the internal opposition in Nicaragua was apparent as early as January, when Sandinista security forces and civilian demonstrators broke up an opposition meeting without the president's consent.[51] Reluctance by then Salvadoran president José Napoleon Duarte to make concessions to leftist rebels and Nicaragua's sluggishness in instituting democratic reforms dampened enthusiasm for the plan even before the Sandinista crackdown in July. The Reagan Administration, moreover, persisted in its efforts to secure aid for the *Contra* rebels despite a reluctant U.S. Congress, which feared that the Sandinistas would justify their non-compliance with the provisions of the Esquipulas II treaty by citing the Administration's rejection of the major security arrangements implicit in the plan. In January 1989 the Administration had rejected Soviet offers to halt aid to the Sandinistas in exchange for the termination of U.S. aid to the *Contra* rebels.[52] The U.S. refusal to subscribe to the major security provisions of the treaty—those regarding outside aid to irregular forces—was confirmation that Washington was counting on the initiative to break down before the Sandinistas could muster a fatal blow to the ailing rebels. Without Washington's acquiescence, the Esquipulas II initiative seemed doomed.

Nevertheless, this state of affairs had precedents in recent Central American affairs. It should be remembered that the Arias plan seemed doomed only a few weeks before its signing in August 1987. Serious doubts about the plan led Arias to consider a personal tour of the Central American capitals in July. Amid suggestions by Nicaraguan president Daniel Ortega that the Contadora peace process be revived, Arias embarked on new efforts to keep Central American security arrangements linked to internal democratic reforms. The Sandinista preference for the Contadora process, which had begun in a 1983 meeting between Mexico, Panamá, Venezuela, and Colombia on the Panamanian island, stemmed from the fact that the Contadora initiative would have provided for guarantees on Nicaragua's security from outside invasion without asking for specific concessions on the issue of internal democratization. The Sandinistas would then have received a political buffer to U.S. invasion of Nicaragua and *Contra* incursions while signing off on more general provisions for Central American democracy.[53]

The Sandinistas were virtually alone in their desire to see the Contadora process revived. Arias and most other Central American leaders saw the plan as unworkable and further complicated by the unrest in Panamá, the principal sponsor of the initiative. The Costa Ricans, moreover, were eager to go to the source of the regional problem; as long as the Sandinistas pursued their internationalist program of subversion and revolution, Costa Rican security could not be guaranteed by anyone but the United States. The regional initiative launched by Arias was an attempt to convince outside actors, including the United States, that Central Americans were themselves capable of addressing the problem of democracy on the isthmus.

To the surprise of practically everyone, the Esquipulas accords were signed by the leaders of Guatemala, Honduras, El Salvador, Nicaragua, and Costa

Rica by August. Nicaragua was among the first to embark on internal reforms and direct talks with the *Contra* insurgents. For the first time in over eight years, *Contra* leaders were able to visit Managua. The talks broke down in June 1988, but a controversial cease-fire agreement signed on March 23 entered its fifth month in September 1988, despite reported violations by both sides.[54] Even after the Sandinista crackdown in July 1988, Nicaraguan rebel leaders expressed confidence that talks would resume in the fall. Indeed, direct talks between the rebels and Nicaraguan officials resumed in Managua during September 1988, after a three-month break.

Such optimism from the rebel side was significant insofar as it reflected a growing concern for the goals of internal democratization in Nicaragua. *Contra* leader Alfredo César admitted that the two sides had already resolved "a number of issues," and he linked the disarming of the rebel forces to democratic reforms inside Nicaragua. The shift in strategic concerns from defeating the Sandinistas on the battlefield to trading away arms for democratic reforms reflected major progress on the other side of the democratic coin in Nicaragua: the democratization of the *Contra* rebel forces, which, at the time, seemed to represent the strongest challenge to Sandinista power in the country.[55]

The Sandinistas had often capitalized on deep divisions in the ranks of the rebel insurgents. The *Contra* movement had always been a heterogeneous mix of ex-National Guardsmen of the overthrown dictatorship, disenchanted social democrats, defected former Sandinista junta members, and disgruntled Nicaraguan peasants revolting against Sandinista rule. Unity was always imposed from above, as a tactical measure under the pressure of Sandinista gunfire or as a political concession to the movement's sponsors in Washington and Langley.[56] The Sandinista regime waited patiently for the expected cutoff of U.S. funding, expecting serious infighting once Washington's leverage was removed and the rebel forces were on the defensive.

There were precedents on which to base such a strategy. The history of U.S. support to the rebel movement is replete with temporary aid cut-offs, limitations, and contingencies. The *Contra* directorate had been a revolving door of strong personalities, some with dubious democratic credentials. As long as military victory was the goal of the movement there would be tactical unity on the ground at least; yet the movement's political front remained divided, its image suffering from the perception that without Washington's aid and direction there would be a further splintering of an obviously discordant political force.

The lack of unity in the *Contra* ranks highlighted Washington's role as the guarantor of rebel political and military viability. Washington's responsibility for what was being touted as a national resistance movement only served to fuel the perception that the *Contra*-Sandinista duel was an East-West showdown in which the Nicaraguan people were the pawns. Edén Pastora, ex-Sandinista Commander and former *Contra* leader of independent forces in the south of Nicaragua, saw the March 1988 negotiations between the U.S.-backed *Contra* leaders and Sandinista representatives in Sapoa, Nicaragua as a meeting between "the monkeys of Washington and the monkeys of Moscow."[57] Unfortunately, this perception was shared by many observers, including a large sector of the U.S. and European population.

Ironically enough, as the goals of the rebel movement shifted from military victory to internal democratization of Nicaragua within the framework of the Esquipulas II accords, the *Contra* directorate experienced a reconsolidation of right-wing leadership. A mutiny against the military leadership of former Somoza National Guard Colonel Enrique Bermúdez in the spring of 1988 was transformed into an overwhelming victory for Bermúdez and his supporters in July 1988 elections for the new rebel directorate in Santo Domingo. The apparent disintegration of the rebel cause was converted into a consolidation of power for hard-line rebel figures, with Bermúdez himself ascending to the ranks of the rebel political leadership.[58]

There was concern, however, that the *Contras'* willingness to negotiate with the Sandinistas reflected a strategic weakness resulting from the U.S. lethal aid cut-off and congressional restrictions on the delivery of non-lethal humanitarian aid to rebel positions inside Nicaragua. The majority of the rebel forces moved back into base camps inside Honduras where supplies were more readily available. The Sandinistas took advantage of the *Contra* retreat by harvesting bumper crops and restoring rural stability. The shift of the battle from the Nicaraguan hills and ravines to the political sphere would inevitably work against *Contra* optimism in the near term. In August 1988, Bosco Matamoros, the spokesman for the Nicaraguan Resistance, the *Contra* alliance, pointed out that the rebels paid a very high price for the negotiations: "Strategically, our situation has weakened substantially. I don't think that we have the capacity to go on the offensive."[59]

The combination of rebel bitterness over the U.S. aid cut-off and the July crackdown by Sandinista hardliners might have cast a shadow of gloom over the situation in Nicaragua if it had not been for the underlying movement of political affairs. The suffering of the Nicaraguan people had forced the Sandinistas into the peace process, making inevitable the democratic reforms that would both alleviate military pressure from outside and permit a more rational functioning of the collapsed Nicaraguan economy. In the view of most Central American diplomats, the shift to strong-arm tactics internally seemed only temporary, affording the Sandinista regime some concessions to make in the negotiating process.[60] The *Contras*, for their part, were forced by financial realities and international pressure to enter into the politics of democracy in Central America. Their appearance in Managua, despite considerable tension, afforded them the opportunity to show the Nicaraguan people that their struggle was not selfish reaction and vengeance but a democratic alternative.[61] The consolidation of hard-line rebel leadership around the democratic platform was perhaps the most significant rebel development of the decade. The making of concessions by a more moderate leadership would have risked the defection of thousands of front-line fighters and thus the eventual collapse of the rebel movement.

THE QUEST FOR DEMOCRATIC FLEXIBILITY

Paradoxically enough, hard-line leadership in Central America was pursuing democratic goals. For the first time since the years of the Good Neighbor Policy, legitimacy for political movements on the isthmus was tied to democratization of national politics. Neither side of the political spectrum could afford the image of inflexibility and ideological paralysis.

Even if democratic visions differ, as they inevitably do when moving across the Central American political spectrum, the granting of concessions in the negotiating process would ultimately lead to a synthesis of positions and a widening of political space. The major hurdle was bringing the confrontation to the political sphere instead of relying on military victory to propel political movement.

At the same time that military solutions seemed more distant than ever, the warring parties in Central America were assessing the limits of this democratic flexibility. Sandinista Interior Minister Tomás Borge stated that his government's flexibility had been "useless,"[62] while some *Contra* leaders saw the negotiations as a sign of rebel weakness.[63] The Sandinistas may have had a secret plan to eliminate the rebel insurgency by 1989–90,[64] but up until that point Sandinista military forces seemed content to reestablish normal economic and social life in former rebel strongholds.

Salvadoran rightists, emboldened by April 1988 legislative election successes and the February 1989 recapture of the presidency by the ultra-conservative *Alianza Republicana Nacional* (Republican National Alliance, or ARENA)-party candidate, Alfredo Cristiani, seemed eager to give the military a green light in its war against leftist insurgents. The guerrilla insurgency gladly accepted this challenge. According to the top guerrilla commander, Joaquín Villalobos, "the choice will be between the right and the army and its repression, and us. It is a war that we can win."[65] The November 1989 rebel offensive in the capital suggested, nevertheless, that the military struggle would produce no clear victor, only more pain and suffering for an already war-weary populace.

Any foreign policy concerned with the peace process in Central America must find a way to participate in the democratization process and thus facilitate the flexibility needed to keep the conflict off the battlefield. European foreign policy had attempted this approach on numerous occasions, with the Spanish achieving some success in bringing the Nicaraguan internal oppositions to direct negotiations with the Sandinista regime.[66]

But the Europeans have generally deferred to regional initiatives, leaving the responsibility with local leaders whose own precarious positions pre-cluded any suggestion of flexibility. The Central American leaders, moreover, were always dependent on superpower willingness to cooperate on the se-curity aspects of the regional initiatives. The main issue was U.S. aid to the *Contra* rebels, if only because Soviet-Cuban aid to rebels in Salvador and Guatemala was, comparatively speaking, less visible.

The expectation surrounding the November 1988 U.S. presidential elec-tions was a further indication of the dependence of the peace and democ-ratization process on United States policy in the region. With the Soviets linking their aid to the Sandinista regime—considered a "regular" fighting force in the framework of the Esquipulas II accords—to the termination of U.S. aid to the *Contra* rebels, and indications from Fidel Castro that Cuban aid to Marxist-led forces in Central America would also end if the U.S. should relent,[67] there was considerable pressure on Washington to call the Sandinistas' bluff by changing its strategy from one of insurgency to one of regional diplomacy. This shift would deprive the Sandinistas of their major justification for internal crackdown and force them to move more quickly on instituting the democratic reforms necessary to meet Nicaragua's obligations under the Esquipulas II provisions. As preparations for February 1990 elec-tions proceeded apace, the Sandinistas reluctantly opened the door to op-position politics.

Much of President Arias's political capital had been spent on efforts to eliminate these "excuses" for not complying fully with the requirements of the peace accord, which provide for cease-fires, a general amnesty, and democratic reforms. While acquiescing to non-lethal aid for the *Contras*, the Costa Rican leader entered the domestic political debate in the United States, asking for a cut-off of military aid to the rebel insurgents.[68] Administration officials were quick to display resentment over this intervention in the U.S. foreign policy process. U.S.-Costa Rican relations reached a low point in 1987 when Washington expressed bitterness over Arias's effort to isolate U.S. policy in the region.

The danger of confronting U.S. policy and intervening directly in the political debate was obvious; what Arias risked, moreover, was the weakening of his own domestic political position. Costa Ricans of all political persuasions were concerned about the country's dependence on the now-threatened U.S. economic aid, while some sectors called for a tougher stance against creeping Central American totalitarianism and for a closer alignment with U.S. policy in the region.

While less risky, Arias's appeal to Cuba and the Soviet Union to halt aid to Marxist-led rebels in the region put the Costa Rican leader in the uncom-fortable position that results from equating the moral posture of the West with that of the East. In a concession to Western security concerns, which are geopolitically more manifest in the Central American context, he also called for a halt in Soviet military aid to the officially recognized Nicaraguan regime, thereby creating a certain asymmetry in his approach to the demilitarization of the region.

The Guatemala Accords (Esquipulas II) provide for the withdrawal of all foreign military forces from the region, which in the U.S. case would include recent deployments in Honduras, but remain vague regarding outside aid to officially recognized Central American governments. The Soviet Union was being asked to halt military aid to the officially recognized government of Nicaragua while there was practically no suggestion of limits on U.S. military aid to friendly governments in the region—including Costa Rica itself.

Referring implicitly to this apparent asymmetry, Soviet leader Mikhail Gorbachev offered, in an April 1988 reply to a written appeal by Arias, to stop arms shipments to the Nicaraguan government if, again, the United States halted its arm shipments to the region. In the Gorbachev letter was a denial that the Soviets were arming Central American guerrillas, thus turning the tables on the U.S. by portraying the Reagan Administration as the only superpower supplier of arms to "irregular" forces. No reference was made, however, to reports that Cuba and the Sandinistas continued to provide low-level support to Central American insurgents.[69]

In October 1989, Foreign Minister Edward Shevardnarze would repeat Gorbachev's offer to cut arms deliveries to Central American actors, but the Soviet push for an expanded political role in the peace process was unlikely to find support in Washington, which rejected any linkage to U.S. forces and bases in the region and any role that would legitimize Soviet power in the Western Hemisphere.

Responding to the regional diplomatic pressure, and still reeling from the setback it received from the congression freezing of lethal aid to the *Contras* on February 29, 1988, the Reagan Administration embarked on a new diplomatic "fallback" strategy in the region. U.S. Secretary of State George Shultz visited four Central American nations in late June 1988 in a long overdue diplomatic mission to isolate further the Nicaraguan regime and gain time for the rebels. Shultz was reminded of his over 4-year absence from the region, and the Costa Ricans were quick to note that his last visit to Costa Rica had been in 1982. The Secretary's absence from the diplomatic stage brought home the reality that Washington's strategy in the region had been primarily military. This focus was not lost on Shultz himself, who was forced to admit that "we have kind of stood back from the diplomatic process to a certain degree."[70]

Forced to accept the *Contras'* apparently autonomous decision to negotiate directly with the Sandinista regime in the context of the regional peace process, the Administration decided on a highly rhetorical diplomatic assault in an effort to give the Nicaraguan rebels more credibility at the negotiating table in a "new era" of diplomatic warfare against the Sandinista regime. During a follow-up visit on August 1, 1988, there were reports in the international media that Shultz was attempting to strong-arm Central American governments into signing a communique that blamed Nicaragua for inviting Soviet-bloc intervention in regional affairs. Guatemala and Nicaragua were reportedly opposed to such a statement, as it suggested a new identification with U.S. perceptions of the Central American crisis after years of hard-earned distance from Washington's approach.[71] Shultz later noted that the statement was originally drafted in July by the Central American foreign ministers—without specifying which—and that they later had second thoughts about issuing it.[72]

Washington's diplomatic drive came within the context of uncertainty over the prospects of unfreezing *Contra* aid in Congress and maintaining control over the political-military affairs of the Administrations's rebel clients. The hard-line leadership of the rebel alliance, especially Bermúdez and political leader Adolfo Calero, was always closer to the Administration's behind-the-scenes operatives in the CIA and the National Security Council. Their public image, complicated by former ties to the Somoza dictatorship and National Guard as well as by their authoritarian and personalistic style, had been nothing less than an embarrassment for the more public facets of U.S. policy.

The more "respectable" Washington recruits, the former Sandinista junta member Alfonso Robelo and the former Sandinista ambassador to Washington Arturo Cruz appeared to have lost the battle over the political-military leadership of the *Contra* alliance, thus making it much more difficult for the rebels to sell their new democratic image to an ambivalent U.S. Congress and a confused American public. The bitter departures of Cruz and Robelo—among others—after the signing of the Guatemala Accords in 1987 put the Administration in the position of having to support whatever force could maintain control on the ground. And when the Administration failed to convince the U.S. Congress to continue funding the rebels, the hard-line leadership of the rebels began to exercise an unprecedented autonomy in their political affairs.

The removal of Washington's financial leverage and the resultant doubts about the credibility of the United States' and Western strategy in confronting world communist revolution propelled the *Contras* into direct negotiations with the Sandinistas, despite considerable consternation on the part of the Administration.[73]

The rebel leaders, nevertheless, claimed that they were "directly defending the interests and the security of the United States." Bolstered by support from the CIA in his role as a rebel negotiator, Bermúdez assured both sides at the negotiating table that he was the rebel leader best able to "make good" on any negotiated accord.[74]

But cease-fire violations continued to occur, as the desperate and hungry *Contras* still remaining inside Nicaraguan territory raided farms for food and supplies. Of the approximately 13,000 rebel fighters, about 15% remained inside Nicaragua, where orders to avoid any form of engagement with the

Sandinistas could not be enforced. This development did not bode well for future arrangements within the context of the Guatemala Accords. There remained the possibility that the rebel alliance would fracture into smaller independent groups that would be difficult to control from either Managua or Washington.[75]

While the diplomatic war proceeded in Central America, uncertainty about U.S. policy after the November 1988 elections cast a sense of tenuousness over the negotiating tables. Nicaraguan rebels made it clear that they feel betrayed by "some liberal people" in the United States who could not see the unity of rebel and U.S. interests.[76] There was also bitter criticism of the Reagan approach: the marketing of the *Contras* to the U.S. public as the "moral equivalent of our founding fathers" had focused attention on their well-documented human rights abuses and opened them up to ridicule. The negotiations may have appeared to be a sign of rebel weakness in the face of the U.S. aid cutoff; but the reorientation of rebel strategic goals from military victory to democratic reforms inside Nicaragua would strengthen their position, especially with a Democratic majority in both houses of Congress.

The Republican victory in the 1988 U.S. presidential race provided additional flexibility inasmuch as funding for the military option would become something more than "potentially possible."[77] Senate Democrats were already planning a rebel aid package in August 1988, after the Sandinistas' July crackdown on the internal opposition, as a means of pressuring the Sandinistas into meaningful democratic reforms and compliance with the provisions of the regional peace process.

For the Sandinistas, the negotiations were the only possible course. The image of weakness displayed by the sacrifice of the previously sacred principle of not negotiating directly or even indirectly with the *Contra* "monkeys" when they should be negotiating directly with the "circus ringmaster" in Washington, was dispelled in July 1988 when Sandinista hardliners cracked down on the internal opposition. But economic realities in Nicaragua were ensuring Sandinista flexibility. Even hardline Sandinista *comandantes* such as Bayardo Arce, who insisted that the Frente Sandinista de Liberación Nacional (FSLN) "will never give up power," would be forced to make concessions to democracy.[78]

The momentum of the Esquipulas peace plan during 1989 was undeniable. The Bush Administration was forced to accept the possibilities of opposition success in Nicaragua as a substitute for the military strategy of overthrowing the regime through *Contra* funding. The Nicaraguan rebel leaders in the Nicaraguan Resistance (Resistencia Nicaraguense, RN) and the 14-party National Opposition Union (Union Nacional Opositora, UNO) met in Guatemala in July 1989 to forge a strategy for victory in the elections scheduled for early 1990.[79] The Sandinistas, meanwhile, promoted their observance with the accords with trips to European capitals and presentations of their plans to demobilize the rebel forces during the inauguration of president Carlos Andrés Pérez in February 1989 in Caracas. The Sandinista effort was paying off, as European leaders including then Prime Minister Margaret Thatcher, a fervent supporter of U.S. *Contra* policy, were resolved to judge the Sandinistas by their deeds and not by preconceived political positions or pressure from Washington.[80]

For its part, Washington shifted to what Bush had promised would be a bipartisan strategy on democratization in Nicaragua. With only humanitarian aid available from Congress, and covert aid a virtual impossibility in the aftermath of the "Irangate" scandal, the rebels were no longer a strategic option. Now the task was to make their weight felt in the democratic struggle within Nicaragua, without tainting the pro-U.S. internal opposition. That goal required good faith observance of the Arias peace plan through orderly demobilization and eventual repatriation.

The five Central American presidents met in Tela, Honduras, in August 1989 and signed an accord to demobilize the *Contras* by December 5. In October 1989 the Esquipulas verification commission made up of the United Nations and the Organization of American States issued a blunt diplomatic message to the Nicaraguan rebels in Honduran territory. "You can stay only as long as the Honduran government lets you," said Fransesc Vendrell, the UN Secretary-General's representative. "You are Nicaraguans and not the object of a U.S. policy that is anachronistic and has been abandoned by the country that helped you." According to Vendrell, the rebel presence in Honduras had "ceased to have any *raison d'etre*." A few weeks earlier, an agreement between the Sandinistas and Miskito Indian rebels, mediated by former U.S. president Jimmy Carter, had bolstered the democratization process. The momentum of the Central American peace plan notwithstanding, the 3,000 to 8,000 rebels inside Nicaragua refused to take Sandinista and UN-OAS guarantees of safe passage and full integration into Nicaraguan political life seriously; fierce fighting raged on, in spite of a 19-month old unilateral Sandinista cease-fire, in the remote areas of rural Nicaragua.[81] The UN Secretary General, Javier Pérez de Cuéllar, realizing the stakes and the delicate sensibilities involved, immediately distanced himself from Vendrell's comments; the UN position was in fact "rigorously impartial," and the international organization emphasized the "voluntary nature" of the disarmament and repatriation plan.[82]

As if to avoid being upstaged and isolated at the October 1989 hemispheric summit in San José, Nicaraguan president Daniel Ortega resorted to shock tactics to draw attention to the fact that the U.S. was dragging its feet on the *Contra* demobilization. After his arrival at the summit he announced an imminent suspension of the unilateral cease-fire, which had been in effect since March 1988, unless the U.S. halted its assistance to the rebels. The Sandinistas took seriously the Bush administration's public position that it would prefer to have the rebels in the field until after the February 1990 elections as guarantors of a free and fair vote.[83] Ortega's reading of the U.S. Congress led him to believe that his using the little leverage he had left would not result in a renewal of military aid to the rebels. According to Ortega, *Contra* attacks during the 19-month unilateral cease-fire had already caused over 2,000 casualties, and the renewal of offensive operations by the Sandinista military forces would be "reversible" if the *Contras* were demobilized by the December 5 deadline.[84] The Sandinistas, moreover, were embarking on a electoral strategy of identifying the internal opposition party UNO, whose candidate was the opposition newspaper publisher Violeta Chamorro, with the armed insurgency.[85] The intensification of the war, the Sandinistas thought, would shift blame for the killing on the internal opposition, which was receiving aid from the U.S. administration, the Congress, and the National Endowment for Democracy, a semi-autonomous foundation funded by the Congress.[86]

Amid polls suggesting a landslide victory for the Sandinistas, the UN approved a plan for the deployment of a 625-person international observer force (UNOCA), to be led by a Spanish general, to aid the Esquipulas Committee on Verification in disarming and demobilizing the *Contra* fighters. The UN force would bolster a small border observer UNOCA force already in the field to monitor Central American borders in an effort to prevent arms transfers and incursions. An impressive array of former presidents and prime ministers was in place to observe the February election in Nicaragua, making it one of the most closely observed elections in history. The force included 450 OAS observers, 240 UN representatives, and over 1,000 members of organizations that included the Council of Freely Elected Heads of Government (led by Jimmy Carter), the European Parliament, and other intergovernmental, human rights, and scholarly groups.[87] The Sandinistas welcomed the scrutiny as they were satisfied that their campaign had succeeded in discrediting UNO and that their fulfillment of the Central American peace initiative would be rewarded by the popular vote. Only observers and analysts who had access to the depth of anti-Sandinista feeling among the Nicaraguan people could contradict the many public opinion polls, which pointed to an overwhelming Sandinista victory.[88]

NORTHERN WINDS

The 14-percentage point margin in the stunning defeat of the FSLN in the 1990 elections raised hopes for a relatively smooth transfer of power. President-elect Violeta Chamorro, widow of the now legendary opposition newspaperman who was murdered by the Somoza regime during the Nicaraguan revolution, shrugged off threats by Sandinista hardliners to retain power. Before taking power she announced sweeping economic reform, which included privatization of businesses and farms, compensation for Sandinista confiscations, and free market financial and foreign sector policies.

She also appealed to the *Contra* rebels to put down their arms and join the political rebirth of Nicaraguan democracy, promising aid for their reintegration into the political, social, and economic life of the country. On March 28, Sandinista opposition to handing over power was largely overcome by an agreement in Honduras between the government elect, the Roman Catholic primate, Cardinal Miguel Obando y Bravo, and a new RN leadership to allow the UN, and OAS to supervise the disarming and repatriation of Honduran-based rebel fighters by late April in designated security zones. Although the agreement did not address the disbanding of the bulk of the rebel forces, who had moved into Nicaragua after the elections and were still skirmishing with Sandinista forces, it allowed for an orderly transition of power to be reached with the Sandinistas a few days later. A definitive truce between the rebels and the Sandinista government was not signed until April 19, less than a week before Chamorro's inauguration on April 25, 1990.

The historic agreement between the RN, the government-elect, and the Sandinistas provided guarantees on all sides for an "effective and definitive" truce that would be verified by Cardinal Obando y Bravo and the UN forces. A separate but similar agreement was reached with the Miskito Indians on the Atlantic coast; both agreements made arrangements for the establishment of security zones within Nicaragua from which Sandinista forces—almost immediately—would be pulled back at least 20km, and in which the rebel forces would begin regrouping in preparation for demobilization by June 10. Many rebels were still insisting, in concert with Washington, that the Sandinista army first be put under the new government's control before the fighters would give up their arms.[89]

Both the rebels and Washington were shocked into practical immobility by Chamorro's decision to retain Humberto Ortega Saavedra, the former Sandinista defense minister and brother of the outgoing president, as chief of the Nicaraguan army. Ortega's resignation from the FSLN party directorate, his promises to break links between the army and the FSLN, and his plans to cut the Nicaraguan army (the region's largest) in half within 18 months were not enough to placate hard-line opposition leaders and reassure rebel fighters who had agreed to demobilize.[90] Chamorro's decision also provoked two members of her 14-party alliance to refuse cabinet positions, thereby leaving her cabinet without representation from her political campaign allies. The choice of businessmen and technocrats, moreover, suggested a continuation of elite rule from above, a perception that Chamorro would do little to dispel during her first year in power.[91]

A meeting between Chamorro, the RN, and Cardinal Obando y Bravo in mid-May, when the rebels were given further security assurances and offers of land, helped insure that the rebels would meet the June 10 deadline. The effective usurpation of hard-line rebel leadership months earlier by Israel Galeano (alias Comandante Franklin) and Óscar Sobalvarro (*alias* Comandante Rubén) facilitated the demobilization and would reward the newly

legitimized rebel commanders with official government positions as super-
visors of rebel integration. Ironically, the debate in the capital over the
retention of General Ortega seemed distant, as thousands of rebel forces had
already begun to enter the security zones by late April. But the process was
slowed by a breakdown of the agreement after a false report of a Sandinista
attack on unarmed rebels, until another meeting on May 30 yielded a definitive accord that established a "development pole" in southern Nicaragua
for rebel integration. A 100-day austerity and anti-inflation program was announced in late April, committing the government to a free market economy,
and the government braced itself for the coming demobilization deadline
and the inevitable protests against economic austerity.[92]

As Sandinista unions took to strikes and street violence to counter government austerity measures, the June 10 deadline for demobilization was
met by the *Contras*. President Chamorro hailed the demobilization of the
rebel forces and the simultaneous reduction of the Sandinista-dominated
army as the beginning of a "new era of peace that would consolidate our
democracy."[93]

But the battlefield was shifting to the streets, where the Sandinistas retained control through their unions and mass organizations. Chamorro's first
100 days were punctuated by increasingly violent strikes, including a general
strike during the first two weeks of July, which threatened anarchy and the
collapse of the government. Although strains within the government emerged
as Vice President Virgilio Godoy, a former Sandinista labor minister, set up
an unauthorized and extra-governmental emergency squad, the primary victim of the chaos was Chamorro's austerity plan, whose strict implementation
was needed to speed up delivery of President Bush's promised $300 million
in emergency aid.[94]

A call by former president Daniel Ortega to civil disobedience in September went largely unheeded by the masses, as a call for another general strike
in October produced more government police than protesters. Yet the Sandinistas were slowly groping their way back to power, themselves avoiding
the predictable splits in FSLN party leadership. Their cause was furthered
by increasingly frequent attacks by disgruntled former rebels who were still
awaiting their land grants and by the continuing economic crisis made worse
by their own disruptions. The January 1991 election, with Sandinista support,
of ex-*Contra* leader Alfredo César to the presidency of the Nicaraguan parliament suggested that the Sandinistas were still resolved to play the role of
"reasonable opposition"; but the obvious signs of *desgaste*, or collective burn-
out, among the population and the government were ominous. Such an
erosion of confidence could only favor the Sandinistas, whose penetration
of society was practically impossible to root out.[95]

The Sandinista leadership, moreover, proved capable of withstanding the
inevitable internal upheavals within the party. The Chamorro government
and the U.S. administration expected the growing factionalism within the

FSLN to lead to a party split at the first FSLN party congress in July 1991. Instead, the party leadership was reinforced by the election of former vice-president Sergio Ramirez, and René Tellez, a long-time member of the party inner-circle, to the nine-man party directorate to replace Humberto Ortega, who had resigned from his party functions in order to retain his post as Defence Minister, and Nuñez's brother Carlos, who died of cancer in 1990. The rest of the directorate remained intact, vowing to disrupt Chamorro's economic and political programs, while searching for a "new economic-social model." Sandinista-led strikes, sit-ins, and land seizures continued to plague the embattled Chamorro government through the summer of 1991, as the ruling UNO coalition began to weaken. Meanwhile, disgruntled former *Contra* rebels, known as *Re-Contras*, rearmed and initiated guerrilla actions against Sandinista targets in the rural areas. By August 1991 a major clash in Nueva Segovia, near the Honduran border, suggested an explosive situation. The increase of human rights violations by the Sandinistas and the *Re-Contras* provoked an OAS investigation of the more than 1,000 cases of human rights offenses and 50 murders of disarmed *Contras* since the inauguration of the Chamorro government.[96]

ECONOMICS AND OTHER DEMONS OF DEMOCRACY

Perhaps the most profound irony of democratic politics in Central America is that while economic realities were reinforcing the transition to democracy in Nicaragua, similar if less drastic economic problems were undermining democracy in other countries on the isthmus.

The theoretical dimensions of this problem are obvious. Much progress has been made in establishing formal democratic institutions and democratic legality in places where authoritarianism had been firmly entrenched. Former Assistant Secretary of State for inter-American Affairs Elliot Abrams credits the Reagan Administration for overseeing democratic transitions in Brazil, Uruguay, Argentina, Guatemala, El Salvador, Honduras, Suriname, Guyana, and Chile.[97] With or without specific recipes or formulae, the *pro forma* aspects of democracy were established in these countries. Whether the inspiration came from the Spanish model or from the default of authoritarian rulers whose failures were catastrophic, the structure and rules of democracy have spread across the Americas in a way that has not been seen since the era of the Good Neighbor Policy in the 1930s and 1940s. Yet there is little indication that economic democracy has been installed in any of these places.

One is tempted to ask, as EEC commissioner for North-South relations Claude Cheysson did in 1987, how long these formal structures of democracy will last in countries plagued by debt, low growth, inflation, and declining terms of trade.[98] Even those scholars whose vocation is lauding such apparent transitions to democracy realize that democratic legitimacy is, more often than not, retained by at least acceptable levels of economic performance. Under the present circumstances, countries that have gained political democracy at a high cost are then pressured into making free-market economic reforms that would secure them aid from Western financial and development institutions. The austerity measures that are subsequently applied are often mortal for democracy: radical and sometimes totalitarian alternatives emerge to "save" the masses from the poverty and misery that democracy has afforded them.

Even if democracy's internal momentum is able to ward off radical alternatives, authority will break down through the loss of democratic legitimacy. At best, the country will muddle through interminable periods of instability, fighting not for the concerns of the peasants or workers but for the survival of the democratic process.

In short, political democracy is not a panacea for Latin America's problems. Human rights groups are kept busy in these "democratic" countries where torture, political assassination, death squad killings, and summary executions are sometimes on the increase. In some of the Latin American countries cited by the Reagan Administration as "success stories," levels of political violence in 1988 were at levels that threatened either a return to authoritarianism or a regime breakdown that creates a revolutionary situation in which totalitarianism would hold an advantage. Examples of this process can be found in the most lauded examples of democratic transition in the 1980s: Brazil, Philippines, Haiti, Peru, Guatemala, El Salvador, and Nicaragua.[99]

NO MORE MODELING

In the first case ever tried by the Inter-American Court on Human Rights in which a government has been put on trial, Honduras was accused in January 1988 of maintaining army death squads that caused the disappearance of suspected leftist citizens. Two key witnesses in the trial were murdered shortly after the hearings, which were the first juridical effort by the Organization of American States to condemn the activities of government-linked death squads in Latin America. The United States, which continued to maintain that Honduras has had an acceptable human rights record, was implicated in training the Honduran soldiers who worked in the death squads. For human rights officials, the killing of witnesses in the trial constitutes "a direct threat to the integrity of the inter-American system."[100]

In Guatemala, a sense of democratic impotency descended over national affairs. Former President Vinicio Cerezo's decision not to prosecute members of the military responsible for the reign of terror during the early 1980s symbolized democracy's impotence in the face of authoritarian power. Civilian power, which has deferred to the military in matters of internal security, must condition its policies on the reaction of the Guatemalan army, whose links to paramilitary death squads have not been severed. The government's attempts to punish offenders in the security apparatus for the execution of opposition politicians and labor leaders have met with humiliating failure.

The trial of four members of the Treasury Police in 1988 resulted in the implication of another 25 members, including the Director. The judge and prosecutor were subsequently kidnapped: the prosecutor was murdered, and the judge, who was set free, ordered the release of all the accused. According to the coordinator of the Guatemalan Commission on Human Rights, "there has been impunity, and there continues to be impunity, for those who commit the crimes," and that Cerezo was "an accomplice who shares the responsibility."[101]

The question of whether Guatemala is further away from democracy than ever cannot be answered by citing only data from Guatemala's political landscape. The conspicuous absence of an agrarian reform program under the democratic regime led the ordinarily conservative hierarchy of the Catholic Church to emit in 1988 a pastoral letter entitled, *The Clamor for Land*. With about fifty percent of the population unemployed, a life expectancy of 56 years in the cities and 46 years in the countryside, an illiteracy rate that reaches almost 95 percent in some rural areas, and 70 percent of the land under cultivation in the possession of 2 percent of the population, Guatemala could hardly boast of proximity to economic democracy. The Inter-American Development Bank (IDB) was just as frank in 1990: "In this context, it is not realistic to expect dramatic economic and social progress in the medium term."[102]

The economic situation may not be as critical as it was in Sandinista Nicaragua, but Guatemala's history has shown that until such socioeconomic issues are addressed, there is no chance for peace or democracy. Politics will remain explosive, and alternatives will be violent and extreme.

The transition in El Salvador seemed to have come full circle by 1991, with rightist extremists and the military asserting their dominance and threatening the much lauded progress in human rights and democratic reforms. After over $4 billion dollars of U.S. aid since 1979, the Salvadoran democratic system has fallen into a now familiar quagmire. Human rights abuses by the military and rightist paramilitary groups reached a level that approached that of the 1979 revolutionary chaos, which had provoked U.S. involvement. In the view of most Central American observers, including Salvadoran government officials, there will be "no more modeling for El Salvador."[103]

Unfortunately for Central American democrats, the same dismal picture can be observed in most other countries on the isthmus. Representative indices of the Central American tragedy can be found in the 1988 report from the Second Contadora Conference on Health and Welfare, which met in Madrid in April 1988. The report, whose subjects include Guatemala, El Salvador, Honduras, Nicaragua, Costa Rica, Panamá, and Belize, suggests that the recent democratic transitions in Central America have done little if anything to improve the basic living conditions of the Central American people. Reported cases of malaria doubled in the past decade; ten million Central Americans have no access to permanent health care facilities; of the

850,000 infants born every year on the isthmus, 100,000 die before reaching five years of age (12 percent); and of those infants that survive, about two-thirds suffer from malnutrition. In Honduras, about 80% of the children who survive infancy suffer from malnutrition. And in war-torn Nicaragua, the infant mortality rate reached 88, compared to the 10.6 rate for the United States, which ranked only 17th in the world in 1988.[104]

For the would-be democratic models of Central America, international economic and financial forces impinge on them in such a way that there seems to be little cause for optimism. The foreign debt burden of the Central American countries may appear to be only a small fraction of the total Latin American debt of $429 billion at the end of 1990; yet on a per-capita or percentage of GDP basis, Central America compares with sub-Saharan Africa as one of the most indebted regions in the world. Lower prices for the region's principal exports, especially sugar and coffee, meant devastating terms of trade for practically the entire decade of the 1980s. Capital flight from war, instability, and hyperinflation only added to the region's misery.

During the 1988 presidential campaign in the U.S., spokespersons for the Democratic Party challenged the Republicans to move decisively on the strategic issues of debt and development. Sol Linowitz reminded the Bush campaign that fragile democracies in Latin America were on a "treadmill of painful austerity, economic stagnation and rising debt." Their failure to meet the basic needs of their populations would result in a collapse of the democratic project in the Americas, thus presenting the United States and the West with an historically unprecedented strategic challenge.[105]

CARIBBEAN *PERESTROIKA* AND *YANKEETROIKA*

The fear is that the profound changes in the strategic context brought on by Soviet reform and the democratic revolution in the East will shift the focus of U.S. and Western concerns to other parts of the world. After over 40 years of strategic confrontation between the superpowers on Central American soil, regional democrats were faced with a curious overlap of strategic interests. Intervention, which had been explained in the past by threats from a superpower rival, was now justified as part of a ineluctable march of democracy led by those very same superpowers. To the dismay of the realists, U.S. secretary of State James Baker suggested such a crusade when he admitted the logic of possible Soviet intervention in the 1989 Romanian revolution as consistent with American behavior in Panamá.[106]

The burning question for Central Americans was whether the new strategic unity of interests would shift attention away from the development crisis that did not end with the withdrawal of Soviet troops from Eastern Europe. There was ample evidence throughout history that U.S. policy for the past two centuries had oscillated between intervention and neglect. Only when perceived strategic interests were threatened, whether by Britain, Germany, Spain, or the Soviet Union, was the U.S. compelled to engage in major strategic initiatives. With the Soviet strategic threat diminished, if not removed, Latin Americans had good reason to doubt whether the United States had begun an era of "new thinking" for the hemisphere.

An urgent warning was issued almost immediately by the pessimists. Third World instability would draw both the United States and the Soviet Union into the fray whether or not the battle between capitalism and socialism was over. The North/South dilemma would easily outlast and perhaps outdo the East/West struggle.

Both subjective and objective concerns existed. Third World leaders expressed distrust of the West's commitment to development in the context of the new *détente* while they pointed to the finite nature of funds available from multilateral sources.[107] Even if the West were still willing to sponsor development programs in the Third World, there would not be enough capital to satisfy the needs of both the Third World and the reborn nations of Eastern Europe. For the Third World nations, the massive and financially unprecedented effort to bail out the Polish economy signalled a shift in development concerns.[108]

Some, like Malaysia's Prime Minister Mahathir bin Mohamad, went so far as to express fears of "total domination" of the Third World by a united group of Eastern and Western nations.[109] Mahathir, who led a June 1990 meeting of the Group of 15 developing nations from the Nonaligned Movement, was expressing the pessimism that many in the Third World shared in the face of a changing international system. Nairobi's Finance Minister and chairman of the International Monetary Fund's (IMF) development committee, Bernard T. G. Chidzero, warned that Eastern Europe's credit demands "pose a challenge to the international community," and that they threaten "an explosion . . . in the North-South relationship."[110]

The optimists responded with assurances that increased demands for funding were already taken into account. The World Bank president, Barber Conable, promised that the bank's "human and financial resources will not be reduced in continuing to fight poverty wherever it exists."[111] The World Bank later weighed in with about a 20% increase in available lending funds, from $20.7 billion in the 1989–90 fiscal year to $24 billion in 1990–91.[112] Michel Camdessus, the IMF managing director, pointed to the painful process of raising IMF quotas by as much as 50%, thus adding at least $60 billion to available resources.[113] And the Inter-American Development Bank offered further comfort: "Even if the attention of the world's policymakers during the 1990s shifts to solving the economic problems of Eastern Europe and the Soviet Union, this shift will not necessarily be detrimental to the interests of Latin America, which may actually benefit from the incorporation of these formally centrally planned economies into a more open system of trade."[114]

The elimination of ideological and strategic conflict in the Third World was an opportunity to address the detailed and complicated issues of economic development that were not easily discussed in the rarified atmosphere of the Cold War. The reciprocal relationship between economic and political development would be set into motion without the interference of regional or global security concerns.

And there was no doubt that the strategic situation in the Caribbean had changed drastically by mid–1990. As the Soviet Union looked to its own internal "international" problems, it left behind weak strategic links to the Western Hemisphere. The February 1990 Sandinista election defeat in Nicaragua, where their former allies in the Soviet-line Partido Socialista Nicaraguense (PSN) had already professed "Felipe González style" social democracy, left significant state-to-state relations only with Cuba. The Soviet Union announced a suspension of arms transfers to Nicaragua in January 1989, leaving Cuba as the Sandinistas' main supplier.

But even before the February 1990 elections the Soviet leader, Mikhail Gorbachev, had appealed to the Sandinistas to move away from Cuba's vision of communist orthodoxy and towards political and economic pragmatism. A gradual falling out with Castro's Cuba began to occur in Managua as the Sandinistas faced the realities of their shattered economy and the Soviet retreat from Central America. Castro had criticized the Sandinistas' 1989 IMF-style austerity plan, and Sandinista leaders began to make veiled attacks on Castro's own failures. Henry Ruiz Hernández, a member of the Sandinista directorate, called on the Marxist countries to "renovate old models of leadership" that had caused them to "fall into technological and political immobility." Suddenly the hundreds of Cuban advisors in Nicaragua were made to feel uncomfortable in the Nicaragua of *perestroika*.[115]

Meanwhile, the Soviet-Cuban relationship was undergoing a profound transformation. For the first time since 1967–68, when Castro clashed with the Soviet Union over Cuban sponsorship of guerrilla adventurism in Latin America, Fidel Castro went on the offensive with regard to Soviet policy. As early as July 1988, Castro was making vitriolic attacks on the idea of a *perestroika caribeña*, lashing out at anything that "reeks of capitalism." According to Castro, Cuba was "against the servile copying of recipes to solve evils that we have not committed."[116] When in 1989 it appeared that the Brezhnev Doctrine of protecting socialism through Red Army intervention had been forever laid asunder in the flowerbeds of East European democracy, Castro faced the reality that Cuba could be sucked into the vacuum of the Soviet strategic retreat.

Cuba's economic dependency on the Soviet Union had always been the key to the relationship. Castro's assertion of political independence was nothing new; there were still many points of convergence that he and Gorbachev would stress in their otherwise difficult meeting during the Soviet leader's brief visit to Havana in April 1989.[117] Castro's real fears were the deteriorating Soviet economic situation, which reminded him of his own attempts at liberalization that had brought the island to "total discontrol and chaos." Against the backdrop of his own foreign exchange problems and Western debt, the last Caribbean guardian of communist orthodoxy contemplated the probability of cutbacks in Soviet aid.[118]

In December 1990, Cuba and the Soviet Union signed a new trade accord for 1991 in Moscow; there was no indication that the rumors of Soviet punishment for Castro's inflexibility had come true. Although the Soviets had been insisting for the first time on hard currency payments at market rates for oil, they also pledged to import significant quantities of Cuban raw materials— including 4 million tons of sugar at above world prices—and $73 million in medicines and medical supplies. Everything but sugar was to be priced at world market rates, with Cuba for the first time contributing 10% of the transportation expenses. More Soviet loans would finance the inevitable negative trade balance for Cuba, and oil shipments were to be kept at 10 million tons, or in any case, "not less" than in 1990. Technical advisers would be reduced by two thirds to about 1,000 in a process of "optimizing and perfecting" Soviet economic cooperation.[119] Despite the surprisingly firm Soviet commitment in the face of pressure from Washington, Castro remained preoccupied, if not with "the political will of the Soviet authorities," then with the possibility that the politically embattled and economically strapped Soviet Union would not be able to make good on the trade deal, which was ominously cut back from the usual five years to one.[120] Looming in the background was the massive Cuban debt to the Soviet government, which was just as unpayable as Latin America's commercial and official debt to the West, and the ominous behind-schedule deliveries of Soviet oil throughout 1990.

Yet those who were ready in 1989 to usher in a new era of strategic balance and restraint were jolted back to reality by the U.S. invasion of Panamá on December 19. The irony of the intervention was its most profound aspect: only *détente* and the new international climate could allow for such an anachronism to prosper. Soviet criticism was muted, and U.S. allies, with few exceptions, felt obliged to accept the *telos* of intervention as part of the new democratic crusade.[121]

From Washington's perspective, the democratic crusade was nothing new; only the context had changed. The Bush Administration had initially provided policy continuity from the last months of the Reagan Administration, when then Secretary of State George Shultz pledged a "new diplomacy" to fight dictatorship and totalitarianism.[122] The Bush Administration stood fast throughout most of the administration's first year, despite the surprisingly ironic cries from liberal Democrats to use force to overthrow the Noriega regime in Panamá.

The military intervention, when it finally occurred, was justified by the familiar appeal to the U.S. government's responsibility to protect American lives and property. The anachronistic justification could not, however, mask the fact that complex strategic factors were involved in Bush's decision. The importance of the Canal to Western trade and commerce was always a constant, even if the direct economic and strategic benefits to the United States had diminished over the past few decades. What was remarkable about the December 1989 strategic initiative in Panamá was that there was a clear message sent about the linkage between U.S. strategic interests and *democracy*. There were no *Contras* with their attendant moral ambiguities (as in Nicaragua), no America-backed dictator waiting in the wings (as there had been throughout the history of the Caribbean), and no strategic adversary to which to send blunt messages (as in Grenada). In the Panamá case, the best guarantor of U.S. strategic interests was the democratically elected Endara government, which had been defrauded at the polls by a vicious military dictator.

At least this view was the implication of Secretary of State James Baker's offer to the Soviets in Romania. And it explained in good part the muted reaction from Moscow and America's European allies, who would ordinarily have reacted strongly against such military intervention in Central America. The strategic link-up between democracy and strategy may not have been convincing to the Left in Latin America, but the international backlash against the United States was buffered by a new international context in which the superpowers were perceived to be acting decisively on the side of democratic outcomes.

NEW CARROTS, NO STICKS

The Bush Administration realized that military intervention, however necessary in the Panamá case, could not be the leading edge in any new strategic initiative. A "new deal" was already in the air when Bush arrived at a hemispheric summit in San José, Costa Rica in October 1989 to announce an unprecedented restructuring and reduction of Costa Rican debt. This bold implementation of the Brady Plan for debt reduction was all the more significant inasmuch as it was taking place in a country that had provoked the wrath of the Reagan Administration for its pursuit of diplomatic solutions to regional conflict not two years before. The new rhetoric of the coming era was introduced in San José, as Bush referred to a new relationship among "partners" and a push for the first completely democratic hemisphere in the world.[123]

But after the Panamá invasion, the Bush Administration was confronted with a hemisphere where democracy was holding its breath, waiting for the next signal from the world's lone superpower. A January 1990 diplomatic mission by Vice President Dan Quayle was scaled back in the face of lingering sensitivities over the Panamá intervention and the sluggishness with which Latin American countries were responding to Washington's calls to recognize the Endara government.[124] After U.S. troops made their way out of Panama City and the Pentagon made its final, though controversial, revisions to its count of the war dead, the time was right for another of the many bold hemispheric initiatives that have come out of Washington throughout the course of history. And this one could not afford to be seen, like the Alliance for Progress thirty years before, as having a security dimension that might bring up recent images of Yankee troops in Panamá, Grenada, or anywhere else in Latin America—including the coca growing regions of the Andes where Washington was fighting a war against powerful drug cartels.[125]

When in June of 1990 George Bush announced his Enterprise for the Americas Initiative, an offer to establish a free trade zone from Alaska to Tierra del Fuego and to reduce by over half the region's debt to the U.S. government,[126] there was reason for optimism on all sides. The announcement of the initiative followed a White House review of U.S. policy, which concluded with a need for President Bush to become more directly involved in Latin America. With the exception of Cuba, there were democratically elected governments in power throughout the hemisphere. With the Soviets in strategic retreat and Castro's survival in question, attention could be shifted to the pressing economic and financial problems that would remain as the only strategic threat to the many fledgling democracies. In Central America, the guerrilla wars in El Salvador and Guatemala raged on, but with the armed Left cut off from its sponsors in Managua and Moscow, the major threat to democratic rule in those countries came primarily from the right wing and the security forces who continued their assault on human rights. The Endara government in Panamá, having taken power on the heels of a U.S. invasion, was bound to be weak, and popular support declined precipitously by the end of 1990 as the task of reconstruction and the ineffectiveness of the country's leaders took their toll on public opinion. And the Chamorro government in Nicaragua became increasingly embattled as economic reforms were watered down by Sandinista opposition in the streets as well as by internal dissent within an unstable government coalition. Yet there was a sense that the problems no longer required military and covert instruments, nor direct intervention. With the proper dose of trade, aid, and reform under the aegis of Bush's Initiative for the Americas, Central American democracy would remain on track.

A DECADE LOST, A DECADE FOUND

The optimists in the White House could base their perceptions on some hard economic facts that had become apparent by 1990. Although the Latin American economic picture revealed unprecedented devastation after what the Inter-American Development Bank has called the "lost decade" of the 1980s, there was reason to believe that the policy reform and adjustment process, a "silent change" brought on by the debt crisis, had put the region in a position for resumed growth.[127] After suffering a shrinkage of economic growth from an average 5.9% in the 1970s to 1.1% in the 1980s. Latin American leaders had adopted a broad-based consensus on the need for "a more outward orientation of the region's economies, with greater importance on being competitive in world markets and on reliance on market forces to determine prices." As long as the pace of reform continued, there would be "improved prospects" with greater external financing continuing to be linked to liberalization and deregulation.[128]

If the Bush Administration's offer for a new "partnership," was spurred on by the "quiet revolution" in economic policy in Latin America, it was also provoked by external stimuli. The failure of the Uruguay round in the General Agreement on Trade and Tariffs (GATT) global trade talks had moved the United States closer to its Latin American neighbors in an effort to confront the economic and commercial challenges of European and Japanese protectionism in the food trade. It was no coincidence that Bush's first promotional trip to Latin America in December 1990 was to the biggest food exporters—Chile, Uruguay, Argentina, Brazil—where anti-European sentiment was the strongest. Also included was Venezuela, where a debt-reduction plan of about 30% had been agreed on in March 1990, reinforcing a similar Brady Plan reduction of 35% for Mexico in 1989 and President Bush's productive visit to Mexico a month before his five-nation tour of South America.[129] With Latin America's major economies enlisted in Washington's strategy, the rest of the region's governments, especially those in the ever-expanding Río Group—the permanent consultative mechanism for regional integration and international relations—would inevitably follow suit.

Healthy skepticism in academic and private circles notwithstanding, the idea of a free trade zone was gaining momentum. The U.S.-Canada free trade zone was already a reality, and the Bush visit to Mexico in November 1990 put Mexico and its northern neighbor closer to an historic free trade accord (FTA). With the Administration's "fast-track" authority for trade legislation without congressional amendments extended beyond the March 1, 1991 deadline, prospects looked bright for approval of the FTA by the summer of 1991. With the Canada-U.S. accord already in place, Mexican President Carlos Salinas de Gortari boasted that "we will create the largest trade area in the world."[130]

But the free trade idea did not stop at the Mexican-Guatemalan border. The five Central American presidents had already met by June 1990 at a summit meeting in Antigua, Guatemala to propose a revival of the Central American Common Market, which had been moribund for over a decade. Trade among the five countries had declined from $1.1 billion in 1981 to about $600 million in 1990, and there was a perception that the regional conflicts that had led to the decline, although far from over, were winding down.[131] In an effort to reinforce the integration process on the Central American isthmus, Salinas invited five Central American presidents, the foreign ministers of Venezuela and Colombia, and a Spanish delegation led by Luis Yáñez, then secretary of state for international cooperation, to a kind of economic "Contadora" summit in Tuxtla Gutiérrez, Chiapas. The Mexicans held out the offer of a continuation of the San José Pact of the 1980s, which had provided Venezuelan and Mexican oil at subsidized rates in exchange for the establishment of a free trade zone from Mexico to the border of Panamá. The major note of discord was the exclusion of Panamá, whose U.S. installed government was still not recognized in Mexico City.[132]

Prospects for Latin American integration received a major boost in March 1991, as Argentina, Brazil, Uruguay, and Paraguay signed a free trade pact to integrate the Southern Cone economies. Moreover, there was optimism that Chile, the most successful economy in Latin America, would soon join the group. At the July 1991 Ibero-American summit in Guadalajara, Mexico, Colombia, Venezuela, and Mexico signed a free-trade accord that would enter into effect in January 1992. For the first time since the 1960s, the healthy *Bolivarian* skepticism of Latin American observers over integration was beginning to soften.

Meanwhile, the United States was grappling with the issue of foreign aid to the region in the context of recession and massive budget deficits at home and the inevitability of a costly war in the Near East. Free trade prospects for the Caribbean were boosted when, in August 1990, the U.S. Congress voted to make the Caribbean Basin Initiative, a 1983 plan to promote non-traditional exports to the U.S. from most Caribbean nations, permanent legislation.[133] Although implemented in 1984 as a direct counter to Cuban and Soviet influence in the Caribbean, its economic results were surprisingly positive. By mid–1989, non-traditional exports had increased by 88.6% across the region, with some countries, including Costa Rica and Guatemala, registering exponential increases.[134]

The Central American countries, nevertheless, were looking to Washington for cash to rebuild war-torn economies. A rather curious battle thus broke out in Washington over U.S. aid commitments to the region, with the Administration fighting for a supplemental 1990 budget request of $800 million for Panamá and Nicaragua. Democrats in the house proceeded to slash the supplemental aid to $300 million for each country, citing, in the words of Senator Patrick J. Leahy, the fact that $800 million was "simply too much money" for "two countries of slight economic, security, and foreign policy importance to U.S. national interests." Although the Democrats were being consistent with their earlier views, which questioned Ronald Reagan's obsession with Central American events as a national security concern, they were not following through on their oft-stated conviction that the fundamental causes of regional crisis of the 1980s were socioeconomic in nature. More disturbing than the Democrats' hypocrisy was their plan to redistribute the rest of the aid request to Eastern Europe. "From this supplemental budget," continued Leahy, "the average American would think Panamá and Nicaragua, legacies of failed American policies in Central America, are far more critical to overall American national interests than the dissolution of communism and the Soviet military threat in Eastern Europe."[135]

The Bush Administration was more than prepared to enter into the strategic debate. If communism was the problem, they why was the Congress so reluctant to fund the Salvadoran government in its war against the Marxist-Leninist insurgency? A one-off arms transfer of surface to air missiles, a "gift" from renegade Sandinista military officers who were desperate after the Sandinista election defeat, strengthened the Administration's case when two Salvadoran government aircraft were downed during a rebel offensive in November and December 1990.[136] The Administrations's military aid request of $85 million had been cut by Congress to $42.5 million in October 1990, with the other half on hold until significant progress on human rights could be shown. The slow progress in bringing Salvadoran military officials to justice for the November 1989 murder of six Jesuit priests was cited as the major obstacle to further funding.[137] But if the strategic challenges presented by the missiles were not enough, especially amid signs of the guerrillas' willingness to negotiate them away, then the downing of a U.S. helicopter and the murder of two injured American military advisers who survived the crash, were certainly enough to present the Congress with a "Jesuit case" for the FMLN guerrillas. Secretary of State James Baker presented the Congress with this dilemma by setting a March 10 military aid resumption deadline for the guerrilla alliance to show its willingness to make concessions to end the civil war, and all parties awaited the results of United Nations-sponsored talks between the Cristiani government and the FMLN in Mexico City and San José. As those talks dragged on through the summer of 1991, Baker quietly released the remainder of El Salvador's military aid.[138]

The U.S. aid programs were clearly suffering from the traditional problems of partisan approaches that tend to produce mixed signals—what former Assistant Secretary of Defense Richard Perle once characterized as the propensity of senators and congressmen to "shape any legislation into an opportunity to come down squarely on both sides of an issue."[139] Perhaps more significant than that, however, were the administrative and bureaucratic logjams that were delaying the timely arrival of already approved funds to their Central American destinations. Panamanian aid for fiscal year 1991, which after the supplemental aid package was approved by Congress in May 1990 totalled $420 million, was seen not only as dangerously late in arriving but also as insufficient to cover the billions in war damages and economic losses from the U.S.-led boycott of the country during efforts to oust the Noriega dictatorship. And for those who saw the aid as generous, there were the problems that such a massive, one-shot amount (which in fact dwarfed the government's own budgets) would be difficult to integrate into the system.[140]

Public discontent bore these fears out, as the U.S.-backed Endara regime made a poor showing against the former dictator's forces in January 1991 by-elections for nine vacant seats in the legislative assembly and 160 local government posts. The massive absenteeism that aided the opposition victories was an expression of declining support for the U.S. intervention in the context of unfulfilled expectations. Already by May 1990, public opinion which saw the *invasion* as a *liberation* declined from 86% to 75%.[141] In the vacuum of local authority caused by the transition to civilian rule, the drug trade was reported to be thriving, thus helping to fuel corruption and a crime wave that the new police force was unable to check.[142] Corrupt military officials were being replaced by corrupt civilian officials, bringing up memories of the 1968 military coup that General Omar Torrijos justified with accusations of corruption in the civilian government.[143]

The Nicaraguan aid package presented similar problems, but it was also complicated by political factors that served to highlight major gaps of understanding between the U.S. administration and the Chamorro coalition government. U.S. aid was slow to arrive in Managua, amid reports that the U.S. was deliberately holding up payments until Nicaragua officially dropped claims to $17 billion from the World Court's ruling against the Reagan Administration for the CIA mining of Nicaraguan ports in 1984.[144] Administration officials were also unhappy about President Violeta Chamorro's decision to retain Sandinista defense minister Humberto Ortega in his post and her backtracking on economic reforms in the face of Sandinista pressure from the street. In any case, by the end of the first year of the democratic government, the aid was doing relatively little to improve economic conditions in Nicaragua. Washington became so concerned about the possible resurgence of the Sandinistas that diplomatic meetings with the Soviet Union were held in Madrid in March 1991 to reiterate Washington's concern that Soviet aid was still reaching the Sandinista-controlled army and that Sandinista officers were again arming rebels in Honduras and El Salvador. The murder of former *Contra* leader Enrique Bermúdez in Managua in February added to the administration's concern that the Sandinistas were slowly regaining power.[145]

Moreover, issues of political leverage and bureaucratic wrangling served to disguise the main cause of concern for Central Americans: the actual decline in U.S. aid to the region. Without counting the special $300 million package to Nicaragua, U.S. aid to Central America had dropped from $702 million in 1989 to $565 million in 1990. There was a growing perception that, with strategic threats practically eliminated from the isthmus, the United States was going to pocket the Central American peace dividend.[146]

The perception that Washington was cutting costs, even before the Persian Gulf crisis, was reinforced at the Antigua summit in June 1990, when Secretary of State Baker revealed a plan to coordinate aid to Central America through a multilateral group of OECD donor nations and development organizations, to be known as the Partnership for Development and Democracy. Modeled on the Group of 24, which was established in response to the development challenge in Eastern Europe, the new group would coordinate aid for the reconstruction of Central America. Baker insisted that the plan would not lead to a reduction of bilateral U.S. aid but that it would "complement" U.S. efforts.[147]

The greatest controversy, however, was over the nationality of the group's executive secretary. Baker's insistence on an American stirred not only old resentments but also a new concern that the United States was shifting its own responsibilities and costs to others in Japan and Europe while maintaining political control over regional outcomes.

On the other hand, the initiative could be seen as an unprecedented strategic retreat for the United States. Not since the American deferral to British power in the early 19th Century was the United States ever disposed to seeing European and Pacific powers become decisive in Central American affairs. Filibusters and gunboats had carved out an exclusive role by the turn of the century; preventive intervention and dollar diplomacy had kept Europe's financial role from becoming decisive; good neighborliness had warded off threats from the Germany-Italy-Japan axis; and American global strategic and economic power had given the United States practically a free hand in Central American affairs. By allowing for a formal development role, however, the United States was not only "cutting costs," but also sharing strategic responsibility with other great powers, especially with the now prosperous and assertive European Community.

EUROPE ON THE MARCH?

Europe had already asserted itself in strategic affairs by attempting to open political space for arms control agreements between the Cold War superpowers. Only top levels of NATO leadership and the British Conservatives seemed to be satisfied with the bipolar order of the international security system, while European public opinion forced Christian Democrats, Socialists, and Social Democrats into more active arms control stances. As a major international security issue, Central America was of concern to European governments whose relations with the United States were under heavy pressure from disarmament groups and leftist nationalists inflamed by Soviet-bloc propaganda. A deep-seated longing for an end to the bipolar world was evident, as the Reagan Administration engaged in a rearmament process that, to the European eye, shunned any measure of arms control. The increasing involvement of the United States and the Soviet Union in the Central American crisis, and the threat of direct U.S. intervention in Nicaragua, damaged the usually solid support for U.S. leadership in Europe. European governments dreaded having to make a choice between their increasingly demanding constituencies, which rejected the U.S. global role, and the strategic sensibilities of the U.S. Administration, upon whose forces and pocketbook Western European security rested.

European concern over U.S. involvement in Central America reached such levels that the European input began to figure strongly in the Administration's calculations. A veritible trans-Atlantic debate had opened, and European and American differences seemed magnified.[148] American commentators close to the Administration added a certain rhetorical violence to the debate, accusing the Europeans of "appeasement" on a global scale. These same voices pointed to a gulf in values that separated social democratic, non-interventionist Europe from the liberal individualism and assertive nationalism of the United States. The brash and often crude diplomacy of Reagan political appointees, led by his Assistant Secretary of Defense for International Security Policy Richard Perle, and later by Assistant Secretary of State for inter-American Affairs Elliot Abrams, further alienated European sensibilities. The Reagan Administration sensed a profound threat to its leadership in international security affairs at a time when it was attempting to reestablish its great power credibility in a region of perceived vital interests.[149]

The depth of European concern over America's reassertion of strategic leadership was evident in Europe's reaction to the U.S. invasion of Grenada in 1983. Political support from most NATO allies for the U.S. was forthcoming, but it was immediately recognized as the kind of lukewarm, tacit approval that comes as a result of the adherence to the principles and obligations of strategic solidarity. The only exception to this rule was Great Britain. This time the Administration would not find itself in favor with Prime Minister Margaret Thatcher's government or with British public opinion. One can hardly speak of outrage when characterizing the British reaction to what was perceived as great power unilaterialism; yet British opprobrium was significant insofar as it represented a breach in what had been the only manifestation of complete trans-atlantic strategic unity. The decisive support given by the United States to Great Britain during the Falklands/Malvinas war had created expectations in the United States that Britain would reciprocate in the Grenadian case. The British reaction proved that despite overlapping strategic interests and ideological harmony on the personal and official levels, Europe's views of Western Hemisphere problems were different.[150]

Again, the issue was great power credibility. Great Britain's image as a great power and leader of the Commonwealth was deeply offended by the strategic "bypass" implicit in the independent decision by the United States and some small Caribbean Commonwealth micro-states in a little-known regional organization to intervene on the side of democracy in Grenada. For the United States, moreover, the decision to intervene was motivated by not only the desire to reestablish superpower credibility in its "strategic rear" but also by perceived stakes that were extended to include a reassertion of *Western* credibility. The latter is precisely where European and American perceptions part ways. Not only were the Europeans more sanguine about the strategic threat in the Caribbean; they were eager to assert their own perspectives and priorities in an area where they have historical, political, and economic ties.

The ties between Europe and Central America cannot be easily dismissed simply by comparing them to the massive presence of the United States on the isthmus. The European Economic Community remains as the second most important export market and source of foreign investment for Central America. While Japanese activity is on the rise, and EFTA countries in Europe supply a significant amount of direct development aid while buying a sizable amount of Central American commodities, the EEC countries are the only states outside of North America that have established the kind of ties that can be considered politically significant—and perhaps decisive—in the long run. Total EEC trade with the region, which had deteriorated throughout the 1980s, was $1.95 billion in 1988, with a favorable balance of $461 million for Central America but small deficits for Guatemala and Nicaragua. Regional crisis and the EEC integration of Spain and Portugal (which produce similar products) in 1986 helped drag trade with Central America down from a decade high of about $3 billion.[151]

By far, Germany is in the forefront of the West European countries in its ties to Central America. German influence, which has been of considerable strategic importance throughout the late–19th and the first half of the 20th Century, continues on the economic, social, and political levels. The German Social Democrats have led Europe's attempt to democratize Central America, serving for most of the 1970s as the bridgehead of the Socialist International.[152] The German Christian Democrats, moreover, have lived up to their perception of strategic responsibility in Central America by giving the region an extremely high priority in their foreign relations, even in the context of high costs for German unification and contributions to the Gulf War effort. The political significance of the Kohl government's February 1991 pledge of about $60 million in aid to the pro-U.S. Chamorro government in Nicaragua, followed by a July 1991 package of $75 million which included the $15 million withheld from the Sandinistas when they took power in 1979, was certainly not lost on the Central Americans.[153] It is worth noting that the tragic explosion of the U.S. space shuttle *Challenger* in 1985 was a blow to U.S.-West German strategic cooperation inasmuch as the previous mission, which included the placement in orbit of a spy satellite over Central America, had been financed by the FRG. The SPD had accused the Kohl government of "perversion" of the FRG's first major space mission.[154]

It is not enough, however, to speak of direct European relations with Central America. Europe exerts its influence through multilateral institutions that decide everything from debt rescheduling and commodity prices to developmental aid. European behavior in these forums has been in conjunction with both economic interests and the goals of democratization; there have been economic punishments for the military dictatorships in Guatemala, and votes against the rightist regime in El Salvador. Most of these rewards and punishments have arisen from purely national priorities. Nevertheless, where reward and punishment were most important in a strategic sense, in the World Bank, the International Monetary Fund (IMF), and the Inter-American development Bank (IDB), the EEC has shown deference to the strategic agenda of the United States. Despite public manifestations of even-handedness toward Sandinista Nicaragua in the context of the Contadora peace process, the European countries did not mount a concerted effort to keep multilateral financial channels open with Nicaragua. When out of power, bitter Sandinistas would accuse Europe of cynical abandonment. "We never really felt accompanied by these European governments," complained former interior minister Tomás Borge. "We felt pressured to make concession after concession . . . why didn't they pressure the perpetrators [the United States] instead of the victims?"[155]

The European failure to stand up for Nicaragua in the most important international and regional developmental institutions gives reasons to believe that the provocative rhetoric that came out of the 1984 meeting in San José (San José I) of the EEC foreign ministers, the Central American governments, and the members of the Contadora Group (Mexico, Panamá, Venezuela, Colombia) was to be for public consumption. The leaders there had gone so far as to declare the Monroe Doctrine, the historical U.S. strategic tool for hegemony in Latin America, defunct. The evidence, nevertheless, suggests that however much the Latin Americans look to Europe as an alternative to recognizing U.S. hegemony, the Europeans have their own national interests at heart. The exigencies of intra-community policy, which include the incorporation of relatively backward southern Europe into EEC trade and development schedules, inhibits the kind of trade concessions to Central America that would signal a sacred commitment to Central American development. The consensus from the European side is that EEC relations with Central America will continue to grow, but that those relations should be regarded "without illusions."[156]

It is no secret that Latin American opinion has turned toward the EEC in venting its wrath over protectionism and other trade issues, including the steadily declining terms of trade for Latin America. The prospects of EEC expansion were of special concern to such influential organizations as the United Nations' Economic Commission for Latin America (ECLA/CELA), where the leadership of Enrique Iglesias voiced grave concern over the possibility of trade diversion to Spanish and Portuguese suppliers of primary goods. To many observers, especially the Latin American elites, the European stance is transparent: communiques that support regional peace efforts reveal an impotence caused by divisions within the Community on fundamental strategic perceptions and by the demands of EEC expansion, whose dynamics resemble those of the Latin American development challenge.[157]

It should be remembered that the dimensions of the challenge *within*

Europe are sometimes as great as those of the Third World. Europeans are cognizant of the fact that democratic transition in Europe is a fairly recent phenomenon. Italy, West Germany, Greece, Spain, and Portugal all have undergone this process in the past forty years or so. The democratic tradition in these countries was indeed stronger than it is in Latin America, yet the Spanish and Portuguese cases still represent unfinished democratic business for Europe. The North-South dimension of international relations is not just a reference to the relationship between the developed "First World" and the underdeveloped "Third World." The internal politics of the EEC are likewise influenced by the developmental issues of the North-South dialogue. The Community budgets represent a massive reorientation of European resources toward the relatively backward southern flank, which includes most of Spain, most of Greece, all of Portugal, and a large part of southern Italy.

This sharing of democratic experience accounts for a good part of the international solidarity that Europeans display rhetorically toward Latin American democrats. Paradoxically, the urgent democratic and developmental agenda in Europe limits the resources that the countries of the EEC can afford to divert to areas such as Central America. Such resources are not just material, whether in the form of trade preferences or direct developmental aid. They also include diplomatic and political energy, which is in short supply in many European countries. When strategic issues impose their weight on European allies of Central American democracy, the tendency has been to avoid direct confrontation with the United States. The *sine qua non* of this deference to U.S. concerns was the military and strategic isolation of Nicaragua, which since 1984 has been cut off from European sources of military and defense aid and cooperation.

It is significant that the first major document on EEC-Latin American relations did not appear until June 1987, when the EEC Council of Ministers approved the conclusions of a European Commission study on policy orientations towards Latin America. This was the first major study of the crisis and the first integrated approach to the problem. Urged by Spanish and French commissioners, it was designed to reflect a common vision of the problems of Latin America, to echo the concerns of Latin American democrats who had looked to Europe for help in establishing new priorities for the international political agenda.[158]

While Latin American perceptions and priorities were echoed in the highest levels of the European Economic Community's policy-making bodies, the tangible, material benefits of this solidarity were not forthcoming. Even on the political side, European pessimism was manifest. After a meeting of delegates from the EEC, the Contadora negotiating group, and five Central American nations in Guatemala in February 1987, one European delegate was quoted as saying that "there is no willingness to settle their differences. The chances of a negotiated settlement are about nil."[159] Such pessimism was motivated not only by the seemingly irreconcilable differences between the Central Americans but also by a palpable tension over the role that was being offered to the EEC countries by the Latin Americans. Despite its reluctance to make tangible commitments to the task of Central American democratization that would put it directly at odds with U.S. policy, the EEC still demanded an active role as intermediary. Indeed, European observers have criticized the Contadora process precisely because, in the European view, an active role was not assigned to the EEC. There was enough resentment over the passive role delegated to the European interlocutors to provoke a crisis when the Contadora countries invited the Grupo de Apoyo (Contadora support group of Latin American countries including Peru, Brazil, Uruguay, and Argentina) to the Third Contadora Conference. Europe insisted on being more than an outside force of support. These tensions contributed to the eventual collapse of the Contadora peace process and its replacement with an initiative led primarily by the Central American governments and Oscar Arias, the former Costa Rican president. In this process, which culminated in the signing in August 1987 of the Esquipulas II peace plan (Guatemala Accords), the Europeans were once again relegated to an outside role as a supporting force.[160]

While differences abound over evaluating the efficacy of European intervention in the Central American crisis, the supporters of such a process continue to draw attention to the strategic implications of European involvement in Central American affairs. The concrete results of such involvement will be slow to come, but the changes in attitudes and in legal/institutional orientations, especially within the EEC, signal profound developments in trans-Atlantic affairs. While these same observers—who include a wide spectrum of the European and Latin American elite—recognize a disturbing "disequilibrium" between the political and economic aspects of the European intervention, they see this intervention as a necessary element of Western global strategy. For the West cannot permit a one-sided interpretation of its values, which in the Latin American case would be resignation to the dictates of the Monroe Doctrine. Western values must be enriched by alliance participation in regions outside of the Western European context.

The analysis, once again, must return to the question of credibility. If there existed such a disparity of opinion between the U.S. Administration and Europe over the strategic implications of the crisis in the Caribbean, it was due to a fundamentally different perception of the methods and mechanisms of establishing strategic credibility. Europe, in fact, *agreed* that the credibility of the West was at stake in the Americas. But the European definition of credibility was quite different from that of the U.S. administration. While the United States saw its credibility tied to its willingness to use military force to achieve strategic goals—as the invasion of Grenada and Panamá and the rapid deployment of U.S. troops to Honduras in 1987 would suggest—, the European perception was that Western credibility is directly related to its ability to foster democratic institutions and then back them up with solid economic and development cooperation. Only then can the Latin American countries form the third leg of the strategic triangle that would safeguard Western values.[161]

The notion of a "strategic triangle," as utopian as it may appear, is what did motivate Western strategic input in the Americas. The slow and painful incorporation of the Latin American countries into Western security arrangements, according to the Europeans, could no longer be a matter that is under the exclusive control of the United States. Europe bases this perspective on its generally accurate historical analysis of U.S. policy in the hemisphere, from which it concludes that strategic housekeeping in Latin America was often conducted without regard for democratic values and human rights. Even the West German Christian Democrats, who have shown no evidence of wanting a confrontation with the U.S. administration over Central America, point to U.S. policy's past support for ruling oligarchies and military dictators. The Europeans consensus is that Western credibility can be lost in Central America and the Caribbean if the West cannot prove that social change and development can transpire with its support.[162]

It should be pointed out that, in all fairness to U.S. policy, the European critique is historical and that few observers doubt, especially with George Bush in the White House, that democratization is the ultimate strategic goal of the United States in the region. The differences are over the operational means to this end and the international political ramifications of the operational aspects of security policy in the Americas. The U.S. Administration's commitment to democracy in the region remains unconvincing to many foreign observers who cannot see a fundamental change in the way the United States views its own role in the hemisphere. Unfortunately for U.S. policymakers, most Latin and European opinion agrees with the former U.S. Assistant Secretary of State for Inter-American Affairs, Elliot Abrams, who grudgingly admits that "the weight of history is great."[163] The credibility of the United States in questions of democratic strategy in the Americas remains, at best, uncertain.

What, then, can be said for European credibility in this context? The Latin American view is ambivalent. While Europe brings with it the historical weight of centuries of colonial and neo-colonial exploitation, it has generally been absolved from the interventionist crimes of the 20th Century. Europe, nevertheless, has been criticized for not using its influence to modify United States policy. It has been accused of passive acquiescence to United States hegemony in the area. At times it has been identified with U.S. "imperialism" in the most direct ways, as the British learned in the Falklands/Malvinas war. Yet nowhere is Europe so vulnerable as in the widening gulf between words and deeds, especially with respect to the imbalance between the economic and political contributions towards the resolution of the Central American crisis.

There seems to be general agreement on both sides of the Atlantic that

Europe could do more for Central America with respect to economic and commercial cooperation. According to data from the EEC-funded Instituto para Relaciones Europa-America Latina (IRELA) in Madrid, total EEC development, economic cooperation and humanitarian aid from 1977 through 1989 was $607 million ECUs (approximately $790 million at the inflated 1990 exchange rates).[164] Bilateral aid from the seven EEC members of the OECD Development Aid Committee, which in the 1986–87 period gave a total of $359 million to Central America, helped to offset the relatively small contribution from the EEC budget; and on the eve of the December 1990 EEC-Latin America Conference in Rome, the EEC voted an ECU2.7 billion ($3.5 billion) five-year plan for all of Latin America, two thirds of which would be in credits.[165] Europeans are fond of pointing out that their joint and bilateral aid to Central America is economic and humanitarian in nature, and that in recent years it has roughly equaled U.S. non-military aid to the region. What these analysts fail to recognize is that the aid from European countries is usually locked into contracts with European producers, making such transfers and credits seem like welfare programs for European industry. And these same analysts admit that Europe's contribution to multilateral institutions pales in comparison with U.S. efforts. It is useful to compare, for example, the billion dollar U.S.-Costa Rica debt deal with the ECU150 million in aid for Central American integration that the EEC pledged during a EEC-Central American summit in San Pedro Sula in February 1989. The Spanish organizers of the summit and the Central American presidents had been expecting the announcement of a European "Marshall Plan."[166]

The Community agricultural policy, the recent incorporation of Spain and Portugal, and the inherent protectionism of the European customs union have created well-founded concern that national interests in Europe will overwhelm the humanitarian values of the European Community. Evaluations of the effects of development aid from the European Community are notable for their suggestions of what more the EEC can and should do for Central America. Despite a series of economic and development agreements between the EEC and Central America (the most significant of which is the December 1985 "Agreement of Cooperation Between the European Economic Community, and the Countries of the General Treaty of Central American Economic Integration" (Costa Rica, El Salvador, Guatemala, Honduras, Nicaragua, and Panamá), the overriding perception, especially on the Latin American side, is that Europe lacks a comprehensive strategy on Central American development. The fiercest critics, some of whom are from the major regional powers, accuse the EEC of propagandizing its contributions while failing to (1) address the serious debt problems of the Latin American countries; (2) find ways to stem the actual decline in trade between the regions; (3) foment direct investment in the region; (4) account for the negative effects of Community enlargement; (5) reform Community agricultural policy, which causes massive trade diversion; and (6) stem the rise of protectionist measures in EEC trade policy.[167]

The most embarrassing component of the EEC's orientation toward Central America is its Common Agricultural Policy (CAP). Through tariff and non-tariff protection, subsidies for production, and trade-distorting export subsidies, this policy keeps world food prices low and European consumer and producer prices high. Many food-exporting Third World countries like those in Central America, which do not enjoy the privileges of access to the EEC market that the Lomé Convention affords, not only find themselves locked out of the prosperous European market but also out of third markets where the EEC sells its surpluses through the mechanism of export subsidies. The resultant glut of agricultural goods, moreover, brings down world prices for the Third World exporters while European prices remain high. Out of this strategic economic showdown has arisen the unorthodox alliance between the United States and the Third World food producers represented by the Cairnes group in the Uruguay Round of GATT negotiations. Former president Raúl Alfonsín of Argentina, who for years led the Latin American charge against European agricultural protectionism, summed up the alliance *raison d'etre* by stating that "More than the United States, it is the EEC that does us harm . . ."[168]

A demand by the United States and the 14-nation Cairnes group to effectively eliminate agricultural production and export subsidies by the end of the century revealed Europe's inability to move beyond its own economic interests to what European leaders refer to in their rhetoric as an "integration of Latin America into the international economic system."[169] The GATT round had become such an acute source of embarrassment for the EEC that there were signs that big concessions in the CAP would be made to save face when the talks, which had officially expired without agreement at the end of 1990, was resumed in early 1991.

Europeans counter with an almost patronizing long-term perspective. They magnify political relationships with Latin America that are characterized more by their domestic policy content than by their foreign policy instruments. European politics have internalized Latin America's problems to such an extent that positions on Central America and the debt crisis, to name just two issues, are part of national and Community debates. Yet the foreign policy resources given over to the solution of these problems is minimal by any standard. European leaders seem to feel that small amounts of precisely directed aid, such as the $600,000 technical aid for the 1991 Panamanian by-elections or the provision in 1990 of election and disarmament observers in Nicaragua, buy them enough influence to make a credible attempt to challenge U.S. hegemony. Ironically, opposition parties such as the German SPD are quietly at work transforming Central American politics while EEC leaders engage in rhetorical platitudes as they protect member states' economic interests.[170]

The realization that there is a profound asymmetry in European/Latin American relations has had a sobering effect on those observers who saw a strategic opening for Europe on the Central American isthmus. If there is something that can be called a European strategic initiative in Central America, its operational components are yet to be put into place. Moreover, there remains the doubt that Europe would want to be strategically decisive in an area that has always been the domain of the United States. The current policy is one of low-risk endeavor to capture a moral high-ground and to inject a dimension of European internationalism as a counter to both communist influence and U.S. isolationism and unilateralism.

A ROLE FOR DEMOCRATIC SPAIN

European proponents of a greater role for the EEC see the key to addressing the problem of asymmetry as one of finding the proper interlocutor for constructive and meaningful relations. All eyes seem to have turned to Spain as the only EEC member capable of addressing the otherwise assymetrical relationship. The reasons for this outlook go beyond the romantic notion of a New World role for the Old World mother country, although romance is always a component of such suggestions. One should also discount the rather flamboyant official rhetoric directed toward Central American and Latin American relations, which is almost constantly broadcasted from the Spanish Foreign Ministry and the Moncloa Palace. Taking into account the fact that Spain, also, is quite limited in its foreign policy resources, especially now that it is bound in the economic and commercial obligations of the EEC and the strategic demands of NATO, the only meaningful credential remaining for a strategic role is its experience with democratic transition.

That an international political metaphor can substitute for more traditional foreign policy instruments is by no means certain. While celebrating Spain's political inroads in Latin America, *The Economist* admits that Spanish economic and commercial means are too sparse to meet the challenge.[171] Spanish image-makers and democratic practitioners have aspired to a larger role in Latin American affairs; yet at the same time that religious, cultural, language and political bonds are being reinforced, "economic ties are fraying."[172] Nevertheless, Central American experience illustrates that even great power intervention of considerable means is often not decisive.

DEMOCRATIC REALISM

What the lure of such initiatives as the Spanish democratic campaign suggests is not that the Spanish experience with democracy can teach the Central Americans how to establish and consolidate democratic systems, but that the goal of democracy remains strategically paramount in the region. Other policy vehicles, including military intervention, are either too costly or more likely to be counterproductive. Even hard-line guerrilla leaders in El Salvador, whose experience has been forged by over ten years of violent struggle, have reluctantly accepted the need for broad-based attempts at establishing democratic legitimacy. Their not entirely successful attempts to establish Dimitrov-style "popular fronts" are a concession to the powerful magnet of pluralistic politics in societies characterized by extreme polarization.

Central American strategists of the left and right can no longer afford to ignore the diminishing international and local appeal of inflexible political ideology. In Nicaragua, where such inflexibility on all sides resulted in a strategic stalemate and unspeakable suffering for millions of Nicaraguans, the former Soviet-line Socialist Party, the Partido Socialista Nicaraguense (PSN), shifted its strategy towards "Felipe González-style" European Social Democracy where Marxist precepts can exist side by side with capitalist efficiency and free market incentives to produce.[173] There is more here than just opportunism. Totalitarian and quasi-fascist ideologies are losing ground in the Central American context, despite desperate attempts on the part of hard-line Sandinistas, dissident Guatemalan militarists, and the Salvadoran ARENA party to assert extremist hegemony. Extremists may achieve or remain in power, as the Sandinistas and D'Aubisson's ARENA party have shown, but they serve merely to perpetuate the turmoil that has yielded not a single strategic victor.

If democracy is the key to strategic success in the Central American context and if all players seek to establish their democratic credentials through revision of ideological platforms or by new high-level initiatives, then one must still ask why the target has not been reached. The answer lies not only in the formidable forces of extremism of both the left and right but also in particular characteristics of Central American society that make democracy so elusive. To those *sui generis* factors must be added the unfortunate economic and trade position of the Central American nations with respect to the world economy. As mighty as these economic forces may seem, however, they are not invincible—unless one succumbs to economic determinism. The strategic forces that have been mustered in pursuit of Central American democracy, which include those of the United States, Europe, and Latin America, are powerful enough in their own right to counter local extremism as well as the relatively weaker efforts by Cuba to raise the costs as high as possible. If democratic forces have failed on the isthmus, as it indeed seems they have, then it is simply because there has been little or no significant coordination among the major players on the means to the strategic ends in the region.

At the center of the debate over these means had been the U.S. Administration's *Contra* policy. The credibility problems that this policy engendered led to a virtually complete lack of strategic coordination on the part of the West. Notwithstanding such an ambiguous initiative, the United States has come to see democracy as the *sine qua non* of its strategic interests in Central America. Such change, or *Yankeetroika*, began with a programmed announcement of a "New Diplomacy" to the Organization of American States in November 1988, when then U.S. Secretary of State George Shultz pledged U.S. support for "the aggressive advocacy of democracy by democratic states."[174] And under the Bush administration, with "Northern winds" clearly blowing in Central America in the wake of the Panamá invasion and the Sandinista election defeat, a great deal of optimism has been generated on both sides of the Atlantic over the prospects for peace and development in Latin America as a whole.

Europe has always had the target within sight, but its credibility problem stems from its inability or reluctance to commit sufficient means. Washington has exploited this weakness by allying with Latin American agricultural exporters in the GATT negotiations. The Bush administration, in effect, held Inter-American economic and trade integration hostage to the success of the GATT round, where the EEC was perceived to be the major obstacle to a just accord. The message from Washington was that regional integration depended on the resolution of global trade issues. Europe was clearly on the defensive, thus allowing the United States to divert attention from the many remaining obstacles to trade liberalization in the Western Hemisphere.[175]

The Spanish presidency of the EEC in the first semester of 1989 heralded some meaningful initiatives in the economic and developmental sphere, but the kind of massive "Marshall Plan" that the isthmus needs may never be forthcoming. Events in Central America permit neither strategic drift nor the paternalism of Old World democrats. The spiritual challenge for Europe, according to the Mexican novelist Carlos Fuentes, is to find a locomotive of multipolarity in international relations. "The alternative is death; a wealthy death, perhaps, but death to the finish, as there will be nothing to do but hoard treasure of dead money, dead labor, exhaustion, and lethal belly-laughs."[176] Thus the challenge to Western strategic credibility in Central America will demand a coordinated strategy to establish, as the Marshall Plan in Europe did over 40 years ago, the foundations for Central American democracy.

Part III

The Push Outward

The impulse to move outside national geographic frontiers is shared by all nation-states, but in the causes of this phenomenon and in the degree to which power is sought in the international sphere, countries will differ substantially. Geopolitical realities are perhaps the only immutable characteristics that can determine behavior, and the observation of even these seemingly pre-programmed impulses are conditioned by time and space. Nation-state behavior may be determined to a great extent by geopolitical realities, but the manifestations of geopolitics are for the most part *glacial* tendencies that must be observed over long periods of time in order to detect meaningful effects on the international system.

At times during history a nation-state will explode geopolitically, thrusting itself into the international sphere within the span of a few years. The rise of the unified, militaristic German nation in the late 1900s or the American naval ascent in the 1890s are the most striking examples of these phenomena. Nevertheless, most countries find their international role growing over time, conditioned by geography but subject to shifts that reflect the demands of both domestic and international politics. There is continuity and change, with geopolitical realities accounting for much of the continuity, and myriad sometimes unaccountable political, economic, and ideological variables propelling change.

There are also, undeniably, *sui generis* aspects of foreign policy and process. To admit to the uniqueness of a nation-state, of its people or peoples, of its politics and its historical experience seems at first to be an admission of defeat, a sign of weakness in the battle to develop a science of politics that would explain behavior. Often one will attempt to break down the idiosyncracies into their component parts—ideological, historical, anthropological, etc.—in an effort to account for the differences that can be observed from one nation-state to another. Yet these differences still bother us, for political science aspires to systematize and generate theory that would apply to all nation-states in spite of apparent idiosyncracies. The bothersome disparities, the *nuances*, and the all too frequent "exceptions to the rule" may well be resolved by future applications of computer science, but until such programs are developed that would account for and weigh hundreds of variables, foreign policy analysts will remain mystified by the behavior of some nation-states.

While Spain has not exactly *exploded* geopolitically, its democratic transition has enabled it to integrate rapidly into Western political, economic, and security institutions. Despite the predictable moves to regain its place, *su sitio*, in the international sphere, Spain still presents the analyst with its compelling uniqueness. Any analysis of Spain's foreign policy must begin with an assertion that Spain, as a nation-state and a unit of analysis, is very idiosyncratic. The 19th Century Spanish novelist, Benito Pérez Galdós, spoke of "a nation *sui generis*, a natural force," when placing Spain in the international sphere. Throughout modern history, Spain's international role has been extremely difficult to assess. Today, Spain challenges the foreign policy analyst with the profound ambiguity of its international position.

Sometimes, literary devices seem to be the most adequate of methodologies. The Spanish experience is replete with paradoxes that confound political science theory. The most profound of these paradoxes is that which concerns Spain's most prominent geopolitical feature: the insularity of the Iberian peninsula, with its hundreds of miles of coastline, is interrupted by a continental corridor that ultimately connects Spain to the European heartland. The Pyrenees Mountains tempered the geopolitical urge throughout history, but the barrier has not been strictly physical. It did not stop Napoleon's armies from conquering and occupying Spain. Nevertheless, the Spanish, whose monarchs were at one time the sovereigns of a good part of Western Europe, have been cut off from the European mainstream. The geopolitical schizophrenia that this physical feature has produced is only one of the many paradoxes that characterize the Spanish historical experience.

Another major paradox of concern for the foreign policy analyst is the seemingly contradictory disposition that Spanish culture and society display with respect to foreign affairs. Reflecting its insularity, Spain's culture has developed almost autonomously. Isolation *within* the Iberian peninsula of one region from another produced layers of insularity. Meanwhile, Spain's ambitious monarchs and explorers broke out of this isolation, discovering and colonizing continents, forging European and New World empires, spreading Western values by force and example.

As Spain looked outward, her peoples looked ever more inward to a rich culture and tradition. The Inquisition, at first an international Catholic movement, became the force by which Spain would purify her blood. There may have been neglect of socioeconomic realities while Spain's kings, bishops, and adventurers plundered the New World and struggled for European hegemony, but within Spain's diverse regions, culture was flourishing. Reinforced by the liberation movement against Napoleonic occupation, as well as by the loss of empire by 1898, Spain's idiosyncracies were well advanced by the turn of the century. Thus the autarky of the 1940s and 1950s under the Franco dictatorship was hardly an unnatural state of affairs. To this day, the Spanish people revel in the thought that their culture remains impermeable, and they jealously guard their cultural inheritance lest it should be "contaminated."

It is not uncommon for "insular" nation-states to manifest these paradoxes. One has only to look at great Britain, where outward expansion was accompanied by a tremendous inward focus. The point here is that Spain manifests these phenomena to a degree that no other European nation-state seems capable.

What these fundamental paradoxes amount to is a profoundly ambiguous international position for Spain. Is Spain an insular nation-state, whose aspirations are met through discovery and predominance in faraway lands reachable only by sea? Is it an amphibious continental power, whose aspirations lie in the European context where tangible economic, social, political, and security advantages abound? Or is Spain a unique "natural force," a *sui generis* entity in search of a meaningful international role?

Any analysis of Spanish foreign policy must at least address these questions, if not answer them. The present focus on Central American policy, it is hoped, will highlight the paradoxes of Spain's international role and help clarify what at first glance appears as intense ambiguity. By studying Spanish foreign policy in such a remote region of the world, a well-defined picture of Spain's new international role will emerge. This image may not be the one that is propagated by the Spanish authorities, nor the one assigned to it by Spain's new partners in the European Economic Community or by U.S. policy. But it will be a realistic image that takes into account Spain's capabilities as well as her aspirations. It will not necessarily be a completely positive picture; analyses of this sort rarely lead to such conclusions. Of necessity it will be an incomplete picture, as Spain's volatile internal dynamics permit neither a wide-angle nor a perfect focus.

DESPERATELY SEEKING DEMOCRACY IN CENTRAL AMERICA

Any nation-state whose foreign policy is caught up in the quest for democratic outcomes in parts of the Third World risks not only failure—which is to be expected in the difficult Central American case—but also the accusation that the policy is disingenuous. When the relationship between rhetoric and realities becomes asymmetrical, suspicion about the motives of policy-makers may arise. The lack of results, if it cannot be blamed on a more powerful regional player, will engender questions about the policy's domestic sources and its self-serving aspects. At best, over the long term the policy will take on a quixotic image that will debilitate the international role and further highlight the embarrassing fact that the country's influence is not decisive. Paradoxically enough, these dangers notwithstanding, Spain cannot afford the loss of moral force that the adjustment of rhetoric and goals to reality would imply.

Testing the International Waters

If Spain is the problem, then Europe is the solution.
—*José Ortega y Gasset*

The ambiguity of Spain's geopolitical position has had the effect of pulling Spanish economic, military, and diplomatic resources in different directions. Its privileged strategic position not only controls the access to the Mediterranean at the Straits of Gibraltar but also combines outposts in the South Atlantic (Canary Islands), North Africa (the enclaves of Ceuta and Melilla), and the Mediterranean (the Balearic Islands) with the secure redoubt of the continental *meseta* behind the wall of the Pyrenees. These factors make Spain the object of international security arrangements sometimes dictated by the great powers. The "strategic depth" that Spain offers cannot be ignored by superpower planners who see Spain's role as that of bolstering—or undermining—alliance strategy. Because of this strategic importance throughout modern history, Spain has always retained some form of foreign involvement. Even if Spain did not initiate such involvement, the international system impinged on her, making her responses inevitable, though never predictable in their character or degree.

It can be said that Spain's first and greatest push outward was provoked by foreign stimuli. The Reconquest of the Iberian peninsula, a process that facilitated the unification of the Spanish kingdoms, did not stop at the expulsion of the Moors in 1492. It continued in the New World, where Spain found not only plunder and riches but also a vehicle for national aspirations.[1] Empire was not thrust upon Spain but neither was it a calculated, autonomous decision. It should be remembered that the Reconquest of Iberia took over

500 years, with the final expulsion of Islam from Granada taking place over 800 years after the Moorish conquests. It is no wonder that the newly unified, if disparate, kingdom of Spain "reconquered" vast territories in the New World in the short span of 50 years.

If "empire" implies a strong international role, the loss of that empire would imply tremendous psychological trauma and diminished international influence. While protecting Spain's uniqueness and character, the insular geographic position also provided for immunity from the technological and economic advances of northern Europe. Gold and silver inflated costs of production, exacerbating an already deep-rooted reluctance to produce. The peninsula and her colonies were weaned on Dutch and British manufactures, as her liquid wealth was transferred to other European powers to pay for goods and to finance foreign wars. As economic and productive power became of supreme importance in world affairs, Spain confronted the world completely disarmed.

The loss of the last of Spain's overseas colonies in the Spanish-American War of 1898 was the culmination of centuries of slow economic, political, and military decline. Such a fact, as obvious as it may seem to even the casual student of world history, is worth repeating only insofar as it shifts the focus of the analysis to internal Spanish dynamics. The "Generation of 1898," an elite literary movement that made an effort to redefine Spain's international role, made public the Spanish trauma by focusing on societal shortcomings. The new inward focus may not have saved Spain from domestic political instability, but it did keep the Spanish out of the trenches of the first World War. Nevertheless, the prosperity of the war trade, where Spanish industrialists in the North prospered from the suffering of millions of Europeans was not translated into international influence. Joaquín Maurín, the Catalonian anarchist, ridiculed the "mediocrity of our industrial bourgeoisie," while José Antonio Primo de Rivera, the visionary fascist leader, lamented the existence of a "mediocre conservative bourgeoisie" that was incapable of forging a new international role for Spain.

Spain's backwardness, however, was not perceived as a weakness by all segments of Spanish society. The traditionalist forces, led by the land-owning oligarchy and the church, drew strength from Spain's inability to participate in a primarily liberal international environment. The reactionary right-wing had struggled throughout the 19th Century to hold its own against the onslaught of European liberalization. The expulsion of the French occupiers did not come without concessions to the "rights of man" and the notion that sovereignty lies with the people of a nation, but the traditionalists were able to identify reformers and liberalizers with foreign interests. This identification enabled the reactionary elite to maintain the *status quo* despite the quickened pace of modernization and liberalization in the rest of Europe. Suspicion of modernizers and liberals was automatic in this context. Spain would sacrifice power in the international sphere if it meant the retention and protection of its traditional values at home. Anti-Europeanism became a political reflex of the right.

The irony here is that many of these reactionary elites were equally reluctant to renounce their own imperial pretentions. They sought empire but empire on their own terms. Like the quixotic leaders of the Holy Alliance, who in vain sought to wipe out the "virus of Republicanism" after the defeat of Napoleon, the Spanish traditionalists of the 20th Century remained true to their anti-liberal crusade. More importantly, they were willing to pay whatever price the international system would exact.

SPAIN AND EUROPEANIZATION

General Francisco Franco, who often described Spanish liberal tendencies as "bastard, Frenchified, and Europeanizing," was willing to pay such a price.[2] At first, his tacit alliance with fascist forces in the Axis seemed to guarantee a prominent international role in the coming New Order. When the Allied victory dashed such hopes, Franco stood fast to his principles. The ideology of the bunker retained its anti-liberal, isolationist components as international pressure forced the Franco regime to move to the offensive. The international critics were motivated by anti-Spanish feelings, not inconformity with a particular regime; international communism was fanning the flames of an historic "ill-will" towards Spain and the Spanish. Freemasons and Jewish liberals were intent on undermining traditional Spanish society. "Eternal" Spain would not relent; it would stand alone as the last bastion of Catholicism and traditional conservativism.

Franco's appeal to isolationist, nationalist sentiment has often been portrayed as a cynical political device employed to ensure that international opprobrium did not receive a dangerous echo from the traumatized post-Civil War Spanish society.[3] Franco's political behavior was not, however, so simply Machiavellian. Franco showed every sign of believing the things he said and was perfectly aware of the international price that Spain would have to pay. The maintenance of his regime was indeed the first priority, and something had to buffer Spain from international criticism. But Franco would reenter the international system only in a way that would not threaten the underlying values of Spanish society. When the Cold War afforded him this opportunity, he joined the conservative, anti-communist crusade led by the United States, signing historically decisive bilateral treaties with the United States in 1953.

Franco was probably not aware that the relationship with the United States would begin a process of economic modernization and international participation that would acquire such momentum that the institutions of Francoism would not be able to withstand the onslaught. Even by the early 1960s, Spain's burgeoning industry, led by significant U.S. and European foreign investment made possible by the 1959 Foreign Investment Decree Law,

sought wider markets and access to imports. A petition to join the European
Economic Community was put forth by the Franco regime in 1962. Franco
mistakenly believed that one can derive economic benefits from customs
unions without suffering political effects; it was an economic issue with no
connection to politics. The petition was rejected on the grounds that Spain's
political system was incompatible with the democracies united in the community. Such a government, it was announced, "cannot aspire to be admitted
into the circle of peoples which forms the European communities."[4]

The significance of the Spanish petition goes beyond the mere economic
benefits that Spain stood to derive from EEC membership, or the issue of
whether Spain would be able to maintain the authoritarian character of its
regime in the context of a customs union. What is of profound importance
for the foreign policy analyst is the fact that Spain was once again looking
toward Europe for realization of its national aspirations. Although Franco
denied the political significance,[5] Spain was suggesting, first through its U.S.-
sponsored petition to join NATO and then in its application for EEC membership, that its political future and international role was tied to Europe.
Europeanization would be inevitable, if not entirely desirable.

GAUGING SPAIN'S INTERNATIONAL PRIORITIES

By Franco's death in 1975, it was apparent that European integration would
be inevitable. There were, nevertheless, voices on the extreme right, characterized by the first post-Franco foreign minister as "mentally constipated,"
that preferred a Spain that was on the defensive against Europe.[6] But King
Juan Carlos I, in his first major address after taking over as head of state,
had already set the tone:

The idea of Europe would be incomplete without a reference to the presence of the
Spaniard, and without a consideration of the activity of many of my predecessors.
Europe should reckon with Spain, and we Spaniards are Europeans. It is a present
necessity that both sides understand this to be so and draw the consequences that
derive therefrom.[7]

By making references to his royal predecessors in both the Bourbon and
Habsburg houses, King Juan Carlos reestablished European linkages that
date to the 16th Century. His appeal to Europe to "reckon with Spain" was
also an appeal for Spain to reckon with Europe. With the King leading the
European charge, the extreme right in Spain, which saw much of its privilege
and position threatened by European standards and competition, was powerless to stop the process of European integration.

Given this priority, it is by no means surprising that the lion's share of
Spanish diplomatic and policy resources have gone to the European project
at the expense of Spain's projection in other spheres. Once the domestic

opponents of European integration—which included those on the extreme left as well as the extreme right—were "reckoned" with, Spanish diplomacy became almost single-minded in its European orientation. Application was made in 1977 for EEC admission, and by 1978 EEC memoranda and reports were reflecting favorable prospects for Spain's accession. When French President Giscard d'Estaing froze negotiations in June 1980, Spanish Foreign Minister Marcelino Oreja raised the stakes even higher: Spain will integrate into the NATO alliance if EEC integration continues as scheduled.

The invocation of the Atlantic Alliance was a departure for Spanish foreign policy. Before the French froze the EEC negotiations on Spanish accession, Spanish diplomacy was careful to cultivate its relationships with areas of the world that were still important to Spain. Prime Minister Adolfo Suárez did not have NATO as one of his highest priorities, and instead looked at Spanish interests in and special relations with the Arab world, Latin America, and other parts of the Third World. He sent an observer to the summit of the non-aligned states in Cuba in September 1979 in an effort to bring a neutralist identity to a Spanish foreign policy already perceived as profoundly Western. Yet neither Suárez's vision of Spain's new international role nor his government would prevail. After Suárez's successor, Leopoldo Calvo Sotelo, rebounded from the failed coup attempt in February 1981, he established a primarily Western and European political agenda, calling his project "Plan Occidente." Calvo Sotelo was convinced that Spain's influence was limited if she were to remain outside the major Western political and security organizations; he committed Spain to NATO and EEC integration before the scheduled elections in 1983. By June 1982, a simple majority vote in the Cortes made Spain the sixteenth member of NATO.

The Spanish prime minister also acknowledged that his strong Atlanticism was conditioned by other foreign policy concerns, namely the negotiations for EEC accession. French opposition could be overcome by eliminating all political obstacles to Spanish integration. Only then would the French be pressured into bargaining the details of the economic agreement; as long as Spain remained somewhere outside Western political and security arrangements, France would be able to find more than just narrow economic arguments to keep Spain out of the EEC.

Early elections in 1982 brought the Spanish Socialist Workers Party (PSOE) into power with an unprecedented absolute majority. Socialist bonds between Prime Minister Felipe González and French President François Mitterrand proved to be much more instrumental in breaking down French opposition to Spanish EEC accession than was the NATO membership. Then Foreign Minister Fernando Morán was dispatched to Paris and Brussels to present the Spanish case. Morán's persistence and professionalism won him the French Legion of Honor. Many Spaniards still believe, however, that his concessions to French agricultural interests accounted for French gratitude and that Spain won a Pyrrhic victory in the lengthy and costly EEC negotiations, which did not end until the signing on June 12, of the Treaty of Accession.

Spain, nevertheless, joined the EEC on January 1, 1986. A promised referendum on NATO was held later that winter; on the heels of the victory of the government's position, the Socialists were voted into power with another absolute majority. The fortunes of the PSOE were intimately linked to Europeanization. Despite outright rejection of NATO during González's stint as leader of the parliamentary opposition during the Suarez and Calvo Sotelo years,[8] the Socialists merely halted the process of Spain's incorporation into the NATO integrated military command, although Spanish participation in important forums such as the Nuclear Planning Group suggests a firmer military commitment to the Alliance. In the referendum, the Socialists called for support of Spain's permanence in the Atlantic Alliance under certain conditions, which included complete withdrawal from the integrated military command, the prohibition on nuclear weapons in Spanish territory, and a significant reduction of the U.S. military presence in Spain. Their victory in the referendum helped them defeat a completely off-balance opposition in general elections in July 1986. The Socialist thrust was well-defined: Felípe González had thus become the most "Europeanized" Spanish leader in many centuries.

SPAIN AND THE REST OF THE WORLD

The powerful dynamics of Europeanization, nevertheless, must be put in their proper context. If there is any continuity in Spanish foreign policy during this century, it can be found in Spain's concern for regions of the world where economic and geopolitical interests have demanded diplomatic attention. The Arab world, from which practically all of Spain's energy resources come, and North Africa, where Spain's colonial outposts at Ceuta and Melilla demand serious official consideration and resources, are two areas of primary importance to traditional Spanish foreign policy. Latin America, where Spain has the pretentious hopes of creating a Hispanic commonwealth, is another area that has traditionally received a great deal of diplomatic attention. Even under the Franco regime, multifaceted ties were developed not only in authoritarian states that saw Francoism as a model but also in nation-states as politically opposed as Cuba, where business was conducted cordially and with great profit for both sides.

The importance of Spain's Europeanization during the 1980s is that it represents a major shift in Spanish priorities. The identification of the Socialist government with the European project and European standards may even be deemed a typically un-Spanish phenomenon. While González and the Socialists have found a *sui generis* way of remaining in the NATO alliance—no nuclear weapons, no incorporation in the integrated military command—, the thrust of their policy is clear: the future of Spain and its hegemonic party, the PSOE, is fused to that of Europe. As early as 1983, the Madrid press was debating "a radical pro-Western turn in our foreign policy."[9]

It was at about this time that one could begin to talk of the "internationalization" of domestic politics in Spain.[10] "Understanding" for NATO cruise and Pershing II missile deployments and a friendly meeting with U.S. President Ronald Reagan in June 1983, where González expressed his support for Western defense initiatives, were evidence of an effort to remove the uncertainty surrounding Spanish attitudes towards the West. In 1987 Spain quietly signed the Treaty of Nonproliferation, for the first time renouncing its sovereign right to manufacture and deploy nuclear weapons. By the end of 1988, with relatively little domestic controversy, Spain would become a member of the Western European Union, a traditionally conservative European defense organization that has gained vigor within the context of EEC integration and the post-Cold War international system. To traditional Spanish foreign policy advocates, the new orientation would ultimately disarm Spanish diplomacy. Spain had always drawn strength from its ambiguous international position. Thrusting her into a regional context in which she is clearly inferior in economic, political, and military means would be dangerous if not fatal.

What the shift amounts to for observers of Spanish policy in Latin America is a clear definition of priorities. The dimensions of the European project are so immense that it would be difficult to speak of significant foreign policy resources being directed elsewhere for anything but extremely short periods of time. This is not to say that other priorities are not being met. In order to meet the potential Moroccan challenge at the colonial outposts of Ceuta and Melilla, the Socialist defense establishment poured tremendous resources into the redeployment of Spanish naval forces from the North Atlantic towards the Straits of Gibraltar and the creation of a potent carrier-led rapid deployment force at the southern Atlantic port of Rota. Only the multibillion dollar deal with the U.S. and McDonnell Douglas for F–18 air superiority jets during the early 1980s could compare in scope and expense to this naval redeployment. Clearly the Mediterranean and the potential threats from the Maghreb were never far from Socialist strategic and defense planning. Spanish dependency on North African oil and gas would demand no less from Spanish policy-makers. But the concern went beyond trade with the region and the historical relationship that Spain has with the Arab world. It did not take the melting of the Cold War to highlight the fact that practically all of Spain's strategic, economic, and demographic threats come from North Africa.

Amid the September 1990 Gulf Crisis, Spain and Italy announced an initiative in Malta that led to an October meeting in Rome between France, Spain, Portugal, and Italy from the EEC, and Algeria, Tunisia, Libya, Morocco, and Mauretania from the North African-Mediterranean littoral. The object of the meeting, which included Malta as an observer, was to garner support for an Italo-Spanish proposal for a Conference on Security and Co-operation in the Mediterranean. Luis Fernández de la Peña, the director of the cabinet of the Spanish foreign ministry secretariat and the official en-charged with the diplomatic initiative, saw the effort as an attempt to con-tinue the momentum of the Conference on Security and Cooperation in Europe (CSCE) in Helsinki to a region that has been largely ignored by NATO and formal Western security arrangements, with the possible excep-tion of the U.S. Sixth Fleet. Spain, according to Fernández de la Peña, has "primordial" interests in forging cooperation around shared values in a region characterized by instability, underdevelopment, and extremism. A draft doc-ument for the Conference was ready by the end of January, but the Gulf War served only to highlight the heterogeneity of the 45 potential partici-pants. Major obstacles, such as the requirement for an explicit recognition of Israel—which Spain had done only a few years earlier—would make the initiative look even more ambitious than the Helsinki process looked in the early 1980s.[11]

Moreover, Spain's significant collaboration in the coalition war effort against Iraq, which included a small naval contingent, intelligence coordi-nation, and use of Spanish bases for logistical support and hundreds of B–52 bombing raids, threatened the moral high ground of the Spanish position on cooperation and security in the Mediterranean. Popular protests through-out the region in support of Saddam Hussein directly threatened the Spanish position, especially in Morocco where earlier protests against the regime of King Hassan II for domestic reasons suggested that the monarchy's survival was in doubt. Spanish diplomats knew that an opposition overthrow of the monarchy in Morocco would mean almost certain confrontation with Spain over the colonial outposts of Ceuta and Melilla on North African soil. With anti-Spanish feelings reaching a peak during the allied bombings of Iraq and Kuwait, Felipe González dispatched foreign minister Francisco Fernández Ordoñez to the region on a largely successful damage-control mission.

Spanish diplomacy, nevertheless, like much of Spanish society, lags be-hind that of other powers in both material resources and experience. The foreign minister was forced to clarify Spain's position after a near fatal dip-lomatic gaff by the cabinet-level government spokesperson, Rosa Conde, who stated that the NATO treaty should not be invoked to protect Turkey from a possible Iraqi attack. Conde's *lapsus* was typical of Spanish attitudes towards the international system; the correction by Ordoñez, amid tremen-dous pressure from Turkey, the U.S., and the EEC, was a reminder to the many people in Spain who feel that Spain does not have foreign enemies and thus would never have occasion to itself invoke the NATO treaty in the event of a Moroccan attack on Spain over Ceuta and Melilla.

Too often the daunting tasks of Spanish foreign relations have been left to Ordoñez himself, whose repeated admissions of exhaustion are not surprising given his merciless travel agenda. His job is less difficult in the Western Hemisphere, as personal diplomacy by Prime Minister Felipe Gonzàlez substitutes for chronic bureaucratic weaknesses there. The largely successful European foray, moreover, has required not only scarce diplomatic resources, but also the voluntary and involuntary cooperation of Spanish producers and consumers. Clearly there is no other foreign policy initiative in Madrid that would require such a popular and official effort.

Why, then, is so much importance given to Latin American relations in official pronouncements and in the national and international press? One may find that foreign policy, even when not put into operation, answers some deeply-felt national needs at the same time it attempts to satisfy some pressing international ones. One of these psychological needs is a kind of political narcissism that divorces reality at home (where there is crisis, uncertainty, and a lack of "realistic" foreign policy resources) from the image of a country abroad. Like many other peoples, Spaniards, and especially Spain's leaders, express this narcissism in missions of diplomacy and conflict resolution abroad.

It may also become clear that, in an operational sense, Spanish foreign policy in Latin America has now become *European* foreign policy—not as a result of EEC impositions, but simply because Spanish identification with Europe has given even the most traditional Spanish relationships a European tint.

Democratic Transition, Spanish Policy, and the Crisis in Central America

Spanish policy's preoccupation with Europe after the death of dictator Francisco Franco in 1975 was a political, economic, and strategic reflex. Franco's rejection of the political and social realities of Europe and his desire to protect Spanish culture and society from the decadence of the West was to a great extent a geopolitical obstruction whose resistance was bound to be temporary. When the democratic leaders of the transition assumed power, there was an institutional vacuum that could only be filled by a conscious identification with European and Western civilization. There was uncertainty and fear. The leaders of the Spanish democratic transition looked to Europe for more than inspiration and guidance; they looked for protection against their own failures and defense against powerful enemies of the democratic project.

It is not in the interest of any nation-state to display such dependence on other political systems. No democrat, no matter now desperate, can ignore the effects on the international position of his country that would inevitably result from employing an agenda that is not national. Hence, Prime Minister Adolfo Suárez, while following an agenda set centuries ago by European and Western civilization, was careful to define Spanish interests as strictly national. Drawing from the European democratic experience a moral force and a corresponding backdrop for the national democratic project, Suárez charted an international course that would preserve Spain's historical independence from the rigid dictates of Western strategy and foreign policy. Spain's relatively privileged relations with the Arab world and her historical and cultural ties with Latin America were to be the areas to which Spanish diplomatic resources were oriented. In this way, there would be both continuity and a consolidation of Spain's unique position in the international system, without the potentially debilitating image of a nation-state dependent on validation from greater powers.[1]

Soon, however, the geopolitical gravity of Europe pulled the Spanish democratic experiment into its orbit. The government of Suárez's successor, Leopoldo Calvo Sotelo, and the three administrations of Felipe González allowed Spain to gradually slip into the European system, casting Spain's future in with that of a united, integrated Europe. For Calvo Sotelo, the pro-Western impulses were a matter of personal conviction as well as a means for Spain to secure the economic benefits of the European Economic Community. For Felipe González, who spent many years in European exile, the European orientation was more of a vocation; Spanish democracy is measured almost strictly by European standards.

To all leaders of the Spanish democratic transition, moreover, Europe held out a vague promise of protection from anti-democratic forces. Spanish democrats believed that if the young institutions of democracy were not capable of dealing with internal threats, then perhaps European opprobrium would ward off the enemies of democracy. The threat of a military *coup d'état* never disappeared from Spanish politics until well into the Socialists' first term. The failed *coup* attempt on February 23, 1981 brought stern responses from Spain's European neighbors, but Spain's democrats sought even more solid preventive mechanisms. European integration was and is viewed as the most affordable means to insure that Spanish politics, no matter what the ideological nature of a regime might be, would follow a democratic course.

FROM EUROPEAN MENTORS TO LATIN PUPILS

While the European and pro-Western *deslizamiento* proceeded apace, Spanish foreign policy turned its rhetorical resources toward areas in which Spain could conceivably exercise the kind of moral and political hegemony that was impossible in the European context. Latin America became the main target as Spanish leaders and the King invoked nostalgia and empathy for the Latin American experience. Once again, the vehicle would be Spain's democratic transition, a cherished political phenomenon that would recommend Spain to its former colonies without calling up ghosts of the *conquistadores* and authoritarians.

The thrust outward to Latin America, as natural as it may seem for a country with such a grand colonial heritage in the New World, responds to a deeply felt need on the part of the Spanish people to assert leadership in world affairs. Modern political realism, which would present Spanish foreign policy as a function of specific national interests, does not provide a complete explanation for the nature of Spain's foreign policy in Latin America, although it does suggest something about the degree of involvement and the potential for influence there. It is in fact quite realistic to speak of an overwhelming psychological drive on the part of Spanish policy that has no bearing on the amount of tangible and material interests that Spain can claim to possess in Latin America. Moreover, this psychological drive, which is expressed mostly in the form of rhetoric, need not command the resources that are ultimately required for any nation-state that seeks influence. It should be remembered that political rhetoric has its domestic audience and that this national audience may well be the ultimate target.

A realistic appraisal of Spain's interests in Latin America would show that the region's importance is in relative decline. Trade, that most profound and revealing of indicators, is perhaps the most significant symptom of this trend. Spain's trade with Latin America, as a percentage of total Spanish international trade, has declined significantly since the democratic succession. Latin America provided only 6.2 percent of Spain's imports in 1987 and took only 4.3 percent of its exports. From about 10 percent of total Spanish trade in 1965, Latin American trade declined to about 5 percent in 1987. By comparison, Spain's trade with Europe grew by over 600 percent from 1965 to 1987, while Latin American trade has grown by only about 300 percent in the same time frame.[2]

Detailed studies of Spain's commerce with Central America reveal serious problems, both subjective and objective. In the 1980s, Spanish trade with the region represented an insignificant portion of Spain's total trade; Central American exports to Spain ranked seventh as a percentage of the region's total exports, and Spain ranked forth behind Japan, the FRG, and the United States in exports to the region. This asymmetry, which has only been reinforced during the latter half of the decade and into the 1990s, had led to the determination that any improvement in the relationship would have to be politically motivated. Spain's imports from the region were almost exclusively made up of primary products, especially coffee, cotton, and wood products. Glaring in their absence were bananas and more importantly, manufactured goods. Spanish protectionism, reinforced by the EEC trade policy, kept the increasingly important Spanish market closed to Central American exports of textiles, shoes, plastics, processed food products, and handicrafts. The only relative improvement was in coffee imports; Spain substituted Central American coffee for African coffee, leaving Central American producers with about 15% of the market.[3]

The subjective aspects are perhaps the most important. Inasmuch as Central America was about as important to Spanish traders as Zaire, there was, and still is, little if any commercial momentum. The region's political instability kept Spanish producers and consumers away, and booming opportunities in Europe shifted whatever remaining focus there was. Only in the Canary Islands is there any evidence of a Latin American trade orientation. In an effort to stimulate the Spanish private sector's interest in the region, Spain launched a "strategic" financial initiative in the region with a $500 million loan to the Inter-American Development Bank. But the money, which was tied to Spanish firms' participation in infrastructure projects, has been characteristically slow in being disbursed, and few Spanish entrepreneurs have shown interest in taking risks in the unstable Central American context.[4] This pessimism has led some observers to talk about a strategic "retreat" of the Spanish private sector from the region.[5] In any case, with respect to Central America, surely some observers are overstating the case for an "Iberian-Latin American connection."[6]

The short-term rise in investment from Spanish industry and banks in the late 1970s and early 1980s is misleading. Only banks and construction companies have invested in Latin America during the rest of the 1980s, but many Spanish banks were in retreat, especially in Central America, and these banks were among the early holders of the seemingly unrepayable Latin debt. Technical and communications agreements abound, but these commercial arrangements are more notable for their symbolic effects than for their long-term ability to alter or reorient trade and technological patterns. The major deals have been in Mexico and in the more developed countries of South America, with the takeover of Aerolineas Argentinas by Iberia Airlines and the activities of the Spanish state-controlled telecommunications monopoly Telefónica suggesting a new Spanish thrust. The skeptical London weekly, *The Economist*, pointed out that, in fact, "weak economic ties threaten to defeat attempts to organise *hispanidad*, especially now that Spain's economic priority is Europe."[7]

Spain's security arrangements with NATO provide for a European focus for Spanish defense planners in addition to Spain's already well-defined defense posture in North Africa. NATO membership also brings with it an identification with the global strategic interests of the United States, something that would rarely be an asset in the Latin American context.

Thus the instruments of Spanish foreign policy in Latin America have been reduced to three relatively intangible resources: diplomatic contacts, rhetorical assets, and the moral force behind the image of Spain's democratic model. One need not belittle these instruments, however; the more tangible aspects of nation-state foreign policy have rarely been successful in the Central American context. Billions of dollars in U.S. aid and superpower military intervention have yet to prove that such "realistic" instruments are guarantors of democracy and development in Central America. The crisis in Central America beckoned, and Spanish policy answered the call with the only resources it could muster.

It should come as no surprise that there were also formal invitations for Spanish intervention; the formidable ideological currents made such intervention inevitable. These aspects may not be decisive in the long run, but they reveal much about Spanish foreign policy and democratic politics in the Americas. The Spanish involvement in the Central American crisis may also raise in value the intangible aspects of foreign policy, thereby serving as a lesson to those who rely on more blatant forms of intervention.

INTERNAL AND EXTERNAL CONGRUENCE

The foreign policy process in Spain has no doubt been complicated by the concurrent domestic political process, which has kept Spanish politics relatively unstable and fluid. In seeking a new international position, Spain has looked inward at its own struggle with democracy and has made a conscious effort to maintain an equilibrium between its internal project and its developing international role. This congruence is important to all nation-states, especially to developing ones; if there should be a contradiction between the internal project and the international role, there will be a threat to the coherence and credibility of the nation-state in the international system. Furthermore, psychological dissonance can develop on the part of Spanish voters who are increasingly sensitive to Spain's role in foreign affairs.

In previous discussions, a link was established between strategy and a democratic project for the United States in Central America. There is an emerging consensus that U.S. policy goals must reflect the national character of the American people and remain consistent with a democratic political culture in order to remain coherent and retain credibility. Although Spain's policy interests in Central America are not as vital as those of the United States, Spanish foreign policy nonetheless seeks the same equilibrium. In the Spanish case, however, the initiative is much more deliberate.

Spanish foreign policy has sought this congruence to establish a means by which all policy goals can be achieved. According to former Socialist foreign minister Fernando Morán, "the ideas that enforce our democratic restoration—rule of law, peace, dialogue, suppression of the concept of enemy for that of competitor, social solidarity and cooperation, respect for cultural characteristics—correspond to those lines that sketch our international behavior." Such congruence between the "external definition" and internal political culture "lends coherence and credibility to international action and affords considerable support in international opinion."[8]

The many contradictions between the Spanish internal project and its international behavior escaped the attention of Morán and will be the subject of commentary in ensuing discussions of Socialist foreign policy in Central America. There is little doubt, however, that in general, Spanish foreign policy makes the deliberate attempt to establish congruity between its internal and external projects.

PROJECTING THE MODEL

The main vehicle is the Spanish democratic model, whose potential international role has been exploited by all Spanish leaders since 1975. Suárez was the first to purvey the model as an international commodity. His rhetorical interventions suggested that Spain could give nation-states in Latin America an education in democracy. Latin Americans were, no doubt, wary.

They were familiar with Spain's lofty and overtly arrogant attempts to establish leadership in Hispanic affairs. Talk of an "Hispanic Commonwealth" drew even more skeptical responses. Well-trained in the patronizing politics of colonialism, Latin Americans were less than enthused. Indeed, there was little symmetry between Spain's means and its pretentions. Latin American interests, moreover, called for increasing autonomy in world affairs. Spain's informal suggestions of an Hispanic voting-bloc in the United Nations and its offer to serve as a "bridge" for European-Latin American relations even before Spain's EEC accession puzzled more Latin Americans than they inspired. The anti-Americanism inherent in such initiatives was not much of a rallying point either; until Spain could offer some real benefits, the Latin American countries would not jeopardize their vital ties with the United States. Thus it seems that Suárez's invitations were more for domestic consumption, to enhance self-esteem during difficult and trying times.

The signals sent by the Calvo Sotelo administration to the Latin American community were not ones of leadership. Rocked by the February 1981 attempt to overthrow the democratic regime, the UCD government sought protection inside the European fold. Spain's international position was once again tenuous: dependent on Western security and economic arrangements to guarantee her own democratic sovereignty, Spain could not aspire to a leadership role in any hemisphere. Solidarity from the Hispanic community would be forthcoming, but even the diplomatic gaffs of the United States' Secretary of State Alexander Haig, who suggested that the attempted *golpe* was an "internal matter," were not enough to forge any kind of Hispanic democratic alliance. Spain looked to Europe for protection in an admission of weakness that would later have serious implications for her international role.

The radical pro-Western drive of the UCD government by 1981 was in part responsible for setting into motion a domestic political dynamic that would result in what seemed at first to be an equally radical reorientation of priorities in the Socialist opposition's foreign policy platform. The original Socialist platform, while owing much to established policy within the Socialist International (where Felipe González was Vice President and confidant of leader Willy Brandt), also responded to traditional isolationist sentiments shared by the right-wing. Like Suárez, who envisioned a unique international role for Spain that would be more consistent with her historical experience, González expressed reservations about the European project. Membership in the EEC would not necessarily require NATO membership as long as French Socialism was there to support Spanish accession to the Community. (The case of Ireland is instructive here.) Open and unabashed sympathies for the Palestinian and Polisario causes signaled a new, more activist, non-aligned stance for Spanish foreign policy. Latin America, where the Socialist International already was working in conflict resolution, would be the main target of Spanish diplomatic resources within this new framework. For Felipe

González, who had established personal and working relationships with Latin American social democrats and leftists through his vice-presidency of the Socialist International, an unbridled advance into the U.S.-dominated security arrangements of Western Europe would send the wrong message to potential partners and clients in Latin America.

With the Central American crisis beckoning for third power intervention at this time, Felipe González, who was well positioned to move his party into the vacuum created by the collapse of the UCD coalition in 1981–82, carefully cultivated the perception that his intervention would not be associated with U.S. policy dictates. Spanish prospects were perceived to be riding on the trust that González could establish with his Central American counterparts. Poised at the gates of power, the Socialists reasoned that perceived independence from Washington and Brussels was key to the success of any Spanish intervention in the polarized politics of Central America. But Central American leaders would soon learn that such independence was illusory; Spain had already begun her plunge into Europe and subsequent events would only heighten her dependence on Washington-led Western security arrangements. Felipe González would inevitably have to bring this European and North American baggage with him on any diplomatic initiative in Central America.

Socialist Policy in Central America: Parameters and Constraints

> The medium-powers do not have the same capacity for action in foreign affairs as the superpowers, but on the other hand they possess a flexibility and a series of possibilities that the superpowers lack.
>
> —*Fernando Morán, 1984*[1]

A convincing victory such as that of Felipe González's Socialist Party (Partido Socialista Obrero Español, PSOE) in the 1982 general elections usually brings with it significant authority and momentum for bold foreign policy ventures. With an absolute majority in the Cortes (Spanish parliament), and public focus on the serious economic crisis inherited from the UCD government, Spanish foreign policy seemed as if it would be bolstered by a mandate for change.

For many Spaniards, the 1982 Socialist victory represented the consolidation of Spanish democracy. For the Socialists had been the big losers in the Spanish Civil War. While presiding over a Republic that was about to provoke the most extreme forms of reaction, the PSOE saw its hegemony over the left eroded by anarchist provocation and Communist imposition. The party and its leaders were legally and literally eliminated under Francoism, whose major task was to erase the memory of the Second Republic from the minds of a brutalized and hungry population. In 1977, the PSOE returned from exile to dominate the opposition to Suárez's UCD coalition. The 1982 elections gave the party more than 10 million votes (almost half of the electorate) in a field already characterized by party proliferation. As the first months of Socialist rule passed by, confidence was built up slowly because many still feared a reaction from the military. The fact that the reactionary forces within the country had not risen up to challenge by force their old Civil War enemies was proof that the Spanish democratic experiment had worked. As the economic crisis in the country worsened, the moral victory over involution was perhaps the only energy upon which the Socialists fed.

That energy, nevertheless, was not enough for more than cautious movements in foreign affairs. The consolidation of democracy was to be the major international resource for the Socialist government, yet the possibilities of a democratic breakdown still weighed heavily on the minds of government strategists. Like its democratic predecessors, the PSOE consciously and unconsciously sought protection for what seemed to be even younger and more vulnerable democratic institutions. Participation in NATO became a vehicle for channeling military ambitions from praetorian ventures to professional missions. The successful negotiations with Socialist France on EEC accession were to occupy conservative business sectors with a formidable economic challenge that would later serve to keep their minds off politics. Felipe González and the Socialists spent on a good deal of political capital advocating the affirmative position in a 1986 referendum on NATO membership—a promised referendum that had been delayed for over three years.[2] Safely tucked into the European fold, and confident that democracy was protected by the most powerful Western international organizations, the Socialists embarked on a Latin American policy venture that could not but be conditioned by Spain's other international commitments.

Such international commitments became bothersome for many party policy-makers who wished to maintain the flexibility and freedom to maneuver of a non-aligned middle power in a bipolar world. González answered critics in his party with the suggestion that his government was pursuing a policy that took into account the interests of all of Spain, not just those of the PSOE. The government's position would have to be wider and less partisan; reasons of state demanded that the narrow party approach to relegated to the status of general principles: autonomy; the defense of human rights; and the vague but operational principles of peace, non-discrimination for political motives, security, and democracy.[3] Many of these principles were intangible enough to permit policy flexibility; the non-discrimination clause, which committed Spain to the maintenance of diplomatic relations with all Latin American countries,[4] was not a burden. (The United States, engaged in an undeclared war with Nicaragua, still maintained diplomatic relations with Managua.) Yet the change of tone in Spanish policy was nonetheless disturbing to some party militants. The first to react against this less *comprometida* policy was the Socialist Foreign Minister himself, Fernando Morán.

There was indeed some irony in Morán's position. After all, it was he who had worked so diligently to remove the political and economic barriers to Spanish accession to the EEC. Perhaps he ignored the fact that with economic ties to Europe would come commensurate security arrangements and other political and strategic ties. He seemed to have mistakenly believed that European integration could come without some kind of acceptance of the role of the United States in Western security. González and his deputy prime minister and vice president, Alfonso Guerra, were quick to censure Morán's partisan views. A fatal breakdown in Spanish foreign policy was narrowly avoided when Morán was replaced in a July 1985 cabinet shuffle and was later given the secondary post of Ambassador to the United Nations.

Morán's replacement, Francisco Fernández Ordoñez, a social democrat and key player in the transition under Suárez, was more inclined to implement a policy that would admit to Spain's pro-Western stance and its strategic and political subordination to U.S. interests. His diplomatic skills were employed in the task of giving Spanish foreign policy credibility in regions of the world where the perception of alignment with United States policy interests would have to be avoided.

Under Morán, Spanish policy had taken on an independent, almost provocative tone. His appeal to the Third World, and especially Latin America, was both ideological and emotional. To Morán, relations with the United States were perfectly manageable in spite of Spain's agenda in Latin America. The critique of the United States was for the most part historical, and the Reagan Administration had plenty of time to learn from the mistakes of the past. Moreover, the Spanish approach could only be in the interests of the United States, as cooperation and accommodation in places like Central America would restore stability in a region deemed "vital" by the U.S. president.

The content of Spanish foreign policy in Central America at this time was perhaps less important than its mere existence. For Morán and many others in the PSOE the content did indeed matter, yet any kind of diplomatic foray into Central American geopolitics at this time would have to be noticed. The American administration had already moved decisively to establish a political pole that would offset the revolutionary leftism of the Sandinista regime and the Salvadoran and Guatemalan guerrilla alliances. As Central American affairs gravitated toward either of the two poles, an unprecedented amount of political space opened up for diplomatic intervention. In 1983–84, the medium was the message in Central America, and Spanish policy, despite its problematic content, was put firmly on the map of Central American politics.

As time wore on, however, and as the Spanish and European diplomats began to realize that their intervention could in no way be decisive in an area of superpower confrontation, the Spanish began to look seriously into the content of their policy and its effect on the vital U.S.-Spanish relationship.

Here Morán was vulnerable. There was nothing inconsistent about his basic principles and Spain's support for the interests of the West in Central America. The problems came about as a result of the particular choices that

Spain would make regarding who best upholds those principles in Central America. Unabashed solidarity with the cause of Edén Pastora, the former Sandinista commander, at the expense of the CIA's *Contra* clients was an acceptable diplomatic *matiz* in the Central American context. But Spanish support extended to the Salvadoran left, already linked in an alliance (FDR-FMLN) with the Marxist-Leninist guerrilla groups, and to the Sandinista regime itself, to which it had already given significant humanitarian donations, as well as trade credits.[5]

The economic and humanitarian aid should have been excusable, given the dimensions of Western aid to the Nicaraguan regime even after 1984; yet the Reagan Administration, engaged in the sabotage of Nicaraguan ports and shipping and in the arming of *Contra* rebel armies, was sending both oblique and direct warnings to NATO allies and other European countries that were pouring aid into Sandinista Nicaragua.[6] The political support of the left was even more troubling to Washington because the absence of truly democratic forces on the ground made the battle for democratic credentials an open contest. With its support resting with the Somoza-linked Nicaraguan rebels, the right-wing ARENA regime in El Salvador, and the military regimes of Honduras and Guatemala, Washington was not winning the propaganda war against Latin American and Western social democrats who were parading Central American leftists through European capitals. It would take considerable pressure from Washington and the resultant NATO discord to cause the Europeans to relent.[7]

Other NATO countries could withstand the pressure without too much destabilization of domestic politics. Spain, however, could not afford that risk. The right-wing of the political spectrum, the principal opposition to the Socialist government of Felipe González, could not be enlisted in the fight against a deteriorating economic situation if it felt betrayed by a foreign agenda that suggested a departure from the norms of behavior in the capitalist world. Spanish democracy, although consolidated, was not in any position to deal with a hostile U.S. administration. Foreign investment, moreover, had become a major contributor to the Spanish recovery. A radical foreign policy at odds with NATO and the United States would eventually destroy investor confidence. The price could be very high indeed: high technology, badly needed by Spanish industry, would not flow to Spain as readily if there was concern over the direction of Spanish foreign policy.

The Socialist government was more willing to placate the political opposition than to make concessions to the left-wing of its own party. Prime Minister González could afford to ignore the noisy protests from the Communist Party and from the left-wing of his party, as there was no need for him to draw power from leftist positions. The government was looking for legitimacy and credibility on the right, where formidable, if disorganized, opposition remained. The positions of Foreign Minister Morán were by no means radical for a nation-state that had achieved democratic autonomy. But

Spain was still vulnerable to internal and external forces. The French Socialists could provoke the U.S. by offering to sweep CIA mines in Nicaraguan
harbors and then see their domestic position bolstered by significant support
on the left. Spain risked not only opprobrium but also the prospects of
economic and political destabilization that could come in both overt and
subtle forms. If González were to err, he would err on the side of his NATO
and U.S. ties. His foreign minister would have to be replaced.

TOWARDS SOCIAL DEMOCRACY, AGAIN

The choice of a recognized social democrat who had once participated in
the UCD center-right coalition marked a significant turning-point in Spanish
foreign policy toward Central America. Already by 1984 critics on the left
were decrying Socialist hypocrisy regarding relations with Latin American
countries. Even under Morán the rhetoric was not backed up by concrete
action. In international forums such as GATT and the United Nations,
Spanish diplomacy was engaged in securing primarily national or European
interests, sometimes at the expense of the Third World. The reticence of
former Economics Minister Miguel Boyer to put Spain in the forefront of
Latin debt renegotiation is perhaps the most obvious manifestation of Spain's
sometimes hypocritical stance. Boyer refused to attend the Lima round of
debt talks in 1984; he drew criticism from within his own party, but there
was no sign of a struggle over the issue within the government.[8]

The government was counting on the realism of Latin leaders to lead them
to forgive Spain for not taking up positions that would threaten Spain's own
standing in important international forums. There was an appreciation, moreover, that Spain did not have much weight to bear in these forums and that
such a quixotic effort would be counterproductive. What Latin America was
looking for was a change in attitude towards the region. There were signs
that Latin American democrats were tiring of the demogoguery and empty
rhetoric of earlier years, especially that of the leaders of the Spanish transition, who seemed to be addressing their own political constituents rather
than the Hispano-American community. The democratic project in Latin
America could accept constraints on Spanish freedom of operation; what was
unacceptable was the kind of arrogance and demogoguery that had characterized Spanish policy for centuries.

One of the ways to restore Spanish credibility in spite of acceptable constraints was to make a concerted effort to transcend the purely *missionary*
character of Spanish policy. Not that the missionary spirit was by any means
a liability; considerable inroads into Latin American culture and society had
been made by the Catholic Church and religious orders. (The Jesuit presence, ironically enough, has contributed to the radicalization of the Latin
American left, especially in Colombia, Peru, and Central America. Key figures in the Andean guerrilla groups are former Spanish Jesuits.) In many

places in Latin America—most particularly in Central America—the church constituted the only evidence of the Spanish presence. Nevertheless, there was a need for a more official and material presence, one that would suggest a high priority for the region in official Spanish affairs.

Such a real and material presence was a formidable challenge given Spanish economic and technical constraints. Before the 1980s, the Spanish experience in Latin America was limited primarily to informal commercial cooperation and a small number of symbolic programs of educational exchange and development. Independent anarchist and cooperative groups in Andalusia had more experience in Latin American cooperation than did the government.

The efforts by religious and charity groups, which sometimes had an economic or technical component, would become a major stepping stone for Spanish official policy. The inherent efficiency in channeling official funds through these non-governmental organizations (NGOs), and the non-ideological nature of such aid, were appealing to Spanish development aid officials.[9] By 1990, the government was channeling about $4 million to Spanish NGOs for projects in the Central American countries.[10] This amount represented a sizeable portion of total Spanish aid to the region, which had been averaging about $25 million dollars a year.

INSTITUTION BUILDING

The Socialists felt the need to establish semi-autonomous official institutions that would serve as the *punto de encuentro* for Hispano-American relations. The Instituto de Cultura Hispánica, a vestige of the condescending notion of *hispanidad* from the Franco regime, had been rebaptized as the Instituto de Cooperación Iberoamericano (ICI) in 1981 during the UCD years. Its library, technical cooperation offices, think tanks, and the editorial offices of *Pensamiento Iberoamericano*, the journal of Latin American political economy, serve as Spain's institutional basis for Latin American policy. In 1985 the Socialists raised the status of the institution by elevating its first socialist director, Luis Yáñez Barnuevo, a close aide of Felipe González and Alfonso Guerra, to the newly created position of Secretary of State for International Cooperation, and president of the commission for the celebration of the V Centenary of the Discovery of America. Again, this appointment would have been merely cosmetic if priority had not been given to Spanish-Latin American relations. If only through Yáñez's closeness to the prime minister and the deputy prime minister as a member of the "Andalusian clique," the new position of Secretary of State had *de facto* cabinet rank. Yáñez and his brother Juan Antonio were perhaps the most influential members of González's administration, with the exception of Alfonso Guerra before his resignation in early 1991. But the primacy of Latin American affairs was threatened by these political connections. Yáñez and his brother were perceived in the press and political circles as domestic political advisors, with

Juan Antonio serving as a bridge between the Moncloa and the Santa Cruz (foreign ministry), often playing the role of a "chief of staff" charged with limiting political damage to the prime minister in foreign policy matters. Juan Antonio maintained a low public profile while exercising decisive influence on the prime minister, who was the country's most important foreign policy resource.

While seemingly competent and energetic, Luis Yáñez has not been inspirational. His involvement in domestic politics undoubtedly limited his effectiveness as one of the chief practitioners of Spanish foreign policy. His association with the *Guerrista* faction of the PSOE put his political future at risk during the 1990–91 governmental corruption crisis. Although he survived the ensuing government shake-up, the party was eager to position him for the mayoralty of Seville in the May 1991 municipal elections. He would later succumb to pressure from opposition candidates in Andalusia to give up his national position as president of the commission for the celebration of the V Centenary of the Discovery of America, whose showcase display would be the 1992 Expo in Seville.[11]

The political fortunes of Juan Antonio also changed during the government crisis of 1990–91. At the end of 1990, after almost ten years of service in the Moncloa as the prime minister's principal foreign policy advisor, he was given the ambassadorship to the UN, where Spain had positioned itself as one of the so-called "friends of the Secretary General" as a result of Spanish participation in UN peacekeeping operations in Namibia, Angola, and Nicaragua. He came to the job with a reputation for having been instrumental in cultivating the international image of Felipe González, but he also boasted credentials as a diplomat and expert on international law.[12]

From the outset, the ICI's role in Spanish foreign policy was limited by its budget, its distance from policy-making circles in the foreign ministry, the idealism of its staff, and by a visible absence of leadership within the organization.[13] The restructuring of the foreign aid apparatus at the beginning of 1989 put the ICI under more direct control of the foreign ministry, and the cooperation programs were fashioned to follow the interests of Spanish foreign policy more closely. While government officials still assert the autonomous nature of the ICI and its oversight agency, the Spanish Agency for International Cooperation (AECI), the restructuring seemed to be a deliberate attempt to reign in the ICI staff, which was often at odds with the growing conservatism of Spain's Latin American policy and the "Europeanization" of Spanish foreign relations. Apart from providing the excellent academic journal, *Pensamiento Iberoamericano*, a publishing house, an energetic think tank in the Spanish Center for the Development of Latin America (CEDEAL), and some important conferences in Spain and Latin America, the ICI has attempted to promote the image of Spanish democracy in Latin America. Its occasional series of *encuentros*, the "Iberoamérica: Encuentro en la Democracia," unites Latin American and Spanish democratic leaders and scholars around the theme of democracy. It is interesting to observe, however, that at the first *encuentro* in Madrid in April 1983 there were only eight representatives from Central America. Argentina alone boasted nine, and Spain was represented by 70 people.[14]

The second *encuentro* in Madrid brought together politicians, intellectuals, and experts from over 23 countries to study the future of relations between Europe and Latin America. Out of this meeting have emerged a number of permanent research projects and institutes, including the Institute of European-Latin American Relations (IRELA), which is funded almost entirely by the European Commission and whose mission it is to instigate and evaluate Europe's forays into Latin America. In addition to its public relations functions, IRELA has also sponsored conferences and research on Latin American integration, democratization, debt, and transatlantic relations, among other issues. There is little question of the institute's effectiveness as a research organization and academic forum, yet it remains vulnerable to the charge that it has an almost vocational tendency to overstate the case for Europe's role and influence in Latin America, which most probably reflects the source of its funding and/or the enthusiasm of its international staff.

For its part, the Spanish foreign ministry in the Plaza de Santa Cruz exercises control of Latin American policy not only through its director general of Iberoamerican affairs but also directly through the foreign minister's oversight of the AECI and the Secretary of International Cooperation himself. Yáñez shared with foreign minister Fernández Ordoñez direct access to the Moncloa, so there was little need for close supervision, but the institutional dependency of the AECI and ICI on the foreign ministry was more apparent by the end of the decade.

The directorship of Iberoamerican affairs, created in 1983, developed throughout the three Socialist administrations into a major source of input on Central American policy. The first director, Carlos Miranda, was an over-exuberant party militant whose resignation was a result of a major gaff he committed in Brazil by allowing quotes from Felipe González to enter a prepared speech by King Juan Carlos. His replacement, Mercedes Rico, injected a strong analytical and rhetorical component before she was named Spain's ambassador to Costa Rica (in fact, Spain's first female ambassador ever), and later, director general of human rights. Her successor, Juan Pablo de la Iglesia, and his team never developed much influence. His involvement in political infighting over Central American policy, where he was identified with the more idealistic positions of the ICI, led to his replacement by the diplomat Yago Pico de la Coaña, who quickly established himself as an authority within the Moncloa and Santa Cruz staffs. His measured public interventions reflect the cautious and conservative character of Spanish foreign policy heading into the 1990s. His assumption that internal forces at work on the Central American isthmus were primarily responsible for developmental problems and instability allowed him to avoid the more polemical references to U.S. policy in the region and set the tone for a non-ideological *acta de presencia* (act of presence) for Spain.[15]

A countervailing influence to the realism of the diplomatic corps could be expected from the PSOE's party apparatus, which asserted its foreign policy prerogatives through its International Department. Elena Flores, the international secretary since 1986, took advantage of the prime minister's position as a vice-president of the Socialist International (SI) and helped establish the PSOE as a major force in European Socialist and Social Democratic debates on Central America.[16] Her energy and enthusiasm won influence in policy formation, but there was no way she could avoid the eventual institutional conflict between the government and the party, which would grow to crisis proportions towards the end of the 1980s. By 1990 Felipe González was suggesting a separation between government and party in the context of party corruption and the backlash of leftist opinion over economic and foreign policy. Unfortunately for Flores and her team, who had progressively moderated their department's positions on Central American affairs in order to respond to the responsibilities of state policy, the PSOE as a party identified with the more left-leaning socialist and social democratic parties in Europe. Official Spanish policy led by González, however, had been moving markedly to the right of such parties as the German SPD and the Swedish Socialist SAP. The prime minister's relations with Socialist International leaders, moreover, were not always on the best of terms, despite the effective campaign in the Moncloa to limit the visibility of political damage. Spain's relations with Costa Rica and its social democratic leadership were often strained during the tense years of the *Contra* war over policy towards the Sandinistas and aid issues. Severe strains in the long-term friendship with Carlos Andrés Pérez appeared after the Venezuelan president legitimized ETA terrorism in 1989 and criticized Spain's handling of the celebrations of the V Centenary of the Discovery of the Americas.[17] And even Oscar Arias, the initiator of the 1987 regional peace plan and the most prominent Central American leader in the SI, would deliberately push González out of the final Esquipulas peace process in favor of a strictly regional solution.

INTERNAL COMPETITION

Socialist policy in Latin America has also been challenged by the emerging power and autonomy of Spain's ethnic homelands as organized in the current system of administrative autonomy known as the "State of Autonomies." Regions with ruling parties different from that of the Madrid central government have embarked on commercial, cultural, and social relations with Latin America. Of these, the Catalonian regional authorities are the most energetic, followed by the Basque and Andalusian autonomous administrations.

The regional governments are primarily concerned with trade relations and in nurturing the cultural linkages they find in the large colonies of Spanish immigrants in the New World. But they also see in Latin America a means by which to move out from under Madrid's administrative and political control. The impulse to move outward is manifest especially in the Catalonian and Basque regions, where nationalism is a powerful force.

Catalonian "foreign policy" is concerned primarily with establishing privileged relations with Europe within the framework of European regional integration. Enjoying a compatability with European culture, economy, and institutions to which other Spanish regions cannot hope to aspire, the Catalonians see themselves as the bridge that would link Spain to the European mainland.[18] By virtue of this position, links with the Third World, especially Latin America, offer the promise of a triangular trade relationship, recalling Barcelona's role as a major center of Mediterranean trade and exploration during the 14th and 15th Centuries. The 1992 Olympic Games in Barcelona are the spearhead for Barcelona and Catalonia's *relanzamiento* as a center of Mediterranean civilization. Beyond the chauvinistic aspects of such aspirations is the reality of Catalonian potential: the region remains the most advanced and politically mobilized autonomy within Spain. Barcelona has been and will be a cultural lighthouse for Latin America; in literature and art, it is the Iberoamerican crossroads.

The strong leadership of Jordi Pujol, the president of the *Generalitat*, or Catalonian autonomous government, is key to the success of the region in establishing itself as the cultural, commercial, and political bridge between Latin America and Europe. Most of Pujol's energies have been directed toward Europe, where Catalonia has cultivated multilevel ties.[19] The Catalonians see in the concept of the "Europe of regions" an opportunity to break out of the confines of the nation-state where they have never been comfortable. There is reason to believe that once European ties are secure, especially those with other European "regions" trapped within the borders of nation-states, and Catalonian integration with Europe is an economic, social, and political reality, Pujol will turn toward other parts of the world, especially Latin America. Madrid has much to fear as Barcelona positions itself to become the *puente* that all Spain has aspired to. Already Catalonian scholars and writers have dominated the research and professional activity of Spain's relations with Central America.

The Basque Country's "foreign policy" obeys similar national concerns, but it is orientated toward addressing the more immediate needs of the sizable Basque community in South America. Official visits by the *lehendakari*, the president of the Basque autonomous government, are usually organized around the vast colonies of Basques in places like Buenos Aires, Montevideo, and the 180 or so outposts of Basque cultural centers throughout 15 Latin American countries. Trade ties are cultivated, as is the Basque language and culture. While the Basque government does not have the same pretentions of leadership as other regional governments, the effort in Latin

America is equally serious. As part of its war against political dominance by Madrid, Basque parties of the right and of the left invest in the promotion of Basque culture and language, drawing international support for nationalist aspirations.

In Seville, the Andalusian government, or *Junta*, absorbed in the 1992 Expo, has pretentions of establishing a Latin American "presence" that would be commensurate with the region's historical role in the discovery and colonization of the New World. According to the former *Junta* president José Rodríguez de la Borbolla, "the possibilities of influence, incidence, and presence" in Latin America "are important."[20] A number of technical and educational programs have been approved for the region, but most Andalusian resources are being put into the effort to make the 1992 celebrations an event of global importance. The difficulties that Seville has encountered in preparing for the Expo are typical of most large Spanish public works projects. Yet so much political energy is being invested in the program that it is difficult to believe that the problems of infrastructure, communications, and local cooperation would not somehow be resolved.

The lofty rhetoric used to refer to the event is at times disturbing. There seems to be little sense of proportion, as if—again—the audience were not the Latin American nations, but Spanish citizens and *sevillanos*. Latin America, it seemed, had become a facet of domestic Spanish politics; divorced from its own context, it took on strictly Spanish national dimensions. If "the future begins in 1992," as Luis Yáñez suggests,[21] then Spanish foreign policy would have to do something in the meantime to cultivate the infinite patience necessary for those Latin Americans—and Spaniards—who demand that the future begin immediately.

Desperately Seeking Social Democracy: The Conduct of Spanish Foreign Policy in Central America

> Spain is an unconditional ally of no one in Central America, but everyone in Central America accepts Spain as a friend.
> —*Francisco Fernández Ordóñez*[1]

The climate of confidence and optimism generated by the signing in June 1985 of the Treaty of Adhesion of Spain and Portugal to the EEC afforded Felipe González the opportunity to change the face of Spanish foreign policy. A day after the signing of the treaty in Lisbon and Madrid, González announced a change in his cabinet that would replace Foreign Minister Morán, who was largely responsible for the breakthrough with the French on the European front. Morán believed that Spain was already *"en su sitio"* (in its rightful place), but it was evident that González was determined to take Spain further into Western political and security institutions than Morán's convictions would allow. The Spanish economy, moreover, was in deep crisis because the difficult process of *reconversión* (restructuring) of inefficient state-owned and private industries was wreaking havoc on working people. For the prime minister, Spain would have to bury its problems in Europe and minimize the risk-taking in foreign policy ventures lest his government not survive the next elections.

The replacement of Foreign Minister Fernándo Morán by the social democrat Francisco Fernández Ordóñez would change the face of Spanish foreign policy towards the rest of the world, but the government of Felipe González was concerned with the internal structure of the foreign ministry itself. The internal "modernization" plan was consistent with a generalized effort throughout the government bureaucracy, where years of Francoist petrifi-

cation had produced an inertia that was complicating all attempts to improve
and streamline public administration. The Spanish foreign service, in particular, had always suffered from an elitist reputation that was exacerbated
by the cronyism of the Francoist ruling social groups.[2]

For many years the foreign affairs portfolio was a concession to the Opus
Dei, a mafia-like politico-religious group with fascist overtones. Into the
foreign service were sent the prodigal sons of the Spanish ruling class. In
Latin America, the Spanish embassies had earned the reputation of being
exile colonies for Spanish domestic embarrassments: alcoholics, *vivedores*
(playboys), and sodomists.[3] High ranking secretaries and ambassadors were
chosen for their loyalty to Francoism or for the proximity of their family to
the centers of power in Madrid. In Latin America and especially in the
remote, isolated, and poorly endowed embassies of Central America and the
Caribbean, Spanish diplomats suffered from a reputation that would be difficult to improve simply by a policy change.

Fernándo Morán had been appointed more for his vision of Spanish foreign
affairs than for his administrative and management abilities. His energies
were not directed inwardly, in spite of his desire for "congruence" between
the internal and external Spanish projects. Morán inherited a foreign ministry
that was essentially Francoist; petrified and immobile, it would not easily
adapt to change. From the onset, the foreign minister demonstrated a propensity to bypass the bureaucratic mechanics of foreign policy. Some profound changes were made at the highest levels to add a degree of
professionalism where it was indispensable. But Morán left the foreign ministry essentially as he had found it; responsibility for leadership in foreign
affairs remained at the top of the official pyramid. According to ministry
sources, there was a "divergence" between the image of a democratic and
modern Spain and that of a deteriorating diplomacy at the embassy level.[4]

The appointment of Francisco Fernández Ordóñez was thus part of a wider
strategy to achieve what Morán, ironically enough, had been calling for:
ideological and administrative consistency between internal and external
political projects. A former Minister of Justice under the last Suárez government, Ordóñez was best known for his work in promulgating Spain's first
divorce statute, which was approved by the Cortes in 1981. His ability to
withstand extreme pressure from the still powerful Catholic Church and
conservative groups and push through what became a moderate divorce
statute by Western standards recommended him well for the equally controversial foreign affairs portfolio. His reputation as a pragmatic but firm
arbiter of competing ideologies and interests preceded him. His calm, pen-
sive demeanor would take the heat off the controversial Socialist policy
agenda.[5] Although effected in a climate of crisis, the appointment of Fernández Ordóñez was not designed for damage control. The choice of "Paco"
Fernández Ordóñez was a deliberate attempt to reinforce the internal and
external projects of modernization.

For that modernization would be not a generic process devoid of political content. Spain would have to be modernized in a political framework, with policy positions reflecting ideological propensities. If some orientation were not given to policy, other political actors would certainly ascribe political positions according to their own perceptions, whether or not these positions actually corresponded to Socialist intentions.

The evidence was overwhelming that the Socialists' orientation toward the modernization process was already being identified with conservative political positions. The austerity and tight-money programs imposed by the Socialists to combat high inflation, the reconversion of Spanish industry to restore competitiveness and reduce output, and the astounding privatization programs of state-owned companies all constituted a political program that answered more to business and banking interests than to those of the working class. Spain was being modernized within a liberal economic framework that had more to do with *Thatcherism* and *Reaganomics* than with socialism.[6]

To the dismay of Fernándo Morán and other party members who still harbored dreams of European socialism, the Spanish "internal project" was moving toward the right. In the most profoundly ironic way, Morán's own prophecy would be fulfilled: there would be congruence between the "internal" and "external" projects, but that congruence would reflect increasingly conservative positions. At best, Felipe González and his executive cabinet would be able to sell the policy package to the Spanish people—who in their voting habits tend to reflect left-wing or center-left positions—as "social democracy." But even Socialist party members were complaining that, if indeed it were social democracy, the policies were those of right-wing social democrats.

In Spanish Central American diplomacy only one major adjustment had to be made. Under Morán, Spanish support for Latin American "liberation movements" had been somewhat unqualified. Spanish policy in Central America had attempted to position Spain in such a way as to be "an unconditional ally" to no particular party but as a "friend" to "almost all."[7] While not directly supporting Cuban or Soviet interests, or those of hard-line Marxist-Leninist guerrilla groups, Spain had nevertheless identified itself with the revolutionary movement. Under Spanish democracy, relations between Central America and Spain had "expanded to the left of the political spectrum." For Morán, "the legitimization of Spanish socialism" in Europe would serve as "a catalyst for the Latin American left's opening to more western-style definitions."[8]

But just as Spanish diplomacy after Franco needed to move great lengths to arrive at the left of the political spectrum, Central American ultra-leftists had a distance to travel before they could position themselves anywhere near the center. It could be said that U.S. policy had helped provoke a radicalization of leftist groups in Central America. The reality in 1984 was that the Salvadoran guerrillas were under the command of a radical ultraleftist; the

Guatemalan guerrilla movement had been severed almost completely from democratic groups operating in the country; and the Sandinista regime was firmly under Cuban tutelage in the military and security spheres. That Washington's policy was facilitating the process of radicalization is beyond dispute; nevertheless, many of these groups had shown their disposition towards extreme positions even before the Reagan Administration. Soviet policy was also mired in the internal between the revolutionary forces; research has shown that the choices were not always for Moscow to make.[9] Soviet policy, content with sapping U.S. political and strategic resources in the area, emerged as a moderating force in the revolutionary context. In any case, it could be said that Washington's policy had been a constant. Radicalization of the revolutionary movement predated the Reagan Administration's hardline policy in Central America.[10]

The attempt to avoid the perception that Spanish policy was "unconditional" was not successful by Washington's standards. To Washington, such unqualified support of the revolutionary movement was tantamount to support of a communist takeover on the Central American isthmus. Fortunately, Spanish policy enjoyed the security of vagueness and ambiguity, which kept it from being accused directly by Washington and U.S.-aligned Central American regimes of complicity in the international communist plot to subvert Central America. The high-level Sandinista defector, Roger Miranda, later confirmed that Spain had refused to discuss the issue of arms sales to the Sandinistas during negotiations for a trade deal in 1983.[11] Still, the pressure to qualify Spanish support for the revolutionary movement was palpable. Spain would have to make clear its position regarding possible outcomes in the Central American conflict. Eventually Spanish policy would find it politically imperative to suggest that Marxist-Leninist dictatorships were not the desired outcome and that the revolutionary movement be channeled into a pluralistic democratic project.

The risks involved in such a change in policy orientation were evident. Relations with the Sandinista regime, the Marxist-led Salvadoran and Guatemalan revolutionary movement, and with the Castro regime in Cuba would inevitably be strained. In Spain, these forces were looking for a capable European interlocutor, which by its own democratic credentials would lend credibility to the Marxist-Leninist revolutionary programs. To fill this role, Spain was forced to compete with Socialist France, whose aid programs and diplomatic resources were considerably greater and whose freedom of maneuver *vis à vis* the United States was much greater. In 1984 there was a growing concern among the Socialist foreign policy establishment that Paris— or even Rome—would eclipse Spain in influence in Latin America. By 1987 the French and Italian investments in Latin America would pay off: Spanish diplomacy began to respond directly to the efforts of its European rivals instead of to the Latin American stimuli themselves.[12] To be sure, in 1984 Vice President Alfonso Guerra pledged that "Spain cannot permit anybody to snatch away its role in Iberoamerica."[13] But that protagonism would have to be reoriented if it were to secure Spanish interests elsewhere, in more important international spheres.

It became evident by 1984–85 that Spain, whose interests were more and more Western and Atlanticist and whose vulnerabilities *vis à vis* the United States were more apparent, could no longer afford unqualified support for revolutionary movements that ran counter to Western political values and interests. Spain's right to differ with Washington over the roots of the crisis in Central America would not be relinquished by the simple qualification of its support to the revolutionary movement. Morán was aware of such limitations but strained at the margin of them. Sending mine-sweepers to Nicaraguan coasts during the CIA-sponsored mining in March-April 1984 was an example of these limits. France could afford to make the offer in the face of U.S. opprobrium; the price Paris had to pay was remitted during the 1960s when French nationalism clashed with U.S. global leadership. But even for Morán, such a move "marks the limits of solidarity beyond which no Spaniard would want to overstep."[14]

Such realism at the margin was not enough for the United States, however. Washington made it perfectly clear in 1984 that any support for the Nicaraguan regime was accommodation and appeasement to the Soviet and Cuban project in the Americas. Spanish policy was forced to clearly demarcate the limits of its confrontation with the United States. This meant that it would have to focus on outcomes that were satisfactory to Washington and at the same time preserving Spanish credibility as an autonomous actor.

For many in the revolutionary movement in Central America, little more could be expected from a lesser power. Many on the extreme left concluded, moreover, that even the qualified support was significant insofar as any triumph for the revolutionary movement as a whole in Central America would be a Trojan horse for communist hegemony. Washington's policy was based on this premise; thus its acceptance of the "new" Spanish policy was reluctant at best.[15]

Yet Spanish policy had undergone a subtle but significant shift under Ordóñez. As long as diplomatic activity was focused overtly on facilitating pluralistic, democratic outcomes, it would remain immune to U.S. pressure. Washington could suggest that Spanish policy suffered from naiveté, but it could not accuse Madrid of directly supporting outcomes that were not consistent with Western interests and values.

PROTAGONISTS AND PIVOTS OF THE NEW REALISM

Spanish foreign policy in Central America was centered on the degree of support for the Sandinista regime in Nicaragua and for the Salvadoran revolutionary movement, whose spokesmen in the Frente Democratico Revolucionario (FDR) were considered to represent Social- and Christian Democratic roots in the movement. Prime Minister Felipe González was the key playmaker in Spanish diplomacy; his status as a vice-president of the Socialist International had allowed him access to most Central American government leaders, as well as to many prominent revolutionaries. Spanish policy exploited González's personal ties with the Central American elite until it was clear that Spanish policy would have to build from the embassy level if it were to achieve anything on the ground in the Central American conflict.

Personal Diplomacy

The dependence on the prime minister's persona and international standing were understandable given the resources of the Spanish foreign policy apparatus. Members of the Foreign Ministry complained that González conducted foreign policy on the De Gaulle model: direct responsibility for implementing policy, leaving for the diplomats only the affairs of protocol.[16] The danger of this situation was not lost on the Socialist executive. Foreign policy is an area where successes are rare, and the chances for failure great. Central America, moreover, was a region where even the superpowers were flirting with disaster. As the Socialists confronted severe economic crisis within Spain, there was a need to limit González's exposure to any additional policy failures. Much would be made of Spain's protagonism in Latin America, but responsibilities, spiritual and day-to-day, would be shared.

The creation in 1985 of the post of Secretary of State for International Cooperation as coordinator between the executive, the Foreign Ministry, the ICI, and the Arab Cultural Institute transferred some of the responsibility to an institutional structure. Ordóñez, moreover, took control of day-to-day affairs at the Foreign Ministry and was able to implement, with the strong backing of González, a new organizational development plan. Yet the problem of Spain's diplomatic corps remained: the Socialists would have to wait for Francoists to retire at the mandatory 65-year retirement age, while embarking on a massive training program to fill vacancies. Paradoxically, this led to a lowering of academic standards for new foreign service recruits. Senior-level diplomats rebelled, and Socialist appointees complained that "nobody has dared to make true reforms in the Foreign Ministry."[17] By the end of 1987, the ministry's morale was at its nadir. The Independent Labor Confederation of Functionaries (CSIF), which represents the majority of ministry personnel, opposed the lowering of standards as a threat to the professionalization of the foreign service. A high-ranking ministry official and CSIF member, Carlos de Benavides, pointed out that it was curious that at a time when competitive exams for jobs such as janitors and concierges were getting more and more difficult, the ministry was cutting out almost 50% of its entry exam.[18]

The decidedly *Third World* character of Spanish diplomatic missions abroad would not be addressed until Spain's presidency of the EEC during the first half of 1989. Even then the approximately $50 million facelift was directed for the most part towards European missions and to a lesser extent its representations in the Soviet Union and Eastern Europe. A large part of the money was spent in Madrid at the Santa Cruz palace, where security and communications technology needed an urgent update. Given the limited resources of an austerity budget, the best Spanish diplomacy could hope for, especially in its far flung Latin American missions, was a change of human face.[19]

Spiritual Crusaders

Meanwhile, King Juan Carlos, the titular chief of state, was leading Spain in the spiritual sphere, all the while highlighting the impulses and general tendencies of Spanish *state* policy. His frequent trips to Latin America brought attention to the Spanish democratic project, and his warm and sincere demeanor made him a popular man in the hemisphere. While Juan Carlos and his entourage do not bear gifts of tremendous import, the good will left in his wake should not be undervalued. His willingness to be identified with the causes of democracy and human rights, witnessed most closely by Uruguayans and Argentines in his 1983 and 1978 trips, endeared him to the Latin American masses.

There was, nonetheless, an important and substantive diplomatic component of the King's travels. Without being explicit, the Royal House was in the business of legitimizing those regimes it deemed worthy of democratic credentials. Through his quest to visit every Iberoamerican country, Juan Carlos promised to be consistent with the general proposition of Spanish policy that diplomatic relations would be maintained with all Spain's former colonial domains. The King's promise to visit every Latin American country was almost fulfilled: by 1985 only Paraguay, Cuba, Chile, and Nicaragua remained. The fact that human rights and democracy were in question in those countries may have had something to do with their being absent from the Royal family's agenda. Yet the perception was that these visits were merely postponed; the monarch optimistically predicted that he would make good on his promise to visit Nicaragua and Cuba by the symbolic year, 1992.[20] By the end of 1990, Juan Carlos would bless the democratic transitions in both Paraguay and Chile, and a state visit to post-Sandinista Nicaragua sent a blunt message to the former rulers in April 1991.

Foreign observers tend to minimize the effect that such a figure can have on international relations. It should be remembered that for Spain, too, the weight of history is great. With Juan Carlos as chief of state, Spain has been able to overcome much of its negative imagery in Latin America. It is difficult, if not impossible, to associate such a figure as Juan Carlos with a dark, cruel colonial past. Even Cuban propaganda, which has a propensity to remind the world of colonial barbarism, has not been able to taint the image of the King with images of past brutality and exploitation.

Yet even Juan Carlos could not escape the burden of history. On a January 1990 state visit to Mexico, the royal couple was met with a typically schizophrenic reception. While there was warmth for the Spanish monarch, especially in light of the signing of a five-year, $4 billion trade and credit deal, there was also open hostility towards the symbol of past colonial oppression. Mexican Indian groups organized demonstrations to protest Spain's plans to celebrate in the 1992 V Centenary in Seville the "pillage and genocide of which we were the object 500 years ago." Fueling the hostility was Spain's rapid slide into Europe, a geopolitical fact that had already cost the Mexicans about 50% of their exports to Spain as a result of EEC requirements to relinquish preferencial trade agreements with many Latin American countries.[21]

While the King set the democratic backdrop for Spanish *state* policy—providing for the *continuity* so desperately sought by the realists—, González plunged into the Central American quagmire and became an official observer to whatever diplomatic initiative was in motion. His signature appears on Central American diplomatic documents, and he or his personal representatives were present at the major meetings. His frequent travels to Latin America have cost him dearly in domestic politics, where his presence is sorely needed. On the other hand, his cancellations of scheduled visits to Latin American countries often take on an importance that is far from commensurate with the purpose of the visit. The Prime Minister's decision to cancel his trip to Peru and Cuba in 1985, for example, provoked a notable deterioration in Spanish relations with those countries.

It was to be expected that the Prime Minister would be able to establish firm working relationships with such Central American social democrats as Alberto Monge and Oscar Arias in Costa Rica, but even those relationships proved to be almost as problematic as those with less ideologically compatible leaders. Key to González's success was his uncanny ability to separate his *persona* from some of the more controversial tendencies that had come under Morán's foreign ministry. While rhetoric that was strongly sympathetic to the Sandinista regime in Nicaragua and to the FMLN guerrilla insurgency in El Salvador radiated from the Palacio de Santa Cruz (home of the foreign ministry) during the first few years of the Socialist government, González's pronouncements and behavior were much less provocative. He shared his ministry's critique of U.S. policy and had open sympathies for the Nicaraguan revolution, but his pronouncements were much less ideological, his behavior less strident and extremely pragmatic.

Creeping Realism

The rhetoric was of concern to the United States and its allies in Central America, yet Spanish behavior did not reflect many of the quasi-Marxist positions of Morán and his ministry. In fact, the PSOE's love affair with the Sandinistas ended as far back as early 1983, when the party noted a deviation from the original project of the Nicaraguan Revolution (a veiled reference to the Puntarenas declaration by the Sandinista Group of 12 in 1979), which was understood to be a promise of political pluralism. Much of this debate took place internally, both within the party and within the Cortes, because Spanish policy still could not afford to lose its influence with the Sandinista leadership. In 1983, official contacts with the Nicaraguan opposition were made in Madrid, despite diplomatic notes denying the official nature of contacts with leaders such as Edén Pastora, the former Sandinista *comandante* and then *Contra* leader.

Behind the Smokescreen: The Nicaraguan Pivot

During this time Spain openly supported the Contadora Peace plan, which offered a convenient vehicle for participating in a solution that would keep U.S. policy from being decisive. The Contadora initiative carried with it the implicit acceptance of political conditions within each Central American country. Security guarantees would be given on all sides, but concerns over human rights and repression were regarded as interference in the internal affairs of sovereign countries. Spain probably shared the widespread pessimism over the prospects for success of the initiative,[22] yet González saw a convenient way to maintain Spanish prestige in the region by being an observer to the process. Such an initiative, moreover, would focus the debate not on the thorny internal regime issues where Spain would eventually have to take a stand, but on the more general and mutual aspects of regional security. In this way, clashes with the communist world and with the United States could be avoided.

Spanish policy hinged so much on the Contadora process—wherein González was a formal observer—that the slow pace of the negotiations was often debilitating. While the position was comfortable for Spain insofar as the regional political dynamics were concerned, Spanish policy was nonetheless linked to the prestige of the project itself. When the process broke down completely at the end of 1985, Spain began to criticize all parties involved. The Nicaraguans were urged to come back to the negotiating table, and the U.S. was accused of avoiding direct talks with the Managua regime. The then-director general of the Iberoamerican desk at the Foreign Ministry, Juan Pablo de la Iglesia, advised Managua that it could not "use Contadora as a bargaining chip" to force the U.S., which was outside the process, to stop aiding the *Contra* forces.[23] Spain also blamed the U.S. for maintaining that the dialogue should be between the rebels themselves and the Managua regime. Gradually, Spanish policy was finding its own space in Central American affairs.

Events in Central America, moreover, would make it easier for González to find the distance necessary for a more realistic relationship with Central American revolutionaries. On the eve of a visit to Madrid by the Sandinista Interior Minister Tomás Borge in November 1983, a member of the Basque terrorist organization ETA was detained in San José and accused of complicity in a plot to destabilize the Costa Rican government and to assassinate *Contra* leaders within Costa Rica. Press reports from San José linked the ETA terrorist to the FSLN in Nicaragua, thus opening an intense debate within the Spanish government.[24] Edén Pastora, the Costa Rican-based *Contra* leader—as well as former Sandinista *comandante* and junta member—was reportedly one of the targets; he confirmed the Sandinista political relationship with ETA but stopped short of asserting military ties between the two "revolutionary" organizations.[25]

No official public notes were exchanged by the Madrid and San José governments, but an investigation into the alleged links between the Sandinistas and ETA was opened. Testimony by the Spanish ambassador to Nicaragua suggested that there was an ETA presence in Nicaragua but did not offer evidence that the FSLN was collaborating with ETA militants in international plots.[26] Nevertheless, the testimony served to chill relations between Spain and Nicaragua. Morán himself threatened to "extract all the consequences" if evidence was found.[27]

Neither the Costa Rican government nor the Spanish government could find proof of the FSLN-ETA connection, but Nicaragua's fervent denials were not convincing to many within Spain. ETA was perhaps the most sensitive internal issue in Spanish politics, and any suggestion of official Spanish support for a regime that kept such company could provoke the downfall of the government. A July 5, 1985, NBC report on ETA terrorists camps in Nicaragua provoked yet another round of debate within Spain. Interior Minister José Barrionuevo was called on to repeatedly deny that there was evidence of such Sandinista involvement in ETA activities. Spanish-Nicaraguan cooperation in the economic sphere would nevertheless be affected by the debate.

The burden of proof, moreover, was on the Sandinista regime: their credibility with regard to previous denials of support for the Salvadoran guerrillas in 1980–81 was practically nil.[28] Although there was no evidence of a direct relationship between the leadership of ETA and the FSLN, Managua at this time was certainly the kind of place in which groups of this sort could find a home. Sandinista denials notwithstanding, the mere suggestion of an ETA connection in Nicaragua was enough to chill Spanish diplomacy.

The ETA incident was all but forgotten in a few months, but the idealism that had characterized Morán's original policy towards the Sandinista version of the Nicaraguan Revolution was never recovered. Criticism—implicit and explicit—of U.S. policy would remain, as this was the only way Morán could hold onto political space within the context of the Central American conflict and thus remain competitive with other European actors who were more intrepid in their embrace of the Sandinistas. France was already making deliveries on a small but significant arms deal during 1982–83; in April 1984, the French would offer to sweep Nicaraguan ports of CIA/*Contra* mines.[29]

Even before the replacement of Fernando Morán by Francisco Fernández Ordóñez, Spanish policy was displaying a reluctance to sanction the internal Nicaraguan project. Diplomatic activity would begin to focus on developing relationships with other Nicaraguan parties to the conflict, implicitly recognizing the need for internal changes in the nature of the Nicaraguan regime. The existence at this time of *Contras* that were outside the control of the CIA provided the means by which Spanish policy could maintain its distance from U.S. policy and still secure political space somewhere in the middle of the Central American conflict.

The first clear message that Spanish policy would not support the Sandinista project in its current form was in Spain's decision not to send observers to the 1984 Nicaraguan elections. Prime Minister González himself took up the cause of the participation of opposition leader and former Sandinista junta member Arturo Cruz in the campaign, making it clear that Spanish support for the elections was conditioned on guarantees that Cruz would be able to campaign without official interference. When it was clear that the Sandinistas could not offer such guarantees, González announced in Río de Janeiro that Spanish observers would not be sent.

By 1985, the original theoretical framework for Socialist Party foreign relations had all but disappeared from Spanish diplomacy. To many Socialists, the recognition of the armed opposition to the government of Nicaragua, especially after the 1984 elections, was a violation of the principles of sovereignty and non-intervention upon which Socialist policy was initially conceived. The Spanish were careful to distinguish between the Costa Rica-based rebels under the direction of former Sandinistas Edén Pastora and Alfonso Robelo and those on the Honduran border who had fallen under CIA direction after initial dependence on Argentine advisors. Despite the distinction, Spain was still legitimizing an armed force bent on overthrowing a government that Spain recognized. Spanish policy now saw itself as a mediator in Nicaraguan internal affairs.

As difficult as this new role may have seemed in an increasingly polarized climate, it was a convenient position for Spanish policy. As a mediator that would bring all parties to the conflict together in political solutions, Spain was distancing itself from military solutions to the crisis. The concerns of U.S. policy would be addressed, at least obliquely, by Spain's focus on the goal of "democratization" in Nicaragua. Implicit in this effort was the recognition that Nicaragua was not satisfying Western criteria as to what constitutes a democratic system. Revolutionary concerns, on the other hand, were addressed by Spain's reluctance to support U.S. funding of *Contra* rebels in the north.

Material aid from Spain to the Sandinista regime during the Contadora time-frame reflected realistic concerns in Madrid over the degree of confidence that the Managua regime merited. Apart from humanitarian donations of food and medicine, and the dispatch of dozens of teachers to aid in literacy programs,[30] the Madrid government offered only about $85 million in credits during the first few years of the Nicaraguan Revolution. Madrid attributed its reluctance to continue offering credits and financing to the arrears in Nicaraguan payments to Spanish creditors, who by the end of 1985 were owed 1,100 million pesetas (about $100 million).[31] In 1985, moreover, Nicaraguan transfers out to Madrid were running at a higher pace than Spanish financing to Managua.[32] More revealing, however, is that by 1988, Spain had only provided a total of about $100 million in credits during the more than eight years of Sandinista rule.[33] The Nicaraguan debt to Spain reached about 120 million unpayable dollars.[34]

The Sandinistas recognized that Spain itself had been a net aid recipient country until the mid–1970s, yet they could not have seen the meager sums from Spain as anything more than a deliberate political message in the light of such things as billion-dollar Spanish arms deals with the U.S. government and aircraft industry.[35] Reluctant to lose Spanish support on general regional issues, the Sandinista leadership was careful to complain only privately to Spanish officials. Spanish officials, for their part, were in a long-term process of ingratiating themselves with Spanish bankers and investors as a guarantee for continued high economic growth rates. Deputy Prime Minister Alfonso Guerra promised that Spain would not press Managua for repayment of debts, but that "Spanish interests" would be secured.[36]

Spanish policy began to bear fruit just as the Contadora initiative reached its nadir. After warning Managua that its decision to abandon Contadora negotiations in December 1985 was an "error," the new Spanish ambassador to Managua, Luis Cuervo y Savregas, confirmed a *New York Times* report that, on instructions from his Prime Minister, he had arranged for the Sandinistas and prominent members of the internal opposition to meet directly under his auspices at the Spanish embassy.[37] The first meetings had been held in September of that year and were continued throughout the fall, bringing together for the first time since the beginning of the Sandinista Revolution members of the Sandinista directorate, the Social Christian Party, and the Independent Liberal Party. In Madrid, the Foreign Ministry and the Socialist executive were enraged by the breaking of the confidentiality of the discussions, claiming that the already moderate hopes for success were further jeopardized by all the publicity.[38]

In explaining why the United States had not been informed of the Spanish initiative, the Foreign Ministry repeated its view that the success of the negotiations depended on their confidentiality. In a gesture that represented the strongest support for the U.S. position in Central America, the Spanish ambassador professed to be "acting as loyal allies" of the United States.[39] The then-Assistant Secretary of State for Inter-American Affairs, Thomas

Enders, who would later become U.S. Ambassador to Spain, responded in kind: "Whatever process that could lead to an international dialogue in which all Nicaraguans take part can be useful."[40]

For most observers of Spanish policy, the understanding between Washington and Madrid at this time marked the turning point at which the crisis in Central America was no longer a discordant, bilateral issue. In Washington, there could be found the usual irritation that accompanied such European efforts at finding peace in Central America. Yet at the State Department there was also a certain conviction that Spain had seen the threat inherent in the Sandinista regime. The Spanish initiative in Nicaragua was welcome insofar as it implicitly recognized the need for change in the nature of the Nicaraguan regime. Washington was thus able to find a way to shrug off the accusations on the part of Spanish diplomats that the U.S. had leaked the news of the negotiations to the *New York Times* after finding out from the opposition parties.[41]

While enjoying the prestige that publicity over the Spanish embassy talks afforded, Spain nevertheless denied that it was acting as a "mediator" in Central America. The initiative was not a result of "disillusionment" with the Contadora process.[42] Foreign Minister Fernández Ordóñez insisted that the talks were not "an alternative" to Contadora and that Spain was only seeking the "presence that was commensurate" with the Spanish role in Latin America.[43]

The Spanish role was welcomed by the *Contra* coordinating directorate Unidad Nicaraguense Opositora (UNO). Alfonso Robelo, Adolfo Calero, and Arturo Cruz signed a letter to Fernández Ordóñez thanking him for the "good offices."[44] The *Contra* leaders added that "in addressing you, we do it inspired by the example that Spain has given the world with its own process of invigorating democracy." However, Robelo noted that the initiative was incomplete "since there are still opposition forces in exile that should be taken into account"—a reference to the more than 15,000 *Contra* rebels on Nicaragua's borders. They asked the foreign minister to put forth the idea of national reconciliation during his January 1986 visit to Managua.[45]

Spain's prestige, nevertheless, was not uniform across the Central American isthmus. Public opinion in Costa Rica was highly critical of what was seen as Spanish accommodation of the Sandinista military buildup. Costa Ricans were looking for a harsh condemnation of Managua from Spanish diplomacy. A meeting between Fernández Ordóñez and then Costa Rican foreign minister Carlos José Gutiérrez in January 1986 revealed some clear differences in perspectives over the Nicaraguan problem. Without an army, Costa Rica was seeking security guarantees from the regional peace process. The Costa Rican government and public opinion believed that Spain's focus on internal Nicaraguan affairs would not address those concerns in the short term.[46]

The Costa Rican view was confirmed over the course of the following eighteen months as the Spanish initiatives in Nicaragua faded to the background of Central American affairs. As Central American leaders, led by Costa Rican President Oscar Arias moved outside the Contadora context and into regional and bilateral negotiations, Spanish policy struggled to find a role in Central America. When the Central American leaders shocked the world with the announcement that a peace plan had been signed in Esquipulas, Guatemala in August 1987, Spanish policy moved back into Central America. This time Spain would act as the conscience of the Esquipulas accords, lending support and pressure on the signatories to abide by the terms of the agreement.

By this time, Spain was firmly within NATO, having approved by referendum *permanencia*, with some conditions, the Atlantic Alliance. The Socialists took advantage of the victory of their NATO policy by calling for early general elections in 1986. They returned to power with another absolute majority in the Cortes—which was tantamount to a blank check for foreign policy. Spanish integration into the EEC customs union began in January 1986, and the government survived a brief backlash from the imposition of value-added taxes and other Community regulations. By the end of 1986, Spain had emerged on the world scene as a major Western player, whose European and Atlantic perspective had been ratified twice at the polls.

The pragmatism of Felipe González instructed him that for European and Atlanticist Spain, Central America was not worth damaging bilateral relations with the United States. Pending were referendum-mandated cutbacks in the U.S. military presence in Spain, a thorny enough issue within the NATO alliance and the bilateral relationship. Both sides were best served by keeping the focus within the European context, as global interests would only complicate the problems further.

The PSOE, nevertheless, was concerned with the image of a conservative, pro-American foreign policy that would ultimately alienate important Third World actors. Many critics saw Spanish foreign policy as "dependent" on the United States, and the still vocal left-wing in Spain echoed these concerns in scathing parliamentary attacks, peace marches, and private initiatives.[47] Spanish policy was risking a disequilibrium within its own constituencies by pursuing a course that was identified with U.S. policy. The Movimiento por la Paz, a broad-based national organization of Church, women's, socialist, communist, and union groups, has kept steady pressure on the González government to keep its *compromiso* with Nicaragua.[48]

The Esquipulas accords provided an adequate vehicle for Spanish policy to reenter the peace process and reassert its relationship with Nicaragua. Madrid was aware that Washington did not welcome the Central American peace plan; yet almost universal international support for it shielded Spanish policy from direct conflict with the U.S. Spain could not be singled out as long as the regional peace plan was the vehicle of Spanish intervention. The engineers of the peace plan were the Central American leaders, not Felipe

González and the Spanish Foreign Ministry. Although the political space that Spain sought was not necessarily neutral from Washington's point of view, any critique of the Spanish role in observing the accords would have seemed mean-spirited and thus would not have helped the Reagan Administration's position.

In a "eminently political" initiative, then deputy prime minister Alfonso Guerra was dispatched to Central America in November 1987 to secure the political space that Spanish policy had cleared in the context of the Guatemala accords.[49] He thus became the highest-ranking official of the European Economic Community to have visited Sandinista Nicaragua in an official capacity. Not known for his diplomatic skills either at home or in foreign capitals, Guerra went well beyond the parameters of González's policy in Central America. The Sandinistas, aware that Guerra's personal convictions had more to do with the left wing of his party than with the González-Ordóñez line, were able to turn the visit into a major public relations coup. Guerra affirmed that "the greatest effort amongst the Central American countries has been the effort of Nicaragua, which has gone forward at perhaps a faster pace than other countries have gone, and has even entered into a process that the Guatemalan Accords did not contemplate."[50] He avoided references to Managua's refusal at the time to negotiate directly with the *Contras* and the denial of entry to the country for *Contra* leaders, saying that "I don't want to give Nicaragua lessons. I came here to be informed, not to give lessons."[51]

The Sandinistas used the Guerra visit as proof of lasting "solidarity" between European socialism and the Sandinista experiment in Nicaragua. The Sandinista Vice-President Sergio Ramírez declared that the visit in itself was the "greatest gesture of solidarity."[52] Only a few months before, however, the Sandinistas were expressing disillusionment with European "socialism," complaining that Bayardo Arce, the Sandinista *comandante* and leading revolutionary ideologue, had been rebuffed at a meeting of European socialist and social democratic parties in Madrid in March 1987. Apparently, the Europeans were sensitive about the possibility of damaging vital ties to Washington and were frustrated by Sandinista inflexibility regarding democratic reforms inside Nicaragua. The Sandinista foreign minister, Miguel d'Escoto, was forced to intervene in Bonn when the Sandinista ambassador to West Germany published scathing articles that referred to the Madrid rebuff of Arce. The ambassador, Heberto Incer Moraga, was replaced in July 1987, after D'Escoto declared that the ambassador's views "do not correspond with the policy of the Revolution."[53]

The "policy of the Revolution," of course, was to maintain as much support as possible from Europe in spite of the widening ideological gulf. Such support, as lukewarm as it might have been, was in the Sandinista view the margin of survival for the regime. Without European intervention, there would be no buffer to U.S. power in the region because most Central American nations had moved closer to Washington's position by 1987. The

Esquipúlas II accords returned the momentum to Central American leaders in August of that year, but there was a sensitivity to Washington's concerns among all of the signatories except Nicaragua. Managua embraced Guerra in a way that revealed Sandinista vulnerability. They treated the visit as if he were a chief of state.

Ideologically, Spanish policy was in a difficult position. Some members of the *Contras* who were in exile in Costa Rica were closer ideologically to the PSOE than were the Sandinistas. Afredo César, for example, had participated as an observer at important Socialist International meetings. The *Contras* had solicited, through their mediator Cardinal Miguel Obando y Bravo, a meeting with Guerra in Costa Rica during Guerra's Central American stay. Guerra managed to meet privately with the by then retired leader Edén Pastora in San José; but the Spanish dignitary missed the opportunity to participate, or even mediate in the first indirect negotiations that began in Managua between the *Contras*, the Sandinistas, and Cardinal Obando y Bravo. Those negotiations were facilitated in great part by another European socialist, the West German Social Democrat Hans Joergen Wischnewski.

Spanish policy cleverly sought shelter from the U.S. Administration's reaction by having Guerra appear at an official dinner with the Costa Rican president Oscar Arias and a delegation of U.S. congressmen led by then house majority leader, Jim Wright. Again, Spain found refuge from U.S. opprobrium by identifying Spanish policy with that of a major legitimizing source: the U.S. Congress.

Alfonso Guerra left Central America with his support for Nicaraguan progress intact, but he could not hide the disarray in which the Spanish foreign policy establishment found itself at the end of 1987. Serious divisions in the Latin American policy teams were beginning to cause morale problems at the Foreign Ministry. Much of it was bureaucratic infighting of the sort found in most industrial democracies. But there was an ideological flavor to some of the squabbles. The former director of the Latin American desk at the Foreign Ministry, Juan Pablo de la Iglesias, had been replaced two months earlier in a move that was widely interpreted as a rebuff to the ICI, where de la Iglesias played a significant role. The Foreign Ministry was reasserting its primary role in Spanish foreign policy, citing "interference, meddling, and distrust" on the part of the Secretariat of International Cooperation, the ICI's *de facto* cabinet level agency.[54] It was no secret in Madrid that the ICI was promoting an activist role for Spanish policy, one that committed itself more strongly to development and the struggle for democracy. The Foreign Ministry at this time confessed a "certain vacillation" in Spanish policy despite Guerra's recent protagonism.[55] The ministry sought to postpone Felipe González's upcoming visit to Central America, which was projected for the end of 1987 or the beginning of 1988. With the Latin American directorate in disarray from the ouster of de la Iglesia, Spanish foreign policy was in no condition to take on new initiatives in Latin America.

The Sandinistas, nevertheless, could not afford to let their own internal divisions jeopardize European support for their struggle to stop U.S. funding of the *Contra* rebels. In March 1988, on the spur of the moment, Daniel Ortega, the Nicaraguan president and moderate leader of the FSLN directorate, embarked on a diplomatic tour of Europe in an effort to secure political and economic support for Nicaragua. His hastily arranged first stop was Madrid, where he stayed for two days on what Spanish officials called a "working visit." The most significant event of his trip was a photo opportunity with King Juan Carlos and Queen Sofia; the photo, published in newspapers across the world, was outdone only by the film clips and photos of Ortega in the Vatican the next day with the Pope.[56]

Ortega's access to such important international figures and his success in securing economic aid for Nicaragua was viewed as a result of European recognition of the fact that Nicaragua was moving faster than any other country in implementing the Guatemala Accords. European diplomats, moreover, felt that Ortega's position was vulnerable with respect to hard-line Sandinista *comandantes*. Some *comandantes* were already threatening that the FSLN would never give up power even if it meant violating the Guatemala Accords. Europeans saw Ortega as the only link to the success of Guatemala Accords; thus the success of his European trip could not remain ambiguous in the eyes of his Sandinista colleagues.[57]

With Spanish policy more in line with that of the European Community with respect to the Guatemalan peace process and Nicaraguan progress, Spanish diplomacy was emboldened. Washington's irritation with the Spanish role in Central America would have to be applied to practically all European countries and to the EEC itself. The Reagan Administration, in any case, had its hands full with Congress, which defeated the *Contra* aid bill a day after Ortega returned from his European tour. Spain called the decision in the U.S. Congress "positive," while a spokeswoman for the ruling Socialist Party expressed her party's "great satisfaction" with the results of the congressional vote. The German Social Democratic leader Hans Jochen Vogel suggested that the European call for the aid cut-off was decisive in the voting.[58]

A private visit to the United States in May 1988 by Felipe González brought attention back to the role of Spain in the Central American crisis. The visit came at a time when González's presence was desperately needed in Spain to confront a government crisis over scandals in the Ministry of the Interior, its economic policies, and its hard-line position toward an increasingly bitter nation-wide teachers strike. Ironically, the response from a Washington diplomat when asked about "Marco Polo González Márquez" was revealing: "Felipe González tends to believe that all the solutions to all the problems of the world pass through him."[59] The millions of Spaniards who were demanding a new cabinet might have suggested that the prime minister was concerned only with solutions to problems in countries other than Spain.

The Sandinista crackdown in July 1988, which destroyed prospects for the fulfillment of the Guatemalan promise of peace, was received in Madrid without comment. The breakdown in the Esquipulas process was a blow to Spanish policy because there was no other framework within which Spain could show its support for democratization in Central America. As an unofficial observer of the Guatemala accords, Spanish policy could not be perceived as supporting the crackdown on the internal opposition. Nor could Spain make any gesture of support for the expulsion of the United States ambassador in Managua, despite strong evidence that the diplomat was indeed meddling in the affairs of a sovereign state. At the same time, however, Spain did not want to blandish the Sandinistas to such an extent that there would be no way to influence an increasingly radicalized regime. Spain feared losing the little leverage it had over the Sandinistas as much as it feared a Washington reaction that, this time, would go beyond the usual irritation.

The August 1988 inauguration of the new Ecuadoran president, the Social Democrat Rodrigo Borja, provided Spain with an opportunity to express its view of the reasons behind the breakdown of the Guatemala peace process. Again, the task was assigned to Alfonso Guerra, who took advantage of the generally anti-American atmosphere in Quito to criticize the United States for the failure of the Sandinista-*Contra* talks. There was no mention of the Sandinista crackdown and its repercussions in the context of the Esquipulas accords, perhaps in deference to the warm welcome that Daniel Ortega received in Quito as Borja officially reestablished diplomatic relations with Nicaragua, broken off by ex-president León Febres Cordero in October 1985. U.S. policy was perhaps even more concerned with the reception that Fidel Castro received at the reunion of Latin American leaders. Castro became a self-appointed master of ceremonies, embracing Latin leaders and appearing in newspaper photos across the Americas.[60]

The only Latin leader with the courage to criticize the Sandinista crackdown was Costa Rican president and Nobel laureate Oscar Arias. However, to Washington's dismay, he also criticized the U.S. administration for its focus on military aid to the Nicaraguan rebels. Guerra's criticisms were thus lost in the symphony of leftist rhetoric in Quito, as Castro and Ortega clearly stole the show. U.S. Secretary of State George Shultz encountered a hostile climate in which Spanish policy was but one voice in a crowd.[61]

Perhaps more interesting was Guerra's general comments about the United States and Latin America relations. When asked about the feasibility of gaining influence without friction with Washington, Guerra displayed rare diplomatic skill:

The problem is that for a long time the United States has considered that a sector of the [American] continent was its backyard. That is changing, because the people do not accept it, although the U.S. at times . . . [shows] its incomprehension of social realities. A country like Spain does not have these problems. We are a country that is a friend of many countries, and one of them is the United States.[62]

If Guerra still left some suspicion among U.S. policy-makers about Spain's motives and objectives, then Felipe González was sure to tidy up after his deputy and *alter ego*. At the February 1989 inauguration of President Carlos Andrés Pérez in Caracas, González, who headed the international dignitaries who were defending against a prancing Fidel Castro, made it clear in private conversations with Daniel Ortega that the EEC could act on aid only when the Sandinista regime took concrete steps toward peace and democratization. The Spanish leader, acting as president of the EEC during the first six months of 1989, was no doubt referring to the Sandinista crackdown on domestic opposition and the expulsion of U.S. diplomats the previous summer. The Sandinista crackdown had been a major setback in the peace process, especially with respect to the *Contras*, whose demobilization now seemed increasingly remote.[63]

In the view of many Central American leaders, the European attitude, as expressed by Felipe González, had definitively solidified around the proposition that the nature of the Nicaraguan regime was what fueled the regional crisis. Then President José Asconas of Honduras concluded that the international pressure had "detained the totalitarian process" in Nicaragua, and he politely suggested that Ortega's request for $40 million from Spain during his April 1989 trip be tabled until there was further proof of Sandinista progress in reestablishing democratic pluralism in Nicaragua.[64]

The multilateralism that was forced upon González by virtue of the Spanish presidency of the EEC marked the beginning of a shift in Spain's Central American protagonism. The EEC was a logical vehicle since Spain had wrested the Latin American portfolio away from the French shortly after Spanish integration in the Community in 1986. But the vagaries of Central American politics were such that even a powerful regional organization could not control events, as the Sandinista crackdown in the summer of 1988 had proven. Spanish diplomacy could not afford the responsibility for such failures. In the Moncloa it was not forgotten that in the months preceding the Sandinista crackdown, Spanish diplomats and the deputy prime minister had been praising the Sandinistas for going beyond their responsibilities under the Esquipulas II accords. The announcement in October 1989 that the Sandinistas would end the unilateral truce in effect since March 1988 only confirmed the need to share protagonism and responsibility.

As early as December 1988 the UN Secretary General Javier Pérez de Cuellar asked Spain to join Canada and the FRG in a Central American border observer force that would monitor arms transfers, refugee flows, and armed confrontations. All parties, including the Spanish, gave positive responses but made it clear that they were not disposed to sending peace-keeping troops to such a volatile area.[65] But when in November 1989 the

UN Security Council unanimously approved the creation of the United Nations Organization, Central America (UNOCA/ONUCA) force to monitor Central American borders for arms transfers to irregular forces and cross-border rebel incursions, there was no way to characterize the mission but as one of peacekeeping. Pérez de Cuellar, however, had already reserved the leadership position among the forces for Spain; in late November the UN ratified the nomination of General Agustín Quesada Gómez as commander of the 260-man UNOCA forces, which were comprised of military representatives from Ireland, Canada, Spain, Colombia, Venezuela, and civilians from the FRG. The Spanish contingent was 50 army officers and three helicopters. Although Spain was already participating in similar, and in many ways larger, peacekeeping missions in Namibia and Angola, the prestige that Spanish leadership afforded in the Central American context was not lost on policy makers in the Moncloa and Santa Cruz.[66]

The multilateral momentum was such that Spain immediately responded positively to the UN request to extend the UNOCA mission to the verification process of *Contra* disarmament after the February 1990 Nicaraguan elections that ended over ten years of Sandinista rule. Up until that point, Spanish participation in the UN-OAS verification commission of the Esquipulas accords was limited to the activities of such Spanish individuals as Fransesc Vendrell, the secretary general's personal representative, who had embarrassed Spain and the UN with his anti-American and anti-rebel remarks in a speech delivered to *Contra* rebel troops in Honduras in October 1989. This time Spain would send an additional 100 officers to help disarm the rebels in designated security zones.[67] The success of the combined efforts of the 800 or so verification observers lent more weight to a previous call on the part of other Central American leaders for an extended mission and a presence of indefinite duration for UN forces in the region. After all, the Salvadoran and Guatemalan civil wars continued, despite some diminution of intensity. In Spain's mind, of course, an extended mission and longer presence for the peacekeepers would be tantamount to a continued Spanish Central American presence sanctioned by the United Nations.[68]

Arm's Length Revolutionary Solidarity in El Salvador

Spain's relations with El Salvador had long been complicated by the fact that Felipe González's closest affinities have been with fellow vice president of the Socialist International, Guillermo Ungo, who before his untimely death in February 1991 became one of the two principal leaders of the Frente Democrático Revolucionario (FDR), the political front group to the Salvadoran insurgency. Thus, when the elections that brought Christian Democrat Napoleon Duarte to the Salvadoran presidency were held in 1984, Spain withdrew its support when the FDR decided that it would not participate.

Two scheduled trips by Duarte were cancelled before he finally visited Madrid in November 1985.

Duarte and his party were clearly bitter about Spain's decision not to send observers to the 1984 elections. The Spanish government had alleged that "their presence would serve to legitimize elections that cannot be controlled."[69] During Duarte's November 1985 visit, Salvadoran diplomats complained of what they felt to be "second-class" treatment of a visiting chief of state. The message to Duarte was that he was responsible for the failure of negotiations with the FMLN guerrillas and the FDR political front. Madrid indirectly accused Duarte of avoiding the reestablishment of a "national dialogue for peace."[70]

The Salvadoran president arrived in Madrid amid reports that the Spanish diplomatic pouch had been used by the FMLN-FDR for communications between the different groups of the rebel alliance. The use of the diplomatic pouch was an "open secret in San Salvador," according to Spanish opposition observers to the 1985 legislative elections, who were informed during their private visit to El Salvador. The Spanish government did not deny the accusations, but officials insisted that the pouch had been used only for "humanitarian reasons" to facilitate communications between Salvadoran refugees and their families.[71]

On a more personal level, Duarte was disturbed by the prevailing perception that Spain had done nothing to facilitate the release of his daughter, Inés Guadalupe, when she was kidnapped and held by the guerrillas for 44 days. The Spanish Foreign Minister Francisco Fernández Ordóñez denied the charges, citing certain initiatives on the part of Spanish diplomacy.[72]

Fortunately for Spanish diplomacy, Duarte himself did not make issue of either the kidnapping, the protocol of his visit, or the use of the diplomatic pouch. The issue of the kidnapping and the Spanish role in getting his daughter released was defused when he thanked the Spanish government for its help; he claimed to possess "no information" concerning the diplomatic pouch; and he blamed himself for the protocol problems, confessing that he had postponed his trip three times. He shrugged off Spanish support for the Salvadoran guerrillas, suggesting that the FDR front was successful in getting other European governments to listen also. Felipe González, he said, had assured him of continued support in his democratic project.[73] The most solid support that Duarte received in Madrid came from King Juan Carlos, who asserted that El Salvador "had given examples of its commitment to peace and reconciliation, in the regional context as well as in the internal context, where it has initiated a path of dialogue to overcome the painful confrontation that divides the Salvadoran people." The King promised Spanish support for Duarte's commitment to peace and reconciliation.[74]

Spanish policy-makers were concerned, nevertheless, that Duarte was not going to avail himself of Madrid's mediation of the Salvadoran conflict. Duarte's trip to Madrid coincided with a stopover by the FDR's leaders,

Guillermo Ungo and Rubén Zamora, who were returning from a European trip. The Spanish Foreign Ministry hoped that Duarte would take advantage of the coincidence to meet with the leaders of the Salvadoran left and make good on his claim to be open to a new round of negotiations. Ungo and Zamora came to Madrid expressly for a possible meeting with Duarte, according to the FDR. But Duarte left Spain a few hours before the FDR leaders arrived; he claimed that he never had received a formal invitation from the FDR.[75]

On the eve of the March 1989 presidential elections, the government of the terminally ill Napoleón Duarte renewed the call for Spanish mediation in the Salvadoran conflict. Fearful of major disruptions in the electoral process, the Salvadoran government asked Madrid to use its influence with the rebels to obtain a cease-fire during the balloting. The guerrillas accepted the mediation of Spanish diplomats in Madrid and Mexico City but flatly rejected Duarte's offer. Nevertheless, Spanish policy, with the help of Socialist International pressure, was able to press Ungo and Rubén Zamora of the FDR rebel political front to pursue their decision to participate in the 1989 presidential elections in a democratic left coalition, Democratic Convergence (Convergencia Democrática, CD), despite the absence of even the most basic security guarantees. International pressure also secured a tenuous but nonetheless important distancing of the FDR from the hard-line positions of the guerrilla alliance leadership, especially around the issue of an election ceasefire. Ungo remitted his gratitude for the Spanish peace efforts and criticized his former allies on the extreme left for playing into the hands of the ARENA rightists.[76]

After the rightist ARENA party's victory in the elections and the extremely poor results of the Democratic Convergence ticket, Madrid, sensing an unbridgeable gulf in Salvadoran politics, remained cautious. Sobered by previous efforts to facilitate negotiations between centrists and leftists, Spain saw the effort to bring together extreme rightists and embittered, militant leftists as a serious risk to its prestige. Spanish policy would defer to regional actors, especially Mexico, Costa Rica, and Venezuela in this difficult enterprise. Implicit in this deferral was a judgment that the talks between the rebel alliance and the Salvadoran rightists were destined to failure. The wisdom of the Spanish decision to defer to regional actors was borne out by the collapse of September 1989 talks in Mexico, an October round in Costa Rica, and the November renewal in Caracas, which took place amid a new rebel offensive on the streets of San Salvador and one week after the savage murder of six Jesuit priests (five of whom were Spanish nationals) at the Central American University (UCA) by members of the Salvadoran security forces.

The wave of domestic and international outrage over the Jesuit killings served to focus Spanish policy on the more traditional concerns of protection of Spanish nationals and their property. Spain's embassy in San Salvador, nevertheless, was active in trying to find a solution to the tense hostage crisis in the San Salvador Sheraton, where 13 U.S. military advisors to the Salvadoran government were trapped in a *Mexican stand-off* with FMLN guerrillas who had taken control of the hotel. Spain had offered its embassy as refuge for the Americans, but the crisis was finally mediated by the Catholic church and the Americans were set free.[77]

Concern for Spanish life and property was nothing new at the time of the Jesuit killings. Spain's patience with the FMLN guerrilla alliance, already worn thin by their extremist positions during the 1989 elections, was further eroded by reports received during the closure of the V San José EEC-Central America summit in February 1989 that two employees of the Spanish embassy in San Salvador (one of whom was a Spanish national) had been robbed, abused, and raped by FMLN guerrillas.[78] Outrage over the Jesuit killings, however, was politically easier to pursue, given the European and Spanish position on the causes of the violence, which put most of the blame on ARENA and the government-linked death squads who acted in the interests of the Salvadoran oligarchy. Spain joined the United States and Great Britain in an investigation, as embassy officials made available air transport for the over 500 Spanish citizens still in El Salvador.[79] Few Spaniards, nevertheless, accepted the offer to leave, despite renewed intensity of the guerrilla offensive and visible signs that the crackdown on relief workers was a systematic plan by the Salvadoran rightists to turn the conflict into a total war against domestic and international foes.[80] The Spanish under-secretary of foreign affairs and number two man in the Foreign Ministry, Inocencio Arias, attended the tense funeral of the slain Jesuits in San Salvador and pressured President Cristiani to open a serious and thorough investigation that would lead to punishment for those responsible.

Previous investigations did not bode well for the Jesuit case. Successive Salvadoran regimes, both military and civilian, were notoriously incapable of guaranteeing independent judicial review, cooperation of official institutions, and protection for witnesses. It was not lost on the members of the international investigation commission that the December 1980 slaughter of American nuns and the March 1980 murder of Archbishop Oscar Arnulfo Romero had gone unpunished. Thus there was little surprise that the U.S.-trained special battalion linked by the Salvadoran president to the murder of the Jesuits and two others would be able to fend off prosecution. Crucial evidence against the battalion commander, Colonel Guillermo Alfredo Benavides Moreno, and seven other officials disappeared along with witnesses; judicial officials accused the government of obstructing the investigation; and the United States Congress threatened a military aid cut-off if progress was not made.[81]

The investigation dragged on throughout all of 1990 amid revelations that previous warnings about the assassinations had been issued to U.S. advisors in San Salvador.[82] Three prominent U.S. jurists were invited by Cristiani to observe the process from inside the Salvadoran Supreme Court, and the renewal of United States military aid, which had been cut in half by the Congress, seemed to be the only motivating factor in the case. Such sluggishness, which would carry the investigation well into 1991, would eventually become a bilateral issue between Spain and the United States. In November 1990, Spain openly criticized the U.S. government for its treatment of witnesses and its inability or unwillingness to speed up the investigation and trial. Spain's ambassador to El Salvador, Francisco Cádiz, was already under pressure from the Spanish and Jesuit communities for not adding his own and EEC influence to the struggle to bring the murderers to justice. Two high-level foreign ministry emissaries, the under secretary Inocencio Arias and the director general for Iberoamerican affairs, Yago Pico de Coaña, promised that Spain would not "sit back with its arms crossed" and that it would pursue the issue with the EEC and the United States if there were no results in four or five months.[83]

The negotiations with the guerrillas, meanwhile, were being managed by the United Nations, which convened the Salvadoran government and the FMLN in Geneva in April 1990. In Geneva there was talk of a UN supervised cease-fire that would possibly involve peacekeeping troops and human rights observers, but intransigence on both sides of the table kept the negotiations moving through cycles of optimism and pessimism, which continued in San José and Mexico City. An agreement on mutual respect for human rights was signed in San José in July 1990, but the dispatch of UN observers was dependent on the establishment of a cease-fire. The off-again, on-again talks were held in an increasingly deteriorating human rights context wherein the Salvadoran rebels were accused by Americas Watch of summary executions of suspected government collaborators, while Amnesty International reported a marked increase in killings by death squads, which took the 1990 death toll well past the previous year's figures.[84]

Hopes were raised in April 1991, when in a UN-sponsored meeting in Mexico City, the Salvadoran government and the FMLN rebel leadership reached an agreement on a package of constitutional amendments that would clear the way for democratic reforms in the armed forces, the judicial system, and the electoral process. The outgoing National Assembly ratified the amendments, but approval from the incoming Assembly was held hostage to an elusive cease-fire accord. Both sides of the struggle expressed optimism at the prospects for peace, but the war in the countryside continued as the Mexico talks dragged on through the summer of 1991. The United States, sensing a deadlock in the talks, and a renewed offensive from the guerrillas, quietly released frozen 1990 military aid to the Salvadoran military.

Spanish policy, nonetheless, remained optimistic. In June 1991, Foreign Minister Ordóñez took the bold step of meeting in Madrid with Joaquín Villalobos, the supreme guerrilla commander, who praised the Spanish intervention in the peace process. While the visit did not go unnoticed in the

U.S. State Department, Spanish policy was operating in a safe, if tenuous, strategic space in Latin American affairs. Earlier in the year, the new Secretary of International Cooperation, Inocencio Arias, had arranged the first official meetings with Miami-based Cuban exile leaders when he received the Democratic Platform, a moderate coalition of anti-Castro politicians and academics. The even-handedness of angering both Castro and the U.S. State Department was a calculated risk; Spanish policy was clearly looking down the road to democratic transitions in El Salvador and Cuba, wherein Spain could position itself as the only potential mediator between ideological poles.

Potential Spanish mediation in El Salvador was embodied by the presence of a Spanish army colonel, Francisco Javier Zorzo Ferrer, at the Mexican negotiating table. Zorzo, a military advisor to the UN secretary general, was further evidence of the influential Spanish presence in the so-called "group of friends of the secretary general," an international committee whose function it is to facilitate the mediation of conflict in Central America. Command of the UNOCA forces remained in the hands of Spanish *hombres buenos* when in May 1991, General Victor Suances Pardo, a member of the Spanish General Staff, relieved General Augustín Quesada, who had successfully overseen the disarming of the *Contra* armies in Nicaragua. Suances Pardo took command of forces whose mandate was extended by the UN Security Council by six months, but whose forces were cut by about 40 percent to some 360 men.

Spain's multi-lateralism was enhanced by the arrival in July 1991 of ONUSAL (United Nations Organization, El Salvador, UNOSAL), a permanent UN observer team in El Salvador, to begin verification of the human rights accord signed by the government and the FMLN in 1990. Again, the military component was headed by a Spanish officer, Colonel Ignacio Balbín Meana, and another four Spanish military officers formed part of a military group of 15. The threats from Salvadoran rightist extremists made the military group's mission strategic in relation to the observer team's 100 other civilian and police members. The upcoming trials of Salvadoran military leaders in the Jesuit case, which were postponed until the Fall of 1991 after new incriminating evidence from U.S. army major Eric Buckland, threatened to complicate a mission that was already hampered by the resurgent violence between the rebels and government troops. The foundering, 15-month long peace talks, which were bogged down by guerrilla reluctance to accept a call by the Central American presidents to lay down their arms as well as government reluctance to begin a purge of the armed forces, had compelled both sides to improve their negotiating position on the battlefield. The best Spain could hope for was that the Spanish presence in the ONUSAL forces would help insure that the trials of Salvadoran military leaders in the Jesuit cases would be conducted under a high degree of international scrutiny.[85]

Spanish policy-makers wisely concluded that securing political space in the Salvadoran context was a risky venture with little chance of success. As representatives of the Socialist International paid homage to the slain Salvadoran social democratic leader, Hector Oquelí, who had been murdered by a death squad in Guatemala in January 1990, there was a realization that little room existed for a European solution to the Salvadoran civil war. Only time, the leverage of the United States on the Cristiani government, and the changing strategic picture that led to guerrilla reassessments of their revolutionary goals, would move the conflict to a stage where United Nations management could be effective.

Treading Lightly in Guatemala

As the Guatemalan insurgency was brought under control toward the mid–1980s, Guatemala moved out of the international focus on events in Central America. Yet the country's geopolitical and economic importance to Central America, as well as the infamous human rights violations committed by its succession of military governments, could not be ignored by Spanish policy. Guatemala was a prime testing ground for democratic transition in Latin America and the world, for its particular strain of authoritarianism was perhaps the most virulent in the world.

Spain had already joined the international criticism of human rights abuses in Guatemala before the Socialists took power. This was a low-risk venture, as even U.S. policy was forced to tread lightly in the face of universal condemnation of the Guatemalan military regime. But the Spanish had a bilateral issue pending with the Guatemalan regime. In 1980, the Spanish Embassy in Guatemala City had been stormed and burned by Guatemalan security forces in an attempt to capture some Guatemalans who had entered the compound as political refugees. When the Socialists took power in 1982, Guatemala was the only Latin American country that did not have diplomatic relations with Spain.

It should be remembered that one of the primary goals of Spanish policy under the Socialists was to maintain friendly relations with all Latin American states, regardless of their political orientation. Fernando Morán had promised that Spain would not "be guided by the kind of pedantry that would disqualify, neither a regime, much less a country, just because it is in a concrete circumstance."[86] The Socialists never attempted to explain how they would resolve the contradiction between their principles of support for democratic outcomes and human rights on the one hand, and on the other, friendly relations with the various and sundry authoritarian regimes that ran the affairs of many Latin American countries.

Following his literary instincts, Morán was looking for a political paradox that would resolve this contradiction. To the realists, however, diplomacy did not afford such a vast supply of nuance that governments would not know how other governments thought about them. Since Spain could not hide behind its policy, it hid behind the fact that in most places its policy was not decisive in the affairs of other states.

Nevertheless, the Socialists moved to restore diplomatic relations with Guatemala. When an agreement was reached with the military government in Guatemala City in September 1984, the move was interpreted more as an an insult to the foreign policy of the Suárez government than as a sincere desire to work constructively with the military authorities in Guatemala.[87] The Socialists were attempting to disqualify all the foreign policy that had come before their election victory in 1982. There would be continuity with traditional Spanish foreign policy only in the broad aspects of national strategy; the operational side—public face—of Socialist foreign policy was directed at creating a perception that the only valid foreign policy for Spain began with the Socialist victory in 1982.

Events in Guatemala would, however, make it easier for the Socialists to bring their policy more in line with realistic national interests. Spanish diplomats and broad public opinion were uncomfortable with the reestablishment of diplomatic relations with a regime that not only violated human rights with impunity but also destroyed the Spanish embassy without apology. The *idealpolitik* of maintaining good relations with all Latin American countries could not endure such acts of barbarism. The decision to renew diplomatic relations with the Guatemalan military regime was popular neither within the Socialist party nor with the general population. Spanish policy was hoping for signs of a democratic transition that would make relations with Guatemala more compatible with both national dignity and stated principles. A combination of U.S. pressure, guerrilla weakness *vis à vis* the military, and economic crisis, brought Guatemala on the road to democracy.

The victory of Christian Democrat Vinicio Cerezo in the Guatemalan elections of December 1985 gave Spanish policy the opportunity it sought. Though Cerezo had been received in Madrid the previous summer without much consideration,[88] Spanish policy did not have many other democratic options in Guatemala. The social democrats who had survived the decades of repression were integrated with the armed insurgency, where Cuban political control was manifest. Edén Pastora had warned Spain of Cuban hegemony in the Guatemalan guerrilla movement when recounting his failed attempt to lead the social democratic guerrilla organization, Organización Revolucionaria del Pueblo en Armas (ORPA), in its strategy to overthrow the Guatemalan regime in 1981–82.

The situation was different from that of El Salvador inasmuch as there was no separation of the political and military fronts of the Guatemalan revolutionary alliance (Unidad Revolucionaria Nacional Guatemalteca, URNG) as there was between the FDR political front and the FMLN guerrilla alliance. Ungo and Zamora exploited this ambiguity within Europe, and they used it within El Salvador to legitimize the FDR's candidacy for the 1989 presidential elections and the 1991 legislative elections. In El Salvador, the left was a force to be reckoned with, whether it was armed or not. In Guatemala, however, the only credible democratic force available was the battered Christian Democratic Party.

Cerezo made Spanish support of Christian Democracy in Guatemala a reasonably painless position. He quickly distinguished himself from his Salvadoran counterpart by distancing himself from U.S. policy and turning to Europe for support. The new Guatemalan president became a faithful ally of Oscar Arias in efforts to find a regional solution to the Central American crisis. Guatemala became host to the negotiations that would eventually result in the signing of Esquipulas II accords in August 1987. Spain refrained from criticizing the slowness of Cerezo's promised social programs and his failure to bring human rights violators to justice, while praising his efforts to find regional solutions to Central American problems. During a failed coup attempt in Guatemala in the spring of 1987, Spain was among the first to voice support for the democratically elected government of Guatemala.

But Spanish prestige demanded a more active role in the Central American context. The urge to mediate the peace process would make itself manifest when it appeared that Spanish policy might be left out of the negotiations. Spain's opportunity came when the Guatemalan guerrilla alliance URNG solicited the mediation of the Spanish government in October 1987. The Guatemalan government and the insurgency were looking for the proper conditions and locale for initiating the "national dialogue" stipulated under the Esquipulas II accords.[89]

Behind closed doors and in the midst of a media blackout, the Guatemalan government and the URNG guerrilla alliance met in Madrid. After little more than two days of discussions, the sessions broke down, along with the media blackout. The Guatemalan foreign minister stated that the talks were "senseless" in light of his government's projected program of amnesty, and the existence of the necessary "conditions for the insurrectionary groups to incorporate themselves in the democratic process, including the opportunity to form their own political party in order to participate in the political life of the country." The guerrilla demands for a demilitarized zone, respect for constitutional guarantees, respect for human rights, and suppression of repressive military activities, "did not make any sense" as all those conditions had already been met.[90]

For its part, Spanish foreign policy had to content itself with the gratitude of President Cerezo, who described the talks as "very positive."[91] As in the Nicaraguan case, Spain had risked little—if anything—to bring the talks off. The image of Felipe González as Central America's *hombre bueno* was bolstered, and Spanish foreign policy was firmly out in front of Europe in the role of observer to the regional peace process.

But Cerezo had already made too many concessions to the military and the right-wing. Direct negotiations with the guerrilla alliance were ruled out for over two years. Only the upcoming January 1991 presidential elections prompted the government to sanction an unofficial commission of political parties (which included the president to be, Jorge Serrano, of the Solidarity Action Movement, MAS) to meet with the URNG in El Escorial, the famous monestary outside Madrid, in June 1990. No cease-fire was arranged, but the Spanish had mediated an agreement, later known as the El Escorial agreement, that promised no guerrilla interference in the voting.

The elections, however, were not without incident. Again, as in the Nicaraguan and Salvadoran cases, the risks inherent in agreements such as the El Escorial accord could outweigh the prestige gained through mediation. The frustration, moreover, was cumulative. With crisis at home requiring the attention of the Prime Minister, things Central American would be better managed by a competent international organization such as the UN, through which Spain could secure international prestige while sharing the risks. By the summer of 1991, three rounds of UN-mediated talks failed to produce an agreement between the newly elected Serrano government and the guerrillas. This time, however, Spanish policy could not be identified directly with the seemingly inevitable failure of peace efforts.

Castro and the Limits of Revolutionary Solidarity

Lurking behind any relationship with Central America was the inevitability of confrontation with Cuban policy in the region. It should be pointed out that, in the complex and sometimes inscrutable historical relationship that Spain has had with Cuba, the state to state aspects of the relationship are probably the more salient features. Even Franco maintained stable—and often good—relations with Castro's Cuba since both parties found it difficult to transcend five hundred years of intimacy. By the 1980s, moreover, Spain had become Cuba's largest Western trading partner, and Spanish investment, especially the relatively massive effort in the tourist sector, was crucial for the Cuban economy.[92]

The Socialists in Spain entered into the relationship with an ideological advantage that previous governments had not enjoyed. Fernando Morán's frequent trips to Cuba were evidence of a compatibility that would facilitate smooth discussion of bilateral issues. The Socialists, moreover, wanted to prove to the Spanish opposition that only a socialist foreign policy could secure Spain's interests. On the bilateral agenda, Spain's most pressing interest was to resolve the issue of indemnification to Spanish citizens for property taken from them after the Cuban Revolution. The satisfactory resolution of this question, which had eluded former Spanish governments, seemed to be proof of an ideological compatibility that would complement the already solid historical relationship. Castro may have been motivated by the promise of trade credits and access to the Spanish and European markets, but this *realpolitik* was no doubt facilitated by Morán's open, if qualified, sympathies for Cuba's revolutionary role in the Caribbean.

The continual crisis in Central America, however, has a history of disturbing even well established bilateral relationships. After all, supreme national interests were at stake in the crisis, and Spain's relationship with the United States was more important to it than the consummation of tenuous ideological affinities with Castro's Cuba.

The first sign that Spain's government had wisely prioritized its foreign relations was its conspicuous delay in condemning the U.S. invasion of Grenada and its reference to the Cuban presence there as a problem. That same year, Felipe González referred to the "imbrication" of Cuba and the Soviet Union in the regional affairs of Central America.[93] The case of Cuba was highlighted as the Prime Minister criticized the military and security assistance that Cuba was giving to parties to the regional conflict. Even Morán, displaying his realism, admitted to Cuba's position on the margin of hemispheric affairs. It was not flattering for the Cuban communists to hear that the Spanish foreign minister believed that Cuba's power was merely a result of the "historic failure" of U.S. policy in the Caribbean.[94]

To add injury to insult, Morán stated that "if the Cuban Revolution has lost prestige in Europe, it is certainly because of its own errors and as a result of its outworn propaganda."[95]

With Fernández Ordóñez at the head of the Spanish foreign ministry, Cuba would not fair any better. A series of diplomatic incidents with grave repercussions sent government to government relations into a tailspin and even managed to threaten the foundations of the historical relationship.

The first incident occurred in December 1985, when a high-level functionary from the Cuban Central Planning junta was assaulted in the streets of Madrid by Cuban embassy officials who attempted to kidnap him. After the attempt was broken up by onlookers and a security guard, the functionary, Manuel Antonio Sánchez Pérez, revealed that he had asked for political asylum in Spain in November when he arrived for a trade exposition. He claimed that he had in his possession secret economic data on the Cuban economy along with information concerning a network of financial dealings that enabled high-level Cuban functionaries—including himself—to take money out of Cuba. Cuba demanded the extradition of Sánchez from Spain, but the Spanish Interior Ministry responded with the expulsion of the four Cuban embassy officials involved in the incident.[96]

The Spanish Foreign Ministry was guarded in its declarations regarding the incident, but the damage to Spanish-Cuban relations could not be hidden. Spain rejected another formal petition of extradition in March 1986, despite the growing Spanish perception that Sánchez was an opportunist attempting to abscond with a large bank account of official Cuban funds transferred from London to a Madrid bank. According to Cuba, the embassy officials assaulted him just as he emerged from a Madrid bank with the money.[97]

These diplomatic incidents took place in an atmosphere already rarified by a profound clash of perceptions. In July 1985, in a reply to an official invitation for Cuba to build a pavilion for the 1992 World Expo and V Centenary of the Discovery of America in Seville, Castro erupted with a scathing critique of the Spanish historical legacy in Latin America:

[October 12] was when one of the most shameful pages in universal history was opened. It was *infamous* and nefarious... It clashes with all the values that we most appreciate... We know what they did, because here they arrived with the sword. They blessed the Conquest with the cross. I respect the cross more than the sword ... I believe that that part of history requires a critique and that the *conquistadores* who today are proud of their forebearers should exercise a bit of self-criticism of the conquests, of colonialism, of themselves.[98]

The remarks, of course, provoked a scandal in Spain. For over a week the national media debated the issue, with all the soul-searching one would expect. Although many on the left applauded Castro's remarks, even they did not disguise their wounded pride. The overwhelming public and official reaction was outrage; criticism of Spain's effort to make Seville 1992 the crowning achievement of Iberoamerican cooperation was a low blow. Spanish officialdom reeled at the thought that the *black legend* still lived in the hearts and minds of the Latin Americans and that there could be even a hint of hypocrisy implicit in the 1992 celebrations. Castro had popped the rhetorical balloon that Spanish policy had been blowing up since the decision to make Seville the single site of the 1992 Expo.

As a distinct chill settled over Cuban-Spanish relations, Spain provoked Castro by excluding Cuba from a reunion of Latin American democratic parliaments in Madrid in December 1986. The spokesman of the decision to exclude Cuba from the meeting, the speaker of the Cortes, Félix Pons, in turn became the target of Castro's venom. The Cuban dictator called Pons a *tipejo fascistoide*, an insult that deeply wounded the Socialist leader who was sensitive to any reference to his already unpopular style as leader of an implacable absolute majority in the Cortes. The subject was not broached with Castro during his Havana meeting with Luis Yáñez in January 1987; Yánñez claimed that it was an issue that had been "overcome," although given Castro's pride, the Cuban dictator probably could never overcome Yáñez's own qualification of him as "Gallego through and through" (*"Gallego por los cuatro costados"*), a sneering reference to Castro's Galician ancestors.[99]

Although Spanish policy did manage to separate the issue of Cuban intervention in Central America from the purely bilateral relations between Spain and Cuba, the souring of those relations made it much more difficult for the PSOE to defend Cuba's hemispheric role. The Spanish government had been careful to keep its rhetoric of support for the Central American peace process as vague as possible. There were more references to the cut-off of U.S. aid to the *Contras* than direct criticisms of Cuban policy.

Whatever criticism Spain made of Cuban intervention was implicit in its support for peace plans that called for the withdrawal of foreign military personnel and advisors and the cessation of foreign support for irregular forces. Spain recognized the influence that Fidel Castro had over the guerrilla forces in El Salvador and Guatemala, Cuba's growing influence in Panamanian policy, and that Cuba was at times a moderating force among some extremely virulent strains of Central American ultraleftism. In short, Spanish policy avoided direct criticism of the Cuban role in the region in order to insure the support of Castro and his guerrilla clients for the regional peace process.

Felipe González and the ruling party seemed willing to maintain this truce with Cuban Central American policy even while bilateral relations between Spain and Cuba were deteriorating. The Spanish position on the bilateral issues was firm; Spain would defend its sovereignty and national dignity against Castro's irresponsible attacks on representatives of Spanish democracy and against criminal acts on the streets of Madrid. Cuba's attempt to appeal to apologist sectors and leftist critics within Spain by offering lectures on Spain's dark historical role in Latin America and on the "inconvenience" of Spain's NATO membership were regarded as interference in the internal affairs of a sovereign state. Like Francoist foreign policy, the foreign policy of the PSOE attempted to strengthen the perception that criticism of its own performance was tantamount to an attack on Spain as a nation. And in this case, Castro's venom struck directly at national pride.

When a European delegation of human rights activists from Cuban poet Armando Valladares's Cuban Human Rights Committee was refused entry into Havana in November 1988, the Spanish government immediately lodged an official protest of the Cuban action. Two opposition Spanish senators were among the delegation traveling to Cuba from Madrid on tourist visas. The delegation was frisked by Cuban security personnel, then abused and insulted by the popular militias. According to Cuba, the tourist visas were not valid for political missions and the presence of Valladares in the Madrid airport to see the delegation off was proof of the political character of the visit. Again, the Spanish government moved to protect national interests and dignity in the face of blatant attacks on Spanish representatives. As the opposition called for sanctions against Cuba for the inhuman treatment of its two senators, the PSOE limited its reaction to an official protest to the Cuban ambassador in Madrid.[100]

The conservative opposition in Spain was attempting to force the PSOE's hand in its Cuban policy by accusing the Socialists of being soft on Cuban totalitarianism. Reports surfaced in November 1988 of a secret agreement between Spain and Cuba to share intelligence data on terrorism. The agreement was a result of Spanish efforts to infiltrate the international networks of the Basque terrorist organization ETA. Castro had shown his willingness to cooperate on this issue in 1984 when he did not rule out the acceptance of Basque exiles deported from France. The opposition reminded the government of ETA's past connections with Central American revolutionaries, and of Cuba's role in revolutionary political-military activities across the globe.

Under the surface of all these disputes was the reality of Cuban isolation. By late 1989, even friendly voices in Spain were questioning the wisdom of the Castro regime in resisting the tide of democratic reform that was sweeping the globe.[101] Soviet aid was in question when deliveries of oil were cut back by 20% in 1990 due to shortages in the Soviet Union. The ideological gulf that had opened up a few years earlier with the implementation of *perestroika* and *glasnost* in the former Soviet bloc was by mid–1990 a gaping hole.[102] The weekly *Moscow News* characterized the former fraternal socialist state as an impoverished police state where stability was assured "thanks to a network of committees for the defense of the revolution that permeate the country" and where Cubans, "especially the young intelligentsia, are watching our *perestroika* closely and with clear sympathy."[103]

It might not have been the "young intelligentsia" that sought refuge in the foreign embassies in Havana throughout the month of July 1990, but the desperate stream of asylum-seekers who entered—or tried to enter—the Czechoslovak, Spanish, Italian, Swiss, and U.S. embassies was no less disillusioned with Castro and Cuban socialism. Thus began, on July 11, the 1990 Embassy Crisis, which only a year after the fall of the Berlin Wall seemed to threaten the Castro regime with a fate similar to that of East European dictators.

For Spain, the Embassy Crisis was the true test of its government's democratic convictions. Felipe González was already under bitter attack by opposition leaders in the Cortes for his friendly meeting with Castro in Brasilia in early 1990, which took place, responded González, "with the knowledge and approval of all the Western leaders present, including the Vice President of the United States, Dan Quayle."[104] His mission had been to convince the Cuban dictator of the need to join the global democratic bandwagon. But now, in the face of armed Cuban police intrusions on Embassy grounds, which had prevented one asylum-seeker from gaining refuge, and the insertion of *forjidos*, or government agents, into the embassies, which eventually brought the total number of Cubans inside to 18, Spanish diplomacy was forced to take one of its few truly unambiguous stands on principle.

After attempting to work with Castro—who in his rage was threatening another *Mariel* style boatlift, this time to Europe—, the Spanish foreign minister, Fernández Ordóñez, went on the offensive: "The crumbling of the communist regimes in Europe transpires when someone opens the door. I suppose that one thing is what [Castro] says he will do, and another is what he does, and he'll be careful not to open the door."[105] The Cuban secretary of the Central Committee of the Communist Party, Carlos Aldana, did not delay his crude response, accusing the foreign minister of "cheap sensationalism" and "irresponsible and lamentable" statements. In response to the astounding news that his own nephew was among the refugees, Aldana went below the belt: "Anybody can have a Juan Guerra in his family [a reference to the then Spanish deputy prime minister's brother whose corrupt practices tainted the Socialist government and sent it plunging into deep crisis in 1990], although this guy is only a tiny Juan Guerra... In Spain there can also be delinquents and antisocial elements called González and Ordóñez."[106]

A shocked and confused Spain, which in the past had seen Spanish diplomacy refrain from harsh attacks on the Cuban leadership, now demanded a full accounting. Spain canceled a meeting on economic cooperation set for the end of July and consulted with its European colleagues on further measures. Undeterred, Castro authorized his foreign ministry to issue a personal attack on the Spanish foreign minister:

Señor Ordóñez seems to be under the—we hope temporary—effects of an attack of historical amnesia; this is the only way possible to comprehend his judgement, warnings and lamentations, whose paternalisms evoke the edicts of the captains general who governed Cuba in name of his Spanish majesties. It is difficult, therefore, to take seriously this scolding of an anguished colonial administrator, especially when he deigns to speak for the European Community. Nor is it possible to attribute to him that endowment that the most illustrious proconsuls used to boast of, because to his confessed ignorance of the Cuban situation, one must add a scandalous illiteracy in questions of international law...[107]

Stunned, Spain recalled its ambassador to Madrid for consultations. But against all odds, the Spanish government wanted to keep channels open with the Castro regime; the Spanish were intent on establishing their diplomats as future mediators in an apparently inevitable transition to democracy on the island. Spain reinforced its embassy by dispatching five additional specially trained police who received visas from an increasingly more cooperative Cuban administration. Madrid also suspended its modest $2 million aid program and convinced, with little difficulty, the EEC to do the same to its tiny, but symbolic, humanitarian aid program. When at the end of July other embassies released their refugees, after securing guarantees from the Cuban government that they would not be punished and that they would be free at some point in the future to leave the country "legally," Spain responded to a more conciliatory tone from Castro in the following weeks by releasing all the nine refugees and nine suspected *fornidos* by September 4. Spanish diplomats expressed their satisfaction that, in contrast with other European embassies, the highly trained special police force known as *geos* was able to avoid confrontations between the suspected government agents and the real asylum-seekers, and they assured a bewildered Spanish public opinion that the release was voluntary and not the result of negotiations with Cuba.[108]

Spanish policy-makers promised that there would be no clean slate with Cuba after the 55 days of tension and diatribe. Aid would not be restored any time soon, and there would be residual effects in Cuban-Spanish relations. "I don't believe, I'm sorry to say, that we could say, erase it and start all over," affirmed Inocencio Arias, who would eventually replace Yáñez as secretary of international cooperation in early 1991.[109]

Nevertheless, Spain immediately plunged into the ambiguity its policy had always enjoyed, until events like those of July 1990 demanded firmer positions. From Paris, a day after the last refugees left the Spanish embassy in Havana, Luís Yáñez declared that Spaniards wanted "to continue being the best friends Cuba has abroad."[110] And in October 1990, Felipe González received Cuban Vice President Carlos Rafael Rodríguez in a private visit at the Moncloa. Questioned afterwards about the state of relations between the two countries, Rodríguez, who two months before blamed Spain for the Embassy crisis, apparently took his signals from the Spanish leadership: "they are normal, which means that they are good."[111]

The Cuban case serves as a paradigm for the difficulties of a foreign policy that uses *idealpolitik* to shield itself from the realities of conflicting interests. To be a friend to all Latin American countries while pursuing defined ideological and national interests leads to contradictions. The watered-down Marxism of Morán's foreign ministry was no match for Castro's revolutionary program. And the social democratic orientation of González's foreign policy could not avoid the eventual clash with Cuban totalitarianism.

At the highest levels, González and Castro could agree to agree on certain broad issues in Central America—such as opposition to U.S. military intervention—as a tactical arrangement, but the strategic interests of the two nation states were different. González received encouragement from the Bush Administration and his European colleagues for keeping channels open with the Cuban dictator, but the apparent obsession with maintaining an image of good relations may only backfire when the Cuban democratic transition finally does come. Moreover, it confuses and disorients public opinion at home, where the Socialists must contend with strong pressures on the left to embrace Castro, the undermining influence of a traditional foreign policy establishment that is vulnerable to insult, and an increasingly active conservative opposition that is successful in embarrassing the Socialists on matters of principle. As if this principle were not enough, there was also the issue of Cuban arrears on indemnification payments, which the conservatives in the Cortes attempted to present as a threat to the historically cozy *state to state* relationship.

The laudable effort on the part of González to channel Cuba's virulent nationalism into democratic outcomes, clashed with Spain's own heightened nationalist sensitivities. Even the left-wing of the PSOE had grown weary of Castro's antics. Former foreign minister Fernando Morán gave the eulogy during the embassy crisis: "As a consequence of great and profound historical changes, Castroism has wound up having no function in the international scene."[112] For many observers of the relationship, especially in the conservative opposition, there was no reason to lament the Cuban decision, on alleged economic grounds, to pull out of its planned pavilion to Spain's former "pearl of the Caribbean" in the 1992 Expo and V Centenary of the Discovery of America.

Like many of his adversaries on the right, Morán suggested that there may be a need to draw some clearer lines around issues of principle. Ambiguity provides policy flexibility, but convictions generate real support for foreign policy initiatives. If Spanish Latin American policy is to mature, it must address the disequilibrium implicit in its desire to be a friend to all on the one hand while insisting on basic Western democratic norms of behavior on the other.

RISKS AND REWARDS

The chronic instability on the Central American isthmus keeps the door open to the intervention of lesser powers, whose prospects for success at conflict resolution are much dimmer than those of the great powers but whose risks are minimal. Spain's efforts at mediation in the Central American conflict ran the risk of angering U.S. hardliners who advocated military solutions to the threat of totalitarianism in Central America. But Spain found immunity from these attacks by cultivating its bilateral relationship with the United States and by Westernizing its defense and security relationships through NATO and Western European Union (WEU) participation. Spain also finds safety in numbers among the EEC members who share the Spanish perspective on Central America. By carefully modulating policy so as to make the Spanish position as responsive as possible to the wide ideological spectrum in Central America, Spanish policy is viewed as inoffensive and at times vague.

When the clash with U.S. policy is too obvious to ignore, Spain makes deliberate efforts to reassure its senior partner and Western ally. In the wake of the *Contra* aid cut-off by the U.S. Congress in February 1988, the Reagan Administration went on a diplomatic offensive to pressure allies and Central American governments into supporting a hard-line stance on Nicaragua. Washington was concerned that the Esquipulas accords would serve to consolidate the Sandinista regime under a democratic guise. The González government, sensitive to these concerns, dispatched a high-level delegation to Washington in early March to explore the dimensions of possible Spanish mediation in Central America.[113] In his subsequent trip to Central America in late March, where he again avoided a visit to Nicaragua, González referred ironically to his agenda in Central America: "I always make my trips in accordance with the itinerary that the U.S. Department of State organizes for me."[114]

The apparent clash between Spanish and U.S. foreign policy in Central America must be put into perspective. Both parties have been able to separate their differences over Central America from the difficult and prolonged negotiations over the bilateral issues of the U.S. military presence in Spain. This maturity on both sides was indicative of the strength of Spanish democracy and the confidence that Spain had generated among European and Western allies. Such confidence was bolstered by González's strategic collaboration with the United States in the Gulf War, where great political risks were taken at home in order to strengthen Western ties and recognize U.S. strategic leadership.

For Spain could no longer be pressured by the United States in the same way as some Central American countries who were struggling for their very survival. Costa Rica, for example, had felt the destabilizing aspects of U.S. pressure. Angry over Costa Rica's decisive efforts to limit the management of the regional peace process to local leaders and the Costa Rican decision to prohibit the *Contra* forces from operating out of Costa Rican territory, the Reagan Administration began to delay economic aid and impose petty restrictions on exports while refusing to aid the economically strapped country in debt rescheduling negotiations. The resignation of a close Arias aide and architect of the Esquipulas peace plan was also attributed to U.S. pressure. Costa Rican aides warned that the Reagan Administration's obsession with Nicaragua was not going to succeed in overthrowing the Sandinistas, but that "in the end, [the Americans] are going to destroy Costa Rican democracy."[115]

Administration officials did not admit to a systematic effort to undermine Arias, but evidence of mutual animosity is impossible to bury. Many former Reagan Administration officials believe that Arias "single-handedly undid U.S. policy in Nicaragua." The tension between the two democracies dramatizes the dangers of a confrontation between a weak democracy and a superpower. But while Arias had "very few cards to play" in return, Felipe González had the modality of NATO membership, the reduction of the U.S. military presence in Spain (along with the prohibition on port calls for ships with nuclear weapons), and influence on the trade policies of the EEC to ward off U.S. threats. The fact that Spain has not felt it necessary to defend itself from U.S. pressure testifies to the level of maturity that Spanish foreign relations have achieved in the strategic sphere, and the degree of respect that Spanish democracy has inspired even in the most powerful of competitors.[116]

Immunity from outside destabilization is not, however, the only key to Spain's ability to reap the rewards of prestige in its Central American policy without major risk. The answer lies in the actual content of the policy, the message that transcends the diplomatic shuffle and the vagaries of rhetoric. To the dismay of many of the over 10 million voters who expected to see a shift to the left in Spanish foreign policy after the 1982 Spanish general elections, Felipe González has moved into the mainstream of European foreign policy. Despite its words of encouragement to the Sandinistas in Nicaragua, Spanish foreign policy still entertained prominent members of the Nicaraguan resistance, and by the end of 1989 Nicaragua was still awaiting signs that either King Juan Carlos or Prime Minister Felipe González would make an official visit to Nicaragua. Only a year after Violeta Chammorro's opposition coalition defeated the Sandinistas in 1990 did the King schedule his Nicaraguan visit.[117]

Whether the means employed are the same or not, Spain's focus on the democratization of Nicaragua was consistent with U.S. and Western interests. The level of material and technical aid to the Nicaraguan regime was negligible relative to other European and Canadian contributions, and Spain collaborates economically, politically, and even militarily with U.S. allies in the region. It is enough to point out the sale of CASA jet aircraft to Honduras, Washington's firmest ally in the region; the six modern aircraft boosted Honduras's already decisive advantage in air power over Nicaragua. Military cooperation with Honduras expanded after a 1990 visit by then Secretary of Defense Narcis Serra, who promised aid for the professionalization of Honduran forces.[118] In short, Spanish behavior in Central America can be characterized as essentially conservative, especially when held up against some of the idealistic positions that Socialist rhetoric had carved out for Spanish policy.

THE QUEST FOR YANKEETROIKA

The Bush Administration recognized this salient feature during the crisis in Panamá, when the U.S. president consulted repeatedly with González on the international community's options in its efforts to remove General Manuel Noriega from power and restore Panamanian democracy. González also had some prophetic words of advice on the Nicaraguan situation. On an official visit to the White House in October 1989, he urged the U.S. administration to "rationalize its options" in the Nicaraguan peace process. "Instead of keeping the *Contras* in an armed situation, let them be repatriated. After all, they are voters and citizens whatever their ideology." For González the 1990 Nicaraguan elections were a "way out"; it was "much healthier politically to gamble that they will work rather than gamble that they won't work and create obstacles."[119]

Less prophetic was González's advice on Panamá. Frequent high-level contacts between Spain and the U.S. during the crisis served to warn the Bush Administration of the Spanish and Latin American view that under no circumstances should the U.S. intervene militarily. González insisted that "we must seek a Panamanian solution which involves respect for the popular will."[120] To facilitate the process, Spain offered on a number of occasions to extend political asylum to Noriega as a way to defuse the crisis. Panamanian opposition leaders were appreciative, but Noriega's violent refusals and the questions of possible extradition to the U.S., where Noriega faced felony drug trafficking charges, made the offer untenable.[121] When U.S.

troops invaded Panamá on December 20, 1989, there was shock and dismay in Madrid and throughout Spain.

On 23 December, González sent Bush a diplomatic message protesting the U.S. action. In Spain there was an immediate groundswell of anti-Americanism that could be better interpreted as misplaced nationalism. For Spain's national pride had been wounded by an American administration that ignored the repeated advice of the Spanish head of government and Europe's most influential Latin Americanist. González, moreover, had portrayed the Bush Administration as one that had adopted a "new style" of foreign relations characterized by "a great deal more consultation—prior consultation and not after the fact—than we are used to in previous administrations."[122]

Spanish public opinion was also seething over the sacking by U.S. troops of Spanish company offices in Panama City, and the killing of Spanish nationals, including Juantxu Rodríguez, a Spanish photographer for *El País*, the Madrid newspaper of record and forum of democratic debate in Spain. The political storm was such that Madrid dispatched two military transports to Panamá to evacuate about 60 Spanish nationals as well as the photographer's body. On 29 December, Spain became the only member of the EEC, and with Sweden, one of two in Europe as a whole, to vote against the United States on a UN resolution condemning the invasion.[123] The vote prompted an apology, which Spain accepted, from the U.S. Army over the treatment of Spanish interests during the invasion,[124] and Bush moved to repair the damage to bilateral relations by holding two long telephone conversations with González over a ten day period. In their conversations, Bush attempted, with some success, to explain to the Prime Minister the reasons behind the U.S. military intervention. The Spanish position may have been softened by reports that four exiled ETA terrorists had been invited into the Vatican embassy along with Noriega by the *nuncio*, who was of Basque origin.[125] González described the talks as "very cordial," and Bush, in a January press conference, used the personal contact with the Spanish Prime Minister as a point of departure in repairing relations with the many Latin American governments that shared Spain's concerns.[126]

The depth of public outrage in Spain over U.S. behavior is difficult to interpret without an understanding of the extreme sensitivity of Spanish nationalism. Given their internationalist concerns and the regional and ethnic differences that divide them internally, Spaniards see themselves as less nationalistic than their European neighbors. Nevertheless, forty years of pent-up nationalist aspirations under the Franco dictatorship exploded on the international scene after the dictator's death. The Socialists exploited these energies while making compromises to French power in the EEC and to U.S. strategic leadership. Latin America became a rich hunting ground for relatively intangible Spanish aspirations. The displaced nationalism inherent in the identification of a war reporter with official Spanish interests and policy was understandable given the Socialists' largely self-appointed role as conscience and guardian of Latin American democratic development.

Spanish policy-makers, nevertheless, were careful to put events into their proper context. Incidents such as those involving individuals in Panamá and churchworkers in El Salvador would be seen as isolated cases that could not be allowed to poison the otherwise good relations with the United States. For its part, the U.S. would be forced to understand that occasional rhetorical lapses on the part of Spain's leaders were for the most part designed to assuage volatile public opinion and domestic political pressure on the left, where the Socialists had trouble within their own party. Spanish collaboration in the strategic bombing of Iraq during the Gulf War, in the face of tremendous domestic political risks, proved that differences of opinion on the means toward democratic ends in Latin America would not threaten Spain's commitment to Western values within an increasingly unstable international system.[127]

Conclusion: 1992 and All That

There is no doubt of the sincerity in Spain's efforts to find peaceful solutions to the many crises in Latin America and in its desire to create a kind of Latin American *commonwealth*. Yet these intentions are for the most part intangible and must be measured in deeds. For all the rhetoric and hyperbole regarding Spain's new international role in Latin America, Spanish public opinion is aware that the intended audience is within Spain's domestic political context; a good part of the benefits are reserved for Spain and its Socialist leadership. Confronted at home with continuous challenges to its own democratic credentials, Spain's Socialist leadership has sought its democratic image abroad. Narcissus looked at his own reflection and thought it was somebody else; Spain's Socialists preferred to see in their Central American foreign policy initiatives a democratic picture untainted by the corruption, mismanagement, and economic and social crisis at home.

Spain's impulse to validate its democratic transition often becomes an obsession that has been tempered only by the limitations of available policy instruments. Domestic pressures force leaders to orient foreign policy initiatives to national priorities. Reminded of the work that remains to be done to solidify *Spanish* democracy, the Socialists have looked outside the country for the legitimization of their democratic credentials. Although welcome in an area of desperate crisis, the echo Spain receives from Central Americans is not always flattering. Spain's plunge into European and North Atlantic economic and political institutions has not gone unnoticed. Central Americans are wary of all kinds of paternalism, especially that of Old World democrats.

1992 AND BUST?

Meanwhile, the promotion of the 1992 Olympic Games in Barcelona, and more importantly, the Expo 1992 and V Centenary of the Discovery of the New World in Seville, became more of a national project than international *puntos de encuentro* for Ibero-America. Inasmuch as Catalonia's foreign policy is oriented toward Europe, the Olympic project is one that will link Spain more to Europe than to the rest of the world. Barcelona's infrastructure projects are directed at improving not only the city's ability to play host to millions during the games but also at a higher degree of European integration. Trans-Pyrenees tunnels and major port and highway improvements are part of a well-financed and well-orchestrated effort to put Barcelona in the international spotlight and restore the Catalonian capital's role as a center of European and Mediterranean civilization.

For Seville, however, the Expo has become a matter of survival. Emerging from the 1980s as the European capital of unemployment and petty crime, the Junta of Andalucia and the municipal authorities, both under Socialist direction, embarked on a grandiose scheme to restore Seville's former glory as the center of the New World. The task was formidable. Seville had become nothing more than a provincial capital even before the Spanish lost their last New World colonies. During the Franco years, Andalusian culture festered in the run-down barrios of Triana and Santa Cruz, providing the occasional tourist with a picturesque spectacle of gypsy eroticism and spontaneous celebration. But Seville could not break out of the boundaries its limited production and administrative neglect had imposed.

A TALE OF ONE CITY

The transition to democracy meant a worsening of the economic situation in Seville until almost one-third of the active population was unemployed.[1] The creation of the autonomous regional government, the Junta de Andalucia, brought high-paid professionals and bureaucrats to a city in severe decay. The influx of Socialist *yuppies* to Seville allowed the ancient but decadent Andalusian bourgeoisie to raise the value of property and to adjust supply of consumer goods to unprecedented income levels. Boutiques and *chalets*, along with fancy cooperative apartments, became the territory of the new, young Seville elite.

The old guard, content with supply-side economic policies and satiated with unprecedented profits from real estate and business dealings with the bureaucratic elite, swallowed their hatred for the Socialists and spent their summers in Huelva and Cádiz. Consumer credit offered the rest of a Seville the illusion that they, too, could participate in the boom that put Andalusian culture in the national spotlight. *Sevilla está de moda* ("Seville is in fashion") was the slogan of the privileged elite even while Spain's industrial crisis wreaked havoc on the working class and small business owners. Tourists from all parts of Spain came to the partially renovated city, only to find their car windows smashed and their belongings gone.[2]

Fueled by intractable, structural unemployment, petty crime and drug addiction became so endemic that the authorities saw social problems as a threat to the very project that was to save Seville from itself: the 1992 V Centenary and Universal Exposition. But that project's difficulties went beyond the city's social crisis. International tour operators would eliminate travel advisories for Seville after an appropriate police crackdown on purse-snatchers and muggers, but the problems of political and entrepreneurial cohesion were more chronic. Ground-breaking for the pavilions in La Cartuja began late because the city and national authorities bickered with entrepreneurs for financing. High-flung rhetoric referring to Seville's historic role in the New World was issued from Madrid and the Junta, but *sevillanos* wondered when the first cement foundations would be poured. Residents also asked themselves how Seville would function in 1992 if in 1990 normal daytime traffic in the city of less than a million people was in a state of collapse.

When the project financing was finally put on track, political feuding spoiled whatever spirit of cooperation remained. The Socialists sought control of all aspects of the project until the Expo international showcase became synonymous with the PSOE public image. Pedro Pacheco, the popular leader of the regional opposition party Partido Andalucista, already marked for his defiance of the partisan justice system in Spain by publicly calling it a *cachondeo* (a big joke), pointed out that the Socialists, not the past, were the most formidable obstacle to a successful and profitable Exposition. "They are not the victims of the decadence," he writes, "they are now the decadence."[3]

The Andalusians ran the risk of seeing their promise for the future sold to international investors while the government in Madrid reaped the propaganda benefits. And even those foreign firms that did invest in the project were nervous about the sluggishness of the preparations and the peculiar political context in which the construction and planning are taking place. Already there was a popular cynicism regarding the celebrations that belied the tremendous official promotion effort. The man in the street asks what Spain can do for Latin America if Spain cannot even employ its own people and invest its own money. Despite the apparent obsession with *Sevilla 1992*, most minds in Seville are focused on what will be in *Sevilla 1993*, when foreign firms pull out with their profits, the construction boom turns to bust, and Seville must face its unemployment, its crime, and the one or two permanent Latin American restaurants.[4] According to Pacheco, "1993, as they [the Socialists] conceive it, is strangling 1992."[5]

Sensing an impending disaster, Felipe González made a trip to Seville in November 1990 to insure that infrastructure projects were put on track, political rifts were ironed out, and additional financing was raised. A battle between independent Expo authorities and government appointed "commissars," ostensibly over the high price of tickets for the Expo, ended in early 1991 with a compromise on special youth and group rates for the expected 18 million visitors. The budget was raised by about $360 million, bringing the total state funded participation to 180 billion pesetas, or about $2 billion at 1991 exchange rates. About 110 countries had contracted to build pavilions, but the Gulf War put a question mark over Arab willingness and financial ability to complete their pavilions on time. On the Latin-American front, Cuba, and more interestingly, Brazil, the Iberoamerican superpower, were absent from the list, both alleging economic difficulties. But for the first time since the project's inception, there was reason for optimism. A shake-up of the Expo administration in July 1991 led to the replacement of the controversial government commissar, improving relations with local authorities. Construction of pavilions and infrastructure would push up against the deadlines, and there would be little space for finishing touches, but by the end of 1990 visitors to the site at the Island of Cartuja in the Guadalquivir River could for the first time find visible signs that progress was being made. Too much time and money was invested in the project to worry about the moral dimensions of the celebrations on the Discovery of America, and the problems of world recession were largely outside of Spanish control. The only cloud hanging over the project itself was the threat by the ETA terrorist group to sabotage the Expo and the Olympic games.[6]

The Socialists were forced to accept the role of the opposition in organizing the celebrations in exchange for the sharing of responsibility. Luis Yañez's defeat at the May 1991 election polls would deprive the Socialists of the opportunity to be identified with a world-class event, but the new mayor, Alejandro Rojas Marcos, will have to shoulder some of the responsibility for whatever failures there may be.

SPAIN AT HOME AND ABROAD

The problems surrounding the celebrations of the V Centenary and the Expo 1992 were illustrative of an emerging pattern in Spanish officialdom. Where the Socialists faced formidable obstacles, they fell back on a rhetorical campaign that appealed to an international audience who was ready to legitimize both their domestic and their international efforts. Bolstered by this international support, the government accused the opposition of undermining Spain's new international role. Meanwhile, the practical aspects of the official projects were either ignored, delayed, mired in political infighting, or implemented in an inefficient, corrupt, or unscrupulous manner.

In many ways, Spanish foreign policy during the Socialist era fit this pattern well. Behind a wall of rhetoric and good intentions, Spain made international commitments to peace and development that it was not always prepared to back up with deeds.

Much of this hypocrisy might be forgiven of a lesser power that was itself an aid recipient less than two decades before; but the gulf between word and deed became alarming in the domestic context where the Socialist performance was not so widely applauded as it was in international circles. Felipe González has been a popular leader both in Spain and in the international community. But his party was under siege within Spain for its inability to deliver on specific economic and democratic promises. The people of Spain wish that *Felipe* would travel more within Spain—or even Madrid—instead of abroad. The PSOE enraged the opposition by purveying a democratic model abroad while failing to satisfy the democratic aspirations of many Spanish people.

Credit must be given, however, to the ability of the Socialist government to muster international support from governments as diverse as those of London and Algiers. The Socialists have positioned Spain in the forefront of Western economic, political, and security institutions, thus satisfying a need for international approval in the wake of Spain's isolated and tarnished past. Felipe González westernized and Europeanized his country to the point at which it could no longer be referred to as the "a great whale stranded on the shores of Europe," as Edmund Burke once remarked. For the Spanish people, however, the benefits do not seem so apparent, and perhaps the expectations that have been released will never be satisfied.

IMAGE AND REALITY IN LATIN AMERICA

In Latin America there seems to be sufficient realism regarding the limits of Spanish policy, as well as a better understanding of Spain's emerging international position. Referring to Spain and its diplomatic intervention in Central America, Oscar Arias of Costa Rica maintains no illusions: "Europe is not a panacea for our problems." Later, Arias would reject a diplomatic role for Spain in the Central American crisis, preferring a regional solution.[7] The president of Venezuela, the prominent social democrat Carlos Andrés Pérez, sees Spain's relationship with Latin America as weak, suggesting that Latin America's voice would not be amplified by Spain's presidency of the EEC in 1989 and by the V Centenary in Seville: "What will happen is that Spain will become more Europeanized, if anything."[8]

Latin Americans are becoming increasingly aware of the Spanish government's exploitations and fictionalization of Iberoamerican relations for domestic political purposes. To the expected diatribes of Fidel Castro has been added a chorus of voices from Latin American intellectual circles who have rejected the idea of the V Centenary. A prominent group of writers and authors, united in the International Forum and Response for the V Centenary denounced the "inept manipulation" of the celebrations by Socialist officials and the general air of "coverup" that Spain has given to the celebrations.[9]

Luis Cardoza y Aragon, the Guatemalan author and Forum member, states that Latin intellectuals are not against the celebrations or the commemoration, but that "the way of commemorating [the Discovery] is the problem."[10] In fact, the debate over the Spanish conquest of the Americas once again began to rage all over the Americas, just as the controversy subsided within Spain.[11] Yet some Spaniards recognized that the rhetoric coming from Seville and Madrid had fallen on incredulous ears.[12]

In Mexico, where anti-Spanish sentiment is strongest, a committee of indigenous Indians was formed to protest the V Centenary celebrations. Made up of seven Indian organizations with 150,000 members, the organization, which calls itself the 500 Years Committee (Comité 500 Años) and claims to represent through the Mexican legislature and civic action the interests of 20 million Mexican Indians, warned in 1990 that "in Mexico there is majority sentiment of rejection of the V Centenary that will be manifested with greater clarity starting next year."[13]

Spanish apologists for the conquests suggest that disease was more virulent than Spanish greed or aggression during the conquests, and that there are many positive aspects that are ignored. The Peruvian novelist Mario Vargas Llosa agrees, advancing the thesis that the rugged individualism of the *conquistador* represented the first rumblings of freedom in the world.[14] The prize-winning author was compelled to defend the positive aspects of the Conquest against threats from a shadowy group called the Association of Indian Cultures, which announced that its members were prepared to conduct acts of "sabotage" in Spain and Latin America in protest of the V Centenary celebrations. Referring to Pizarro's legendary conquest over the Inca empire of millions of soldiers, Vargas Llosa offers the key to what Spain and Europe bestowed upon Latin America:

Those Indians who let themselves be knifed or blown into pieces that somber afternoon ... lacked the ability to make their own decisions either with the sanction of authority or indeed against it, and were incapapable of taking individual initiative, of acting with a certain degree of independence according to the changing circumstances. Those 180 Spaniards who had placed the Indians in ambush and were now slaughtering them did possess this ability. It was this difference, more than the numerical one or the weapons, that created an immense inequality between those civilizations. The individual had no importance and virtually no existence in that pyramidal and theocratic society whose achievements were always collective in nature.[15]

In short, Europe gave Latin Americans the key to freedom. But Latin Americans, who are still struggling for that freedom, refuse to believe that Europe bestows such gifts. Europe bestows gifts upon Europeans, and Spain is now European.

The true meaning of the discovery or conquests will probably never be found, and the debate will continue even after 1992. But the challenge of Spanish foreign policy in the Central American crisis is not an intellectual exercise. The problems on the isthmus cannot and will not be resolved through debate on Spain's colonial past. They will not be settled by a greater Spanish cultural presence or by the otherwise laudable efforts to provide diplomatic support.

SPAIN: A MODEL OF INTERNATIONAL COOPERATION?

Central America needs tangible aid and an active policy of the sort only firmly entrenched powers can afford. The Spanish foreign ministry is forced to seek this kind of aid in Europe, where Spain's EEC partners are preoccupied with the commercial and development interests of their respective former colonial regions in Africa, the Middle East, and Asia. Spain's own aid programs have grown in fits and starts, but the almost symbolic sums of money do not provide leverage.

Spain's aid programs, moreover, are not under the scrutiny of the OECD Development Aid Committee (DAC) because Spain is not a member of the DAC; its total development aid is well below the required .35% of gross domestic product.[16] In the absence of formalized reporting and accounting procedures, Spain evades scrutiny of its aid programs and the actual disbursement of promised aid in promised time-frames. Although the government presents an annual plan of development aid, the Plan Anual de Cooperación Internacional (PACI), which is coordinated by the Spanish Agency for International Cooperation (AECI) under the supervision of the Secretary of International Cooperation, the actual disbursements are difficult to track.[17] Moreover, Spain's credit aid program, known as the Development Aid Fund (FAD), is comprised mostly of credits that are tied to the purchase of Spanish goods and services. Only a small fraction can qualify as development aid in the OECD accounting.[18] According to the informal accounting of Fernando Valenzuela, the AECI president, official development aid to Central America averaged about $25 million a year through 1989.[19] By 1990, however, the Central American Aid Plan (PECA) reached about $80 million, but again some of it was credits for Spanish exports or to finance construction projects by Spanish firms.[20] The same can be said for Spain's 1988 "spectacular thrust" in Latin America, a $500 million loan and $150 million in interest subsidies, in the framework of the V Centenary, to the Interamerican Development Bank, which was not approved by the Cortes and signed by the bank and Spain until 1990. All of the money, for which 25 countries in Latin America are eligible, is tied to Spanish company participation.[21] Spanish businessmen, moreover, have been reluctant to take the handouts, especially in the Central American context.[22] Opportunities still abound in growing European markets where political risk is minimal and economic stability high. Spanish commercial cooperation in Latin America centers on a $12 billion government coordinated investment and aid plan in Argentina, Chile, Mexico, Venezuela, and Brazil. In addition, big Spanish firms acquired a number of high profile firms in those countries during a wave of privatizations at the end of the 1980s. Telefónica, the state-owned telecommunications monopoly, bought controlling interest of the Argentine firm Entel and a large stake in the Chilean CTC. For its part, Iberia airlines bought Aerolineas Argentinas, the large Argentine carrier, in 1990, a controlling interest in Viasa, the Venezuelan carrier, and a major stake in the Chilean Ladeco in 1991. The effort to increase Spain's trade with Latin America, which was less than 5% of total Spanish trade in 1990, would focus on the large economies of South America and Mexico. In 1990, Spain's trade with Central America as a whole was less than half that of Spanish trade with Argentina.[23]

Despite the paltry sums in the Central American context, in a few cases Spain still attempted to use the aid as diplomatic leverage, belying official pronouncements that Spain's aid programs were apolitical in nature.[24] In the case of El Salvador, where Spain was frustrated over lack of progress in bringing Salvadoran military officials to justice for the murder of the five Spanish Jesuit priests, the symbolic 1990 official development aid of less than half a million dollars was kept at the same low level for 1991.[25] In Nicaragua, it was not lost on the Sandinistas that they were not the favored rulers when Madrid contributed $5 million in 1990, after the Sandinista election defeat, to help train Nicaraguan army officers in the profession of a democratic military.[26] Ironically enough, El Salvador—as well as the other countries in Central America—would have been better off if they had accepted ETA terrorist exiles from the Spanish government. In the 1987–88 period alone, Spain gave credits totaling some $400 million and development aid of about $90 million to the seven countries (Venezuela, Cuba, Cape Verde, Santo Tomé, Panamá, Dominican Republic, and Algeria) that took in *etarras*. The Spanish government, however, denies any relationship between aid programs and a country's willingness to accept ETA exiles.[27]

Spain attempted to compensate for its less than spectacular aid programs in Central America by using its scarce diplomatic resources to convince its EEC partners that Latin America, and Central America in particular, are of strategic importance to the West. The absence of its own generous aid program, in spite of burgeoning international reserves (third in Europe behind Italy and Germany at the end of 1990), did not help make the case, nor did Spain's general acquiescence to European protectionism, especially in the agricultural sphere where Spain produces similar products.

At a March 1991 meeting in Seville of EEC and Central American parliamentarians, Enrique Baron, the Socialist president of the European Parliament, summed up Spain's failure to commit sufficient means to its rhetorical ends: "We are no model for international cooperation."[28] His frank admission was confirmed in July 1991, when on the eve of the first Ibero-American Summit, Spain announced a 30 percent cut in its international aid program for 1991. The "soft" credits would remain intact, but the already meager donations suffered the effects of Spanish domestic austerity.

INSIDE THE EUROPEAN FORTRESS

By the end of the 1980s, however, Spain had firmly wrested the Latin American portfolio away from the French on the European Commission. The Spanish commissioner, Abel Matutes, a popular politician of the conservative opposition, led Spain's efforts in Brussels with the help of Angel Viñas, a famous scholar and author. Along with Felipe González and the foreign ministry, Matutes attempted, with considerable success, to position Spain as Latin America's ombudsman and *interlocutor* in the European Community. Such an identification of that role was established that Latin American clients were loathe to criticize Spain for its inflated rhetoric, diplomatic transgressions, or penurious aid programs, lest Spain not make a case for Latin American concerns among the richer countries of Europe. Hence, the European role shielded Spain from the negative output of its diplomatic interventions and diverted rising expectations to the possibilities of an EEC largesse.

While Spain was speaking for Latin America, however, its commissioners were losing power in the important decision-making organs of the European Commission. During a major 1990 reshuffle of the Commission along European balance of power lines, Spain managed to place one of its commissioners, Joan Prat, as director general of North-South relations, which includes relations with Latin America. But according to the Commission president, Jacques Delors, Spain had to pay a high price for the placement of Prat. In other key organs, Spanish candidates lost out to Europe's other powers, leaving Spain with only two directors general with portfolio to France's six and five each for Italy, Germany and the UK. Poor personnel planning was blamed for the loss, and Prime Minister González, who was undoubtedly busy with domestic crises, was criticized for not intervening personally with Delors.[29]

The result of the 1990 power shifts in the EEC was the commensurate weakening of Spain's ability to advocate within the EEC for policies that would favor the nations for which Spain was claiming to speak. Spain's clout would depend on the relative strength of its foreign minister and prime minister in the Council of Ministers and the European Council respectively. Though Felipe González and Francisco Fernández Ordóñez had represented Spain well in these forums, they could not be expected to take on Europe's giants singlehandedly.

The real test of Spain's clout was in the context of the so-called "San

José" summits of the EEC Council of Ministers and the Central American presidents, which began in 1984. In the fifth "San José" conference of the EEC and the Central American countries in February 1989, when Spain held the rotating European presidency, the Spanish delegation was only able to push through an emergency three-year aid plan worth 150 million ECUs (approx. $160 million), while promising a "special effort" during the rest of the year.[30] Aid for 1990, however, was only about $140 million, mostly to finance Central American trade integration.[31]

Expectations were high for San José VII in March 1991, where the Central American presidents were determined to force Europe to move from rhetoric to decisive action. On the eve of the meeting, the Central American countries called for Europe to extend the preferential treatment of exports that it had given to the Andean Group of countries as part of the EEC's contribution to the war on drugs. The Andean countries, in turn, were to shift production of coca to coffee and tropical products that would enter an expanding European market. The Central Americans were seeking the same duty-free entry of similar Central American products to the EEC market. In order to head off a chain reaction, or contamination effect, across the entire Third World, EEC negotiators attempted to convince the Central Americans that the Andean deal was a special case and that the EEC position at the extended Uruguay Round of the GATT negotiations was to offer the elimination of tariffs on tropical products as a concession to the United States and the Cairns group of agricultural exporters.[32]

As a compromise, the EEC promised to set up a commission that would study the possibilities of compensation for lost markets—especially for coffee—as a result of the Andean agreement. On the prospects for a similar agreement for Central America, however, the Spanish commissioner, Abel Matutes, admitted that "our experts did not see sufficient technical reasons to justify such a measure."[33] The linkage with the GATT negotiations in the summit's final declaration, according to Matutes, gave the commissioner for Latin America a clear mandate to argue Central America's case in the European Commission and Council when the EEC finally presented its offer at the GATT table. Matutes also promised that EEC aid, which from 1977 through 1990 totaled some $1.1 billion, would increase by 80% in the 1991–95 period.[34]

In a rare display of compellence, foreign minister Ordóñez threatened his EEC colleagues in Managua with lack of Spanish cooperation in European integration if Europe did not sort out its cooperation with Latin America. Ordóñez said that Spain would not accept "European political union if the issue of cooperation with Latin America is not cleared up."[35] The statement was bolder than it appeared inasmuch as it ignored the fact that Spain had for five years towed the line on EEC agricultural protectionism, and its position on GATT, which supported European intransigence over agricultural subsidies, had been a continuing source of embarrassment for Spanish diplomacy.[36] The statement was probably meant more for the Latin American audience; the foreign minister's European colleagues were well aware of the fact that the threat not to cooperate in European union was empty in the context of paralysis of European political and monetary union due to differences over the Gulf War and the chilling effect of Germany's crisis with its own monetary union.

The most significant development at the Managua summit was the appearance of the FMLN leadership, which used its Nicaraguan hosts to gain access to the EEC ministers for the presentation of a new peace plan. Ordóñez remarked that the peace process was at a "decisive" moment in El Salvador in the wake of mid-term elections, in which the guerrillas refrained from disruptions and the leftist coalition led by former rebel political spokesman Rubén Zamora helped take away the ruling ARENA party's majority in the legislature despite widespread election fraud and counterinsurgency operations by the military. The guerrillas relaxed their demand for political reforms before the establishment of a cease-fire, and the Salvadoran government, after initial anger at the FMLN's appearance in Managua, expressed optimism for the prospects of a cease-fire in the near term. These pronouncements came despite huge constitutional obstacles to the signing of the peace plan which, among other things, would recognize rebel control over national territory. Hinging on the cease-fire was a UN-EEC plan to raise $4.4 billion in financial aid for the region.[37]

The EEC ministers and Central American governments declared the Managua summit a "success," but many Central Americans were not convinced. The meeting, moreover, took place against a backdrop of violent strikes over a new Nicaraguan economic anti-inflation and stabilization plan, which included another massive currency devaluation. A last minute agreement with the Sandinista unions for a short grace period averted sabotage of the summit. It was evident that despite the rhetoric and vague promises, Central Americans remained skeptical about Europe's willingness and ability to help solve their problems. The opposition newspaper *Barricada*, the former Sandinista official daily, expressed what many in Central America were thinking in spite of the diplomatic niceties of San José VII: Central America would continue its struggle "without having faith in Europe."[38]

In July 1991, the European Council took measures to temporarily restore faith in Europe's role in Central America. Responding to a recommendation from the European Commission, the council gave the Central American countries the trade preferences that they had requested in Managua. But the tariff relief for tropical products was to end by January 1992. The council was careful to link the time period to the agreement with the Andeas Group, "without prejudice to the annual nature of the community's system of generalized tariff preferences."[39]

ACTING ON PRINCIPLE

In Latin America, the asymmetry between rhetoric and action debilitates Spanish foreign policy in subtle yet profound ways. Spain's historical experience in Latin America carries with it a tremendous moral and spiritual burden that rhetoric only serves to increase. The desire to maintain good state to state relations with all Latin American countries ran into the inevitable contradictions that government to government relations usually provide. Spanish policy attempted to avoid these contradictions by presenting itself as an impartial observer of, and mediator in, ideological and strategic conflicts. But the impartiality of any government implies a lack of conviction with which Felipe González would become increasingly uncomfortable.

After years of ambiguity, Prime Minister González made it clear that the Nicaraguan and Cuban models of democracy were not what he would want for his own country. "There is a failure in the system [in Cuba], period . . . the system is inefficient and it cannot function if directed from a centralized bureaucracy." With reference to Nicaragua and Cuba, González pointed out that economies without material incentives can function for a year or so "when people act out of enthusiasm, [but later] only the *watery stew* [*cocido*] party remains."[40]

Such declarations would eventually cause Washington, and President George Bush in particular, to concede to the figure of González a position of leadership in Latin American affairs. Confident that Spain and the United States share the same values and pursue the same outcomes, Bush used the *punto de encuentro* of the 1989 NATO summit to personally communicate to González his support for the Spanish Prime Minister's role in the region. González confirmed the new spirit of cooperation, adding that there had already been a number of telephone consultations between the two national leaders.[41] The intense telephone consultations after the Panamá invasion, in which Bush explained the U.S. position, suggested that there was a high level of confidence that Spain had taken its rightful place after all: a firm ally of the United States-led Western democratic coalition.

There was a consensus among Western leaders, as well as among the Latin American and Iberian elite, that Felipe González exercised real influence in the Central American context. Among his colleagues in Spanish officialdom, including those whom he had removed or excluded from power, there was an almost reverential attitude towards the Prime Minister. This admiration may have come simply through the recognition that he was the only Socialist politician capable of winning Spanish elections for the PSOE, but there was little doubt that González's presence was in demand in the Latin American context. It should be pointed out, nevertheless, that respect for the Spanish Prime Minister increased in proportion to his own realism and his willingness to take principled positions in regional conflicts.[42]

BRINGING ON HOME THE IBERO-AMERICAN COMMUNITY

It was no surprise, then, that Felipe would turn toward his realistic trump card during the first Ibero-American Summit meeting in July 1991, in Guadalajara, Mexico. The idea of an annual summit has been controversial enough; at Mexican and Latin American insistence, Spain conceded that the first meeting in Mexico would precede the meeting already planned for Madrid in 1992. Months before the Guadalajara gala, at which 23 heads of state and governments from 21 nations in Latin America and the Iberian peninsula were united for the first time, Mexico's special ambassador for the summit, Alfredo de Mazo, made it clear that Latin America would not allow Spain to monopolize the prestige of the annual summit or set the agenda, either in Mexico or Spain. Leadership of the "rediscovered" *Comunidad Iberoamericana* would not be decided in Seville or the Spanish capital.

The Spanish were also concerned by resistance from their neighbors in Lisbon who were complaining of the *españolización* of the rediscovered community.[43] But the presence of Fidel Castro, who was scheduled to meet with both King Juan Carlos and Felipe González, would provide the true opportunity for leadership to whomever could muster the courage to confront the Cuban dictator for being out of step with his democratic colleagues.

Though all eyes at the summit were on Castro, it was Felipe González who broke the ice with his sarcastic humor and his hard-hitting commentaries on what Castro represented. Before the inauguration of the conference, Castro achieved some diplomatic successes by managing to reestablish consular relations with Colombia and Chile, two former political adversaries. But before Castro could gather diplomatic momentum, González, in his introductory speech at the inaugural session, embarrassed Castro with a reference to the incomplete democratic mission in Latin America: "Without democracy there will be no internal or international solidarity to take on the projects of economic development."[44] In a long interview with Castro, which was later joined by President Carlos Salinas of Mexico, González urged the Cuban dictator to initiate democratic reforms. Castro's response was no different from the one he gave González in Brasilia back in March 1990: there would be no concessions on internal political matters. The Cuban delegation blamed the pressure for reform on "intoxications fabricated from the North,"[45] as González used his sense of humor to engage questions from the press about Castro's efforts to buck the region's new liberal orthodoxy, and Castro's military garb: "We don't want uniformity—not the uniformity of uniforms."[46]

At the close of the summit, however, González lashed out more directly at the Cuban role in hemispheric politics. This time the reference was not even thinly veiled:

Let us permit the parliaments and the people to write their history in a sovereign fashion, and relegate guerrilla adventures to the tales of the imaginative novelists that this continent has in such great supply.[47]

The Spanish prime minister emerged from the summit as Castro's harshest critic, while the King dutifully played the role of state representative, meeting briefly with the other participants and attending the sessions and social activities. González emphasized the value of a long-term *state to state* relationship with Cuba by stating that the King still planned to visit Cuba in the near future. The presence of the King in Guadalajara created a controversy in Spain as the new conservative opposition foreign policy spokesman, Javier Rupérez, accused the Socialists of creating "confusion" around the constitutional separation of powers between the government and the state. Though party chief José Maria Aznar later contradicted the statements by Rupérez, the conservatives were concerned about the skillful use of the King's presence as a foreign policy tool. The powerful combination of Juan Carlos and Felipe was insuring the Socialists with foreign policy successes that would deflect attention from domestic crises that the Partido Popular was eager to exploit.[48]

González had gone beyond skillful diplomatic performance and into the realm of foreign policy substance. Two weeks before the summit, Spain had hosted a high-level meeting of industrialized donor nations to coordinate a European and Canadian contribution to the Multilateral Investment Fund, a major component of President Bush's Enterprise for the Americas Initiative.[49] Whether he acknowledged it rhetorically or not at the Guadalajara summit, González was aware of an ineluctable process of economic liberalization that ran parallel to and reinforced the democratic tide sweeping through the Americas. He needed no reminding, as the presidents of Colombia, Venezuela, and Mexico signed an historic free trade pact at the summit. As in his efforts to involve the EEC in Latin American affairs, González recognized the need to be identified with such processes while getting others to pay the attendant costs.

FROM PERSONAL DIPLOMACY TO MULTILATERALISM

The Prime Minister's realism, moreover, counseled him to defer to other regional and international actors when Spanish prestige was too much on the line. The Arias peace plan in the Esquipulas II summit may have been a *fait accompli*, but Spain's intense collaboration with the United Nations secretary general in regional peacekeeping and observer forces was a recognition of Spain's limited policy resources, which needed to be enhanced by a major legitimizing source. The collaboration with the United Nations was also a recognition that Europe alone could not offer the vehicle through which Spain could realize its aspirations in Latin America. In fact, there was a conscious struggle to balance the frenzied pace of Europeanization with aspirations for a privileged Spanish relationship with Latin America.

THE WEIGHT OF EUROPE

The outcome of the struggle between Spain's European priorities and aspirations in other parts of the world could not have been more decisive. With democratic confidence shaken at home by scandals, corruption, and economic and social crises, Spain sought refuge in the European fold, where its historical aspirations had never been realized and where its economic and political progress had been reinforced. The failures of Spanish democracy would be drowned in the prosperity and time-tested institutions of a powerful, democratic Europe pouring in over open borders. The industrial goods and political force of a united Europe would be the focus of Spanish aspirations for generations to come, especially with new political and economic opportunities of the eastern part in the *viejo continente*. Referring to Spain's serious democratic weaknesses, the *Europeista* Fernando Morán, asserted that "we will never come out of this situation until the economic integration and the development of a common European culture leads to the constitution of a European political society."[50]

For Latin Americans, however, the borders were closing. Determined to prevent Spain from becoming the "Mexico of Europe," through which hundreds of thousands if not millions of Africans and Latin Americans would pour into the wealthy countries of the EEC, the Community police, customs, and immigration authorities pressured Spain into taking severe measures against illegal immigration. Visas for Latin Americans, which were never required even under the Franco regime (except for Communist Cuba) are on the 1992 agenda; economic screening of individuals entering Spain, including minimum financial requirements as well as a return ticket home or to a third country (which must be deposited at the airport police station) were already being imposed by the time of Spain's first semester of presidency of the EEC in January 1989. Under intense pressure from Latin American diplomats, Spain vowed to drop the visa requirements for Iberoamericans and succeeded in early 1991 to gain free access for all Iberoamerican countries except Cuba, and—ironically—the Dominican Republic, where Spain's "Discovery" of Latin America had begun some 500 years before.[51]

Harassment of aliens, nevertheless, continued unabated. Deportations became massive both in numbers and in the dimension of the human tragedy. In May 1990, the EEC Commission published a scathing report accusing the Spanish government of systematic abuse and denial of human rights to the close to 800,000 immigrants in its territory. To make matters worse,

Spanish authorities were not collaborating with EEC efforts to monitor the situation. According to the Spanish police, "the diffusion of such information could provoke diplomatic problems and loss of prestige in public opinion."[52]

An EEC poll in November 1989 confirmed what many long-term visitors to Spain already felt: Spaniards were among the most racist and xenophobic people in Europe. With immigrants representing only about 1.5% of the population, the high scores on racist indicators were all the more alarming. In his characteristically polemical and incongruous style, then deputy prime minister, Alfonso Guerra, defended what he called the "least restrictive measures" in Europe and pointed out that "they criticize us in international forums because we are too permissive."[53]

In Latin America the spiritual and symbolic effects of Spain's love affair with Europe were soon expressed with alarming passion. Nobel laureate Gabriel García Márquez vowed never to come back to Spain, where he had lived for seven years and had published many of his most famous works:

The European Community has decided to convert Spain into the doorman of Europe and they begin to close the door to Latin Americans. They are implementing restrictions, you have to bring a bankbook, a return ticket. We will wind up needing a visa to go to Spain. The first Spaniards who came to America did it without a visa, shooting from both hips. They shacked up with the women they found here and they took away all the gold . . . [54]

Like the Mexican author Carlos Fuentes, García Márquez was disturbed by the increasingly European orientation of the former *madre patria*. In this sense, the Spanish collaboration with the UN and the U.S. in the Gulf War was decisive for some influential Latin American intellectuals:

Now that she sent her little ships to the Gulf, she is now European, now she has passed the test. Five hundred years ago she sent three little ships to find the way to the Indies and she changed the world. We *latinos* know that Europe only forgives of us what we do in her own image. I am obsessed by the idea that Spain is becoming European. It's like one's mother going to sleep in another house.[55]

The sovereign right to protect and control borders, to safeguard employment opportunities, and to limit criminal activity is not at issue here. The affront to Latin Americans can again be found in the asymmetry between rhetoric and actual behavior. The Spanish authorities promised to be a *puente*, or bridge, between Europe and Latin America. But Europe has greatly hindered the advancement of Latin American development by pursuing its own regional economic and trade interests. For Europe, "1992" means the completion of its own regional integration, which is perceived by outsiders not as a reaching out to other peoples but as a consolidation of Old World prerogative and protection of narrow economic and political interests.

Spain's triumph, and that of her leaders, is in Spain's own project of

European integration, which brought Spaniards back into the mainstream of Western economic, social, and political life. This feat, brought off in a miraculously short period of time, afforded Spain's leadership the moral power to embark on conflict resolution and democratization projects in places like Central America. But Spain's own democracy is dependent on Europe's ability to help solve pressing social, political, and economic problems. As that dependency increases, and as Spain looks over the Pyrenees and towards the Mediterranean to fulfill its national aspirations, its rhetorical commitment to an Iberoamerican "commonwealth" will be increasingly more difficult to match in deeds.

To the Latin Americans, the V Centenary of the Discovery of America in Seville in 1992 will be the meeting ground, the *punto de encuentro*, for Europeanized Iberians and the few rich Latin Americans able to afford the trip to the Old World. Spain will host the annual Iberoamerican summit in Madrid, and millions of Europeans will pour across Spain's borders to see the Olympic games in the truly European city of Barcelona. For the hundreds of millions who remain in poverty and desperation in Latin America, there will be very little to celebrate. In their minds, and in the minds of many Spaniards, not since 1492, when Columbus left Spain in search of wealth and glory, did Latin America seem so far from the shores of Spain.

Notes

PART I

Chapter 1: Spain and Latin America: Democratic Models and the Search

1. The political science debate on behavioralism is covered in Albert Somit and Joseph Tanenhaus, *The Development of American Political Science: From Burgess to Behavioralism* (New York: Irvington Publishers, 1982).

2. The post-war guru of this approach is Hans Morganthau, the father of modern power politics and political realism. See his *Politics Among Nations* (New York: Knopf, 1948) and his *In Defense of the National Interest* (New York: Knopf, 1951).

3. See, for example, John Spanier, *American Foreign Policy Since World War II* 10th Ed. (New York: Holt, Rinehart and Winston, 1985).

4. Inis L. Claude puts the power politics, realism, and moral approaches in brilliant analytical perspective in his masterpiece, *Power and International Relations* (New York: Random House, 1962). Claude softens Morganthau's "iron laws" of international relations, while doing political realism justice. See also: Robert O. Keohane and Joseph S. Nye, *Power and Interdependence: World Politics in Transition* (Boston: Little, Brown, 1977). More recent attempts to challenge the realists with the norms of democracy are not the exclusive property of any one ideological camp. See, for example, Joshua Muravchic, *Exporting Democracy* (Washington, D.C.: American Enterprise Institute Press, 1991) and Lynn H. Miller, *Global Order: Values and Power in International Politics* (Boulder: Westview Press, 1990).

5. Henry Kissinger was "deeply troubled" by the suggestion that U.S. and Soviet interests were identical. See Thomas L. Friedman, "Baker's Policy on Soviets: Kissinger Begs to Differ," *International Herald Tribune (New York Times)*, February 3–4, 1990, pp. 1, 5.

6. The foregoing ideas about scarcity and revolutionary transformation in the

Third World are owed to the work of Robert Heilbroner. See *Between Capitalism and Socialism* (New York: Random House, 1970). See also: "Reflections on the Future of Socialism," *Commentary* (November 1969).

7. The scrutiny and scholarly effort given to the Spanish model will be the subject of discussion in Chapter 2.

8. Of the myriad sources, it is enough to mention Seymour Martin Lipset and Aldo Solari, eds., *Elites in Latin America* (New York: Oxford University Press, 1968). See the treatment of elites as "actors" in an international political "game" in Gary W. Wynia, *The Politics of Latin American Development* 3rd Ed. (Cambridge: Cambridge University Press, 1990).

9. No discussion of the intellectual history of Latin America can be conducted without reference to the classic work on Latin American thought: Miguel Jorrín and John D. Martz, *Latin American Political Thought and Ideology* (Chapel Hill: University of North Carolina Press, 1970).

10. Bolívar's speech at the Congress at Angostura. See Vicente Lecuna and Harold A. Bierck, eds., *The Selected Writings of Simón Bolívar*, 2 Vols. (New York: The Colonial Press, 1951). For a handy Spanish language volume see Simón Bolívar, *Escritos Políticos* (Madrid: Alianza Editorial, 1983).

11. Bolívar's famous "Jamaica Letter," *ibid.* (Translation by John A. Crow.)

12. *Ibid.*

13. Rafael Heliodoro Valle, *Valle* (Mexico: Secretaría de Educación Pública, 1934), an edited volume of Valle's works. See also: Franklin D. Parker, *José Cecilio del Valle and the Establishment of the Central American Confederation* (Tegucigalpa: Universidad de Honduras, 1954).

14. Andrés Bello, *Obras Completas* (Santiago: Impresora Pedro G. Ramírez, 1881).

15. Lecuna and Bierck, *op. cit.*, I, p. 118.

16. In Managua in 1984, Latin American diplomats involved in the Contadora Peace Process in Central America admitted privately to the author that one of the objectives was to push the Sandinista Revolution along the same path as the Mexican Revolution.

17. For a treatment of the dizzyingly circular logic of the Sandinistas see David Nolan, *The Ideology of the Sandinistas and the Nicaraguan Revolution* (Coral Gables: Institute of Interamerican Studies, 1984).

18. Ironically enough, the revolutionary movement in El Salvador embarked on a Dimitrov strategy after the failure of the 1981 final offensive. See *Otechestven Front* (Sofia) interview with Salvadoran guerrilla leader Julio Flores (28 October 1983, p. 6) as reported by the Foreign Broadcast Information Service (FBIS).

19. That appeal was disseminated by the Frenchman Alexis de Tocqueville in his classic and still relevant *Democracy in America* (New York: Harper and Row, 1966).

20. The publication in 1900 of José Enrique Rodó's anti-American diatribe *Ariel* marks the final break in the intellectual partnership between Latin American and North American democracy.

21. In Central America, a few examples are the Ejército Guerrillero de los Pobres (EGP) in Guatemala and the followers of Ernesto Cardenal and Father Miguel D'Escoto, a Maryknoll priest and foreign minister of Sandinista Nicaragua.

22. For a discussion of the phenomenon in Central America, see Ricardo Arias Calderón, "Political Systems as Export Commodities: The Role of the U.S. in Central America," *Caribbean Review* 15 (Winter 1986), pp. 20–23.

23. See Kenneth N. Skoug Jr., "Cuba as a Model and a Challenge," *Department of State Bulletin* 84 (September 1984), pp. 73–77. The appeal of Cuban socialism is presented in a favorable light in H. Michael Erisman, *Cuba's International Relations: Anatomy of a Nationalistic Foreign Policy* (Boulder, CO: Westview Press, 1985). See also the critique of Erisman's lack of scrutiny of Castro's socialist practices in Damian J. Fernández, "Cuban Foreign Policy: Scholarship and Double Standards," *Journal of Interamerican Studies and World Affairs*, 28 (Summer 1986), pp. 147–153.

24. Some of the details, moreover, should not be taken for granted. Cuban gains on the health care and education fronts have been so universally recognized that there has not been the proper scrutiny until recently. See Nicolas Eberstadf, "Did Fidel Fudge the Figures?" *Caribbean Review*, 15 (Spring 1986), p. 47, and Sergio Diaz Briquets, "How to Figure Out Cuba," *ibid.*, pp. 8–11.

25. The Nicaraguan economic situation will be discussed at length in Chapters 4 and 8.

26. For a legalistic analysis of the Costa Rican democratic model see Robert S. Barker, "Constitutional Adjudication in Costa Rica: A Latin American Model," *Inter-American Law Review*, 27 (Winter 1986), pp. 249–274.

27. The political pressure in the strategic and local contexts will be addressed in detail in later chapters. For the Costa Rican view see José Figueres, Daniel Oduber, et. al., "Reflections on U.S. Policy," *World Policy Journal*, 3 (Spring 1986), pp. 317–346. The economic situation, which will also be addressed in greater detail in the context of regional issues, is serious. In 1985, foreign debt was taking about 85% of Costa Rica's export earnings (*Panorama Económica Latinoamericana*, no. 271 (May 1985), pp. 12–17).

28. Some have warned of the end of the model itself. See Andrew Reding, "Costa Rica: Democratic Model in Jeopardy," *World Policy Journal*, 3 (Spring 1986), pp. 301–316.

29. See former president A. Monge's statements on this point in *Caribbean Today*, 2 (May 1985), pp. 10–15.

Chapter 2: Groping for Theory: The Spanish Democratic Model as an International Metaphor

1. Robert Dahl makes reference to the impossibility of arriving at anything more than an operational definition of democracy in *Polyarchy: Participation and Opposition* (New Haven: Yale University Press, 1971), pp. 1–10.

2. Some basic references that reflect the fact that behavioralism was nurtured in a democratic environment are: Gabriel Almond and G. Bingham Powell, Jr., *Comparative Politics* (Boston: Little, Brown, 1966) and Robert A. Dahl, *Who Governs?* (New Haven: Yale University Press, 1961).

3. Seymour M. Lipset, *Political Man* (New York: Doubleday, 1960) and "Some Social Requisites of Democracy: Economic Development and Political Legitimacy," *American Political Science Review*, 53 (1959); D. Jaros and L. V. Grant, *Political Behavior* (Oxford: Basil Blackwell, 1975).

4. See, for example, Phillip Cutright, "National Political Development: Measurement and Analysis," *American Sociological Review*, 2 (1963).

5. Stanley Rothman, "Functionalism and its Critics: An Analysis of the Writings of Gabriel Almond," *American Political Science Review*, 57 (Fall 1971), pp. 236–276

and Almond's reply, "Slaying the Functional Dragon: A Reply to Stanley Rothman," *American Political Science Review*, 67 (Fall 1973), pp. 259–268. Also see D. E. Neubauer's critique of Lipset and Cutright in "Some Conditions of Democracy," *American Political Science Review*, 61, 1 (1967).

6. Dahl in *Polyarchy, op. cit.*, pp. 71, 135.

7. D. A. Rostow, "Transition to Democracy: Toward a Dynamic Model," *Comparative Politics*, 2 (April 1970), pp. 337–63.

8. See John Herz, *From Dictatorship to Democracy: Coping with the Legacies of Authoritarianism and Totalitarianism* (Westport, CT: Greenwood Press, 1982).

9. The most basic reference is Juan Linz and Alfred Stepan eds., *Breakdowns of Democratic Regimes* (Baltimore: The Johns Hopkins Press, 1978). See also the latest volumes on transitions: Larry Diamond, Juan Linz, and Seymour Lipset, eds., *Democracy in Developing Nations* (Boulder, CO: Lynne Reinner, 1988); Enrique Baloyra, ed., *Comparing New Democracies: Transition and Consolidation in Mediterranean Europe and the Southern Cone* (Boulder, CO: Westview Press, 1987) for a valid comparative perspective. For an excellent analysis of the empirical onslaught see Joan Botella, "Despedidas de la idea: Perdida del terreno del pensamiento en benficio de los estudios empiricos," *El País*, May 29, 1988, p. 21.

10. Daniel H. Levine, "Paradigm Lost: Dependence to Democracy," *World Politics*, XL, 3 (April 1988), pp. 377–394, a scathing indictment of the almost pseudo-scientific nature of much of the analysis on democratic transitions and, in particular, of the four-volume work of Guillermo O'Donnell, Philippe C. Schmitter, and Laurence Whitehead, eds., *Transitions from Authoritarian Rule: Prospects for Democracy* (Baltimore: The Johns Hopkins University Press, 1986).

11. The many excellent studies of the international and national dimensions of the Civil War (Payne, Matthews, Preston, Carr, et al.) are all overshadowed by Hugh Thomas's *The Spanish Civil War*, 3rd Ed. (Middlesex: Penguin, 1986).

12. Raymond Carr makes reference to this in "The Spanish Transition to Democracy in Historical Perspective," in Robert P. Clark and Michael H. Haltzel, eds., *Spain in the 1980s: The Democratic Transition and the New International Role* (Cambridge, MA: Ballinger Publishing, 1987), pp. 1–3.

13. Address by Felipe González at the Wilson Center, September 27, 1985 in Clark and Haltzel, *op. cit.*, pp. 179–190.

14. Raymond Carr and Juan Pablo Fusi, *Spain: Dictatorship to Democracy*, 2nd Ed. (London: Allen, Unwin, 1981); José Maria Maravall, *The Transition to Democracy in Spain* (London: Croom and Helm, 1982); Victor Alba, *Transition in Spain: From Franco to Democracy* (New Brunswick, NJ: Transaction Books, 1978). The more recent "corporatist" approach to the Spanish transition (Wiarda, Foweraker, *et al.*) has yet to produce a benchmark volume. In all fairness, the scholarly trend shows promise. See note 20.

15. Carr in Clark and Haltzel, *op. cit.*, p. 1.

16. *Ibid.*, pp. 3–8.

17. Maravall, *op. cit.*, p. 203. For an update of his work on the democratic transition see José Maria Maravall and Julian Santamaria, "Political Change in Spain and the Prospects for Democracy" in O'Donnell and Schmitter, *op. cit.*, "Latin America."

18. The party is the Partido Socialista Obrero Español (Spanish Socialist Workers Party, PSOE), for whom Maravall served as education minister until the controversy

over student violence in 1987 and the long teachers strike in 1988 provoked his downfall in July 1988.

19. Alba, *op. cit.*, p. 281.

20. Richard Gunther, "Democratization and Party Building: The Role of Party Elites in the Spanish Transition," in Clark and Haltzel, *op. cit.*, pp. 35–65 and R. Gunther, Giacomo Sani and Goldie Shabad, *Spain after Franco: The Making of a Competitive Party System* (Berkeley: University of California Press, 1985). The politics and policies of the Socialist Party (PSOE) have been central to the investigation of institution building. See Donald Share, *Dilemmas of Social Democracy: The Spanish Socialist Workers Party in the 1980s* (New York: Greenwood Press, 1989) and Richard Gillespie, *The Spanish Socialist Party: A History of Factionalism* (Oxford: Oxford University Press, 1989). Close to this trend is the "corporatist" approach, best presented in Joe Foweraker, "Corporatist Strategies and the Transition to Democracy in Spain," *Comparative Politics* 20, 1 (October 1987), pp. 57–72; Howard J. Wiarda, "Toward a Framework for the Study of Political Change in the Iberic-Latin Tradition: The Corporative Model," *World Politics* 25 (January 1983), pp. 206–235; and Salvador Giner and Eduardo Sevilla, "Spain: From Corporatism to Corporatism," in A. Williams, ed., *Southern Europe Transformed* (London: Harper and Row, 1984).

21. Andrea Bonime-Blanc, *Spain's Transition to Democracy: The Politics of Constitution-Making* (Boulder, CO: Westview Press, 1987). See also: Jordi Solé Tura, "The Spanish Transition to Democracy," in Clark and Haltzel, *op. cit.*, p. 34.

22. Gunther in Haltzel and Clark, *op. cit.*, pp. 35–36.

23. Bonime-Blanc, *op. cit.*, pp. 6–9.

24. *Ibid.*, Chaps. 5–6.

25. *Ibid.*, Chap. 7.

26. Paul Preston, *The Triumph of Democracy in Spain* (London and NY: Methuen, 1986).

27. The glossary is entitled "Dramatis Personnae." Even students of the role of King Juan Carlos tend to succumb to the "elite reformer" thesis. See Charles T. Powell's update of his Oxford Dissertation, *El Piloto del Cambio: El Rey, la Monarquía, y la Transición a la Democracia* (Barcelona: Planeta, 1991).

28. *Ibid.*, p. 158.

29. *Ibid.*, pp. 225–227.

30. Preston does reserve special praise for Suárez. *Ibid.*, pp. 117, 120–121, 187–188. Suárez himself is careful to remind Spanish voters that he effected the most important transition during his stewardship. See his campaign statements in *El País*, June 9, 1989, p. 17.

31. Howard J. Wiarda, "The Significance for Latin America of the Spanish Democratic Transition," in Clark and Haltzel, *op. cit.*, p. 163.

32. Suárez's involvement with the Chilean opposition in 1986–87 produced only some vague references to the goals of transition.

33. Abraham F. Lowenthal, foreword in O'Donnell and Schmitter, *op. cit.*, "Latin America," p. ix.

Chapter 3: Packaging the Model

1. See *The Economist*, December 10, 1988, pp. 26, 31–33 for an analysis of Spain's embarrassing obsession. For González's comments see the *El País* interview, December 9, 1990, p. 16.

2. *The Financial Times*, January 19–20, 1991, p. 3; *International Herald Tribune (New York Times)*, February 2–3, 1991, p. 3.

3. See *El País*, November 15, 1985, p. 14, for Amnesty International's charges.

4. See *Cambio 16*, February 15, 1988, pp. 20–21.

5. *El País*, May 10, 1987, pp. 1, 19.

6. See *Tiempo* (Madrid), October 29, 1990, pp. 47–53 for accusations on sales of weapons of mass destruction and Spanish "merchants of death" in the Middle East, Latin America, and elsewhere. *El País*, August 3, 1990, p. 17 pursues the issue of Spanish chemical-capable munitions to Iraq.

7. *El País*, September 30, 1989, p. 20.

8. A public opinion poll published in *El País* (October 2, 1988, p. 1) indicated that 54% of Spaniards believed that the U.S.-Spain treaty violated the 1986 NATO referendum.

9. See Paul Delaney, "González Defensive on Pact," *International Herald Tribune (New York Times)*, October 3, 1988, p. 2.

10. *International Herald Tribune*, February 2–3, 1991, p. 3. The decision had been made weeks before on January 17.

11. The U.S. press is most guilty of creating an inflated image of Spanish democracy. See, for example, "Spain: Racing into the Future," the cover story of *Newsweek*, May 23, 1988.

12. See *El País* (Domingo Section), December 11, 1988.

13. According to Lt. Gen. Migule Iñiguez del Moral, Chief of the General Staff of the Spanish Armed Forces, Spanish officers have "assimilated the Constitution" and are no longer a factious power. See interview in *El País*, May 28, 1988, p. 18.

14. Promotions and retirements tend to bring the issues to the surface. The voluntary retirement of disgruntled and unpromoted General Fernando Yrayzoz Castellón sparked the debate once again in 1986. See editorial in *El País*, March 23, 1986, p. 10. Narcis Serra, nevertheless, was rewarded with the position of deputy prime minister (vice-president of the government) in a March 1991 purge of the followers of his predecessor, Alfonso Guerra.

15. See the scathing opinion piece by Gabriel Jackson, "Sobre el modelo político socialista," *El País*, October 17, 1985, p. 11.

16. See Edward Schumacher, "An Age-Old (But Still Common) Horror," *New York Times*, December 2, 1984. The article cites Amnesty International's accusations against the Spanish police. See also Amnesty International's 1987 Report on Spain (London: Amnesty International, 1988), which also mentions the encarceration of two conscientious objectors to obligatory military service. By 1991, however, Amnesty International would identify only one case, that of an objector who had been given a six-month sentence.

17. *El País*, April 15, 1988, p. 16. The revelations led to the replacement of Barrionuevo in July 1988. He was quietly given the communications and transportation portfolio.

18. *El País*, November 25, 1988, p. 21; *International Herald Tribune*, July 2, 1990, p. 2 for Miláns de Bosch; *El País*, January 19, 1991, p. 31 for Spanish protests on Videla's retirement plans.

19. "The old story...," as it is known in rural political circles, is described in common-sense, non-ideological terms by Juan Manuel Sanchez Gordillo, mayor of

the conflict-ridden Andalusian village of Marinaleda, in "El movimiento de los jornaleros andaluces: La vieja historia...," *El País*, October 28, 1985, p. 52.

20. See "La larga marcha de los procesos contra los jornaleros," *El País*, March 23, 1986, p. 21.

21. *ABC* (Seville edition), editorial, July 19, 1988, p. 11.

22. See *El País*, December 16, 1990, pp. II, 8–9 for general coverage of lingering farm worker problems.

23. See critique from the EEC perspective in *ABC* editorial, *op. cit.*

24. Of all that has been written about ETA's exploits since the 1960s, still the best source of ETA's motivations and strategy during the Francoist era is Julen Aguirre (*alias* Eva Forest), *Operación Ogro: cómo y por qué matamos a Carrrero Blanco* (Paris, 1974).

25. Much has been written about ETA's own internal struggles, which split the group in 1977. The active group, ETA-Militar (ETA-M), has a much more nationalistic and militaristic view of the "war" against Madrid. The other group, ETA-politico-militar (ETA P-M), is believed to have been infiltrated by Spanish police; those that were not neutralized by the security forces joined the ETA-M.

26. Much of the international linkage is undocumented or classified. The Spanish authorities have made the difficult decision of separating the ETA issue from their international relations, as they appeared to have done with Sandinista Nicaragua. (See Chapter 8.) For the full range of terror network connections (real and imagined) see Claire Sterling, *The Terror Network*, (New York: Holt, Rinehart & Winston, 1981), Chap. 10.

27. *Cambio 16*, December 10, 1990, pp. 15–21 broke the Santo Domingo story. Also see one of González's more forceful reiterations of policy in *El País*, December 11, 1990, p. 19.

28. *El País*, December 16, 1990, p. 17. In fact, in 1990 alone 40 *etarras* were released or paroled in an effort to break ETA control over prison populations. See *El País*, August 12, 1990, p. 12.

29. See *Diario 16*, December 8, 1988, p. 14.

30. See government spokeswoman Rosa Conde's declarations after the first meeting of the reshuffled Council of Ministers in Madrid, *El País*, July 16, 1988, pp. 1, 14.

31. *Cambio 16*, August 13, 1990, pp. 17–21; *El País*, August 3, 1990, pp. 1, 15.

32. *El País*, October 12, 1990, pp. 1, 15; and September 11, 1990, pp. 1, 13.

33. Official figures given to the press tend to be inconsistent due to later revisions on the authorship of attacks. See *Cambio 16*, December 24, 1990, p. 24.

34. See Richard Gunther, "Democratization and Party Building: The Role of Party Elites in the Spanish Transition," in Clark and Haltzel, *op. cit.*, pp. 35–65.

35. See, for example, Ricardo de la Cierva, "La misión de Alfonso Guerra," *Epoca*, February 22, 1988, pp. 65–74.

36. See Pablo Castellanos, "Desde las grutas," *El País*, September 8, 1979.

37. Partido Socialista Obrero Español, *Forjar el Socialismo*, Texto del VI Congreso Extraordinario (Madrid: PSOE, 1979).

38. Gomez Llorente in Eduardo Chamorro, *Felipe González: Un hombre en las espera.* (Barcelona: Editorial Planeta, 1980), p. 188.

39. Interview with Felipe González, *El País*, November 17, 1985, pp. 1, 13–15.

40. The still-clinging Castellanos substantiated the charge again in May 1987.

See *Diario 16*, May 21, 1987, p. 10. Edged out of the PSOE in 1988, Castellanos joined the United Left (coalition of the small communist and other leftist groups) voting bloc in the Cortes in February 1989.

41. It appeared that by the mid–1980s, 32 Socialist bosses controlled all the decision-making of a supposed mass party, and by virtue of an absolute parliamentary majority, they controlled all of Spain. See revelations in *El País*, January 23, 1988, p. 15. See also Donald Share, *op. cit.*, and Richard Gillespie, *op. cit.*

42. See his article, "Poder Institucional y Hegemonía Social," reprinted along with additional commentaries, in his book, Ignacio Sotelo, *Los Socialistas en el poder* (Madrid: Ediciones El País, 1986), Intro. and Chapter II. See also the historical treatment of authoritarianism in the context of the Spanish transition in José Enrique Rodríguez-Ibañez, *Después de una dictadura: cultura autoritaria y transición política en España* (Madrid: Centro de Estudios Constitucionales, 1988).

43. *Epoca*, February 17, 1988, p. 67.

44. *El País*, October 23, 1988, p. 72.

45. See Eusebio. Mujal-Leon, "Decline and Fall of Spanish Communism," *Problems of Communism* (March-April 1986), pp. 1–27.

46. For a sober essay on the "regionalization" of the Right, see ex-Communist and, later, Socialist culture minister Jordi Solé Tura's "Una derecha regionalizada?" *El País*, June 10, 1987, p. 11.

47. Interview in *El País*, May 10, 1987, p. 8.

48. For an account of a particularly nasty day's work see *Diario de Cádiz*, April 29, 1987, p. 1.

49. The author was an eyewitness to practically all of the incidents in 1987.

50. The author was witness to a complete degeneration of the situation towards late April, as an insurrectionary atmosphere appealed to the town's usual enemies.

51. The only substantial investigative report to make it to the national media was written by the well-known leftist journalist Maruja Torres, "La guerra de Puerto Real," *El País*, May 3, 1987, pp. 8–9.

52. The front-page press and prime time TV and radio coverage was incessant during late April and most of May 1987. See, for example, *El País*, May 7, 1987, p. 1.

53. A front-page photo of the situation in Puerto Real, published in *El País* (April 29, 1987), did not include a report on the situation.

54. *El País*, September 6, 1988, pp. 1, 14.

55. For example, see the spate of reports on the *conflictividad* in *El País*, April 28, 1988, p. 1.

56. Ministry of Interior figures reported in *El País*, June 29, 1988, p. 26.

57. See Jordi Solé Tura, "Un poco de calma . . . ," *El País*, July 22, 1987, p. 9. Solé Tura later passed over to the PSOE in an effort to "keep the Left in power in Spain."

58. For a report on the police and student violence see *El País*, January 24, 1987, pp. 1, 12–14; and *International Herald Tribune* (Reuters), January 24, 1987, p. 1.

59. The crisis of *seguridad ciudadana* occupied the front page of *Cambio 16, Tiempo*, and most newspapers throughout the course of 1987–88. There was a perception that petty crime against property was completely out of control in the urban and suburban areas; the rate of violent crime was soaring in the big cities.

60. These observations are based on over three years of living experience in

Seville and Cádiz, as well as on the testimony of many Spaniards during the period 1985–89.

61. See, for example, *Cambio 16*, October 26, 1987, p. 144.

62. *Ibid.*, p. 85.

63. *El País*, October 4, 1989, p. 16.

64. *El País*, December 20, 1990, pp. 1, 20.

65. Official statistics are analyzed in *Tiempo*, February 17, 1986, p. 62.

66. The *New York Times* states that the real number ranges from 54,000–280,000 depending on the source. The public perception supports the higher figure. See *International Herald Tribune*, November 10, 1988, p. 5. Deaths from drug trafficking, including overdoses and poisonings, reached 690 in 1990. See *El País*, February 16, 1991, p. 17.

67. The Spanish media have become bolder in their presentation of the heroin problem. See the nightmarish journey of a young drug victim in Miguel Figuero, "Bajo el caballo," *El País Domingo*, June 26, 1988, p. 2.

68. See *Cambio 16*, August 13, 1990, pp. 63–66 for a chilling survey of the landscape.

69. *International Herald Tribune*, November 10, 1988, p. 1.

70. The Bank of Spain reported 2.3 percent growth in 1985, 3.3 percent growth in 1986, and an impressive 5.2 percent in 1987. See *El País Negocios*, July 3, 1988, for a summary of the economic recovery.

71. Bank of Spain forecasts reported in *El País*, July 22, 1988, pp. 1, 39.

72. Bank of Spain forecast for 1988. *Ibid*.

73. See *The Economist*, December 3, 1988, p. 116; *Financial Times*, March 28, 1991, p. 2.

74. See *ibid.*, *The Economist* and Bank of Spain data on reserves from *El País*, January 8, 1991, p. 34.

75. See Reginald Dale, "Economy of Spain is Suddenly Sunny," *International Herald Tribune*, May 17, 1988, pp. 1, 2.

76. *Ibid.*, p. 2; *Financial Times*, March 28, 1991, p. 2.

77. *TVE* (Television Service, Madrid), December 30, 1988.

78. See for example William Chilslett, "In Spain, a Risk of Overheating," *International Herald Tribune*, September 26, 1988, p. 14.

79. Bank of Spain forecasts in *El País*, July 22, 1988, p. 39.

80. The European financial community's view is reflected in Reginald Dale, "Spain's Managers: Conservative, Jet-Set, Socialists," *International Herald Tribune*, May 19, 1988, p. 1. For Iberia's recuperation see *International Herald Tribune*, January 28, 1987, p. 9. Strikes in 1988, however, hurt earnings, and the plunge in air travel as a result of the Gulf crisis devastated the company.

81. A December 1987 poll reports the opinion of Spanish households in *El País*, December 19, 1987, p. 1.

82. See, for example, *La Vanguardia*, May 21, 1987, pp. 1, 3.

83. *Ibid.*, p. 3.

84. October 1988 unemployment in Spain was 18.9 percent. See *The Economist*, December 3, 1988, p. 115. It dropped to 15.6 percent in 1990, according to Ministry of Economy data published in *El País*, April 14, 1991, p. 5.

85. See Chilslett, *op. cit.*

86. Dale, *op. cit.*, May 17, 1988, p. 2.

87. *Ibid.*

88. See José Luis Leal, "CEE: un primer balance," for an economist's view of the trade performance in *El País Negocios*, June 5, 1988, p. 2.

89. The Socialist government's paradoxical fears are reported in *El País*, September 23, 1988, p. 1.

90. See an analysis by the Fondo de Investigación Económico y Social in *El País*, May 17, 1987, pp. 1, 45.

91. *International Herald Tribune*, May 31, 1987, pp. 1, 45.

92. *El País*, December 16, 1988, p. 1, quotes Felipe González.

93. The historical aspects of the relationship and subsequent rupture are treated in Joaquín Prieto and Carmen Parra, "La ruptura," *El País Domingo*, December 18, 1988, p. 1.

94. *El País*, December 4, 1988, p. 16.

95. For an interesting comparison between *Felipismo* and Thatcherism see Raymond Carr, "Thatcherism, Felipism," in *The Independent* on the eve of the British Prime Minister's first official visit to Madrid since the 1982 Socialist victory. Reprinted in *El País*, September 21, 1988, p. 11.

96. *El País*, November 16, 1988, p. 64.

97. *Ibid.*, pp. 1, 62.

98. *El País*, December 29, 1987, p. 43.

99. *El País*, October 26, 1989, p. 20 for Aznar's critique of Solchaga's position.

100. *El País*, January 16, 1989, pp. 1, 11 carries a leader by Joaquín Estefania, who would later become editor-in-chief of the Madrid daily.

101. See interview with González, "The Left's Saving Grace," *Financial Times*, December 17, 1990, p. 32.

102. Peter Bruce, "Spain's Current Account Deficit Soars," *Financial Times*, March 28, 1991, p. 2.

103. OECD cited in *El País*, December 21, 1990, pp. 1, 57.

104. For the national and EEC implications of such fraud see Peter Bruce, "Spanish VAT Fraud Plot Opens Debate on Policing," *Financial Times*, October 27–28, 1990, p. 2.

105. See, for example, *El País*, November 8, 1989, pp. 1, 23; *El País*, November 20, 1989, p. 22.

106. *International Herald Tribune* (Reuters) March 27, 1990, p. 2.

107. For a good summary of "the year of Juan Guerra" see *Tiempo*, January 7, 1991, pp. 13–16.

108. See interview with Felipe conducted by Joaquín Estefanía, *El País*, December 9, 1990, pp. 14–16.

109. *El País*, December 18, 1990, pp. 1, 19.

110. *El País*, December 16, 1990, p. 19.

111. Apart from some evidence of resumed high rates of economic growth in the construction and services industries, the only positive development on the eve of the Guadalajara summit was the announcement by the Catalonian terrorist group Terra Lliure that it had abandoned the armed struggle. See *El País*, July 6, 1991, p. 1. Spanish police also boasted the disarticulation of ETA's *Comando Barcelona*, but only after yet another bloody terrorist attack in Catalonia. ETA attacks throughout the country and overseas during the summer led to a more sober assessment of the terrorist group's ability to disrupt the 1992 Olympic Games in Barcelona, and the

World Exposition and Celebration of the V Centenary of the Discovery of America in Seville. For the blow against the *Comando Barcelona*, see *El País*, May 31, 1991, p. 1.

112. For the King's rare commentary on domestic affairs, see *El País*, June 27, 1991, pp. 1, 20.

PART II

1. Felipe González at meeting of EEC Commission to announce the upcoming Spanish Presidency of the Community. *Television Española* (TVE), December 12, 1988.

2. For an excellent depiction of this diversity and the profound social, economic and political implications see Griffin Smith Jr., "Guatemala: A Fragile Democracy," *National Geographic* 173, 6 (June 1988), pp. 768–803.

3. See, for example, John A. Booth, "Socioeconomic and Political Roots of National Revolts in Central America," *Latin American Research Review* Vol. 26, no. 1 (1990).

Chapter 4: Democracy's Moving Target: Central American Prospects and the Strategic Dimension

1. Interview with Claude Cheysson, then the EEC's North-South commissioner in *El País*, July 19, 1987, p. 6.

2. Paul Simon, "Baby in a Bubble," *Graceland*, Warner Bros. Recording, © 1986.

3. *The Economist* scoffs at the importance of such bonds in comparison with the power of aid, trade, and commerce (July 30, 1988, p. 20).

4. The international press made much of this symbolism. Nevertheless, later it was announced that *Contra* rebels and Sandinista officials were set to resume talks in September 1988.

5. John Peeler, *Latin American Democracies: Colombia, Costa Rica, Venezuela* (Chapel Hill: University of North Carolina Press, 1985). Among the many scholars in and around this school are Enrique Baloyra, Scott Mainwaring, Guiseppe Di Palma, Guillermo O'Donnell, Phillipe Schmitter, Juan Linz, *et al.* See the discussion in Chapter 2.

6. Martin Needler, *The Problem of Democracy in Latin America* (Lexington, MA: D. C. Heath and Co., 1987).

7. *Ibid.*, p. 15. Here is where the Marxist scholars would part ways: pre-socialist economic production would always involve a degree of coercion based on the prerogatives of ownership and capital.

8. *Ibid.*, pp. 163–64.

9. Much work has been done on this subject, beginning with the pioneering work of Samuel Huntington, *The Soldier and the State* (Cambridge, MA: Belknap/ Harvard, 1957) and Amos Perlmutter, *The Military and Politics in Modern Times* (New Haven: Yale University Press, 1977). In the Latin American context research is also voluminous: See the current state of the art in Martin Needler's review essay, "The Military and Politics in Latin America," *Journal of Interamerican Studies and World Affairs* 28, 3 (Fall 1986), pp. 141–47.

10. Needler, *op. cit.*, p. 15.

11. *Ibid.*, p. 3.

12. See prominent transitionists Guillermo O'Donnell and Phillippe C. Schmitter, *Transitions from Authoritarian Rule: Tentative Conclusions About Uncertain Democracies* (Baltimore: The Johns Hopkins University Press, 1986), pp. 34–37.

13. The Costa Rican land tenure experience is different from that of other Central American countries, but the notion that democracy emerged from the experience of the small *labrador*, or independent small farmer in the countryside, is to a great extent a myth: these independent and poverty-stricken farmers depended on and sold to the *patron*, or large plantation owner, while the *peones*, or peasant laborers, worked the patron's own fields.

14. Enrique Baloyra, "Negotiating War in El Salvador," *Journal of Interamerican Studies and World Affairs* 28, 3 (Spring 1986), p. 139. Also see Baloyra's earlier work (*e.g.*, "Dilemmas of Political Transition," *Journal of International Affairs* 38, 2 (Winter 1985)). Baloyra's definition of democracy is indebted to work by Carlos Huneeus.

15. *Ibid.*, pp. 125–26.

16. See North American Congress on Latin America, *Guatemala* (Berkeley: NACLA, 1974); Stephen Kinzer and Stephen Schlesinger, *Bitter Fruit* (New York: Doubleday, 1982); R. H. Immerman, *The CIA in Guatemala* (Austin: University of Texas Press, 1982); and the long-awaited and honest account from the U.S. Government in U.S. Department of State, *Foreign Relations of the United States 1952–54: The American Republics* (Washington: Government Printing Office, 1984).

17. One of the most widely read reports from Amnesty International was their 1981 Guatemala survey. See Amnesty International *Guatemala: A Government Program of Political Murder* (London: Amnesty International, 1981).

18. The labor component of this strategy, coordinated through the AFL-CIO's American Institute for Free Labor Development (AIFLD), was particularly successful in creating a non-ideological business union constituency for democratic rule. The role of "Project Democracy" in Central American affairs is not well-known or well documented. Despite its vague parameters, its use of covert instruments to redirect U.S. strategy was often successful in avoiding a more visible and hence more controversial role for the United States. Most of the operations were classified or confidential. For example, the U.S. Embassy in Guatemala sent a confidential policy suggestion to the Department of State (May 14, 1984, unpublished) that recommended U.S. funding of Guatemalan business unionism through AIFLD under the auspices of "Project Democracy" as a strategy to counter Christian Democratic and communist unionists.

19. See Konrad Adenaur Stifting (KAS), *Jahresbericht 1980* (Saikt Augustin, FRG), 1981, which reports on Christian Democratic labor activism in El Salvador and Nicaragua.

20. Estimates of as many as 300 Christian Democrats murdered or disappeared (1978–82) have surfaced in the international press. See *Latin America Weekly Report*, May 27, 1982, pp. 6–8.

21. The recent experiences in Uruguay, Argentina, and Spain are cases in point. See "Rights Advocates Bitter Over Argentine Amnesty," *International Herald Tribune*, June 27, 1987, p. 3 and Bradley Graham, "Argentine Amnesty Law Ruled Unconstitutional," *International Herald Tribune* (Washington Post Service), June 13, 1987, p. 2 for the constitutional dimensions of the problem in Argentina.

22. Edén Pastora, the legendary *Comandante Cero* of Sandinista fame, left the revolutionary junta in Managua in 1981 to aid the social democratic guerrilla organization, Organización Revolucionaria del Pueblo en Armas (ORPA). His initiative, however, was frustrated by the presence of Cuban agents, who forced a unity between the social democrats, the Communists, and the ultraleftists engaged in armed struggle.

23. *Latin American Weekly Report*, December 24, 1987, pp. 8–9; Interamerican Development Bank, *Economic and Social Progress in Latin America* (Washington D.C.: Johns Hopkins Press/IDB, 1990), p. 117.

24. The economic and refugee problems are highlighted in Stephen Kinzer, "In Guatemala Terror Persists Despite Civilian Leadership," *International Herald Tribune* (New York Times), February 18, 1988, p. 3. Rising rights abuses were reported by Americas Watch and the United Nations Commission on Human Rights. See *International Herald Tribune* (Los Angeles Times Service), November 26, 1988, p. 2.

25. Jorge Castañeda talks of a rising populist left that "supposedly had been consigned to history's dustbin." See "Latin America's Rising Populist Left," *International Herald Tribune* (Los Angeles Times), September 7, 1988, p. 4.

26. The widely shared views on IMF austerity are incorporated in Juan Guillermo Espinosa, "Outlook for the World Economy: A Latin American Viewpoint," *Journal of Interamerican Studies and World Affairs* 29 4 (Winter 1987–88), pp. 125–45. The Latin American desperation in the face of this issue is reported in Alan Riding, "Latin America Looks to Bush for Debt Relief," *International Herald Tribune* (New York Times), November 30, 1988, p. 1. See also: Ambler H. Moss Jr. ed., *The Miami Report II: New Perspectives on Debt, Trade and Investment—A Key to U.S.-Latin American Relations in the 1990s* (Coral Gables: North South Center/University of Miami), 1988.

27. See, for example, Needler, *op. cit.*

28. Americas Watch reports that in the first nine months of 1988 at least 621 people died in politically related assassinations, most at the hands of the police and security forces who are linked to the private death squads. (See note 24.) President Vinicio Cerezo admitted in January 1989 that 1,706 Guatemalans had disappeared in 1988. See *El País*, January 29, 1989, p. 4.

29. *El País*, May 13, 1990, p. 7.

30. *Reuters* in *International Herald Tribune*, March 31, 1990, p. 2; Lindsey Gruson, "Guerrilla War in Guatemala Heats Up, Fueling Criticism of Civilian Rule," *New York Times*, June 3, 1990, p. 18.

31. Stephen Kinzer, "In Guatemala Terror Persists Despite Civilian Leadership," *International Herald Tribune* (New York Times), February 18, 1988, p. 7; Lindsey Gruson, "Voting Isn't Helping in Guatemala," *New York Times*, June 3, 1990, p. E3.

32. Gruson, *New York Times*, June 3, 1990, p. 18.

33. Lindsey Gruson, "Violence is Again Growing in Guatemala," *International Herald Tribune* (New York Times), June 29, 1990, p. 3.

34. See Covenant House and Amnesty International reports in *El País*, July 15, 1990, p. 8.

35. Gruson, *New York Times*, June 3, 1990, p. E3.

36. *International Herald Tribune* (New York Times), September 21, 1900, p. 2.

37. On Rios Montt's election bid see Richard Johns, "Guatemala Watches Its Born-Again General," *Financial Times*, September 26, 1990, p. 4.

38. *El País*, January 8, 1991, p. 4.

39. See Shirley Cristian, "Decade of Disasters," *The New Republic*, August 29, 1988, pp. 44–49. The Argentine support was withdrawn completely after the election of President Raúl Alfonsín. (Interview with Donald Winters, former CIA station chief, Tegucigalpa, in Miami, September, 1991.)

40. Personal correspondence with the author from David Nolan, a foreign service officer and one of the seven reporting officers expelled from Nicaragua in August 1988 (Rockville, MD, November 28, 1988). See also, Julia Preston, "Another Victim of Nicaragua's War: The Economy," *Washington Post Weekly*, February 1, 1988, pp. 17–18.

41. The minister of agriculture, Jaime Wheelock, one of the pragmatists in the Sandinista 9-man directorate, has been the target of attacks by hardliners like Bayardo Arce. Wheelock attempted to alleviate the suffering of the Nicaraguan peasants by implementing production-oriented mechanisms in the countryside. Wheelock believes that democratization in Nicaragua implies a separation of the state apparatus from the FSLN party. See interviews with Sandinista commanders in Lucia Annunciata, "Democracy and the Sandinistas," *The Nation*, April 2, 1988, pp. 454–56.

42. Interview with Interior Minister Borge in *El País*, July 19, 1989, p. 8.

43. *Ibid.*

44. James LeMoyne, "For Sandinists Economy May Be Worst Enemy," *International Herald Tribune* (New York Times), December 21, 1987.

45. William Branigin, "A Crackdown in Managua," *International Herald Tribune* (Washington Post Service), August 2, 1988, p. 3. The political restrictions were not the only thing feeding discontent in Nicaragua. For the first time in generations, physical hunger was a factor in Nicaraguan politics. See William Branigin, "Let Them Eat Fruit Rinds," *Washington Post Weekly*, October 10, 1988, p. 19.

46. *Ibid.* See also *El País*, July 16, 1988, p. 7.

47. *Ibid.*, *El País*.

48. Erik Ramirez of the Social Christian Party (PSC) in *El País*, July 17, 1988, p. 10.

49. *El País*, November 28, 1987, pp. 1, 15.

50. *El País*, April 15, 1988, p. 10.

51. Stephen Kinzer, "Ortega's Moves Bring Internal Dissent," *International Herald Tribune* (New York Times), January 25, 1988, p. 5.

52. *International Herald Tribune* (New York Times), February 5, 1988, p. 3.

53. James LeMoyne, "Arias's Central America Peace Initiative Appears to Be Near Collapse," *International Herald Tribune* (New York Times), June 25, 1987, p. 3.

54. The most serious of reported violations was the August 3, 1988 attack on a civilian vessel sailing the Escondido River. The death toll included a U.S. Baptist minister. See *Financial Times*, August 4, 1988, p. 3 and *International Herald Tribune*, August 4, 1988, p. 3.

55. César in Stephen Kinzer, "Contra Leader Hopes Talks Resume Soon," *International Herald Tribune* (New York Times), July 26, 1988, p. 3.

56. U.S. officials admit privately to Washington's role as the "glue" that held the movement together. (*Washington Post Weekly*, May 23, 1988, p. 17.)

57. *Diario 16* (Madrid), March 27, 1988, p. 24.

58. *Ibid.* See also *International Herald Tribune*, July 26, 1988, p. 3.

59. Julia Preston, "Peace Pact Participants Are in No Mood to Party," *Washington Post Weekly*, August 15, 1988, p. 18.

60. *Ibid.*

61. *The Washington Post, Ibid.*, quotes Farid Ayales, the Costa Rican ambassador to Managua as asking "When before this, for example, did anyone in Managua know what the *Contras* really stood for?"

62. Borge interview in *El País*, July 19, 1988, p. 8.

63. Julia Preston, *op. cit.*

64. See analysis of Sandinista plans revealed by high-level defector Roger Miranda in William Branigin, "Nicaragua's Leader Plays Down Assertions of Military Buildup," *International Herald Tribune* (Washington Post Service), December 15, 1987, p. 3.

65. Douglas Farah, "No More Modeling for El Salvador," *Washington Post Weekly*, May 23, 1988, p. 18 gives a stern warning to all observers of democratic transitions. See also: Charles Lane, "Death's Democracy," *The Atlantic* (January 1989), pp. 18–25. Later, after the bloody but indecisive offensive in November 1989, guerrilla leaders would admit that the war was not winnable for either side. See Leonel González (member of the FMLN high command) in "A Plan for Peace in El Salvador," *The Nation*, October 15, 1990, p. 407.

66. Stephen Kinzer, "Sandinists, Opposing Parties Meet Under Spanish Peace Plan," *International Herald Tribune* (New York Times), December 26, 1985, p. 1.

67. *El País*, February 9, 1986, p. 5.

68. William Drozdiak and William Branigin, "Arias Urges Communists to Halt Aid," *International Herald Tribune* (Washington Post Service), February 8, 1988, p. 1.

69. *International Herald Tribune*, April 12, 1988, p. 2.

70. David B. Ottaway, "Shultz Trip: A New Strategy on Nicaragua," *International Herald Tribune* (Washington Post Service), July 4, 1988, p. 2. Shultz later called for a "new diplomacy" to fight dictatorship and totalitarianism (*International Herald Tribune*, November 15, 1988, p. 2).

71. Ottaway, *ibid.*

72. *CBS News*, August 2, 1988.

73. Bermúdez boasted of this autonomy, noting that CIA control of the organization was "purely administrative." See *El País*, May 29, 1988, p. 6.

74. Bermúdez in *ibid.*, p. 6.

75. Julia Preston, "In Nicaragua, Fear Returns," *International Herald Tribune* (Washington Post Service), September 20, 1988, p. 3.

76. *Washington Post Weekly*, August 15, 1988, p. 18.

77. Shultz in *International Herald Tribune*, July 4, 1988, p. 2.

78. Bayardo Arce in *El País*, July 17, 1988, p. 2 and *El País*, January 24, 1988, p. 1, 3.

79. *The Times of the Americas*, July 26, 1989, p. 5.

80. See reports on Ortega's meeting with Thatcher, *El País*, May 9, 1989, p. 5.

81. Lee Hockstader, "A UN-OAS Appeal to the Contras: It's Over, Go Home in Peace," *International Herald Tribune* (Washington Post), October 16, 1989, p. 3. For Carter's role see Lee Hockstader, "Nicaragua to Allow Indians to Return," *International Herald Tribune* (Washington Post), September 20, 1989, p. 2.

82. *Reuters* in *International Herald Tribune*, October 30, 1989, p. 2.

83. Lindsey Gruson, "Ortega Says He'll Keep Truce If U.S. Stops Assisting Contras," *International Herald Tribune* (New York Times), October 30, 1989, p. 1.

84. Lee Hockstader, "A Risky Bid to Undermine the Contras," *International Herald Tribune* (Washington Post), October 30, 1989, p. 5.

85. *El País*, November 8, 1989, p. 13.

86. For analysis and calculation of U.S. covert and overt aid, including National Endowment of Democracy (NED) support see Latin American Studies Association, *Electoral Democracy Under International Pressure: The Report of the LASA Commission to Observe the 1990 Nicaraguan Elections* (Pittsburgh: LASA, 1990), pp. 24–29.

87. For analysis of the observer force see *ibid.*, pp. 31–33.

88. See the author's earlier predictions of an opposition victory in the case of free elections in Robin Rosenberg, "Sandinistas Brace for a Showdown," *Miami Herald*, May 16, 1984, p. 15A.

89. *Associated Press* in *International Herald Tribune*, April 20, 1990, p. 1.

90. For Ortega's vows see Lee Hockstader, "General Vows to Half Nicaraguan Army," *International Herald Tribune* (Washington Post), April 28–29, 1990, p. 3.

91. See, for example, Mark A. Uhlig, "In the Democracy of Nicaragua Control Is Still From the Top," *New York Times*, September 23, 1990, p. IV, 2.

92. Lee Hockstader, "In Nicaragua, Eye to Eye Without a Shot," *International Herald Tribune* (Washington Post), April 30, 1990, p. 4.

93. See *Miami Herald*, June 10, 1990, p. 27A; *Los Angeles Times*, June 10, 1990, pp. 1, 10, 13.

94. For a summary of the first 100 days see *Washington Report on the Hemisphere*, August 8, 1990, pp. 1, 6–7.

95. For a look inside Sandinista ranks and psyche see George Vickers, "Out of Power, FSLN Gropes for a Way Back," *Toward Freedom* Vol. 39, no. 7 (October/November 1990), pp. 13–18; and Sara Miles and Bob Ostertag, "Power Outage," *Mother Jones* (November/December 1990), pp. 37–38, 65–68. For government problems in rooting out Sandinistas from public institutions and confiscated private property see Lee Hockstader, "New ABCs For Nicaraguan School Kids," *International Herald Tribune* (Washington Post), July 31, 1990, p. 1; Mary Speck, "In Nicaragua, Social Tensions Unlatched," *Miami Herald*, August 12, 1990, p. 66; Mark A. Uhlig, "Fighting Persists in Nicaragua—Over Symbols," *International Herald Tribune* (New York Times), August 4–5, 1990, p. 1; and William Branigin, "Sandinistas Moved In, Now Will They Leave?" *International Herald Tribune* (Washington Post), April 16, 1990, pp. 1, 5.

96. For the FSLN congress, see Shirley Christian, "Sandinistas Shed a Bit of their Past," *The New York Times*, July 23, 1991, p. 3. For UNO coalition infighting see Agence France Presse report in *El Nueuo Herald* (Miami), June 27, 1991, p. 3. See Ivan Roman, "OEA investigará asesinatos de Nicaraguenses," *El Nuevo Herald*, July 22, 1991, p. 1 for OAS reactions to the human rights situations and Sandinista/Re-Contra violence.

97. Elliot Abrams, "The Reagan Policy for Latin America Has Worked," *International Herald Tribune* (New York Times), July 28, 1988, p. 11.

98. Claude Cheysson interview, *op. cit.*

99. See Americas Watch vice-chairman Aryeh Neir's testimony in "A Dose of Democracy Isn't a Cure All," *International Herald Tribune* (New York Times), July 6, 1988, p. 4.

100. James LeMoyne, "Honduras is Defendant in Rights Trial," *International Herald Tribune* (New York Times), January 20, 1988, p. 1.

101. "Guatemala está aún más lejos de la democracia," *El País*, September 23, 1988, p. 8.

102. IDB, *op. cit.*, p. 118.

103. Douglas Farah, *op. cit.* (Note 65.)

104. *El País*, April 28, 1988, p. 25. See also the report from the Congressional Office of Technology Assessment cited in the *Washington Post* (*International Herald Tribune*), March 10, 1988, p. 3.

105. Sol M. Linowitz, "The Latins Should Top the Agenda," *International Herald Tribune*, September 21, 1988, p. 4.

106. Former U.S. Secretary of State Henry Kissinger was "deeply troubled" by Baker's suggestion that U.S. and Soviet interests were the identical. See Thomas L. Friedman, "Baker's Policy on Soviets: Kissinger Begs to Differ," *International Herald Tribune* (New York Times), February 3–4, 1990, pp. 1, 5. See also *El País*, December 26, 1989, p. 7 for the position of the United States and France on Soviet intervention in the Romanian revolution of 1989.

107. Michael Richardson, "A Third World View: Peril in Detente," *International Herald Tribune*, June 2–3, 1990, p. 5.

108. Lawrence Malkin, "Third World Fears Funding Competition," *International Herald Tribune*, May 7, 1990, pp. 1, 11.

109. Richardson, *op. cit.*

110. Malkin, *op. cit.*

111. *Ibid*.

112. *International Herald Tribune*, September 17, 1990, p. 9 for figures from World Bank annual report.

113. Malkin, *op. cit.* For Third World worries about EEC funding see *The European*, May 25–27, 1990, p. 7.

114. IDB, *op. cit.*

115. Mark A. Uhlig, "The Thrill Is Gone: Sandinistas Fall Out With Castro," *International Herald Tribune* (New York Times), January 19, 1990, pp. 1, 2.

116. *El País*, July 28, 1988, p. 3.

117. See the editorial in *Le Monde*, April 6, 1989 for a rather upbeat appraisal of the meetings.

118. *El País*, July 28, 1988, p. 3.

119. *Reuters* in *International Herald Tribune*, December 31, 1990, p. 9. The Soviet ambassador to Cuba, Yuri Petrov, described the details of the deal in *The Economist*, January 26, 1991, p. 49. See also *Reuters*, *Miami Herald*, January 20, 1991, p. 13A.

120. *El País*, February 5, 1991, p. 14 for Castro's warnings.

121. See the reaction to the invasion in the *Le Monde* editorial (December 21, 1989). For the mixed and muted response of U.S. allies see *El País*, December 22, 1989, p. 7.

122. *International Herald Tribune*, November 15, 1988, p. 2.

123. See coverage of Bush's historic trip in *El País*, October 28, 1990, p. 8.

124. Andrew Rosenthal, "Quayle's Mission to Latin America Is Scaled Back," *International Herald Tribune*, (New York Times), January 19, 1990, p. 3.

125. Vice President Dan Quayle promised Peru that American soldiers would not be sent "for military operations in Peru or the Andes." See Philip Shenon, "U.S.

Troops Won't Fight in Peru, Quayle Says," *International Herald Tribune* (New York Times), August 10, 1990, p. 3.

126. *Reuters* in *International Herald Tribune*, June 28, 1990, p. 10.

127. IDB, *op. cit.*, pp. 5, 29. The Economic Commission on Latin America was also optimistic on future growth of the export sector in Latin America. See *Panorama Económica de America Latina*, 1990 (Santiago: CEPAL, 1990).

128. See summary of IDB report in Robert Graham, "Latin American Growth 'Due to Resume'," *Financial Times*, October 29, 1990, p. 6.

129. For Venezuela and Mexico debt deals see Jonathan Fuerbringer, "Venezuela Deal Bolsters Brady Plan." *International Herald Tribune* (New York Times), March 22, 1990, p. 9. For positive appraisal of Bush trip to Mexico see *El País*, November 27, 1990, p. 11. Later reports put Venezuelan debt reduction closer to 20% with a 50% drop in service payments for most of the 1990s. See the *Washington Post* editorial in *International Herald Tribune*, December 11, 1990, p. 8.

130. Interview with Salinas in *El País*, November 26, 1990, p. 12.

131. Lee Hockstader, "Initiative in Central America," *International Herald Tribune* (Washington Post), June 19, 1990, p. 7.

132. *El País*, January 11, 1991, p. 9.

133. For summary of legislation see Dory Owens, "Caribbean Bill Passes," *Miami Herald*, August 5, 1990, p. 28A.

134. See Peter D. Whitney's upbeat report, "Five Years of the Caribbean Basin Initiative," *Current Policy* no. 1241 (February 1990).

135. See Susan F. Rasky, "Democrats to Test Bush on Aid," *International Herald Tribune* (New York Times), March 22, 1990, p. 2.

136. For aircraft downings see Lindsey Gruson, "Missiles Give Rebels a Boost in Salvador," *International Herald Tribune* (New York Times), December 11, 1990, p. 2. See *Reuters* and *AP* in *International Herald Tribune*, January 5, 1991, p. 3, for details on the Sandinista officers who were swiftly punished by the Sandinista-controlled army. Many of the missiles were immediately returned to Nicaragua.

137. For original aid request see Clifford Krauss, "Baker Campaigns for El Salvador Aid," *International Herald Tribune* (New York Times), April 16, 1990, p. 3.

138. *International Herald Tribune*, January 7, 1991, p. 2 cites Baker's outrage at the FMLN. *The New York Times*, June 27, 1991, p. 3, reports the release of the remaining half of the military aid.

139. Richard Perle, "America's Failure of Nerve in Nicaragua," *U.S. News and World Report*, August 10, 1987, p. 32.

140. See the special report on Panamá in *Financial Times*, February 18, 1991, pp. 19–21.

141. See Gallup poll figures in *El País*, May 13, 1990, p. 6.

142. See Mark A. Uhlig, "Post-Noriega Panama: The Cocaine Still Flows," *International Herald Tribune* (New York Times), August 22, 1990, p. 3; and Michael R. Gordon and David E. Pitt, "Can Panama's Police Cope?" *International Herald Tribune* (New York Times), February 3–4, 1990, p. 3.

143. See Christopher Dickey, "This Is Not Life," *Newsweek*, June 25, 1990, p. 31. See also Antonio Caño, "La Mal 'Paga'," *El País Semanal*, December 16, 1990, pp. 45–61.

144. See Roberto Espindola, "The Unjust Rewards of Loyalty," *South*, (December/January 1990), p. 21. Similar leverage was reportedly being used against the

newly elected Callejas government in Honduras in order to force the government to continue the pace of economic reform.

145. Clifford Krauss, "US to Ask Soviets to End Nicaragua Military Aid," *International Herald Tribune* (New York Times), March 1, 1991, p. 2.

146. Lindsey Gruson, "Baker Reveals Plan to Coordinate Aid to Central America," *International Herald Tribune* (New York Times), June 20, 1990, p. 2.

147. *Ibid*. See also my comments in Luisa Esquiroz Arellano, "Central America Aid Program Making Strides," *International Business Chronicle*, June 24, 1991, p. 5, and the statements of Ford Cooper, U.S. Special Coordinator. Partnership for Democracy and Development in Joaquín Roy, ed., *The Reconstruction of Central America: The Role of the European Economic Community* (Miami: North-South Center, 1991) (Forthcoming).

148. The most influential result was the publication by the Council on Foreign Relations of Andrew Pierre, ed., *Third World Instability: Central America as a European-American Issue* (New York: Council on Foreign Relations, 1985).

149. Irving Kristol, "Should Europe Be Concerned About Central America?" in *ibid.*, pp. 45–69.

150. This essentially strategic debate on the issue of unilateralism *versus* multilateralism in the Caribbean has been—perhaps—the most vigorous in Western scholarly and policy circles. See Joaquín Roy and Robin Rosenberg, "Falklands, Grenada Diminish OAS as Caribbean Problems Linger," *Miami Herald*, December 5, 1983, p. 21; and Elliot Abrams, "The Reagan Policy for Latin America Has Worked," *International Herald Tribune* (New York Times), July 28, 1988, p. 4.

151. The author's figures are calculated from EEC data supplied to IRELA, the EEC-funded agency, and made available in their 1990 report (Madrid: IRELA, 1990), p. 187. See also *Financial Times*, March 21, 1991, p. 9. For a pre–1986 (pre-Iberian integration in the EEC) view of EEC-Central American economic relations, see Victor Bulmer Thomas, "Relaciones entre Centroamérica y Europa Occidental," *Síntesis* 4 (January-April 1988), pp. 286–294. For a later analysis of EEC-Central American relations see Albert Galinsoga i Jordá, "Centroamérica en el marco europeo de la política exterior española," in Centre d'Informació i Documentació Internacionals a Barcelona (CIDOB) and Asociación de Investigación y Especialización sobre Temas Iberoamericanos (AIETI), *Las Relaciones Entre España y America Central (1976–1989)* (Barcelona: AIETI/CIDOB, 1989) and the update (Madrid: IRELA, 1991).

152. See Eusebio Mujal-Leon, "The West German SPD and the Politics of Internationalism in Central America," *Journal of Interamerican Studies and World Affairs* 29, 4 (Winter 1987–88), pp. 89–123 and the earlier "Europa Occidental y los procesos de la democratización en America Latina," *Síntesis op. cit.*, pp. 256–264.

153. For the FRG role in Central America see Alois Mertes, "Europe's Role in Central America: A West German Christian Democratic View," in Pierre, *op. cit.*, pp. 117–119. On the Chamorro-Kohl deals see *El País*, February 23, 1991, p. 16, and the *Miami Herald*, July 9, 1991, p. 4.

154. *El País*, October 28, 1985, p. 9.

155. Interview with the Sandinista hardliner in *Tiempo*, January 7, 1991, p. 67. Also see Wolf Grabendorff, "Las relaciones de la Comunidad Europea con America Latina: una política sin ilusiones," *Síntesis* 4 (January-April 1988), pp. 117–119 and the later rehash "European Community Relations with Latin America: A Policy

Without Illusions," *Journal of Interamerican Studies and World Affairs* 29, 4 (Winter 1987–88), pp. 68–88.

156. *Ibid.*, Grabendorff.

157. The courageous stance by Iglesias began back in 1984 with the Appraisal of the Latin American Economic Conference (January 1984) in Quito. See "Declaration of Quito and Plan of Action," *ECLA Notas sobre la economía y el desarollo de América Latina* 389/390 (January 1984). For later comments (after Iglesias became the Uruguayan foreign minister and then director of the Interamerican Development Bank) see "Nuevas formas de cooperación entre la comunidad Europea y America Latina," Ponencia del coloquio organizado por la Academie Diplomatique Internacional, Paris, June 1987.

158. "Conclusions of the Council and the Representatives of the Governments of the Member States on Relations Between the European Community and Latin America," Council of the European Communities 7120/87 (Press 110), June 1987, in *Europe* (Brussels), 1460, June 26, 1987. For an analysis see Juan Pablo de La Iglesia, "Las relaciones entre la Europa de los doce y America Latina: Un proceso de cambio accelerado," *Pensamiento Iberoamericano* 13 (January-April 1988).

159. James LeMoyne, "EC-Central America Meeting Closes with Hopes for Peace Dimmer," *International Herald Tribune* (New York Times), February 12, 1987, p. 3.

160. Juan Pablo de la Iglesia, *op. cit.*

161. This view is common to all European governments, from the West German Christian Democrats (see Mertes in Pierre, *op. cit.*, p. 128) and the British Conservatives (*International Herald Tribune*, February 12, 1987, p. 3 quotes British Contadora delegates) to the Spanish Socialists (see references in Chaps. 8–10).

162. Mertes in Pierre, *op. cit.*, pp. 124, 128.

163. Elliot Abrams, *op. cit.*

164. IRELA figures are from the EEC Administrative Base Budget Articles (Brussels), August 23, 1990. See the balanced appraisal of EEC development aid by Germán Granda Alva and Victor Mate de Castro, "La cooperación para el desarollo de la comunidad Europea con América Latina," *Sintesis, op. cit.*, pp. 225–237.

165. *El País*, December 20, 1990, p. 10.

166. See, for example, Andrew Crawley, "La Comunidad Europea y América Central," in AIETI/CIDOB, *op. cit.*, p. 172.

167. See, for example, Victor Urquidi, "Hacia una nueva relación economica entre Europa y América Latina," *Comercio Exterior* 7 (July 1986), and Silvia Maria Canela, "Por qué no comerciamos más con Europa? Proteccionismo y discriminaciones de la Comunidad," *Nueva Sociedad* 85 (September-October 1986). After Iglesias, the former Argentine president, Raúl Alfonsín, has been the most outspoken critic of EEC trade policies. See Chapter 8 and Chapter 9 for discussion of Spain's attempt at leadership around GATT and other international trade issues.

168. Interview with Alfonsín in *Tiempo*, July 6, 1990, p. 120.

169. Interview with Giulio Andreotti, the Italian Prime Minister, in Ayuntamiento de Barcelona and Sociedad Estatal del Quinto Centenario *El Libro Blanco: La Nueva Europa y el Futuro de América Latina*, (Barcelona: Ayuntamiento de Barcelona/Sociedad Estatal del Quinto Centenario, 1990), exerpted in *El País, Temas de Nuestra Epoca*, Vol. IV, no. 150 (September 1990), p. 16.

170. *The Economist*, February 2, 1991, p. 45; Eusebio Mujal-Leon in *Journal of Interamerican Studies and World Affairs, op. cit.*

171. "Spain Rediscovers the New World," *The Economist*, July 30, 1988, pp. 17–20.

172. *Ibid*. *The Economist* (December 10, 1988) gives OECD figures on Spanish exports to Latin America in 1977 (10% of total) *versus* 4% of the total in 1987. Spain's commercial relations with the Central American region are comparable to Spain's trade with Zaire, Pakistan, *et. al.* See Luís de Sebastián, *et. al.*, "Las relaciones económicas entre España y América Central: un balance de una década," in AIETI/ CIDOB, *op. cit.*, p. 81.

173. Stephen Kinzer, "Nicaraguan Socialists Move Toward Center," *New York Times*, August 18, 1988, p. 5.

174. *International Herald Tribune*, November 15, 1988, p. 2.

175. Author's discussion with Myles Frechette, Assistant U.S. Trade Representative for Latin America, the Caribbean, and Africa in Miami, July 20, 1991. See his remarks in "The Trade Pillar of the Enterprise for the Americas Initiative," in *North-South: The Magazine of the Americas* (September/October) 1991 (forthcoming).

176. Carlos Fuentes, "La otra cara del continente," *El País, Liber*, December 16, 1989, p. 20.

PART III

Chapter 5: Testing the International Waters

1. The "reconquest" thesis is advanced in James Lockhart and Stephen B. Schwartz, *Early Latin America* (Cambridge: Cambridge University Press, 1987).

2. See citation in Ian Gibson, *En Busca de José Antonio* (Barcelona, 1980), p. 314.

3. See, for example, Paul Preston, *Spain, the EEC and NATO* (London: Royal Institute of International Affairs, 1984), p. 27.

4. European Parliament, Birkelbach Report, Brussels, January 15, 1962.

5. Francisco Franco Salgado-Araujo, *Mis conversaciones privadas con Franco* (Barcelona, 1976), p. 334.

6. José Maria Areilza, *Diario de un ministro de la monarquia* (Barcelona, 1977), p. 27.

7. *Radio Nacional de España (RNE)*, November 2, 1975.

8. González explained his position as that of the Socialist International—in which he serves as Vice President—which opposed all military blocs. While military blocs exist, he said, there would be no "ideological attack" on NATO. His opposition was to Spain's joining NATO, which was "different." "From a defense and security point of view, there is no need for Spain to join NATO. Our party is committed to a referendum on NATO" (*Cambio 16*, June 20, 1983).

9. *Cambio 16*, June 27, 1983.

10. For a view of such internationalization as a vehicle for domestic political hegemony see Otto Homan, "In Search of Hegemony: Socialist Government and the Internationalization of Domestic Politics in Spain," *International Journal of Political Economy* Vol. 19, no. 3 (Fall 1989), pp. 76–101.

11. Author's interview with Luis Fernández de la Pena, Director of the Cabinet of the Secretariat, Foreign Ministry, Madrid, November 26, 1990.

Chapter 6: Democratic Transition, Spanish Policy, and the Crisis in Central America

1. This continuity has intrigued scholars and has led—unfortunately in this author's view—to an unwillingness to recognize the significant changes in the Spanish posture over the course of the 1980s. Every foreign policy or political phenomenon is characterized by "continuity and change"; scholars must, however, note those changes that significantly alter the national and international contexts. For the continuity theme see: Eusebio Mujal-Leon, *Continuity and Change in Spanish Foreign Policy* (Washington: American Enterprise Institute, 1985); and William Salisbury, "Spain's Foreign Policy," in Thomas D. Lancaster and Gary Prevost eds., *Politics and Change in Spain* (New York: Praeger, 1985). For the purposes of this analysis, it is useful to regard the distinction between continuity and change as that which characterizes the differences between "government" or "party" policy, which enjoys a certain margin of operational freedom, and "state" strategy, which is determined by the particular geographic, historical and other tangible factors of the nation-state, and is not subject to fundamental revision.

2. *The Economist*, July 30, 1988, p. 20.

3. See the impartial analysis of Luis de Sebastián, Emilí Sánchez Díaz, *et. al.*, "Las relaciones económicas entre España y América Central: balance de una década," in *Las Relaciones entre España y América Central* (Barcelona: CIDOB/AETI, 1989), pp. 97, 107–10.

4. This author's interviews and conversations with Spanish development officials and scholars in November 1990 confirmed the European orientation of the Spanish private sector and the difficulties surrounding the IDB "multilateral" initiatives that are tied into Spanish company contracts.

5. Luis de Sebastián, *et. al.*, *op. cit.*, p. 109.

6. Even Howard Wiarda's careful and realistic analysis overstates the trade dimension. See Howard J. Wiarda, "The Significance for Latin America of the Spanish Democratic Transition," in Clark and Haltzel, *op. cit.*, p. 170.

7. *The Economist*, July 30, 1988, p. 20.

8. Fernando Morán, "España en el mundo," *Cambio 16*, October 26, 1987, p. 110.

Chapter 7: Socialist Policy in Central America: Parameters and Constraints

1. Fernando Morán, "Principios de la política exterior español," *Leviatán* 16 (Summer 1984), p. 8.

2. The decision to support NATO membership with certain conditions was adopted at the PSOE party congress in December 1984.

3. These principles are outlined, discussed and operationalized with Latin American case examples by Fernando Morán in *Leviatán, op. cit.*

4. The issue here was Guatemala. Diplomatic relations between Spain and Guatemala were cut off after the military government, in an effort to capture refugees, stormed the Spanish embassy in Guatemala City in 1980.

5. See *Central America Report*, May 20, 1983 and ACAN-EFE (Madrid-San José), September 27, 1983. In 1984 a modest aid package was approved amid heated debate in the Spanish Cortes. The package included technical (computer training), cultural,

educational, and sanitary aid. An office of cooperation was established in Nicaragua to administer to the aid. See the debate on the pact in *El País*, June 14, 1985.

6. See Robin Rosenberg, "Soviet Aid for Central American Guerrilla Movements as a Strategic Initiative," *Soviet Armed Forces Review Annual* 8 (1983–84), pp. 348–389; *The Jacobsen Report: Soviet Attitudes Towards, Aid to, and Contacts with Central American Revolutionaries*, Report Commissioned by the U.S. Department of States (Washington, D.C.: GPO, 1984), pp. 26–28.

7. See, for example, *Miami Herald*, April 7, 1984, and *New York Times*, April 27, 1984.

8. See Marcos Roitman, *La política del PSOE en América Latina* (Madrid: Editorial Revolución, 1985) for a strong critique of this hypocrisy. Alan García, president of Peru, has suggested that Spain's position must be clear on the debt problem. See Instituto de Cooperación Iberoamericana, *Encuentros en la democracia* (Madrid: ICI, 1983), p. 62.

9. Much attention has been directed towards NGO cooperation. See, for example, Alfredo Arahuetes and Alonso Game, *Aproximación a la realidad de los ONGs en España* (Madrid: CEDEAL, 1989).

10. "Relación por países de proyectos subvencionados, Convocatoria IRPF" (Madrid: Instituto de Cooperación Iberoamericana, 1990).

11. A court-case during the mid–1980s in which Luis Yáñez sued economist and Communist deputy (member of parliament) Ramón Tamames for defamation of character is a perfect example of this involvement in domestic affairs. During a dispute over the PSOE's domestic policies, Tamames had publicly accused the Socialist secretary of state of being a user of cocaine. Tamames was let off after a public apology, but Yáñez's involvement in domestic affairs only intensified during the 1990 government crisis, where he remained one of the Prime Minister's closest advisors on everything from government remodeling to a controversial property tax reform. His candidacy for the mayoralty of Seville in May 1991, which caused him to give up his national posts with the foreign ministry and the V Centenary, was widely interpreted as a move to strengthen the party position in Andalusia. When Yáñez lost the elections in May 1991, he recovered the largely ceremonial post of President of the Commission of the V Centenary. The new mayor, Alejandro Rojas Marcos, of the Partido Andalucista, the regional party, will open the 1992 celebrations.

12. See F. Morán's generous characterization of Juan Antonio in his memoirs, *España en su sitio* (Madrid: Plaza y Janes/Cambio 16, 1990), p. 126.

13. These limitations were corroborated during the author's field research in Spain (1985–89). The Institute resembles, at best, a large school of international affairs at a major American university. In the library, the serials collection, moreover, is clearly deficient by any standards. English language periodicals are practically nonexistent. It is a universally known fact that much of its modest budget is used for administrative and bureaucratic costs. See Eusebio Mujal-León, *European Socialism and the Conflict in Central America* (Washington, D.C.: Praeger/Center for Strategic and International Studies, 1989), pp. 45–46.

14. See Instituto de Cooperación Iberoamericana, *Encuentros en la democracia, op. cit.*, pp. 503–511.

15. See his low key, almost conservative address to the 1990 conference on "The Central American Parliament and the European Experience" in Cuenca in *El Par-*

lamento Centroamericano y la Experiencia Europea (Madrid: Frederich Ebert Foundation/ICI, 1990), pp. 43–52.

16. For an excellent analysis of Spanish and European Socialist and Social Democratic parties, including the Socialist International, see Eusebio Mujal-León, *op. cit.*

17. The huge scandal over ETA and foreign policy in Latin America broke out in June 1989 when Pérez said that "it was an exaggeration" to call the 11 *etarras* sent into Venezuelan exile from Algiers "terrorists." He also tested his friendship with González by comparing the struggle of ETA to that of the liberator Bolívar, who was born in Caracas. See *El País*, June 3, 1989, pp. 1, 15; and *El País*, June 7, 1989, pp. 1, 17. The critical remarks about the V Centenary came at a 1988 conference on the topic in Caracas. See *El País*, July 21, 1988, p. 14.

18. See Santiago Petschen, "La política exterior de la comunidad autónoma de Cataluña," *Política Exterior 2*, 5 (Winter 1988), pp. 222–238.

19. *Ibid.* The source speaks solely of Europe.

20. *El País*, December 9, 1987.

21. Luis Yáñez Barnuevo, "El futuro comienza en 1992," *El País*, October 14, 1988, p. 18.

Chapter 8: Desperately Seeking Social Democracy: The Conduct of Spanish Foreign Policy in Central America

1. Interview with the Spanish foreign minister in "Política exterior de España 1987–1990," *Política Exterior* I, 1 (Winter 1987), p. 25–26.

2. See "Una diplomacia del Siglo XIX," *Cambio 16*, July 22, 1985, pp. 25–26.

3. The well-known image of pre-Socialist era Spanish diplomats in Latin America was corroborated by numerous Latin diplomats during the author's field research in Guatemala and Nicaragua (1984).

4. A high-level ministry official is quoted in *Cambio 16*, July 22, 1985, pp. 25–26.

5. See one of the few penetrating personal interviews with the now discreet minister in "Me quedan más convicciones que ilusiones," *Cambio 16*, July 22, 1985, pp. 21–24.

6. This development, the other side of the foreign policy coin, was treated in Chapter 3.

7. Fernando Morán, "Europe's Role in Central America: A Spanish Socialist View," in Pierre, *op. cit.*, p. 40.

8. *Ibid.*, p. 37.

9. Robin Rosenberg in *SAFRA*, *op. cit.*

10. Ambler H. Moss, Jr. "Reflections on U.S. Policy Towards Central America: The Transition from Carter to Reagan," (Coral Gables: Institute of Interamerican Studies, 1983).

11. *El País*, December 16, 1987, p. 21.

12. The *empuje francés e italiano* is discussed in *El País*, October 28, 1987, p. 20.

13. *El País*, April 28, 1983, p. 1.

14. Morán in Pierre, *op. cit.*

15. Washington's repeated warnings to Europe were stern. See *Miami Herald*, April 7, 1984.

16. *Cambio 16*, July 22, 1985, p. 26.

17. See the cover story "Los diplomaticos se rebelan," in the conservative weekly *Epoca*, February 22, 1988, pp. 12–15.

18. *Ibid.*, p. 13.

19. See *El País*, February 3, 1989, p. 18 for government renovation plans.

20. A meeting between Juan Carlos and Fidel Castro in Mexico was planned for the first Iberoamerican summit in 1991. A visit to Cuba was planned "by 1992." See *El País*, January 8, 1990, p. 14.

21. See Larry Rohter, "A Mixed Welcome for Juan Carlos," *International Herald Tribune* (New York Times), January 13–14, 1990, p. 4.

22. The prospects were dim for Contadora by 1984. It was cynically viewed as a "smokescreen" for Sandinista hegemony in Nicaragua on the one side and for U.S. intervention on the other. See Robin Rosenberg, "Sandinistas Brace for Showdown," *Miami Herald*, May 16, 1984, p. 23.

23. *El País*, December 13, 1985, p. 8.

24. See *La Vanguardia* (Barcelona), September 20, 21, pp. 1, 15, 18; *El País*, September 17, 1983, p. 1.

25. *La Nación* (San José), September 26, 1983, p. 10D.

26. Lucian Baselga, "Informe ante la Comisión de Asuntos Exteriores del Congreso," *Boletín Oficial del Estado*, March 14, 1984.

27. Fernándo Morán, "Press Conference at Foreign Ministry," Oficina de Información Diplomatica, September 19, 1983, p. 456.

28. It should be remembered that much of the $118 million in U.S. aid to the Nicaraguan regime in the first 18 months of the revolution was hinged on suspicions that Managua was aiding the Salvadoran rebels. On January 9, 1981, the Carter Administration concluded that evidence of such aid was irrefutable and thus terminated U.S. grants and credits to Managua. See Robert Pastor, *Condemned to Repitition*, (Princeton: Princeton Univ. Press, 1988), pp. 217–226.

29. See *New York Times*, April 27, 1983; *El Nuevo Diario* (Managua), April 4, 1984; and *Miami Herald*, March 22, 1984.

30. *EFE-ACAN*, September 27, 1982.

31. See the somber accounting in *El País*, November 27, 1985, p. 49.

32. *Ibid.*

33. *El País*, November 27, 1987, p. 19.

34. *Ibid.*

35. The Spanish FACA program for Iberian air superiority contracted with McDonnell Douglas and the U.S. for a billion-dollar F–18 fighter deal that included co-production, service, and training.

36. *Ibid.*, note 33.

37. *New York Times*, December 25, 1987, p. 1; *El País*, December 26, 1987, p. 2.

38. *El País*, December 27, 1985, p. 6.

39. *Ibid.*

40. *Ibid.*

41. *El País*, January 13, 1986, p. 13.

42. *El País*, December 27, 1985, p. 13.

43. *El País*, January 13, 1986, p. 13.

44. *El País*, January 14, 1986, p. 11.

45. *Ibid.*

46. *El País*, January 13, 1986, p. 13.

47. The analysis of Roitman, *op. cit.*, reflects a view from that side of the political fence. See also Mariano Aguirre, "Between Two Worlds: Spain's Latin America Policy," *NACLA Report on the Americas* XX, 2 (April-May 1986), pp. 12–15.

48. Apart from staging the customary rallies and protests, the Movimiento para la Paz has donated school supplies, medical supplies, books, agricultural supplies, and construction materials. See *El País*, November 27, 1987, p. 6.

49. *El País*, November 21, 1987, p. 21.

50. *El País*, November 28, 1987, pp. 1, 15.

51. *Ibid.*, p. 15.

52. *El País*, November 27, 1987, p. 19.

53. *El País*, July 7, 1987, p. 7.

54. *El País*, November 28, 1987, p. 15.

55. *Ibid.*

56. Julia Preston, "Ortega's European Tour Seen by Diplomats as a Success," *International Herald Tribune* (Washington Post), February 4, 1988, p. 3.

57. For documentation of Sandinista progress relative to that of other Central American countries (until July 1988) see: Stephen Kinzer, "In Nicaragua, Even Sandinist Foes Sense a New Breeze Blowing," *International Herald Tribune* (New York Times), February 4, 1988, p. 3.

58. *El País*, February 5, 1988, p. 4.

59. *El País*, May 1, 1988, p. 18.

60. *El País Internacional*, August 15, 1988, p. 4.

61. *Ibid.*, p. 5.

62. *Ibid.*, p. 4.

63. *El País*, February 4, 1989, p. 4.

64. Interview with ex-president Asconas in *El País*, May 9, 1989, p. 4.

65. *El País*, December 2, 1988, p. 2.

66. See summary of Spanish participation in *El País*, March 25, 1990, p. 2.

67. *Ibid.*

68. *El País*, November 27, 1990, p. 22 for the support of the Honduran president, Rafael Leonardo Callejas, for the UN mission.

69. *El País*, March 25, 1984, p. 3.

70. *El País*, November 2, 1985, p. 11.

71. *Ibid.* The unofficial delegation of observers to the 1985 legislative elections included an array of impartial opposition figures, including ex-prime minister Leopoldo Calvo Sotelo and Carlos Robles Piquer for Alianza Popular (principal opposition party of the right, later reformed into Partido Popular); Pedro Pérez of the Liberal International, and Javier Rupérez, a Christian Democrat. The government sent only an official from the Madrid city hall.

72. *El País*, November 4, 1985, p. 15.

73. See interview with Duarte in *El País*, November 6, 1985, pp. 8–9.

74. *El País*, November 6, 1985, p. 14.

75. *El País*, November 9, 1985, p. 4.

76. *El País*, March 16, 1989, p. 2 for talks with FMLN.

77. *El País*, November 23, 1989, p. 4.

78. *El País*, February 28, 1989, p. 2.

79. *El País*, November 20, 1989, p. 2.

80. See Lindsey Gruson, "El Salvador Presses Crackdown on Relief Groups," *International Herald Tribune* (New York Times), December 9–10, 1989, p. 3.

81. Lindsey Gruson, "Evidence Disappears in Jesuit Killings," *International Herald Tribune* (New York Times), May 8, 1990, p. 2.

82. See initial reports on the testimony of U.S. military advisor, Major Eric Buckland to FBI in *El País*, October 29, 1990, p. 12. Buckland later retracted his testimony, but other reports confirmed the fact that the murders had been a planned attack. See Lindsey Gruson, "New Allegations in Jesuit Killings," *New York Times*, August 12, 1990, p. 9. The trials were postponed until the Fall of 1991 after Buckland's testimony to the FBI was finally released in July 1991. See the devastating report in *The Miami Herald*, July 5, 1991, p. 1.

83. See *El País*, November 17, 1990, p. 11 for Spanish official declarations. For a view of the depth of Spanish outrage see Antonio Caño, "El coronel anda suelto," *El País Domingo*, November 18, 1990, pp. 1–3.

84. See Americas Watch report in *Reuters* in *International Herald Tribune*, May 29, 1990, p. 7 and Amnesty International report in *AP*, *International Herald Tribune*, October 24, 1990, p. 4. Guerrilla promises not to disrupt the March 1991 mid-term legislative elections were kept, but the civil war raged on into the spring of 1991. Zamora remarked after election observers confirmed widespread election fraud against his Christian Democrat coalition that the absence of violence was a small step in the transition to democracy. "We have evolved from Haiti to Chicago," was the former Christian Democratic leader's opinion. See *Newsweek*, March 25, 1991, p. 36.

85. For a report on deadlocked peace talks see *The Miami Herald*, July 26, 1991, p. 16. For Spanish participation in multi-lateral peace efforts see *El País*, April 25, 1991, p. 11; May 13, 1991, p. 11; May 24, 1991, p. 13; and July 28, 1991, p. 2. On ONUSAL's difficult position see *Agence France Presse* in *El Nuevo Herald*, July 26, 1991, p. 3.

86. Oficina de Información Diplomática, January 16, 1983, p. 83.

87. There was some suggestion that Spain was looking to build an arms factory in Guatemala that would supply the rest of Central America and replace the Israelis as the primary arms merchant after the United States. See, for example, M. Roitman, *op. cit.*, p. 87.

88. See *El País*, December 11, 1985, p. 4.

89. *El País*, October 3, 1987, p. 3.

90. *El País*, October 14, 1987, p. 2.

91. *Ibid.* There was another brief but unsuccessful meeting in February 1988.

92. For an analysis of Spain's Cuba foreign policy see Joaquín Roy, *Cuba y España: percepciones y relaciones* (Madrid: Editorial Playor, 1988).

93. See Felipe González, "Declarations of the President" in *Revista de Estudios Internacionales* 2 (1983), p. 593.

94. See Morán in Pierre, *op. cit.*, p. 9.

95. *Ibid.*, p. 11.

96. See interview and article in *El País*, December 20, 1985, p. 13.

97. *El País*, March 21, 1986, p. 16.

98. See Castro's remarks in *El País*, July 21, 1985, pp. 1, 3.

99. *El País*, January 28, 1987, p. 14; *El País*, July 24, 1985, p. 5.

100. *El País*, November 11, 1988, p. 17.

101. Seę the *El País* editorial, "La isla aislada," January 6, 1991, p. 10, which sounds the death knell to the love affair with the audacious Cuban revolutionary.

102. Lee Hockstader, "Forecast for Cuba: Grim Tidings for 1991," *International Herald Tribune* (Washington Post), January 2, 1991, p. 1; and *Reuters* in *Miami Herald*, September 30, 1990, p. 24A.

103. *Reuters* in *International Herald Tribune*, March 8, 1990, p. 1.

104. *El País*, March 28, 1990, p. 16.

105. *El País*, July 18, 1990, pp. 1–2.

106. *Ibid.*

107. The entire text is reprinted in *El País*, July 19, 1990, p. 2.

108. *El País*, September 6, 1990, p. 7.

109. *Ibid.*

110. *Ibid.*

111. See Rodriguez's declarations in *El País*, October 12, 1990, p. 1 and his attacks on Spain in an interview in *Tiempo*, August 20, 1990, pp. 98–99.

112. Fernando Morán, "De bastión de la guerra fría al nacionalismo tradicional," *El País, Temas de Nuestra Epoca*, August 2, 1990, p. 6.

113. *El País*, March 8, 1988, p. 15.

114. *Diario 16*, March 27, 1988, p. 21.

115. See Martha Honey and Tony Avirgan, "Leaning on Arias," *The Nation*, September 12, 1987, p. 27.

116. Remarks on U.S. policy towards Arias by Robert W. Kagan, former aide to then Asst. Secretary of State for Inter-american Affairs Elliot Abrams, in Stephen Kinzer and Robert Pear, "Officials Assert U.S. is Trying to Weaken Costa Rica Chief," *New York Times*, August 7, 1988, p. 1. See also the definitive indictment of Elliot Abrams and the Reagan Administration's Central American policy by Reagan's own ambassador to Costa Rica in Frank McNeil, *War and Peace in Central America: Reality and Illusion* (New York: Scribners, 1988).

117. Also the downgrading of Spanish official participation at the Reunion of Young Democracies in Manila in June 1988 after it was made known that Nicaragua would attend. See *El País*, May 22, 1988, p. 8.

118. See *Cambio 16*, February 15, 1988, pp. 20–21; *El País*, November 27, 1990, p. 22 for Serra's promises.

119. Alan Riding, "González to Offer Advice to Bush on Latin America," *New York Times*, October 15, 1989, p. 18.

120. *Ibid.*

121. See interview with opposition leader and vice-president to be, Guillermo Ford, in *El País*, September 30, 1989, p. 10.

122. *New York Times*, October 15, 1989, p. 18.

123. *El País*, January 5, 1990, p. 4.

124. *El País*, January 2, 1990, p. 3.

125. *El País*, December 27, 1989, p. 13.

126. *El País*, January 6, 1990, p. 3.

127. Author's conversations in Madrid, November 1990 and interview with Luis Fernández de la Pena, Director of the Cabinet of the Secretariat of the Foreign Ministry, November 26, 1990.

Chapter 9: Conclusion: 1992 and All That

1. Andalusia leads other Spanish autonomies in unemployment and has traditionally commanded the lowest percentage of national income (with the exception of the smaller and less populous region of Extremadura). At the peak of Spanish unemployment in the spring of 1987, official statistics put Andalusian unemployment well above the national rate of almost 23%. In the Andalusian capital of Seville, the rate was well over 30% during the course of the 1980s, reaching 31.3% in 1986. See *El País* (Andalucía ed.), April 1, 1987, p. 24; *La Vanguardia*, May 21, 1987, p. 1; *El País*, May 21, 1987, p. 1; and *Diario 16*, May 21, 1987, pp. 1, 19. The construction boom around the 1992 Universal Exposition brought Sevilla's unemployment closer to the national average of about 16% by 1991, but there were grounds for fear that 1993 would represent a regional catastrophe if the state did not provide massive investment after the Expo.

2. Petty crime in Seville was so infamous that tour operators in London, New York, and other Western capitals, as well as travel guide publishers, began issuing travel advisories. Purse snatching and car break-ins were the most frequent, but violent crime was also on the rise.

3. Pedro Pacheco, "La Exposición Universal en Crisis," *El País*, March 4, 1988, p. 20.

4. Seville remains a provincial city with a small resident international community and two months per year of massive tourist influx (Semana Santa-Feria in March/April), which is drawn mostly from within Spain.

5. Pedro Pacheco, *op. cit.*

6. See *El País Domingo*, March 3, 1991, pp. 7–8. For Felipe's trip see *The European*, November 23, 1990, p. 2.

7. Interview with Oscar Arias, *Tiempo*, February 17, 1986, pp. 82–3. On Spain's role see *El País*, May 9, 1987, p. 3.

8. Interview with Carlos Andrés Pérez, *Cambio 16*, December 5, 1988, p. 103.

9. *Diario 16* (Sevilla '92), September 27, 1988, p. 1.

10. *Ibid.*, p. 2.

11. Mexico, for example, agonized over the meaning of the "discovery" during the course of 1987 and into 1988. Foreign Minister Fernández Ordóñez regards this process and the more virulent Cuban critique as an "historical evaluation." See *Politica Exterior* I, 1 (Winter 1987), p. 26.

12. See Eduardo Subirats, "Latinoamérica: el otro mundo," *El País*, April 28, 1988, p. 12.

13. *El País*, October 21, 1990, p. 23.

14. Then president of the Institute of Iberoamerican Cooperation, Manuel de Prado y Colon de Carvajal, offers Vargas Llosa's comments as one of the "reasons for a commemoration." See "Reflexiones sobre el V Centenario: Razones para una conmemoración," *El País*, May 20, 1988, p. 24.

15. Mario Vargas Llosa, "Questions of Conquest," *Harper's* (December 1990), pp. 45, 49.

16. *El País*, December 24, 1990, p. 15.

17. *El País*, July 25, 1989, p. 11.

18. *Ibid.*

19. Interview with Fernando Valenzuela, president of the Agencia Española de Cooperación Internacional (AECI), *TVE*, "La Noche," March 1, 1989. Also see Banco de España, *Información Comercial Española*, no. 2207 (November 1989).

20. *El País*, January 3, 1990, p. 12.

21. *El País*, January 22, 1988, p. 14; see also, Interamerican Development Bank, *Annual Report*, 1989 (Washington, D.C.: IDB, 1990).

22. Conversations in Madrid with Spanish development officials and scholars, November 1990.

23. *Reuters* in *International Herald Tribune*, July 6, 1990, p. 15. Spanish media groups, including the state-owned *TVE* have engaged in a number of programming ventures in Latin America. *TVE* invested about $36 million in South America in the 1987–90 period. Apart from a few popular soap operas from South America and Mexico, the only major penetration of the Spanish media was from *Galavisión*, the Mexican company founded by Televisa, the Mexico City media giant. Even if Panama were included in the 1990 figures (imports, exports, and transhipments), Spain's trade with the isthmus would still be less than one quarter of Spanish trade with Mexico and about one third that of Brazil. See the comparisons in *Latin American Weekly Report* (WR–91–17), May 9, 1991, p. 5.

24. *El País*, December 24, 1990, p. 15.

25. *Ibid.*

26. *El País*, November 25, 1990, p. 15.

27. *El País*, July 22, 1989, pp. 1, 13–14.

28. *Cambio 16*, April 3, 1991, p. 12.

29. *El País*, March 7, 1990, p. 7.

30. *El País*, February 28, 1989, p. 2.

31. *Financial Times*, March 19, 1991, p. 7.

32. *Ibid.*

33. *Financial Times*, March 21, 1991, p. 9.

34. *El País*, March 19, 1991, p. 8; *El País*, March 20, 1991, p. 12.

35. *El País*, March 21, 1991, p. 12.

36. Conversations in Madrid, November 1990; interview with Luis Fernández de la Pena, *op. cit.*

37. *Financial Times*, March 19, 1991, p. 7; *The Economist*, March 23, 1991, p. 62.

38. *El País*, March 20, 1991, p. 12.

39. *Official Journal of the European Communities*, No. c 194/18, July 25, 1991, p. 18.

40. *El País*, June 4, 1985, p. 15; see González's strong statements in *El País*, February 3, 1989, p. 2.

41. *El País*, May 31, 1989, p. 5.

42. Yañez called González's influence in Central America "decisive." See interview in *Tiempo*, December 10, 1990, p. 30. See also Fernando Morán's memoirs, *op. cit.*, in which the former foreign minister seems to have nothing but praise and admiration for the man who fired him in 1985.

43. *El País*, July 15, 1991, p. 10.

44. *El País*, July 19, 1991, p. 3.

45. *Ibid.*

46. Mark A. Uhlig, "For Castro, the Hemisphere Gets Smaller and Lonelier," *The New York Times*, July 28, 1991, p. E5.

47. Mark A. Uhlig, "Castro Gets Attention, but Not Money, From Latin Leaders," *The New York Times*, July 21, 1991, p. 5. For more on Castro's antics and the reactions of his critics, especially the Miami exile community, see the coverage in *El Nuevo Herald*, July 21, 1991, p. 1.

48. *El País*, July 23, 1991, p. 13; July 27, 1991, p. 12.

49. *El País*, July 4, 1991, p. 48.

50. Fernando Morán, "Desprestigio del Estado, indefensión del cuidadano," *El País*, April 27, 1988, p. 12.

51. *El País*, May 26, 1989, p. 23.

52. *El País*, May 26, 1990, pp. 1, 18–19.

53. *El País*, December 16, 1990, p. 14.

54. Interview with García Márquez in *Tiempo*, March 27, 1989, p. 134.

55. Interview with García Márquez, *El País*, September 2, 1990, p. 24.

Select Bibliography

GENERAL

Almond, Gabriel. "Slaying the Functional Dragon." *American Political Science Review III* (Fall 1973), pp. 259–268.

Almond, Gabriel, and Bingham Powell, G., Jr. *Comparative Politics*. Boston: Little, Brown, 1966.

Booth, Ken. "New Challenges and Old Mind-Sets: Ten Rules for Empirical Realists." *The Uncertain Course: New Weapons, Strategies, Mind-Sets*. Edited by C. G. Jacobsen. Oxford: Oxford University Press/SIPRI, 1987.

Botella, Joan. "Despedidas de la idea: Pérdida del terreno del pensamiento en beneficio de los estudios empíricos," *El País*, May 29, 1988, p. 21.

Claude, Inis. *Power and International Relations*. New York: Random House, 1962.

Combs, Jerald A. *The History of American Foreign Policy*. New York: Knopf, 1986.

Cutright, Phillip. "National Political Development: Measurement and Analysis." *American Sociological Review 2* (1963).

Dahl, Robert. *Polyarchy: Participation and Opposition*. New Haven: Yale University Press, 1971.

———. *Who Governs?* New Haven: Yale University Press, 1961.

Diamond, Larry; Linz, Juan; and Lipset, Seymour, eds. *Democracy in Developing Nations*. Boulder: Lynn Reinner, 1988.

Fagen, Richard. "The Politics of Transition." *Monthly Review* 38, 6 (November 1986), pp. 1–19.

Heilbroner, Robert. *Between Capitalism and Socialism*. New York: Random House, 1970.

———. "Capitalism." *The New Yorker*. January 23, 1989, pp. 98–109.

———. "Reflections on the Future of Socialism." *Commentary*. (November 1969).

Herz, John. *From Dictatorship to Democracy: Coping with the Legacies of Authoritarianism and Totalitarianism*. Westport, CT: Greenwood Press, 1982.

Huntington, Samuel. *The Soldier and the State*. Cambridge, MA: Belknap/Harvard, 1957.

Ilke, Fred C.; Wohlstetter, Albert; et. al. *Discriminate Deterrence*. Report of the Commission on Integrated Long-Term Strategy. Washington, DC: Government Printing Office, 1988.

Jacobsen, Carl G. *The Uncertain Course: New Weapons, Strategies, Mind Sets*. London: Oxford University Press/SIPRI, 1987.

Jaros, D., and Grant, L. V. *Political Behavior*. Oxford: Basil Blackwell, 1975.

Keohane, Robert O., and Nye, Joseph S. *Power and Interdependence*. Boston: Little, Brown, 1977.

Levine, Daniel H. "Paradigm Lost: Dependence to Democracy." *World Politics*, XL, 3 (April 1988), pp. 377–394.

Linz, Juan, and Stepan, Alfred, eds. *Breakdowns of Democratic Regimes*. Baltimore: The Johns Hopkins Press, 1978.

Lipset, Seymour M. *Political Man*. New York: Doubleday, 1960.

———. "Some Requisites of Democracy: Economic Development and Political Legitimacy." *American Political Science Review* 53 (March 1959).

Liska, George. "From Containment to Concert." *Foreign Policy*, 62 (Spring 1986), pp. 3–23.

Miller, Lynn H. *Global Order: Values and Power in International Politics*. Boulder: Westview, 1990.

Morganthau, Hans. *In Defense of the National Interest*. New York: Knopf, 1951.

———. *Politics Among Nations*. New York: Knopf, 1948.

Muravchik, Joshua. *Exporting Democracy*. Washington, DC: American Enterprise Institute, 1991.

Neubauer, D. B. "Some Conditions of Democracy." *American Political Science Review* 61, 1 (1967), .

O'Donnell, Guillermo; Schmitter, Phillipe C.; and Whitehead, Laurence, eds. *Transitions from Authoritarian Rule: Prospects for Democracy*, 4 vols. Baltimore: The Johns Hopkins University Press, 1986.

Perlmutter, Amos. *The Military and Politics in Modern Times*. New Haven: Yale University Press, 1977.

Rothman, Stanley. "Functionalism and Its Critics: An Analysis of the Writings of Gabriel Almond." *The American Political Science Review* I (Fall 1971), pp. 236–276.

Rostow, D. A. "Transition to Democracy: Toward a Dynamic Model." *Comparative Politics* 2 (April 1970), pp. 337–63.

Schrems, John J. *Principles of Politics*. Englewood Cliffs, NJ: Prentice Hall, 1986.

Somit, Albert and Tenenhaus, Joseph. *The Development of American Political Science: From Burgess to Behavioralism*. New York: Irvington, 1982.

Spanier, John. *American Foreign Policy Since World War II*, 10th Ed. New York: Holt, Rinehart and Winston, 1985.

LATIN AMERICA: DEMOCRACY, STRATEGY AND THE EUROPEAN EXPERIENCE

Abrams, Elliott. "The Reagan Policy for Latin America Has Worked." The *International Herald Tribune* (New York Times). July 28, 1988, p. 4.

Aguirre, Mariano. "Between Two Worlds: Spain's Latin America Policy." *NACLA Report on the Americas*, XX, 2 (April-May 1986), pp. 12–15.

Amnesty International. *Guatemala: A Government Program of Political Murder*. London: Amnesty International, 1981.

Annunciata, Lucia. "Democracy and the Sandinistas." *The Nation*. April 2, 1988, pp. 454–457.

Arias Calderon, Ricardo. "Political Systems as Export Commodities." *Caribbean Review*. 15 (Winter 1986), pp. 20–23.

Ayuntamiento de Barcelona, Sociedad Estatal del Quinto Centenario. *Libro Blanco: La nueva europa y el futuro de América Latina*. Barcelona: Ayuntamiento de Barcelona/Sociedad Estatal del Quinto Centenario, 1990.

Baloyra, Enrique, ed. *Comparing New Democracies: Transition and Consolidation in Mediterranean Europe and the Southern Cone*. Boulder: Westview Press, 1987.

———. "Dilemmas of Political Transition." *Journal of International Affairs*, 38, 2 (Winter 1985).

———. "Negotiating War in El Salvador: The Politics of Endgame." *Journal of Interamerican Studies and World Affairs*, 28, 3 (Spring 1986), p. 123–47.

Barker, Robert S. "Constitutional Adjudication in Costa Rica." *Inter-American Law Review*, 17 (Winter 1986), pp. 249–274.

Bello, Andrés. *Obras Completas*. Santiago: Impresora Pedro G. Ramírez, 1881.

Bodemer, Klaus. *Europa Occidental-America Latina: Experiencias y Desafíos*. Barcelona: Ediciones Alfa, 1987.

Bolívar, Simon. *Escritos Políticos*. Madrid: Alianza Editorial, 1983.

Booth, James A. "The Socioeconomic and Political Roots of Revolt in Central America," *Latin American Research Review*, Vol. 26, no. 1 (1990).

Booth, John A., and Seligson, Mitchell A. *Elections and Democracy in Central America*. Chapel Hill: University of North Carolina Press, 1989.

Bulmar-Thomas, Victor. *The Political Economy of Central America Since 1920*. Cambridge: Cambridge University Press, 1987.

———. "Relaciones entre Centroamerica y Europa Occidental." *Sintesis*, 4 (January-April 1988), pp. 286–294.

Canela, Silvia María. "Por qué no comerciamos más con Europa? Proteccionismo y discriminaciones de la comunidad." *Nueva Sociedad*, 85 (September-October 1986).

Castañeda, Jorge. "Latin America's Rising Populist Left." *International Herald Tribune* (Los Angeles Times Service). September 7, 1988, p. 4.

Committee of Santa Fe. *A New Inter-American Policy*. Washington: Council on Interamerican Security, 1980.

Christian, Shirley. "Decade of Disasters." *The New Republic*. August 29, 1988, pp. 44–49.

Cirincione, Joseph, ed. *Central America and the Western Alliance*. New York: Holmes and Meier, 1985.

Dahl, Robert. "Social Science Workshop on Transition and Consolidation of Democracy in Latin America and Chile." *Opciones* (January-April 1986), pp. 22–69.

Díaz Briquets, Sergio. "How to Figure Out Cuba." *Caribbean Review*, 15, pp. 8–11.

DiPalma, Guiseppe. *Crafting Democracies: An Essay on Democratic Transition*. Berkeley: University of California Press, 1990.

Drake, Paul W., and Silva, Eduardo, eds. *Elections and Democratization in Latin America 1980–85*. San Diego: Center for Iberian and Latin American Studies/University of California, 1986.

Dunkerley, James. *Power in the Isthmus: A Political History of Modern Central America*. London: Verso, 1988.

Durán, Esperanza. *European Interests in Latin America*. London: The Royal Institute of International Affairs, 1985.

Eberstadt, Nicolas. "Did Fidel Fudge the Figures?" *Caribbean Review*, 15 (Spring 1986), pp. 47–48.

Economic Commission on Latin America. "Declaration of Quito and Plan of Action." *ECLA Notas sobre la economía y el desarollo de América Latina*, 389/390 (January 1984).

Erisman, H. Michael. *Cuba's Interational Relations: Anatomy of a Nationalistic Foreign Policy*. Boulder: Westview Press, 1985.

Erisman, H. Michael, and Martz, John D., eds. *Colossus Challenged: The Struggle for Caribbean Influence*. Boulder: Westview Press, 1982.

Espinosa, Juan Guillermo. "Outlook for the World Economy: A Latin American Viewpoint." *Journal of Interamerican Studies and World Affairs*, 29, 4 (Winter 1987–88), pp. 125–145.

European Economic Community. Council of the European Communities 7120/87. "Conclusions of the Council and the Representatives of the Governments and the Member States on Relations Between the European Community and Latin America." *Europe*, 1460. June 26, 1987.

Farber, Samuel. "The Cuban Communists in the Early Stages of the Cuban Revolution: Revolutionaries or Reformists?" *Latin American Research Review*. (Fall 1983), pp. 59–83.

Fernández, Damian J. "Cuban Foreign Policy: Scholarship and Double Standards." *Journal of Interamerican Studies and World Affairs*, 28 (Summer 1986), pp. 147–153.

Figueres, José. *El Espíritu de 48*. San José: Editorial Costa Rica, 1987.

Figueres, José, and Oduber, Daniel, et al. "Reflections on U.S. Policy." *World Policy Journal*, 3 (Spring 1986), pp. 317–346.

Flores, Elena. "Europa y América Latina: el desafío de la cooperación." *Leviatán*, 27 (Spring 1987), pp. 93–102.

Fried, Jonathan, and Gettlemen, Marvin E., et. al., eds. *Guatemala in Rebellion: Unfinished History*. New York: Grove Press, 1983.

Fundación Friedrich Ebert and Instituto de Cooperación Iberoamericana. *El Parlamento Centroamericano y la Experiencia Europea*. Madrid: Fundación Friedrich Ebert, 1990.

Furlong, William L. "Costa Rica: Caught Between Two Worlds." *Journal of Interamerican Studies and World Affairs*, 29, 2 (Summer 1987), pp. 119–154.

Galvani, Victoria. "El Rey y la Comunidad Iberoamericana. La filosofía y las tesis del iberoamericanismo de España en el reinado de Juan Carlos I." *Colección de Estudios Iberoamericanos*, 5. Madrid: Fundación CIPIE, 1987.

González, Leonel. "A Plan for Peace in El Salvador." *The Nation*, October 15, 1990, pp. 407–408.

Grabendorff, Wolf. "América Latina y Europa: esperanzas y desafíos." *Nueva Sociedad*, 85 (September-October) 1987–88, pp. 126–133.

————. "European Community Relations with Latin America: A Policy Without Illusions." *Journal of Interamerican Studies and World Affairs*, 29, 4 (Winter 1987–88), pp. 69–88.

————. "El papel de Europa Occidental en la cuenca del caribe." *Foro Internacional*, 4 (April-June 1983), pp. 400–422.

————. "Las relaciones de la Comunidad Europea con América Latina: una política sin ilusiones." *Sintesis*, 4 (January-April 1988), pp. 117–130.

Grabendorff, Wolf, and Roett, Riordan, eds. *Latin America, Western Europe, and the U.S.: Re-evaluating the Atlantic Triangle*. New York: Praeger, 1985.

Gutman, Roy. *Banana Diplomacy*. New York: Simon and Schuster, 1988.

Granda Alva, German, and Mate de Castro, Victor. "La cooperación para el desarollo de la comunidad Europea con América Latina." *Sintesis*, 4 (January-April 1988), pp. 225–237.

Harnecker, Marta, and Perales, Iosu. *Guerra en El Salvador: Entrevistas con Comandantes del FMLN*. San Sebastián: GAKOA Liburuak, 1989.

Heliodoro Valle, Rafael. *Valle*. Mexico: Secretaría de Educación Pública, 1934.

Honey, Martha, and Avirgan, Tony. "Leaning on Arias." *The Nation*. September 12, 1987, p. 27.

Huneeus, Carlos. *Para Vivir la Democracia*. Santiago: Editorial Andante, 1987.

Iglesias, Enrique. "Nuevas formas de cooperación entre the comunidad Europea y América Latina." *Ponencia en el coloquio organizada por la Academie Diplomatique Internacional*. Reprinted in *Sintesis*, 4 (January-April 1988), pp. 366–370.

————. "Relaciones entre la Europa comunitaria e Iberoamérica en el marco de las relaciones Norte-Sur y Este-Oeste." *Encuentro en la democracia: Europa-Iberoamérica*. Madrid: Instituto de Cooperación Iberoamericana (ICI), 1986.

Immerman, R. H. *The CIA in Guatemala*. Austin: University of Texas Press, 1982.

Instituto de Cooperación Iberoamericana. *Encuentros en la democracia: Europa-Iberoamérica*. Madrid: ICI, 1986.

Instituto de Relaciones Europeo-Latinoamericanas. *Manual para las Relaciones Europeo-Latinoamericanas*. Madrid: IRELA, 1990.

Interamerican Development Bank. *Annual Report: 1989*. Washington, D.C.: IDB, 1990.

————. *Economic and Social Progress in Latin America, 1990*. Washington, D.C.: IDB/ Johns Hopkins Press, 1990.

Jacobsen, Carl G. *The Jacobsen Report: Soviet Attitudes Towards, Aid to, and Contacts with, Central American Revolutionaries*. Report Commissioned by the United States Department of State. Washington: Government Printing Office, 1984.

Jorrín, Miguel, and Martz, John D. *Latin American Political Thought and Ideology*. Chapel Hill: University of North Carolina Press, 1970.

Karl, Terry Lynn. "Dilemmas of Democratization in Latin America." *Comparative Politics*, XXIII, 1 (October 1990), pp. 1–22.

Kinzer, Stephen, and Schlesinger, Stephen. *Bitter Fruit*. New York: Doubleday, 1982.

Konrad Adenaur Stifting (KAS). *Jahresbericht 1980*. Sankt Augustin, FRG: KAS, 1981.

de La Iglesia, Juan Pablo. "Las relaciones entre la Europa de las doce y América Latina: Un proceso de cambio accelerado." *Pensamiento Iberoamericano*, 13 (January-April 1988).

Lane, Charles. "Death's Democracy." *The Atlantic*. January 1989, pp. 18–25.

Latin American Bureau. *The European Challenge: Europe's New Role in Latin America.* London: LAB, 1982.

Latin American Studies Association. *Electoral Democracy Under Pressure: The Report of the LASA Commission to Observe the 1990 Nicaraguan Elections.* Pittsburgh: LASA, 1990.

Lecuna, Vicente, and Bierck, Harold A., eds. *The Selected Writings of Simon Bolívar.* New York: The Colonial Press, 1951.

Leiken, Robert S., and Rubin, Barry, eds. *The Central American Crisis Reader.* New York: Summit Books, 1987.

Linowitz, Sol. "The Latins Should Top the Agenda." *International Herald Tribune* (New York Times). September 21, 1988, p. 4.

Lipset, Martin, and Solari, Aldo, eds. *Elites in Latin America.* New York: Oxford University Press, 1968.

Liska, George. "The Reagan Doctrine: Monroe and Dulles Reincarnate?" *SAIS Review* (Summer-Fall 1986), pp. 83–98.

Lowenthal, Abraham F., ed. *Exporting Democracy: The United States and Latin America.* 2 Vols. Baltimore: The Johns Hopkins University Press, 1991.

McNeil, Frank. *War and Peace in Central America: Reality and Illusion.* New York: Scribners, 1988.

Malloy, James M., and Seligson, Mitchell A., eds. *Authoritarians and Democrats: Regime Transformation in Latin America.* Pittsburgh: University of Pittsburgh Press, 1987.

Mikoyan, Sergei. "The Particularities of the Nicaraguan Revolution." *América Latina,* 3 (1980).

Miles, Sara, and Ostertag, Bob. "Power Outage." *Mother Jones.* November/December, 1990, pp. 37–38, 65–68.

Mols, Manfred. "La Responsibilidad Europea en el proceso Latinoamericano de redemocratización: Una Perspectiva Alemana." Working Paper DT13–88. Madrid: IRELA, 1988.

Montgomery, Tommie Sue. *Revolution in El Salvador.* Boulder: Westview Press, 1982.

Moss, Ambler H., ed. *The Miami Report II: New Perspectives on Debt, Trade and Investment—A Key to U.S./Latin American Relations in the 1990s.* Coral Gables: North South Center/University of Miami, 1988.

———. *Reflections on U.S. Policy Toward Central America: The Transition from Carter to Reagan.* Coral Gables: Institute of Interamerican Studies, 1983.

Mower, A. Glenn. *The European Community and Latin America: A Case Study in Global Role Expansion.* London: Greenwood Press, 1982.

Mujal-Leon, Eusebio. "Europea Occidental y los procesos de la democratización en América Latina." *Sintesis,* 4 (Winter 1987–88), pp. 256–264.

———. *European Socialism and the Conflict in Central America.* Washington D.C.: Praeger and Center for Strategic and International Studies, 1989.

———. "The West German SPD and the Politics of Internationalism in Central America." *Journal of Interamerican Studies and World Affairs,* 29, 4 (Winter 1987–88), pp. 89–123.

Needler, Martin. "The Military and Politics in Latin America." (Review Essay) *Journal of Interamerican Studies and World Affairs,* 28, 3 (Fall 1986), pp. 141–147.

————. *The Problem of Democracy in Latin America.* Lexington, MA: D. C. Heath and Co., 1987.

Nolan, David. *The Ideology of the Sandinistas and the Nicaraguan Revolution.* Coral Gables: Institute of Interamerican Studies/North-South Center, 1984.

North American Congress on Latin America. *Guatemala.* Berkeley: NACLA, 1974.

Parker, Franklin D. *José Cecilio del Valle and the Establishment of the Central American Confederation.* Tegucigalpa: Universidad de Honduras, 1954.

Pastor, Robert. *Condemned to Repitition.* Princeton: Princeton University Press, 1988.

Paz Zamora, Jaime. "Cómo nos ven, cómo los vemos: las relaciones entre Europa y América Latina." *Nueva Sociedad,* 85 (September-October 1986), pp. 103–107.

Peeler, John. *Latin American Democracies: Colombia, Costa Rica, Venezuela.* Chapel Hill: University of North Carolina Press, 1985.

Perle, Richard. "America's Failure of Nerve in Nicaragua." *U.S. News and World Report.* August 10, 1987, pp. 32–33.

Pierre, Andrew, ed. *Third World Instability: Central America as a European-American Issue.* New York: Council on Foreign Relations, 1985.

Reding, Andrew. "Costa Rica: Democratic Model in Jeopardy." *World Policy Journal,* 3 (Spring 1986), pp. 301–316.

Rosenberg, Robin. "Soviet Support for Central American Guerrilla Movements as a Strategic Initiative." *Soviet Armed Forces Review Annual,* 8 (1983–84), pp. 348–389.

Rothenberg, Morris. "Latin America in Soviet Eyes." *Problems of Communism.* (September-October 1983).

Roy, Joaquín, and Rosenberg, Robin. "Falklands, Grenada Diminish OAS as Caribbean Problems Linger." *The Miami Herald.* December 5, 1983, p. 21.

Roy, Joaquín, ed. *The Reconstruction of Central America: The Role of the European Community.* Miami: North-South Center, forthcoming.

Sanchez, Nestor D. "The Communist Threat." *Foreign Policy,* 52 (Fall 1983).

Skoug, Kenneth N., Jr. "Cuba as a Model and a Challenge." *Department of State Bulletin,* 84 (September 1984), pp. 73–77.

Smith, Griffin, Jr. "Guatemala: a Fragile Democracy." *National Geographic,* 173, 6 (June 1988), pp. 768–803.

Sociedad Estatal Quinto Centenario. *Libro Blanco*: La Nueva Europa y el Futuro de América Latina. In *Pensamiento Iberoamericano,* Volumen Extraordinario, 1991.

Suchlicki, Jaime. "Soviet Policy in Latin America: Some Implications for the United States." *Journal of Interamerican Studies and World Affairs,* 29, 1 (Spring 1987), pp. 25–46.

Tanner, Fred. "From Europe to Central America: Regional Co-operation and Peace Processes." Working Paper WP15–88. Madrid: IRELA, 1988.

de Tocqueville, Alexis. *Democracy in America.* New York: Harper and Row, 1966.

Treviño Huerta, Luisa. "La política exterior del Gobierno socialista hacia Latinoamerica." *Estudios Internacionales,* 1 (January-March 1985), pp. 111–124.

United States Congress, Staff Report, Subcommittee on Evaluation and Oversight, Permanent Select Committee on Intelligence. Washington: Government Printing Office, 1982.

United States Department of State. *Foreign Relations of the United States 1952–1954: The American Republics.* Washington: Government Printing Office, 1984.

United States Embassy, Guatemala City. Confidential Policy Recommendation to
U.S. Department of State. May 14, 1984. (Unpublished).

Urquidi, Victor. "Hacia una nueva relacion económica entre Europa y América
Latina." *Comercio Exterior*, 7 (July 1986).

Valenta, Jiri. "Soviet Policy and the Crisis in the Caribbean." *Collosus Challenged:
The Struggle for Caribbean Influence*, edited by H. M. Erisman and J. D. Martz.
Boulder: Westview Press, 1982, pp. 42–86.

Villagrán Kramer, Francisco. "Encauzamiento y Posible Solución del Conflicto Centroamericano: El Papel de Europa y de las Support." Working Paper DT22–
90. Madrid: IRELA, 1990.

Viñas, Angel. "European-Latin American Relations in the East-West Conflict. A Spanish Perspective." Working Paper WP7–87. Madrid: IRELA, 1987.

Vorozheinkina, Tatiana. "Salvadoran Revolutionary Organizations and the Popular
Movements." *América Latina*, 8 (1982), pp. 18–19.

Wiarda, Howard, ed. *Corporatism and National Development in Latin America*. Boulder:
Westview Press, 1981.

Wilhelmy, Manfred. "Las Políticas Latinoamericanas Hacia Europa Occidental."
Working Paper DT6–87. Madrid: IRELA, 1987.

Wynia, Gary W. *The Politics of Latin American Development*. 3d ed. Cambridge: Cambridge University Press, 1990.

Yañez-Barnuevo, Juan Antonio. "Relaciones entre Europa e Iberoamérica en el marco
de las relaciones Norte-Sur y Este-Oeste." *Encuentros en las democracia: Europa-Iberoamérica*. Madrid: ICI, 1986.

Zagladin, Victor. "World Balance of Forces and the Development of International
Relations." *International Affairs* (Moscow). (March, 1985), pp. 65–75.

SPAIN: DEMOCRATIC TRANSITION, FOREIGN POLICY

Able, Christopher and Torrents, Missa. *Spain: Conditional Democracy*. London: St.
Martins, 1984.

Aguirre, Julen. *Operación ogro. cómo y por qué matamos a Carrero Blanco*. Paris, 1974.

Aguirre, Mariano. "Between Two Worlds: Spain's Latin American Policy." *NACLA
Report on the Americas*. (April-May 1986), pp. 13–16.

Alba, Victor. *Spain: From Franco to Democracy*. New Brunswick, NJ: Transaction
Books, 1978.

Amnesty International. *1987 Annual Report: Spain*. London: Amnesty International,
1988.

Arahuetes, Alfredo, and Gamo, Alonso. *Aproximación a la realidad de las ONGs en
España*. Madrid: Centro Español de Estudios sobre América Latina, 1989.

Areilza, José Maria. *Diario de un ministro de la monarquia*. Barcelona: Editorial Planeta,
1977.

del Arenal, Celestino, and Nájera, Alfonso. *La Comunidad Iberoamericana de Naciones:
Hacia el Futuro*. Madrid: CEDEAL, 1991.

———. *España e Iberoamérica: de la Hispanidad a la Comunidad Iberoamericana de
Naciones*. Madrid: CEDEAL, 1989.

Armero, José Maria. *Politica exterior de España en democracia*. Madrid: Espasa Calpe,
1989.

Baloyra, Enrique, ed. *Comparing New Democracies: Transition and Consolidation in Mediterranean Europe and the Southern Cone.* Boulder: Westview Press, 1987.

Baselga, Lucian. "Informe ante la Comisión de Asuntos Exteriores del Congreso." *Boletín Oficial del Estado.* March 14, 1984.

Bell, David S. *Democratic Politics in Spain.* New York: St. Martins, 1983.

Bernales Ballesteros, Enrique. *El Camino de la democracia.* Madrid: Instituto de Cooperación Iberoamericana, 1986.

Bonime-Blanc, Andrea. *Spain's Transition to Democracy: The Politics of Constitution-Making.* Boulder: Westview Press, 1987.

Carr, Raymond. "Thatcherismo, Felipísmo." *El País.* September 21, 1988, p. 11.

Carr, Raymond, and Fusi, Juan Pablo. *Spain: Dictatorship to Democracy.* London: Allen, Unwin, 1981.

Castellanos, Pablo. "Desde las grutas." *El País.* September 8, 1979.

Centre d'Informació i Documentació Internacionals a Barcelona and Asociación de Investigación sobre Temas Iberoamericanos. *Las Relaciones Entre España y América Central (1976–1989).* Barcelona: CIDOB/AETI, 1989.

Chamorro, Eduardo. *Felipe González: un hombre en la espera.* Barcelona: Editorial Planeta, 1980.

Clark, Robert C., and Haltzel, Michael H. *Spain in the 1980s: The Democratic Transition and the New International Role.* Cambridge, MA: Ballinger Publishing/The Wilson Center, 1987.

Cortada, James W. *Spain in the Twentieth Century World: Essays on Spanish Diplomacy, 1898–1978.* Westport, CT: Greenwood Press, 1980.

Coverdale, John F. *The Political Transformation of Spain after Franco.* New York: Praeger, 1979.

European Economic Community. European Parliament. *Birkelbach Report.* Brussels, January 15, 1962.

Fernández de la Mora, Gonzalo. *Los errores del cambio.* Madrid: Plaza y Janes, 1986.

Fernández Ordóñez, Francisco. "Conferencia Ministerial de San Pedro Sula sobre el diálago político entre los países de Centroamerica y the Comunidad Economica Europea, Discurso del Ministro de Asuntos Exteriores en la Sesión inaugural." Reprinted in *Sintesis*, VII (1989), pp. 404–409.

———. *La España necesaria.* Madrid: Taurus, 1980.

———. "Política exterior de España." *Política Exterior* I, 1 (Winter 1987), pp. 14–27.

Foweraker, Joe. "Corporatist Strategies and the Transition to Democracy in Spain." *Comparative Politics* 20, 1 (October 1987), pp. 57–72.

Franco Salgado-Araujo, Francisco. *Mis conversaciones con Franco.* Barcelona, 1976.

Galinsoga i Jordá, Albert. "España y la Política Centroamericana de la Comunidad Europea." Working Paper DT26–91. Madrid: IRELA, 1991.

Gibson, Ian. *En busca de José Antonio.* Barcelona, 1980.

Gillespie, Richard. *The Spanish Socialist Party: A History of Factionalism.* Oxford: Oxford University Press, 1989.

Giner, Salvador, and Sevilla, Eduardo. "Spain: From Corporatism to Corporatism." In A. Williams, ed. *Southern Europe Transformed.* London: Harper and Row, 1984.

Grugel, Jean. "Spain's Socialist Government and Central American Dilemmas." *International Affairs.* (Autumn 1987), pp. 143–155.

González Casanova, J. A. *El cambio inacabable*. Barcelona: Anthropos, 1986.

González, Felipe. "Declarations of the President." *Revista de Estudios Internacionales* 2 (1983), p. 593.

Gunther, Richard; Sani, Giacomo; and Shabad, Goldie. *Spain After Franco: The Making of a Competitive Party System*. Berkeley: University of California Press, 1985.

Herz, John. *From Dictatorship to Democracy: Coping with the Legacy of Authoritarianism and Totalitarianism*. Westport, CT: Greenwood Press, 1982.

Homan, Otto. "In Search of Hegemony: Socialist Government and the Internationalisation of Domestic Politics in Spain," *International Journal of Political Economy* XIX, 3 (Fall 1989), pp. 76–101.

Hooper, John. *The Spaniards: A Portrait of the New Spain*. London: Penguin, 1987.

Instituto de Cooperación Iberoamericana. *Cooperación Española: Lineas Directrices de la Política Española para la Cooperación al Desarollo*. Madrid: ICI, 1990.

———. *Encuentro en la democracia: Iberoamérica*. Madrid: ICI, 1983.

———. *La transición a la democracia, hoy*. Buenos Aires: Universidad de Belgrano, 1983.

Jackson, Gabriel. "Sobre el modelo socialista," *El País*. October 17, 1985, p. 11.

Jiménez, Inmaculada. *La Ayuda de España al Desarollo*. Madrid: IEPALA, 1989.

Lancaster, Thomas D., and Prevost, Gary, eds. *Politics and Change in Spain*. New York: Praeger, 1985.

Linz, Juan. *España: Un presente para el futuro*. Madrid: Instituto de Estudios Economicos, 1984.

Lockhart, James, and Schwartz, Stephen. *Early Latin America*. Cambridge: Cambridge University Press, 1987.

Maravall, José Maria. *The Transition to Democracy in Spain*. London: Croom and Helm, 1982.

McDonough, Peter; Barnes, Samuel H.; and López Piña, Antonio. "Social Identity and Mass Politics in Spain." *Comparative Political Studies* XXI, 2 (July 1986), pp. 200–230.

Morán, Fernando. "Desprestigio del estado, indefensión del ciudadano." *El País*. April 27, p. 12.

———. "España en el mundo." *Cambio 16*. October 26, 1987, p. 110.

———. *España en su sitio*. Madrid: Plaza y Janes/Cambio 16, 1990.

———. *Una política exterior para España*. Barcelona: Editorial Planeta, 1980.

———. "Press Conference at Foreign Ministry." Oficina de Información Diplomática. September 19, 1983, p. 456.

———. "Principios de la política exterior español." *Leviatán* 16, (Summer 1984), pp. 8–23.

Morán, Gregorio. *Adolfo Suárez: Historia de una ambición*. Barcelona: Planeta, 1980.

Mujal-Leon, Eusebio. *Continuity and Change in Spanish Foreign Policy*. Washington: American Enterprise Institute, 1985.

———. "Decline and Fall of Spanish Communism." *Problems of Communism*. (March-April 1986), pp. 1–27.

O'Donnell, Guillermo; Schmitter, Phillipe; and Whitehead, Laurence, eds. *Transitions from Authoritarian Rule: Prospects for Democracy*, 4 Vols. Baltimore: The Johns Hopkins Press, 1986.

Otero Nivas, José Manuel. *Nuestra democracia puede morir*. Madrid: Plaza y Janes, 1987.

Pacheco, Pedro. "La Exposición Universal en crisis." *El País*. March 4, 1988, p. 20.
Partido Socialista Obrero Español. *Forjar el Socialismo*. Texto del VI Congreso Extraordinario. Madrid: PSOE, 1979.
Perry, William, and Wehner, Peter, eds. *The Latin American Policies of U.S. Allies*. New York: Praeger, 1985.
Petschen, Santiago. "La política exterior de la comunidad autónoma de Cataluña." *Política Exterior* 2, 5 (Winter 1988), pp. 222–238.
Pike, Frederick B. "Latin America." In Cortada, James W., ed. *Spain in the Twentieth Century World*. Westport, CT: Greenwood Press, 1980.
Pons Prados, Eduardo. *Crónica negra de la transición española: 1976–85*. Madrid: Plaza y Janes, 1987.
Powell, Charles T. *El Piloto del Cambio: el Rey, la Monarquía, y la Transición a la Democracia*. Barcelona: Planeta, 1991.
———. "Reform *versus Ruptura* in Spain's Transition to Democracy." Unpublished doctoral dissertation, Oxford University, 1989.
de Prado y Colon de Carvajal, Manuel. "Reflexiones sobre el V Centenario." *El País*. May 20, 1988, p. 24.
Preston, Paul. *The Triumph of Democracy in Spain*. London: Methuen, 1986.
Preston, Paul, and Smyth, Denis. *Spain, the EEC and NATO*. London: Royal Institute of International Affairs, 1984.
Rodríguez-Ibáñez, José Enrique. *Después de una dictadura: cultura autoritaria y transición política*. Madrid: Centro de Estudios Constitucionales, 1988.
Roitman, Marcos. *La política del PSOE en America Latina*. Madrid: Editorial Revolucion, 1985.
Roy, Joaquín. *Cuba y España: percepciones y relaciones*. Madrid: Editorial Playor, 1988.
Share, Donald. "Dilemmas of Social Democracy in the 1980s: The Spanish Socialist Workers Party in Comparative Perspective." *Comparative Political Studies* XXI, 3 (October 1988), pp. 408–428.
———. *Dilemmas of Social Democracy: The Spanish Socialist Workers Party in the 1980s*. Westport, CT: Greenwood Press, 1989.
Solé Tura, Jordi. "Una derecha regionalizada." *El País*. June 10, 1987, p. 11.
———. "Un poco de calma . . . " *El País*. July 22, 1987, p. 26.
Sotelo, Ignacio. *Los Socialistas en el poder*. Madrid: Ediciones El País, 1986.
Subirats, Eduardo. "Latinoamérica: el otro mundo." *El País*. April 28, 1988, p. 12.
Tezanos, José Felix; Cotarelo, Ramón; and De Blas, Andrés, eds. *La Transicion Democrática Española*. Madrid: Editorial Sistema, 1989.
Thomas, Hugh. *The Spanish Civil War*. Middlesex: Penguin, 1986.
Tulchin, Joseph S. "Spain, NATO, and the Western Alliance." *Ideas '92*, I, 2 (January-June 1988), pp. 57–66.
Vargas Llosa, Mario. "Questions of Conquest." *Harper's* (December 1990), pp. 45–52.
Vilar, Sergio. *Proyección internacional de España*. Madrid: Tecnos, 1981.
Wiarda, Howard J. "Does Europe Stop at the Pyrenees or Does Latin America Begin There? Iberia, Latin America, and the Second Enlargement of the European Community." Occasional Paper 2. Washington: American Enterprise Institute, 1981.
———., ed. *The Iberian-Latin American Connection: Implications for U.S. Foreign Policy*. Washington: American Enterprise Institute, 1986.

————. "Interpreting Iberian-Latin American Interrelations: Paradigm Consensus and Conflict." Occasional Paper 10. Washington: American Enterprise Institute, 1985.

————. "Toward a Framework for the Study of Political Change in the Iberic-Latin Tradition: The Corporative Model." *World Politics* 25 (January 1983), pp. 206–235.

Williams, Allan, ed. *Southern Europe Transformed*. London: Harper and Row, 1984.

Yáñez Barnuevo, Luis. "El futuro comienza en 1992." *El País*. October 14, 1988, p. 18.

Select Abbreviations

AECI—Agencia Española de Cooperación Internacional (Spanish Agency for International Cooperation)

AES—Astilleros Españoles (Spanish Shipbuilders)

AIFLD—American Institute for Free Labor Development (U.S.)

AP—Alianza Popular (Popular Alliance) (Spain)

ARENA—Alianza Republicana Nacional (Republican National Alliance) (El Salvador)

CAP—Common Agricultural Policy (EEC)

CBI—Caribbean Basin Initiative (U.S.)

CC.OO.—Comisiones Obreras (Workers Commissions) (Spain)

CD—Convergencia Democrática (Democratic Convergence) (El Salvador)

CDS—Centro Democratico y Social (Democratic and Social Center)

CIA—Central Intelligence Agency (U.S.)

CIU—Convergencia i Unió (Convergence and Union) (Spain)

CSCE—Conference on Security and Cooperation in Europe

DAC—Development Aid Committee (OECD)

ECLA/CEPAL—Economic Commission for Latin America (Comisión Económica para América Latina) (UN)

EEC—European Economic Community

EFTA—European Free Trade Association

EGPGC—Exército Guerilleiro do Poblo Galego Ceibe (Guerrilla Army of the Poor Galician People) (Spain)

EMS—European Monetary System

ETA—Euskadi ta Askatasuna (Basque Homeland and Freedom) (Spain)

FAD—Fondo de Ayuda al Desarollo (Development Aid Fund) (Spain)

FDR—Frente Democrático Revolucionario (Revolutionary Democratic Front) (El Salvador)

FMLN—Frente Farabundo Martí para la Liberación Nacional (Farabundo Martí National Liberation Front) (El Salvador)

FSLN—Frente Sandinista de Liberación Nacional (Sandinista National Liberation Front) (Nicaragua)

FTA—Free Trade Accord

GAL—Grupo Anti-terrorista de Liberación (Anti-terrorist Liberation Group) (Spain)

GATT—General Agreement on Trade and Tariffs

GRAPO—Grupo de Resistencia Antifascita Primero de Octubre (Patriotic Anti-fascist Revolutionary Group) (Spain)

ICI—Instituto de Cooperación Iberoamericano (Institute of Ibero-American Cooperation) (Spain)

IDB—Interamerican Development Bank

IMF—International Monetary Fund

INI—Instituto Nacional de Industria (National Institute of Industry) (Spain)

IRELA—Instituto de Relaciones Europea-Latinoamericanas (Institute of European-Latin American Relations) (Madrid)

IU—Izquierda Unida (United Left) (Spain)

MAS—Movimiento de Acción Solidaria (Solidarity Action Movement) (Guatemala)

NATO—North Atlantic Treaty Organization

NGOs—Non-Governmental Organizations

OAS—Organization of American States

OECD—Organization of Economic Cooperation and Development

ORPA—Organización Revolucionaria del Pueblo en Armas (Organization of the People in Arms) (Guatemala)

PA—Partido Andalucista (Andalucian Party) (Spain)

PACI—Plan Anual de Cooperación Internacional (Annual Plan for International Cooperation) (Spain)

PDC—Partido Demócratica Cristiano (Christian Democratic Party) (El Salvador)

PDD—Partnership for Development and Democracy

PP—Partido Popular (Popular Party) (Spain)

PSN—Partido Socialista Nicaraguense (Nicaraguan Socialist Party)

PSOE—Partido Socialista Obrero Español (Spanish Socialist Workers Party)

RN—Resistencia Nicaraguense (Nicaraguan Resistance)

SI—Socialist International

SPD—Sozialdemocratischen Partei Deutschland (Social Democratic Party) (Germany)

UCA—Universidad Centroamericana (Central American University) (El Salvador)

UCD—Union del Centro Democrático (Union of the Democratic Center) (Spain)

UGT—Union General de Trabajadores (General Workers Union) (Spain)

UNO—Union Nacional Opositora (National Opposition Union) (Nicaragua)

UNOCA—United Nations Organization, Central America

UNOSAL—United Nations Organization, El Salvador

URNG—Unidad Revolucionaria Nacional Guatemalteca (National Guatemalan Revolutionary Unity)

WEU—Western European Union

Index

About the Author

ROBIN L. ROSENBERG is Deputy Executive Director of the North-South Center at the University of Miami, Coral Gables. He has researched this study at length both in the United States and in Spain. He formerly taught at Troy State University and has served in Spain as Adjunct Professor for several institutions.